THE
Watkin Path
An approach to belief
The Life of E. I. Watkin

To My Husband
Richard
who loved his father-in-law

THE
Watkin Path
An approach to belief
The Life of E. I. Watkin

Magdalen Goffin

sussex
ACADEMIC
PRESS

BRIGHTON • PORTLAND

2 4 6 8 10 9 7 5 3 1

First published 2006 in Great Britain by
SUSSEX ACADEMIC PRESS
Box 2950
Brighton BN2 5SP

and in the United States of America by
SUSSEX ACADEMIC PRESS
920 NE 58th Ave   Suite 300
Portland, Oregon 97213-3786

British Library Cataloguing in Publication Data
A CIP catalogue record for this book is available from the British Library.

Library of Congress Cataloging-in-Publication Data
Goffin, Magdalen.
The Watkin path : an approach to belief / Magdalen Goffin.
    p. cm.
Includes bibliographical references and index.
ISBN 1-84519-128-5 (h/b : alk. paper)
  1. Watkin, E. I. (Edward Ingram), 1888– 2. Catholics—
  Biography. 3. Illustrated London news. 4. Catholic
  Church—History—20th century. 5. England—Church
  history—20th century. I. Title.

BX4705.W375G64 2005
282'.092—dc22

                                        2005024373

Typeset & Designed by G&G Editorial, Brighton & Eastbourne
Printed by TJ International, Padstow, Cornwall
This book is printed on acid-free paper.

Contents

Contents

Illustrations

21 Watkin, *left*, talking to Christopher Dawson on the Yorkshire Moors, 1930s.
22 Jack Hornby.
23 The graves dug by the Canadian Mounted Police by the Thelon River in the Northern Territory, Canada, 1929.
24 Watkin's mother, Emmeline Heakes, looking into her crystal ball, 1920s.
25 Perpetua, Teresa and Mrs McDowell with two dogs on the lake at Pantafon, 1932.
26 Watkin's bookplate.
27 Frank Sheed, 1980.
28 Michael de la Bédoyère in his sixties from a sketch by his son, Count Quentin de la Bédoyère.
29 Sir Bruce Ingram, 1950.
30 Perpetua and Hugh Ingram, 1950.
31 "Watkin at the Waterfront". Hoboken, USA. *Jubilee*, 1957.
32 Watkin and Teresa Chapman with her son, Peter, 1953.
33 Catherine Davenport, Fairmead, 1957.
34 Watkin at Torquay, January 1960, aged seventy-two.
35 Helena at Fairmead, 1960, aged seventy-eight.
36 Richard Goffin, *left*, at the Frankfurt Book Fair, 1965. *Centre*: Siegfred Taubert, Director of the Fair; *right*, Dr Schröder, West German Foreign Minister.
37 Samuel Shepheard in old age in the grounds of Abbot Hall.
38 Christopher Dawson talking to Alec Guiness at Boston College, USA.
39 Christopher Watkin (Dom Aelred) when he was appointed Head Master of Downside School, 1962.
40 Magdalen at Silcocks, 1996.

Preface

Edward Ingram Watkin was the only child of Emmeline Paxton Ingram, one of the daughters of Herbert Ingram, the founder of the *Illustrated London News*. His father was the nephew of Sir Edward Watkin, the railway magnate.

Watkin became a Catholic in 1908, his first year at New College, Oxford. He was already well aware of the conflict between science and religion, faith and doubt. "By descent and upbringing," he wrote in 1949 as part of his Translator's Preface to the complete edition of Elie Halévy's *History of the English People in the Nineteenth Century,* "I belong to the Liberal tradition of freedom of which M. Halévy is the sympathetic historian, by religious belief to the Catholic 'Reaction' of which Newman was the outstanding English representative. Are they irreconcilable? Is a synthesis embracing what is true in both traditions impossible? Was not their mutual hostility the tragedy of the nineteenth century?"

He was one of the most original, learned and profound of the group of scholars, writers and artists who arrived on the Catholic scene between the wars. His apologia for Catholicism transcends denominational Christianity, transcends Christianity altogether and reaches out to all religions.

"Why hast thou made me for naught?" the Psalmist cries out. He has not made us for naught, Watkin answers, but so that we can be united to God both here and hereafter. It is for this purpose that institutional religion exists and in Christian understanding the reason why Jesus came into the world. In his opinion the Roman Catholic Church taught this doctrine more fully and more consistently than any other communion in the West. It was the main reason why Watkin became a Catholic and the main reason why, despite many obstacles, he remained one.

His approach was, in emphasis, different from that of Chesterton, Belloc and Ronald Knox, although towards the end of his life, Knox recognized the need for change. They preached the Church as it was, Watkin what it could be. Early in his career he dismayed many British

Catholics by his passionate denunciation of the slaughter on the Western Front in the First War and bishops and clergy were embarrassed by his and Francis Meynell's attempts to publicize Pope Benedict XIV's proposals for a negotiated peace.

Watkin was convinced that the Christian creeds could be presented in such a way that neither denied nor suppressed the certain conclusions of modern knowledge in all its branches. The first book he ever wrote (1915) was a plea that anticipated the words of Pope John XXIII. Catholics, Watkin said, must open the windows and present the faith in terms understood by the modern mind.

Bishop B. C. Butler once described pre-Conciliar Catholicism as the best of all possible religions and everything in it an intellectual scandal. He was writing with conscious exaggeration but expressing an uncomfortable truth. At the most fruitful period of Watkin's life, fear of modern knowledge had caused the Church to fall back on credal fundamentalism. Both clergy and laity were kept in a state of arrested development, encouraged to hold inflated ideas about papal authority and childish notions about the nature of revelation. Watkin was able to complete his books on philosophy, history and literature more or less unmolested. When he came to what he cared about most, the interpretation of the Catholic faith, he was harassed by censors and frequently refused the *Imprimatur* or permission to publish.

However, although Watkin was one of the foremost precursors of the Second Vatican Council, he deeply deplored some of its consequences, particularly the dismantling of the Catholic liturgy.

One "close, warm, breezeless summer night" in 1791, William Wordsworth and a friend climbed to the summit of Snowdon to see the sunrise. They started from Beddgelert and at the mountain's foot awoke the official guide, a shepherd sleeping in his hut, who with his dog, accompanied both men up the mountain. At the top, the beauty and sheer otherness of what he saw above the mist in the moonlight, became for Wordsworth "the emblem of a mind that feeds upon infinity." He used the experience as the climax of *The Prelude*, the long, autobiographical poem on the growth of his mind published after his death. Whether the ascent was made on what is now called The Watkin Path, we do not know.

Just over a hundred years later, in 1892, the four year old Watkin was present at the Path's ceremonial opening and sat on Mrs Gladstone's lap during the speeches. This book is an account of the growth of his mind, his religious belief, his education, the part he played in contemporary politics and his frequently troubled family relationships. It is based upon an extensive collection of letters, diaries and newspaper reports left to the author over twenty years ago. Because these contained so much personal material, it could not be published until after the death of Watkin's second wife, who lived to ninety-six.

The majority of those people who so kindly gave up their time to give me information are dead but their contribution is acknowledged. As always, my deepest debt is to my husband Richard. My friend Barbara Wall managed to read Watkin's handwriting and beautifully typed out his lengthy diaries kept between 1911 and 1912. I am grateful to Dr Giovanna Farrell Vinay for finding and copying letters kept in the Istituto Luigi Sturzo, Rome. I would like to thank Dom Daniel Rees, the former editor of the *Downside Review*, for his memories of my father and his comments on his work.

I would like also to thank my son-in-law Roderick Ives, Alan Keeler, Ronald Blythe, Julian Scott, Rosemary Middleton, Quentin de la Bédoyère, Joanna Plachcinska, Pam Tennent and my sister, Catherine Davenport. The Public libraries of Tunbridge Wells and Rusthall have been unfailingly helpful. The author and publisher would like to acknowledge Glenys Williams, Archivist & Historian, Marylebone Cricket Club, for permission to reproduce the picture of A. N. Hornby and the Tate Gallery for permission to reproduce the portrait of Maria Pasqua in 1863 by Henriette Browne.

Pages xii and xiii set out a simplified family tree, in two parts. The story begins with the drowning of Watkin's grandfather, Herbert Ingram, in Lake Michigan, USA. The fortune he left was to influence Watkin's entire life.

MAGDALEN GOFFIN
SILCOCKS, 2006

Simplified Family Tree, Part One

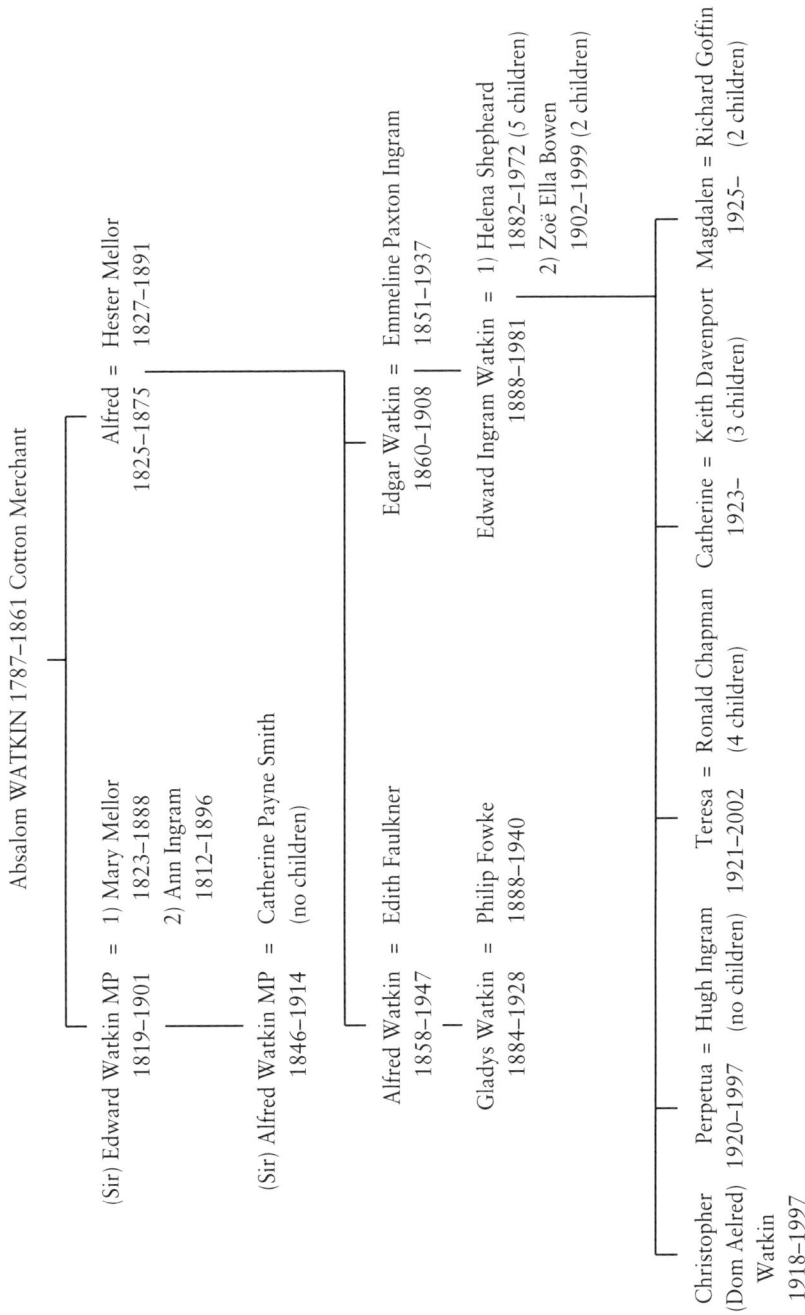

Absalom WATKIN 1787–1861 Cotton Merchant

Alfred = Hester Mellor
1825–1875   1827–1891

(Sir) Edward Watkin MP = 1) Mary Mellor
1819–1901   1823–1888

                        2) Ann Ingram
                           1812–1896

(Sir) Alfred Watkin MP = Catherine Payne Smith
1846–1914   (no children)

Edgar Watkin = Emmeline Paxton Ingram
1860–1908   1851–1937

Alfred Watkin = Edith Faulkner
1858–1947

Edward Ingram Watkin = 1) Helena Shepheard
1888–1981   1882–1972 (5 children)

                       2) Zoë Ella Bowen
                          1902–1999 (2 children)

Gladys Watkin = Philip Fowke
1884–1928   1888–1940

Christopher   Perpetua = Hugh Ingram   Teresa = Ronald Chapman   Catherine = Keith Davenport   Magdalen = Richard Goffin
(Dom Aelred)   1920–1997 (no children) 1921–2002 (4 children)   1923–   (3 children)   1925–   (2 children)
Watkin
1918–1997

Simplified Family Tree, Part Two

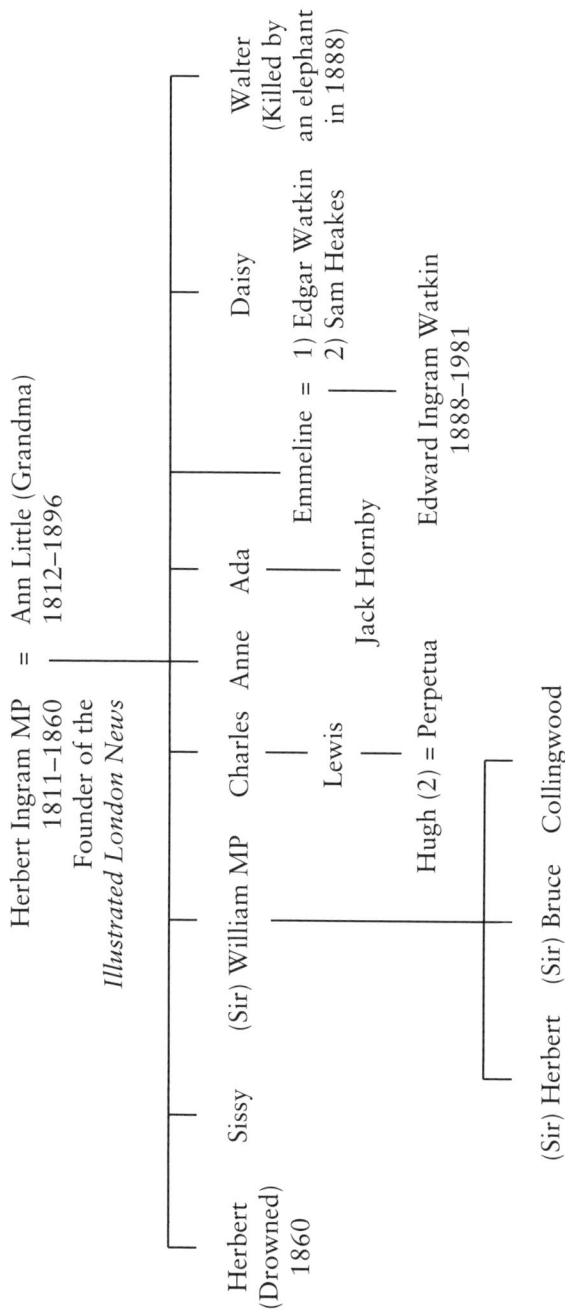

Herbert Ingram MP = Ann Little (Grandma)
1811–1860   1812–1896
Founder of the
Illustrated London News

Herbert   Sissy   (Sir) William MP   Charles   Anne   Ada   Daisy   Walter
(Drowned)   (Killed by
1860   an elephant
                                                                                             in 1888)

                                              Lewis   Jack Hornby   Emmeline = 1) Edgar Watkin
                                                                                     2) Sam Heakes

                                    Hugh (2) = Perpetua   Edward Ingram Watkin
                                                                           1888–1981

(Sir) Herbert   (Sir) Bruce   Collingwood

CHAPTER ONE

Making Money

From his experience in Nottingham, Ingram learnt three important lessons: people enjoy reading about crimes and disasters; newspapers with pictures sell far more copies than those without; that human beings of the poorer sort are exceedingly credulous especially when it comes to matters of health.

Herbert Ingram was the founder, proprietor and managing director of the *Illustrated London News*. He was also Liberal Member of Parliament for Boston, Lincolnshire, the town where he was born in 1811 and which would erect a statue in his memory. An ambitious, energetic, and tenacious opportunist, Ingram revolutionized journalism. Up to his time, newspapers had occasionally used pictures to heighten the reporting of very important or sensational events. Ingram's idea was to produce a weekly periodical whose entire purpose was to illustrate the news and information which it featured.

Ingram's father was a butcher and grazier who died when his son was an infant.[1] The boy was educated at a local charity school and at fourteen apprenticed to a Boston printer. After a few years as a journeyman printer in London he moved to Nottingham where he bought a shop and in partnership with his brother-in-law, Nathaniel Cooke, set up as a cheap printer, stationer, newsagent and dealer in patent medicines. This was probably in 1832 or 1833 after he and his sister had come into a legacy of £150 each, left to them by a great-aunt who had taken pity on the fatherless children and their poverty-stricken mother.

From his experience in Nottingham, Ingram learnt three important lessons: people enjoy reading about crimes and disasters; newspapers with pictures sell far more copies than those without; that human beings of the poorer sort are exceedingly credulous especially when it comes to matters of health.

It has long been a subject for amusement that the founder of such a respectable paper as the *Illustrated London News* should have financed his venture from profits made from the sale of a quack medicine. No one knows how Ingram first learnt that Thomas Roberts, the owner of a chemist's shop in Manchester, was prepared to sell the secret recipe for the famous "Parr's Life Pills." Whatever else was invented, a man named Thomas Parr actually existed.[2] He was born at Alberbury, a hamlet not far from Shrewsbury and until he was lured to London in 1635 lived all his life on a small farm there. He claimed to be 152 years old, born therefore in 1483, to have lived throughout the reigns of ten kings and queens, to remember the dissolution of the monasteries and to have fathered a bastard when he was 95. News of this curiosity reached the ears of Thomas Howard, Earl of Arundel, who had estates in the district and he arranged for Parr to be carried up to London by slow stages on a litter in order to present him to the court of Charles I. The excitement and the rich food proved to be the old man's undoing. He arrived in London in September, he was dead two months later. William Harvey performed an autopsy and declared Parr's organs were in an unusually healthy condition. He was buried in the south transept of Westminster Abbey close to an inscription telling the tale of his extreme longevity.

To us the Tudors seem remote but they were close to those living in the first half of the seventeenth century. Thomas Howard's own father had died in the Tower of London. Let us suppose that Parr was in fact a centenarian, rare in those days.

He was not lying when he claimed to remember the destruction of the monasteries. There were two religious foundations in his own village. If he had been born about 1535 their destruction would be fresh in the minds of those he lived among. The old man was no fool. When at Court he was asked a question about his religion, he answered that it was wiser to follow that of the reigning monarch.

Ingram probably had little real interest in religion. He certainly had none at all in the truth about Parr's life. Having bought the famous pills the secret of whose preparation he now claimed to have acquired from one of Parr's descendants, he set to work swiftly. William Blake, who loved the Abbey and its monuments, had drawn an imaginary picture of Parr at the age of forty. That would not do at all. Ingram commissioned the artist Henry Vizetelly to engrave a portrait of an old man with a flowing beard copied from the one Rubens had painted of Parr from memory. This appeared on the wrapping of every packet of pills. He also employed a schoolmaster to re-write a contemporary account of Parr's life, which was accompanied by illustrations drawn by Vizetelly and John Gilbert showing Old Parr gathering herbs and being presented to Charles I.

Ingram and his partner published the little book themselves with a title page announcing "The Life and Times of Thomas Parr who lived to be 152 years of age: with Remarks on Disease and Health and the Means of Prolonging Life." The book sold in its thousands and so did the pills which, besides longevity, claimed to promote relief from indigestion, gout, dropsy, insomnia and constipation. To give the impression that they were the genuine article each packet bore the signature of Thomas Roberts who, it seems, continued to manufacture the pills from Manchester.

By the end of the 1830s the groundwork for Ingram's subsequent extremely successful venture was already laid. By temperament he was forceful, manipulative, unscrupulous, quick to exploit his own and other people's ideas. He knew about printing and marketing, and how to make contact with skilled artists and engravers. Thanks to Old Parr he had some capital and would borrow more from his wife's brother.

Pioneers, whether consciously or unconsciously, often develop ideas already formed, or half formed, in the minds of others. Ingram had to work quickly. The first number of *Punch* had come out in the summer of 1821 with his friend from early Boston days, Mark Lemon, as one of its editors. There is evidence to suggest that Ingram, although convinced that matching pictures with news would be a commercial success, was at first uncertain about the contents of his paper and to which market it should be directed. Part of him was attracted to the steady selling crime sheets, to accounts of murders, floods, hangings and violent attacks on young women on their way to church. The other part recognized that profits could be made, and more prestigiously made, from a publication which would cover more general topics of interest to a prosperous middle class. By now he was commuting between Nottingham and his offices in Crane Court, off Fleet Street, from where he continued to market Parr's Pills. His circle was widening, he was meeting people more cultured than himself, with different standards, other values and far broader horizons.

The artist Henry Vizetelly claimed to have drawn up the draft prospectus of the *Illustrated London News* and has described how Ingram read it, approved and scribbled across the page "Print one million."[3] Ingram himself was no writer. Some of his surviving letters, although plain and direct, are ill-punctuated and not always correctly spelt but his choice of his first editor was shrewd. Frederick William Naylor was a minor poet and litterateur who wore seedy dress suits and snake-like ringlets. He put into words what Ingram would have written if he could: "Here we make our bow, determined to pursue our great experiment with boldness; to associate its principles with purity of thought that may secure and hold fast for our journal the fearless patronage of families, to seek in all things to uphold the great cause of public morality, to keep continually before the eyes of the world a living and moving panorama of all its actions and influences."

In those days the front page was usually given up to advertisements.

Ingram put them at the back and printed on the front news and pictures under a mast-head which was to become famous throughout the world – an engraving of St Paul's Cathedral looking across to the Lord Mayor's processional barges gliding down the Thames. The original wood blocks for the first edition of the *Illustrated London News* are in the Victoria and Albert Museum.

In a few years time the paper would benefit enormously from photography. In 1842 Ingram had to depend upon artists to draw a picture and skilled engravers to translate that drawing on to the woodblock, before cutting away all parts of the wood except the lines which made up the drawing. The small blocks had then to be assembled with nuts and bolts in order to put the whole picture together. All this had to be done swiftly under pressure from deadlines.

Ingram collected a band of artists, engravers and journalists willing to take part in his great experiment and its launch, on May 14, 1842, is famous in the history of journalism. On the day before publication Ingram employed 200 sandwich men to march up and down the Strand bearing placards announcing "The Illustrated London News. Thirty engravings! Price 6d!" Queen Victoria was in the fifth year of her reign, she had been married to Prince Albert for less than two years; the future King Edward VII was six months old.

Not everyone cared for this translation of human activities into pictures as if educated people were children. Four years after the *Illustrated London News* was published Wordsworth wrote a poor but prophetic sonnet attacking the whole idea.

> A backward movement surely have we here,
> From manhood, – back to childhood; for the age –
> Back towards caverned life's first rude career.
> Avaunt this vile abuse of pictured page!
> Must eyes be all in all, the tongue and ear
> Nothing? Heaven keep us from a lower stage!

The publication had, in fact, been held up in order to feature the Queen's first grand masked ball at Buckingham Palace. The delay turned out to be advantageous. Just as they were going to press a terrible fire broke out in Hamburg and seizing his chance, with the help of a print of the city from the British Museum, Ingram had an engraving made which showed the scene with imaginary spectators watching the smoke and flames in horror from the other side of the estuary: 26,000 copies were sold. In three months the circulation had doubled and by the end of the year figures exceeded a million. This necessitated a change of premises to the Strand. The first issue to contain coloured prints was published for Christmas 1855.

The *Illustrated London News* was created to supply a need. Once read by millions, it contained within its covers a remarkable record of contemporary history and the social attitudes of the largest empire the world has yet known. It also made Ingram a fortune. His rise from poverty to riches was almost as swift as that of a modern pop star. A fatherless boy educated at a charity school, his own family lived in large houses with servants and carriages. His sons were educated at Winchester, Eton and Oxbridge. Of course neither Ingram nor his friend Watkin were gentlemen in the sense that their descendants would have understood that word. But unlike many modern nouveaux riches they strove, not to perpetuate the deficiencies of their background, but to overcome them.

"Is he not living too fast?" a contemporary once asked after listening to Ingram's energetic and forceful description of how he intended to improve the world. Starting with almost no advantages save good health, imagination and a natural push and drive, Ingram had founded a newspaper, bought out three rivals, printed Paxton's plans for the Crystal Palace before anyone else, invested in the very latest steam printing machines and two paper mills, been elected twice as Liberal Member of Parliament for Boston and was one of the Deputy Lieutenants of Lincolnshire. Nor had he forgotten his roots.

In a letter written in response to a charitable appeal a year before he died, he remarks that his sympathies are altogether with the industrial classes and those who earn their bread by the sweat of their brows. The *Illustrated London News* under his management was never a crusading paper but from the first it published articles about pressing social problems of the day. He helped to supply his native town with pure water and railways, obtained a free library for them, and contributed large sums towards the restoration of his parish church and the repair of a medieval chapel, to be dedicated to the memory of John Cotton of Boston, Massachusetts. Cotton was a former vicar who had fallen foul of Archbishop Laud, escaped to New England and there led the Congregation at the First Church in Boston.

To look at, Ingram was short and stocky with protuberant blue eyes and prominent front teeth. He dressed badly, had an abrupt manner, a quick temper which sometimes led to violence, and a liking for brandy and water. He was indeed living too fast, he always had done and always would. When in 1860 it became known that he was about to take a holiday in North America, his enemies suggested that this was really an attempt to escape the consequence of shady financial dealings which had led to a nervous breakdown. The truth was more complicated.

Ingram had had his troubles. In the last decade the business partnership with his two brothers-in-law, Nathaniel Cooke and his wife's brother, William Little, had collapsed. Their withdrawal was accompanied on Little's part with recriminations and accusations of unscrupulous business methods, an unpaid debt and allegations that Ingram twice sexually assaulted William's brother's wife when she was in bed with a heavy cold. This was hardly to uphold the great cause of public morality, and from the evidence available may have been true.[4] But had it been made public the very accusation would have tainted Ingram and if proved, have utterly ruined him, his family and by extension, his newspaper.

Fortunately his competitors knew nothing of this. They had got wind of a scandal of a different nature. John Sadleir, a Member of Parliament, a former Lord of the Treasury and a man of widespread financial interests, had persuaded Ingram to allow him to make use of his name in connection with the launch of various fraudulent companies. In 1856 these were exposed and Sadleir killed himself on Hampstead Heath by swallowing prussic acid from a silver cream jug.[5] Ingram was cited in the court proceedings which followed but declared innocent of any criminal intent. Nevertheless, he had lost money, the matter was unsavoury and caused him a great deal of anxiety. They all said he needed a rest. He was to get a long one.

Ingram wished to visit Canada and the United States. In this he had undoubtedly been encouraged by the example of his high-flying friend and business advisor, Edward Watkin, who had first visited Canada and the United States in 1851 and on his return written a book about his experiences. Watkin had also gone to North America to recuperate after a nervous breakdown, in his case brought on by the stresses and strains resulting from the winding up and amalgamation of various railway companies with which he was involved.

Following Watkin's example, Ingram decided to combine business with pleasure. For part of the journey he intended to follow the same route as the Prince of Wales, later King Edward VII, then aged eighteen, who was making a tour of Canada and the United States. Ingram hoped to observe the Prince and his entourage and be enabled to produce one of the coloured supplements which were making the *Illustrated London News* famous.

For this purpose he took a number of his staff with him together with his eldest son, a boy of fifteen, also named Herbert. The family had an unusually tenacious sense of self-identity for people of their background. The eldest son in the direct line was always named Herbert. There had been seven of them since 1666; four were to follow in the century after young Herbert's death. Whatever the truth about his advances to his sister-in-law, Ingram was a devoted father and as events were shortly to prove, had remarkable confidence in his wife, Ann Little, whom he had married in 1843. They had ten children with eighteen months between each. One of the children died as an infant, another was drowned together with his father. Among the remaining eight was a girl, Emmeline Paxton, the god-daughter of Sir Joseph Paxton, later to be E. I. Watkin's mother.

Judging from his portrait, the young Herbert was a pleasant looking boy. According to his father, he attracted much notice although he was retiring and modest to a fault. If so, it was not one which would occur frequently in that most assertive of families. Ingram had a tremendous drive to express himself. He began a twenty-five page diary letter home even before he embarked and once he set sail threw overboard what he called "a bottle dispatch" stating the time, the date and the ship with a request to the finder to send the contents on to the *Illustrated London News*. He would have loved the telephone, and television would have endorsed all he held about the value of pictorial information and have suited his talents exactly. They arrived at Quebec on August 20, 1860.[6]

The St Lawrence was probably the finest river in the world, Ingram wrote to Edward Watkin who had already seen it, and the situation of Quebec unsurpassed; it reminded him of pictures of Constantinople. The Prince of Wales's visit was causing great excitement in both Quebec and Montreal. Ingram's party received an invitation to the official luncheon given by the Provincial Parliament for the Prince whom Ingram was to describe later as like the Queen, only more lively, with a fondness for dancing and cigars. In fact Victoria always loved dancing and in later life enjoyed a cigarette in the open with her ladies at Balmoral.[7]

He saw the Prince again in Montreal laying the last stone in the great railway bridge over the St Lawrence and he wrote to tell Watkin that the Grand Trunk Railway was nevertheless a hopeless concern and a waste of sixteen millions of English capital. This observation was unfortunate. In two years' time Watkin would be its President. For us, who know what is about to happen, Ingram's next remark was unfortunate too, but for quite different reasons. He went on to praise the excellence of the American Steam Boat system, the most delightful and cheapest means of conveyance he had ever seen. He had sailed on one, he wrote, through Lake Ontario in order to see the Niagara Falls. Excellent breakfasts, dinners, beds and in the bargain splendid saloons with every comfort. Watkin should take the hint and pay more attention on his trains to convenience and pleasure. As for the Falls, the water fell over a rock as high as Boston church. Thank God he had lived to see this most wonderful part of creation. It seemed to soothe his unsettled mind and reconcile him to future struggles; he would go on and not despair.

The Prince of Wales was to visit Niagara too and uneasily watch Blondin cross on a tightrope. By then Ingram was dead. His idea was to separate from his colleagues and to go to Chicago with his son. From there they would go down the Mississippi to New Orleans, then up to New York, the tour ending at Boston, this time in Massachusetts. Ingram remarked in a letter home that the United States would in time have a large population and perhaps in the setting sun of England, the new ruling Empire of the world would rise there. Land was so cheap, two shillings an acre in the wilderness. He could buy a township for Herbert here and now.

The pair travelled together to Chicago and after looking round changed their plans. They were enjoying themselves so much, they could easily prolong their holiday on the Great Lakes for a few more weeks and still be back at Westminster for the next session of parliament. The steam ships were floating palaces, the lakes like seas.

Attracted by a general air of festivity round a paddle steamer, the *Lady Elgin*, Ingram made inquiries and was informed she was going on a trip through Lake Michigan to Lake Superior.[8] The ship was crowded not only with casual passengers but with a contingent of Union Guards accompanied by their wives and children who were returning to Milwaukee from a Democratic Rally in Chicago. She had a passenger list of almost four hundred together with a cargo of freight which included cattle. She was, however, well lit and her life-saving equipment included four yawls designed to carry twenty people each, three lifeboats and four hundred of what were called "preserver floats". Ingram and his son went below.

At two o'clock in the morning, whilst there was still dancing both in the saloon and on deck, the *Lady Elgin* was struck amidships at full speed by the bow of the schooner *Augusta* which continued on her course. The *Lady Elgin* sank in half an hour. Two hundred and ninety-five people were drowned, including Herbert Ingram and his son. The boy's body was never found, his father's was washed ashore some sixteen miles from Chicago. Ingram was forty-nine.

As soon as the news reached them, two of the party who had accompanied Ingram to North America hurried down to Chicago. They saw the body with its countenance in death "perfectly calm and peaceful" and after a macabre and futile attempt to restore life, had the body embalmed and returned with it to Liverpool. From there it was taken to Boston by special train. On the day of the funeral all business was suspended in the town, flags flew at half mast and a procession headed by the Mayor and Corporation, other local officials, fifty of Ingram's associates and employees, together with friends and family, made its way to the cemetery. Here Ingram's widow later erected a polished granite obelisk bearing on it a carved marble relief of her son and the details of her husband's life.

Ingram had been quick to realize the commercial value of catastrophe. His own death was a tribute to his sound judgement. "With trembling hand and sorrowing heart we announce the death of Herbert Ingram, MP, the sole proprietor of the *Illustrated London News,*" ran the beginning of the report in the victim's own paper when the tidings reached England.[9] The number sold out. The next sole proprietor, single executorix and beneficiary of Ingram's entire fortune was discovered to be his widow.

CHAPTER TWO

Spending It

He left everything he had to his wife absolutely "in full and perfect confidence" that she "will continue, as hitherto, to be a kind and affectionate mother to my children and that she will make such a disposition of my property as may be for their benefit and advantage."

Ann Ingram was the only surviving daughter of a prosperous farmer from Eye, now in Cambridgeshire. Presumably she had met Ingram through her brother, William Little, a boyhood friend of his who was to be for many years the printer and publisher of the *Illustrated London News*. He was also the inventor of a successful sheep dip. At the time of her husband's death Ann was fifty-two and living with her eight children in a house near Rickmansworth on the River Chess, close to the Loudwater paper mills. Ingram had built the house in 1852 and his daughter, Emmeline Paxton, then nine months old, had laid her hand on the foundation stone.

Ingram drew up his will seven years before his death. Bearing in mind the complications of his estate, the extent of his family and the length of most testamentary depositions then, it was surprisingly short. There were no elaborate trusts, legacies or minute directions about the future of his beloved paper. He left everything he had to his wife absolutely "in full and perfect confidence" that she "will continue, as hitherto, to be a kind and affectionate mother to my children and that she will make such a disposition of my property as may be for their benefit and advantage." She was appointed sole Executrix.

Few wives of rich men can have been left in such a position of absolute power. Ingram had properties in Hertfordshire, Lincolnshire and Boston and far-reaching interests in the newspaper world, not to speak of his flagship, the *Illustrated London News*. Ann could buy, she could sell, she could marry again. She must have been close to her husband, he must have trusted her to carry out his wishes absolutely.

The eldest of her surviving children was Harriet, a girl of fifteen, always known as "Sissy", an affectionate nursery diminutive of "sister" to survive incongruously right up to old age. The youngest was Walter, a boy of five. He had two elder brothers, William and Charles, aged fourteen and thirteen and four other sisters besides Sissie: Annie, Ada, Emmeline, and Daisy. Even if they had wished or had had the capacity to act, many years were to elapse before any of Ann's sons could take over the management of the *Illustrated London News.*

Ingram had foreseen this difficulty and plainly discussed it with his wife. They had agreed that if he died before his sons became of age, his friend Edward Watkin and his uncle Nathaniel Wedd were to be legally empowered to act under her direction.

We do not know exactly when or where Ingram and Watkin met. They had much in common and each would help the other on the path to worldly success. They shared imagination, drive, a certain ruthlessness, business ability, obstinacy, a flair for publicity and at the very end, a wife. Watkin was more intelligent than Ingram, much better educated, more of a man of the world and came from a different background. His father, Absalom Watkin, was a self-made cotton merchant, a highly-strung, fastidious, bookish man with a tender social conscience who, coming to Manchester as a boy had from the beginning involved himself in a large number of reforming movements in a city that had grown too quickly, too haphazardly and with greater emphasis on personal wealth than the welfare of whose who helped to produce it. He had a deeply religious temperament and had started life as a Methodist lay preacher. He did not pass on to Edward this side of his nature but the inheritance was there, biding its time underground and like a mole would surface in unexpected places.

There was something of the showman in both Ingram and Edward Watkin and it was not altogether kindly suggested that they had met each other through the marketing of Parr's Pills. They were however, close enough friends for Watkin to be employed as a go-between at the time Ingram was accused of "gross and unmannerly conduct" towards his sister-in-law.

Edward Watkin possessed all the energy and drive his father lacked. From an early age he cultivated the right people and attached himself to the middle-class reforming party which had achieved so much for Manchester. He became a Director of the Anti-Corn Law Association and of the Manchester Athenaeum, campaigned and gained consent for the Saturday half-holiday for shops and businesses in the city, wrote *A Plea for Public Parks* and founded the *Manchester Examiner* in 1845, the year he made his escape from the cotton trade. Fortunately for him, he was offered a post as Secretary of the newly formed Trent Valley Railway. He accepted and was just in time to be chosen to push the wheelbarrow for

Sir Robert Peel at the cutting of the first sod. He was only twenty-six and would become one of the greatest railway promoters of the age.[1] *The Illustrated London News* was then but three years old.

Interests common to that particular time brought the two together. Today we are accustomed to a swift and highly structured society. We move at speed from one place to another and expect the government to regulate the means of doing so. But for centuries travel was restricted to the pace of men and horses, distances were conceived in a totally different way and trade controlled by geographical factors largely irrelevant today. Ingram was in his late teens and Watkin eleven years old when the Liverpool to Manchester railway was opened in 1830. By the time Edward seized his opportunity speculators were rife and different railway companies abounded.

If central control was weak, nevertheless it existed. Each claim to open a railway line had to be submitted to the Board of Trade by the company whose prospectus had already attracted sufficient investors. The claim was then examined by a parliamentary committee to which a number of Members of Parliament had been appointed. In 1854 Edward was General Manager of the Manchester, Sheffield, and Lincolnshire Railway and adept at these presentations.

Ingram had been quick to seize the opportunity offered by the outbreak of the Crimean War in 1853 and to send out artists of the quality of Constantin Guys, William Simpson and Joseph Archer Crowe. His was the only picture paper to cover the war both in the Baltic and the Crimea and its sales had soared. In his turn, Watkin's reputation as a fixer had reached the ears of Lord Palmerston who suggested, in response to the general outcry against appalling mismanagement, that Watkin should be appointed head of the Commissariat and organize military supplies for the troops.[2] He had the sense to refuse but such a man was just the kind of person Ingram was looking for to manage the paper should he die before his children attained their majority.

The once popular writer Clement Shorter, a former editor of *The Illustrated London News*, rather sourly pointed out in his autobiography that in Victorian times the proprietor of a paper was in fact the editor-in-chief and the editors under him merely well paid clerks. There is more than an element of truth in this. No one knew better than Watkin that it was vital for *The Illustrated London News* to maintain continuity after Ingram's death and not for one moment to give the impression that standards were in any way threatened. He may have suggested the editorial which, after the account of the catastrophe on Lake Michigan, went on to assure readers that the paper would go on being conducted "on the principles which it has always advocated and in the manner which its founder adopted and approved."

This the paper did. The family got richer and richer and in 1868 moved to a handsome and extensive house on the river at Walton-on-Thames designed by Barry for Lord Tankerville. It was called Mount Felix and here Ann Ingram, under the continued guidance of Edward Watkin, kept an eye on the precious paper, supervised a large domestic establishment and the upbringing of her five daughters and three sons.

It is very difficult, writing so long after all this happened, to describe Ann Ingram or even to think of her as she was then. By the time she died in her eighties towards the end of the nineteenth century, she was known by the younger generation as "Grandma", a little figure wearing a lace cap who held the threads of all their destinies in her plump hands. It has been suggested that she was by nature as forceful as her husband, that it was her managerial skills together with those of Edward Watkin which enabled *The Illustrated London News* not only to survive but to increase its sales during the minority of her sons. It may be so. To judge from photographs she was plain, and like her sovereign, attached to that most unbecoming of all styles, hair parted in the middle and drawn straight back over each temple. Perhaps it was as much her circumstances as her nature that made her what she was. Money had given her power, she was accustomed to being obeyed, experienced in those skills which prompt or entice human beings to carry out one's wishes.

For the most part her children were flamboyant, confident, and enjoyed their money. William was the most intelligent of her sons. He went to Winchester and Trinity College, Cambridge, where he got a First in Applied Science. He was called to the Bar by the Inner Temple, but never practiced.

When he was only twenty-four he followed his father as Liberal Member of Parliament for Boston. He represented what was fast becoming a family constituency until 1880 when his re-election was declared void because of corrupt practices on the part of the Ingram family. Grandma had distributed free coal.[3]

Emmeline was the last of the five so-called Ingram heiresses to get married and it is probably fair to say that the man she accepted did so for her money. However, if her husband was incapable of making her happy, he was by far the most gifted and amusing of Grandma's sons-in-law.

Edgar Watkin was one of the two surviving sons of Edward Watkin's brother, Alfred. Alfred was Absalom Watkin's youngest son and had remained in his father's cotton business. Like many of the family, Alfred was not a particularly steady character, although he succeeded in business, and became Mayor of Manchester. He loved entertaining, books, pictures, music and good port. There was evidently something wrong with his childrens' physical inheritance, whether derived from him or his wife, we do not know. Out of their family of six, three died as infants or young children, and the only daughter in early middle age. Two sons grew to manhood, the elder another Alfred, the younger, Edgar, who was to marry Emmeline Ingram.

No brothers could have been more different. Alfred was to become what seems from the outside to be a typical businessman of a certain type, red faced, sturdy and bluff. Owing to his father's early death he had to leave school early and work very hard to rescue a firm which had gone downhill during his father's long drawn-out illness. He was to be successful in the business, to end up in a fine Queen Anne House, to be appointed a High Sheriff of Cheshire and be the only one of his parent's children to attain old age. But he had had to slave for his money. He held this against his brother.

The gods had given Edgar a great many gifts but strength of character was not among them. He was good looking and amusing, very attractive to women, an accomplished pianist and actor and he drew exceptionally well. He was never robust, he was a homosexual and as time passed, self-ishness and idleness smothered an affectionate nature and a generous heart. He was to die young in a house on the cliffs in Norfolk within the sound of the sea, seeking in vain to make some sort of contact with the son he had neglected when the tide was high.

Utterly unlike as they were, Edgar Watkin shared with Herbert Ingram a strong impulse to express himself. He was always drawing, writing, acting or playing the piano. His father, Alfred, died when he was still at Harrow. Edgar had a weak chest and was probably suspected of having tuberculosis. In any event, his widowed mother, who had good cause to be anxious about the health of her children, arranged for him to make a voyage in the sailing ship *Parramatta* round the Cape of Good Hope to Australia and back. Edgar was just fifteen and he kept a detailed diary of the voyage.[4] Without it, we might assume that what he became he always was.

In a sense this is true. We have a picture of an unusually sharp and intelligent boy who observes and records the manners, clothes, accents and foibles of his fellow first-class passengers, one who grades social nuances as minutely as a woman might match embroidery silks. He has learnt, he writes towards the end of the voyage, more lessons about human nature from living in close proximity in a small community for a few months than he would have done by visiting five continents. He is acutely self-conscious and sensitive, after encouragement he plays the piano and sings although to his embarrassment, his voice is breaking. Above all, he exhibits a passion for theatricals which he helps to organize on board with zest and skill. It is doubtful if he is aware of the direction of his own sexuality. He is an affectionate creature, he misses his home, is devoted to his mother and keeps a photograph in his cabin of his dead father. Those who have in themselves a tendency to insincerity are the first to recognize it in others. He laughs to himself at social lies, is scornful of hypocrites and caustic about the insolent behaviour of the well-bred towards those passengers they consider beneath them.

He describes the Sunday services on board with care and sometimes with the sardonic amusement peculiar to those who know what religion is about. Once he was quite overwhelmed by the beauty of the scene on deck, the intense blue of the sky and sea, the ripple of the waves against the ship's bows and the singing of the simple hymns to the God in whose hands they all were. This was not mere adolescent gush although it is a voice we are not aware of again until not long before his death.

Once more he is writing a diary, this time recording a voyage to India where he is going to meet friends in Delhi to enjoy himself at the Coronation Durbar of 1902. He is, of course, a married man. His only child is a boy of fourteen, not much younger than he was himself when he set out for Australia. The passengers had sailed through the Gulf of Suez and into the Red Sea with the Sinai Peninsula on their left. "The sky was absolutely cloudless, nor was there any stir of breeze nor sign of any living thing. Vast mountain chains rose from the steeply shelving sands in fantastic and terrible shapes, no blade of grass or shrub or tree softening their rugged grandeur – range upon range, pinnacle upon pinnacle." He imagined the Israelites "wandering through that appalling chaos of burning sand and barren mountain till the agony of despair closed on them and they murmured against God." These thoughts were interrupted by a Wesleyan minister who was having a tedious argument with a school-master about the precise route the Israelites took.

Why, Edgar asks in his diary, should the wonderful suggestiveness of Bible History be trammelled by the weight of dates, dimensions and exact geographical position? "My whole soul revolts," he adds, "at the coun-terfeit presentation of God the Father – the incomprehensible one – the great 'I am' as a more or less benign old gentleman with a white beard and blue and red robes – always the same – cut each other's throats and forget entirely the spirit, the kernel, the embodied truth."[5] It might have been his son speaking.

Edgar adopted the law as his profession and qualified as a solicitor. His mother was a Mellor, the daughter of a well-known Lancashire legal and business family. Her first cousin was the distinguished judge Sir John Mellor and this legal connection may have suggested that line of life. If so, he was not to pursue it long. We do not know exactly where or when Edgar first met Emmeline Ingram but they must have been aware of each other's existence for years because his mother and Sir Edward's wife were sisters.

His Uncle Edward had indeed gone from strength to strength and from one grandiose scheme to another. Member of Parliament for Hythe, High Sheriff of Cheshire, Officer of the Order of Leopold of Belgium, Officer of the Order of the Redeemer of Greece, Chairman of the Manchester,

Sheffield, and Lincolnshire and the South Eastern and Metropolitan Railways, he had been knighted in 1868 and was created a baronet twelve years later. Although absorbed in his own projects, the Channel Tunnel and the Wembley Tower, he was still Grandma's right hand and the power behind the throne as far as *The Illustrated London News* was concerned. He was disliked and resented by William and Charles and now their sister was marrying into the enemy camp.

It is impossible to do more than guess what feelings Emmeline had for Edgar. She would not have discussed her marriage with her son. Her natural confidantes were her sisters. But by the time Emmeline's grandchildren were sufficiently grown up to be suitable and eager listeners, their great-aunts were dead. In 1887 Emmeline was thirty-six, small, thin, with the protuberant blue Ingram eyes. She could never have been pretty but she was handsome and in later life looked distinguished. Victorian photographs are so misleading because their subjects rarely smiled. Some of her contemporaries described Emmeline as cheerful and jolly. On one point there was general agreement. She was the most obstinate, wilful and difficult to deal with of all the sisters.

Edgar was twenty-seven. We know from others that he was very attractive to women. We know too that Emmeline gave him every material thing he asked for. She paid entirely for the luxurious style of living in which she had been brought up and that he was so to enjoy. It seems that she loved him and did so to the last. We have no idea whether she really understood what sort of man he was before she married him or if in her heart she forgave his way of life. Nor will we ever know what Edgar's feelings were for her.

Perhaps there is no aspect of human life which demonstrates the ambiguity of moral judgements so much as our attitude to marriage. To marry for money or position where there is no love is considered plainly wrong and as a form of prostitution. But because money is one of the motives for marriage, love is not necessarily absent. "Do not marry for money but marry where money is," was the commonsense advice given by middle- and upper-class parents down the ages. It was taken for granted in a non-contraceptive age. Jane Austen makes plain that Fanny Price's mother ruined her life by marrying a mere lieutenant in the marines when had she been more discriminating she might have enjoyed the ease and pleasures of her sister, Lady Bertram. Lower down the social scale we accept the inevitable consequences which followed when Mr Tulliver's sister threw herself away on a poor farmer. Edgar would not have married Emmeline if she had not been rich. Emmeline would not have married him if he had not come from the right social background. The fact that he had no money and was unlikely to make any may not have bothered her. She probably wanted him to be dependent. Her future husband was offered a life of leisure and he took it.

They were married on November 22, 1887, at St Paul's, Knightsbridge. Neither William nor Charles was present. The youngest son, Walter, however consented to give his sister away. The wedding was a grand one. According to newspaper descriptions and the drawings which accompanied them, the bride wore a magnificent dress of rich ivory duchesse and silver brocade, over which were beautifully arranged flounces of old lace, the gift of her mother, fastened by bouquets of orange blossom, jessamine and myrtle. The very long court train, borne by two page boys, was of massive silver brocade and the bridal veil was fastened by clusters of diamond stars, also given by Grandma.

The honeymoon was spent in Algiers. Emmeline conceived quickly for a woman of thirty-six. Their only child, Edward Ingram Watkin, was born at Stand, Cheshire, on September 27 the following year. Within a few weeks, perhaps days of his birth, the baby was handed over to the care of Grandma. He came to be known among the family as Edda.

CHAPTER THREE

A Public Scandal

Grandma was good, she was kindly, she told the footman
to stop all the grandfather clocks at night as striking might
prevent the child from sleeping. But she was nearly eighty.

Children accept the world they live in because they know no other. Edda's children did not question their father's unusual childhood any more than they did the strangeness of their own. When in old age Edda was pressed on the subject and asked the real reason why his mother left him in the care of Grandma, he looked shifty and did not answer at once. At last, in almost a whisper, he replied that he feared it was money.

It took him almost a lifetime to realize it, but Edda was in fact a small but significant pawn in the power game being played out between Sir Edward and Grandma together with her daughters on one side, William and Charles on the other. Briefly, the problem was how to distribute the spoils of Ingram's successful venture fairly and how to ensure that the business continued to be profitable. By 'fairly' was meant how much each interested party could safely get away with.

Probably no one would have paid much attention to Edda's birth had not Walter Ingram been killed by an elephant.[1] Walter, the youngest of the family, was barely five when his father drowned. The army offered him a more exciting life than the stuffy old *Illustrated London News* and after Eton and Cambridge he became an officer in the Middlesex Yeomanry and started to specialize in military tactics. In 1884 the idea of General Gordon holed up in Khartoum surrounded by what were then called "stinking dervishes" so caught his imagination that with his brother Charles as a companion, he set out for Egypt and chartered a steamer on the Nile. Hiring a band to keep spirits up on board, he and Charles were allowed to follow Lord Wolseley's expeditionary force up the river. Walter was an extrovert, he loved travel and sport and was an excellent swimmer. On the way up his chief engineer fell overboard during the navigation of some cataracts. Walter dived in and saved the engineer's life at some risk to his own. For this he was awarded a silver medal by the Royal Humane Society and he was later mentioned in dispatches for his gallantry at the battles of Abu Klea and Metammeh.

Later he travelled throughout Egypt and in an ill-fated moment during the winter of 1885–6, bought an ancient coffin with a mummy in it from a dealer in Luxor. This he sent home and it was deposited in the offices of the *Illustrated London News* where it was examined by the famous Egyptologist, E. A. Wallis Budge. He identified it as Nes-Amsu, the second prophet of the god Amsu. The name was later corrected by the Oriental Institute in Chicago to Nes-Min.[2] Charles gave the gilded mask to the British Museum and Walter the painted coffin and mummy to a private collector. It was sold at auction in 1910 and poor Nes-Min's remains have never been traced since.

The relationship between body and spirit is intimate and religion recognizes this. A clouded intuition about risen bodies is expressed in the Christian creeds and in a different manner by the Catholic veneration of relics. For this reason, trafficking in bodies is sometimes felt to be distasteful. However, Nes-Min's fate would have been of interest, regret and censure only to Egyptologists and other cultivated people, had it not been for a single circumstance. It was reported that on a papyrus inside the coffin was inscribed a warning that any one who disturbed the mummy would die a violent death. In 1888 Walter went big game shooting in Somaliland with Sir Henry Meux, whose wife had been given the mummy for her collection at Theobald's Park. That April Walter was killed by a charging elephant, thus fulfilling, so it was said, the mummy's ancient curse.[3]

Fantasies of that kind were in the air. An 'unlucky mummy' among the collection in the British Museum was said to have caused the sinking of the *Titanic,* and a few years later it was even suggested that Nes-Min was on board the *Lusitania* and had attracted the German submarines. After the First War, stories about the so-called "curse of King Tut" circulated widely. Conan Doyle, who had abandoned Catholicism, became more credulous in a different direction and mentioned the Ingram mummy in several interviews he gave after the unexpected death of the excavation's patron, Lord Carnarvon.[4]

At this time both Emmeline and Walter's widow were expecting babies, much to the delight of Grandma who, utterly disillusioned with her own sons and their constant financial demands, had become almost obsessed with having a male grandchild. Walter's child was born in July 1888 and turned out to be a girl. In vain did the widow have the baby named 'Walterina Favorita'. In favour she was not and a very disappointed Grandma had to wait for Emmeline's confinement. In the months between

July and September Emmeline and her mother, together presumably with
Edgar, must have agreed that should the baby be male he would be immediately put into the care of his grandmother. And so it was done. Grandma
had that autumn either bought or rented a house in Bournemouth and it
was there, with a small entourage of nurses and chambermaids, that Edda
spent the first Christmas of his life.

It must not be thought that Emmeline and Edgar never saw their son.
They visited him regularly, stayed with Grandma and had news of him
through the post. Nor was the situation quite so odd as it would be thought
now. It was then not so unusual for children to be adopted or sent away
to be looked after by richer friends or relations. What we call social services were rudimentary. No one examined the suitability of people who
adopted children, assessed the material conditions under which the child
would live or questioned the motives of those who had got hold of them;
there was certainly no talk about bonding or emotional deprivation.

We have but few facts. Grandma wanted comfort, she felt like poor
General Gordon, besieged by her surviving sons. She had a fixation on
boys but her own had betrayed her. Her large family had all left home,
she longed for a human being who would again be dependent upon her.
For her part, Emmeline cared for her mother and certainly did not wish
to alienate her. She hoped that by doing what was asked both she and her
child would profit financially. Although intensely possessive about people
and objects, she may not have cared particularly for babies.

A few letters from this period survive. Edda was called 'Toby' until after
seeing a Punch and Judy show at the age of six, he protested vigorously
that he was not a dog. In an undated letter from Mount Felix, Grandma
tells Emmeline that Toby's teeth have very nearly come through and that
he could say almost anything. Edgar needed a rest, Grandma said, he had
been staying at Mount Felix and he would tell Emmeline how clever Toby
is, a darling child and most amusing, they get on so well together. He talks
about his mother daily and his 'Fazder'.

Grandma was good, she was kindly, she told the footman to stop all
the grandfather clocks at night as striking might prevent the child from
sleeping. But she was nearly eighty.

Edda's first solid memories referred to a time when he was just three.
It was 1891 and he was spending Christmas at Mount Felix with
Grandma. Thinking no doubt of her own boys, she gave him a box of toy
soldiers as a present. These he disliked. He wanted to play with dolls but
was not allowed to, dolls were for girls only. Perhaps among the more
sophisticated members of the family there was an unspoken fear that he
might grow up like his father. For some time Edda puzzled over the difference between boys and girls. In the end he came to the conclusion that at
birth the parents chose what sex they wished the child to be and dressed
the baby accordingly. He thought boys rough and noisy and imagined,

mistakenly, as he would add in after life, that girls were always gentle and kind, so he longed for a sister.

What was going on around Edda was far from kind. Emmeline's marriage, Walter's death, the birth of her son and his transference to Grandma on top of the continued presence of Sir Edward forced an agitated William Ingram to take action. He and Charles insisted that the paper should be put on quite a different business footing altogether and that both of them should have greater financial control and more of the profits. After long and recrimatory negotiations, in 1890 it was at last agreed that former trusts and settlements should be abrogated and a private, family joint stock company should be formed. After further disagreements, the profits of the *Illustrated London News* and other papers owned by the family were fixed at £300,000 a year, then a very large sum.[5] But how were the shares to be distributed and how much were William and Charles to be paid for managing the paper? Statements of Claim abounded, Interrogatories multiplied, the British Consul in Cannes attested to oaths, settlements were drawn up and abandoned, Grandma gave Charles notice to quit her house in Onslow Gardens, and Sir Edward uttered a solemn warning about being sucked into Chancery.

For some time rumours had been circulating about a possible marriage between Grandma and Sir Edward. Watkin had made many enemies during the course of his relentless climb upwards. In 1892 he was seventy-two, Ann Ingram was eighty and in many quarters the prospect of their marrying was greeted with subdued hilarity. For years William Ingram had been on the alert. He minded his mother being the subject of jokes, he deeply resented Sir Edward and suspected his motives. He was not alone in this. There were others who hinted that Watkin's finances were not altogether sound, and that he was marrying Ann Ingram to get his hands on her money.

Sir Edward's first wife, Mary Mellor, the sister of Edgar's mother, had died from 'a complication of disorders' in 1888, four years before the proposed marriage became public knowledge. She had directed that a diamond bracelet set with cameo portraits of Sir Edward, herself and the children which Her Royal Highness had once much admired, should be presented on her death to the Princess of Wales. This splendid gift, the newspapers reported, had been accepted gratefully and merited a letter of sympathy to Sir Edward Watkin written in HRH's own hand.[6] One wonders what actually happens to such presents. Mary had had two children, yet another Alfred and a daughter, Harriette. Pushed into it by his father, Alfred had made a respectable but unsatisfactory marriage to a daughter of the Dean of Canterbury. His sister had married Henry Worsley-Taylor.

The paper was now subject to regular board meetings of the family company. This consisted of William, Charles, Edgar, who acted on behalf of the sisters, and Sir Edward, who acted on behalf of Grandma. It was asserted by the enemy party that Edgar used to turn up at Board Meetings wearing powder and discreet lipstick. No doubt this was as mendacious as it was malicious. Since the entire Board spent a great deal of time in the South of France, it was difficult to get them together but Sir Edward did his best to see that when they did meet they were not at each other's throats.

As the winter of 1892 melted into spring and the gossip columns were sniggering about a certain approaching marriage, Sir Edward made a great effort to placate William who was always called 'Willie' by the family. "And now my 'dear Willie'" he wrote, " – *pray*, Mr Ingram, excuse the liberty – let us all work together in support of your management and in the interests of all! And will you let me speak to you on some family matters – in *masonic* secrecy? You *know* I have no selfish views to serve."

William and Charles knew nothing of the kind. They met and without actually stating that Watkin was dishonest, his motives were impugned and words like 'public scandal' and 'disgusting' and even 'carnal knowledge' were bandied about. William informed Sir Edward that in future he would forward all his letters on to his solicitor. He was full of horror and disgust at the proposed marriage, he would certainly not meet him at Mount Felix because if he did he would take a horse-whip to him and the shock would be too great for his mother.

Sir Edward was in the right and acted honourably. All the gossip about pending bankruptcy and getting hold of a dying heiress was totally false. Sir Edward's motives were not mercenary nor were the financial prospects of Grandma's children in any way effected. Ann Ingram was feeble and infirm and needed protection. She was being bullied by her sons. Little Edda could not help her, Emmeline was frequently abroad with her delicate husband, nor were her other daughters inclined to take up residence at Mount Felix. Sir Edward let the scandal-mongering journalists know that Mrs Ingram's entire property was settled on her children to the exclusion of himself and his own property was settled on his children.

So Grandma became Lady Watkin and the ceremony was performed at St George's, Hanover Square, at nine in the morning of April 7, 1892. By an extraordinary chance, an artist from the *Pall Mall Budget* happened to be in the church attending to his religious duties before the wedding party arrived. His pictures are as delightful as his text. In view of their age, the service was tactfully abbreviated and only a handful of people were present to see the couple kneeling at the altar rails. Sir Edward, the reporter wrote, "kept his eyes on the bride, whom he carefully helped down the steps. She was dressed in black silk with a long train, with a heavily beaver-bordered cloak and a bonnet with a light purple ostrich tip upon it. She was blushing like a girl of sixteen and both 'the happy pair' seemed to be enjoying suppressed amusement."[7]

Emmeline and her sisters and their husbands were probably there but not Edda, who ever afterwards regretted that he could not tell people that he had been present at his grandmother's wedding. A letter from Sir Edward to Emmeline from Mount Felix survives, carefully pasted into her scrapbook. "Toby," Sir Edward tells the child's mother, "came into our chamber this morning uninvited – and seemed astonished to find his Grandma in bed – and not alone!"

The marriage effected Edda only in so far as he saw more of the man who was now not only his great-uncle but his step-grandfather. Sir Edward, like Grandma, was very kind to him and treated him as he himself was to treat his own children, a person in his own right. He remembered vividly the joy of going in the carriage with Grandma and Sir Edward to Absalom's old home at Rose Hill and back again to London in a special train. He travelled with the upper servants in their own compartment and had a jolly time. They drank what they told him was 'red lemonade', really wine, and allowed him to have a sip or two before mocking their employer's failure to get on with his Channel Tunnel by singing in sarcastic merriment a verse from an ode composed in Sir Edward's honour a year or two before.[8] This ode, originally of fourteen verses, had been composed to celebrate the opening of Watkin's railway bridge over the River Dee at Hawarden where Mrs Gladstone had started proceedings by blowing on a gold whistle. "All hail Edward Watkin/Pioneer of the world! Who unites great nations/His banners unfurled," the staff sang loudly. "All hail to our hero,/ Great man of the day/ A grand Old Veteran/ So youthful and gay."At this they collapsed into laughter and Edda loved it.

This, surely, must have been before the arrival of Nana. Nurse Walker was a rather formidable Scot who was to play a large part in Edda's early life and by chance to enter it again when he was older. She had left school at fourteen and started life as a nursery-maid in the Duke of Montrose's family. Her main work then was to carry heavy cans of hot water up four flights of stairs. The head nurse wore a gold watch pinned on to her bosom and Nana's great ambition was some day to wear one like it. Emmeline gave her such a watch as a leaving present. Nana had been employed to replace a previous nurse who through neglect, had allowed Edda to develop rickets. Her real love was for babies and she was a little puzzled by Edda, and in after years alarmed her subsequent charges by telling them all about the miraculously clever little boy who could recite the whole of the *Pied Piper of Hamlin* when he was only three.[9]

In September, 1892, when he was nearly four, Edda had his first experience of the public side of his new grandfather's life. He accompanied Grandma to the ceremonial opening of the Watkin Path up Snowdon.

CHAPTER FOUR

The Watkin Path

Sir Edward's dramatic sense had not deserted him. He had chosen to hold the ceremony under the very shadow of Snowdon in a great natural amphitheatre formed by the cwm. Here he had selected a massive glacial boulder, ordered a roofed and carpeted platform to be built on it and a stairway constructed at the side to enable his guests to take up their position on the top.

S ome historians have accused Sir Edward Watkin of being a megalo-maniac, a gambler, an abrasive, ruthless egoist determined to dominate everything and everybody. A perceptive modern critic remarked that he seemed to have been driven by a great urge "to make something utterly stupendous."[1] That was true. A strong character was allied to a romantic imagination.

Watkin thought in large intuitive sweeps like a poet or a visionary. Earlier in his career he was asked by the Duke to Newcastle to sort out the tangled affairs of the Grand Trunk Railway in Canada whose President he became. At once he saw the problem not in terms of an effi-cient railway line merely, but as an essential instrument in the formation of the Dominion of Canada. He wrote that to him "it was the great idea – to be realized some day distant though that day might be – of a great British nation planted for ever under the Crown and extending from the Atlantic to the Pacific."[2] He accepted the challenge, crossing and recrossing the Atlantic, pressing hard for the purchase of that barrier to his expansionist plans, the Hudson's Bay Company. As so often, his achievements did not match his vision, not through his fault but the fault of others who were too slow to share it. It did not matter. When towards the end of his life, Sir Edward came to have his portrait painted by Herkomer, he asked to be shown holding a map of Canada.[3]

The same imaginative flash, a conviction of what could be, underlay his fierce and prolonged fight to complete the tunnel under the Channel which he had started to build in 1891. Manchester could be linked with Paris. Using his Great Central Line people should be enabled to travel on the same train from the North to London, to Dover, to the Continent via the tunnel which already stretched almost two miles towards France. In 1892 he was compelled by a court injunction to put a stop to the enterprise but there was nothing one could teach Watkin about public relations. To gain support he organized fashionable champagne parties beneath the sea.[4]

The guests were lowered in a lift 168 feet down and drawn along in wheeled trolleys to an excavated space furnished with tables and chairs. The Prince and Princess of Wales had been taken down and greatly enjoyed themselves, perhaps it was here that the Princess had taken the opportunity to admire Lady Watkin's diamond bracelet. The Archbishop of Canterbury had made the trip too, and the Lord Mayor of London and the leader of Watkin's own party, Mr Gladstone. Queen Victoria was not amused. She thought the project "very objectionable" and so did Cardinal Manning. Garnet Wolseley was not convinced by Sir Edward's claim that should war break out the whole thing could be blown to pieces by touching a button on Horse Guards. Watkin brought forward bill after bill in the Commons but in his lifetime there was no further tunnelling.

In the year of Edda's birth Watkin was struck by another idea. Eiffel had built a 984-foot high tower in Paris. He would build a tower higher than that in London. As Chairman of the Metropolitan Line he was able to persuade the Company to buy 280 acres of land at Wembley and got himself appointed as Chairman of the Tower Construction Company. He initiated the building of Wembley Park station, during the excavations for which the fossilized remains of an elephant and a hipopotamus were discovered. The tower was to be 1,150 feet high and its design thrown open to competition.

The distinguished engineer Sir Benjamin Baker was appointed the principal judge. Entries poured in from all over the world. Eiffel did not think it patriotic to compete. The London Vegetarian Society put forward a structure shaped like an Egyptian monolith with fruit and vegetables growing from hanging baskets and on its summit a slightly reduced copy of the Great Pyramid of Gaza. Albert Brunel submitted a 2,296-foot high copy of the Tower of Pisa, to be built of granite. The entry finally chosen looked very like its Paris rival, only 165 feet taller. It was designed to house restaurants, a theatre, shops, winter gardens and Turkish baths, all with magnificent views over London. At the top, where the air was clearest, an observatory was to be set up in order to photograph the stars. It was suggested that a sanatorium to facilitate the fashionable "pure air cure" might be established. The Pleasure Park was to be laid out with boating lakes, landscaped gardens and a waterfall.[5]

The Watkin Path

In 1891 the foundations for the Tower's four steel legs were laid in what is now the centre of Wembley Stadium. Making the pleasure gardens went forward according to plan but the progress of the Tower itself was slow. By 1892 the shareholders began to get restive, but Sir Edward assured them that there was plenty of capital to continue building and when the Tower opened it would take three times as many people as the one in Paris. The whole thing would be completed in about eighteen months and then the money would come rolling in. Unfortunately, a year later the Tower had reached only 62 feet and by May of 1894 when the Park was opened the 100,000 visitors were dismayed to find that it had reached a mere 155 feet. That winter the work stopped. In 1907, the year Edda went up to Oxford, the rusting girders were blown up by dynamite.

It is easy to mock Sir Edward because some of the most spectacular of his projects failed. But the Hudson's Bay Company was bought out, a transcontinental railway was constructed and the Dominion of Canada was formed under the British Crown. A Channel Tunnel was eventually completed, the Great Central Railway may yet be revived and whatever the fans may say, his Tower and Pleasure Gardens would have offered far greater variety and enjoyment than mere football. Moreover, he gave his name to something which, if properly maintained, should be imperishable. This is the Watkin Path which leads to the summit of Snowdon.

When he was not at Mount Felix, Watkin lived at Rose Hill, his old home at Northenden, then in the country not far from Manchester. However, he frequently retired to a retreat he had contrived for himself in North Wales. His family claimed to have come originally from that country and Absalom had faithfully attended the annual Welsh dinner held in the city. Sir Edward loved that part of Wales, he relished the emphatic, the sensational, striking contrasts and bold scenic effects, thunderstorms and waterfalls. In 1889, a year after Edda's birth, he had bought a property of some one thousand five hundred acres on the southern side of Snowdon at Cwm y Llan.[6]

Here he built himself a one-storey house constructed of corrugated iron, the then fashionable material, and painted it white. It had solid foundations, brick chimneys and the inside walls were lined with wood. It was usually referred to as 'The Chalet' but sometimes as the 'Hafod', a Welsh term for the temporary mountain refuge to which farmers moved when their flocks came in summer. Sir Edward thought of it as his refuge and often used to visit with his faithful valet and remain there alone, a thousand feet up between Llyn Gwnant and Llyn Dinas, listening for hours to the sound of roaring water. That was one part of his nature. The other part, the showman, the exhibitionist, delighted in people, parties and entertaining. So he had the Chalet built with six bedrooms, a servants' hall and four servants' bedrooms, the whole lit by electric light produced by water power. He had a stone walled garden made with a fountain

25

playing in its centre. The place became a ruin. Sold after Sir Edward's death, at some time fire took hold and nettles, brambles and the encroaching rhododendron covered the solid foundations. The ground was littered with twisted sheets of corrugated iron and blackened bricks from fallen chimneys.

In the summer of 1892 Lord Salisbury asked the Queen to dissolve Parliament which meant a General Election. Sir Edward was quick off the mark. He got Grandma to write to Gladstone and offer him the use of her house at Walton-on-Thames including "servants, cuisine, horses and carriages" for the duration of the campaign. Gladstone won the election without the help of Mount Felix but with a narrow majority. The Conservative government did not resign until Parliament met but in August fell to a vote of No Confidence moved by a young barrister, H. H. Asquith. Gladstone's fourth and last ministry then began.

Sir Edward retired to the Chalet. His property extended to the summit of Snowdon. He had employed his own engineers and workmen to construct a road of local stone from the disused slate works in Cwm Llan to the top of the mountain and wished the public to make use of it. With the help of Tom Ellis, the Liberal MP for Merioneth, he persuaded Gladstone, as part of a visit to North Wales, not only to open his path but to stay at the Chalet with his wife and other members of his family which included his daughter, Mary Drew.[7]

On the evening of their arrival at the Chalet, September 12, 1892, Sir Edward gave a dinner party to which he had invited among others, the young David Lloyd George, the Liberal Member for Caernavon. After dinner they were all entertained by a choir from Portmadoc which sang Welsh hymns and songs outside the house until dusk.

Gladstone was nearly eighty-three, ten years older than his host. Lloyd George was not quite thirty and kept his eyes and ears about him. He was a sincere admirer of Sir Edward's Great Central Railway whose strategic importance was such, he later remarked, that without it we might not have won the First World War. This was true. The Great Central fed the slaughter on the Western Front. It was also ironical. Watkin's great-nephew, Edda, was in the course of time to be one of the comparatively few people who condemned that war almost from its start.

Gladstone, Lloyd George wrote in his memoirs, showed that evening none of the usual symptoms of a man of his age.[8] He did most of the talking in his deep, vibrant voice and told amusing stories about coachmen in the days before the railways, gave a dissertation on the advantages and disadvantages of corrugated iron roofing and pointed out the high cost of sugar candy in his youth. Prompted by some mention of the Channel Tunnel of which he heartily approved, he sang a hymn of praise to the people of France who were so much more enlightened, broad-minded and civilized than those over whose destinies he was then privileged to preside. Presumably Nana and Edda were already in the house. His parents did not arrive until the following day. Edgar had recently returned from a trip to America and wore the faintly sardonic expression he adopted throughout other people's entertainments. It was either then or the day before that Edda of his own accord plucked a flower from the garden and solemnly presented it to the Grand Old Man. Gladstone was delighted and Edda was to remember the occasion and recount it with relish to the end of his days.

The actual ceremony was to take place after lunch. All the morning groups of people had been seen walking up past the house and before long a crowd of some 2,500 were waiting to greet the Prime Minister. Sir Edward's dramatic sense had not deserted him. He had chosen to hold the ceremony under the very shadow of Snowdon in a great natural amphitheatre formed by the cwm. Here he had selected a massive glacial boulder, ordered a roofed and carpeted platform to be built on it and a stairway constructed at the side to enable his guests to take up their position on the top. A Welsh hymn greeted the party and Gladstone stood with uncovered head. They climbed up to the platform to hear the speeches which started with a fiery address from a Welshman. They were one with their Celtic brethren in Ireland, the Church should be disestablished, funds spent on education and a Welsh university, the land should be reformed. Edda sat on Mrs Gladstone's lap during her husband's speech.

He was in tolerable agreement with Welsh aspirations, the Prime Minister answered, the Liberal party would work as hard for Wales as, having regard for human infirmity, men could work. More hymns gave these guarded commitments a glow of credibility. The quarrymen of Llanberis then delivered a Loyal Address, Lloyd George spoke in Welsh, Sir Edward stepped forward and proposed 'A Welcome to Wales' which was greeted by three hearty cheers. Further hymns were sung and it was evening before the crowds dispersed to make their way homeward down the valley.

In time, the Path became so eroded that it was hard to imagine carriages there at all. But then it was new and so soundly constructed of stone from the South Snowdon Slate Quarries that someone suggested they made an attempt on the summit, starting in the landau. Since the weather remained fine, the idea was favourably received and next morning Edward Owen, the chief guide of the Goat Hotel, was summoned from Beddgelert to organize the expedition. Sir Edward's cob, Polly, pulled the landau up the carriage road without difficulty, then Gladstone mounted Owen's own pony, Tommy, taken from the stables of the Goat. Unfortunately when they reached *Bwlch y Saethau*, the Path of Arrows, a mist came down and shrouded the summit and Gladstone's family entreated him to go no further. Reluctantly he agreed to turn back and only Emmeline and Mary Drew made the final ascent.

In 1998 four thousand acres on the Southern slopes of Snowdon, which included the Watkin Path and a third of the mountain's summit, were put on the market. The National Trust launched a successful appeal and the following year the land was bought for the nation. The Path was repaired, extended and slightly re-routed. In the autumn of 2004, one hundred and ten years after its inauguration, it was ceremonially reopened and remains one of the most popular and beautiful of the routes up Snowdon.

Edda lived with Sir Edward and Grandma for another three and a half years. In the spring of 1893, a case was filed before Mr Justice Chitty in the Chancery Division of the High Court of Justice. Dame Ingram Watkin, as Grandma was quaintly called, and Sir Edward were cited on one side, the *Illustrated London News* Ltd and William and Charles on the other. Eventually a settlement was made out of court. At the end of March a Compromise was drawn up and *Ingram v Ingram*, *Ingram v Watkin*, *Watkin v Ingram*, was at an end. Not however the enmity between the two parties. William ordered the *Illustrated London News* never to mention Sir Edward in its pages again. He wrote to the papers making fun of the proposed Channel Tunnel, lobbied against Watkin in the House of Commons and was delighted when in 1893, the bill to permit further excavation was finally lost. The following year Sir Edward had a heart attack and was advised to take things more slowly. He resigned all his directorships but remained convinced that opposition to his tunnel was foolish and obscurantist and that one day he would be vindicated. It would take a hundred years.

Edda was six when he first saw Sheringham in North Norfolk, the place that was to play such a large part in his life and would haunt his children until the end. The east coast had a reputation for bracing air and Nana thought her charge delicate. Sheringham had just started to grow from a small but thriving fishing village into the popular seaside resort it would later become. The railway had arrived there in 1887, the Sheringham Hotel had been built, and there were a few canvas huts and bathing machines on the beach. Some of the impetus for this development had come from a well-known local family called Pegg. Always one to go to the top, Emmeline made arrangements for her son and his nurse to stay with them or in one of their houses for some months. These flint fishermens' houses were right on the sea and Edda loved Sheringham from the very beginning. He enjoyed the freedom of his new life, running over the sands, walking with Nana and half shocked, half envious, watching the naked fisherboys playing about in the water.

We do not know who first taught Edda to read or write but while Nana's boasts about the *Pied Piper* may have been exaggerated, it is plain that from an early age he showed an unusual ability to read almost any book that was handed to him and to retain its contents. Emmeline took what was then the almost unheard of step for a woman of her background, she sent Edda to the local school, in those days called the Elementary or Board School, where boys and girls were educated together from the age of five to fourteen. The school was about a mile away at Upper Sheringham, the original village with its mediaeval church. The Sheringham we know today grew not from that village but from its poor relation, the fishing hamlet by the sea. Maintained in the beginning by the Upcher family, the school had been enlarged when Edda went there and was able to accommodate as many as 200 pupils. What they made of him we have no idea nor how he understood their Norfolk dialect, universal among the working classes then. In after days his own children dreaded the sight of old Pegg coming up the garden path because they could not make out a word he said. But to their surprise their father would hold long conversations with the local fishermen, he speaking in his manner, they in theirs. Edda must have been accepted and treated well because he was very happy at the school and remained grateful to his mother for her unconventional approach. The headmaster was a Mr Savage, whose son, years later, was to become Director of Education at County Hall, London.

It may be that Edda's health was less of a problem than the fact that since Sir Edward had been ill and Grandma more frail, Emmeline simply did not know what to do with the child. Soon she and Edgar would have total charge of him for the first time. In 1896, when Edda was eight, Grandma died at Mount Felix and was buried at Boston beside her first husband and the memorial to their drowned son. While the family gathered and expectations sharpened, Edda was left alone at Mount Felix with Nana and the servants.

William and Charles received nothing. They immediately complained that their mother had not been of sound mind, took the matter to court, and lost the case. Almost the entire estate was left to be divided equally between her five daughters with trusts drawn up in favour of her grandchildren and great-grandchildren. Such is the ambiguity of wealth and the frailty of good intentions, it was these trusts which were to become the subject of bitter and disastrous contention between Edda and his mother.

That year Emmeline bought Edgar a property called Pantafon.

Pantafon was a world in itself. Built high up in Snowdonia between Caernarvon and Llanberis, the house was large with some twelve bedrooms set in nearly sixty acres of ground. It had a trout lake, a golf course, a small farm, streams, woods, pergolas, parterres, stables, an extensive kitchen garden and magnificent views at the back over lawns to the Menai Straits and Anglesey. At the front the ground rose sharply up and away towards Snowdon.

It was to be Edgar's playground, the place where he could entertain artists, actors and above all, opera singers; he held house parties, concerts, fancy dress balls and provided excellent shooting for his younger friends. There we see him in photograph after photograph: debonair in a smart suit and trilby hat, cane in hand, in breeches and gaiters, on horseback, fishing on his lake, picnicking on a boat at sea, looking solemn with an arm round Jim Worsley-Taylor, laughing with one round the waist of a girl named Molly Robbins.

At one of the fancy dress balls Edgar so enjoyed, Molly dressed up as a nun. There is a photograph of her in her habit, eyes heavenward, prayer book in hand. Strangely enough, she later became an actual Catholic nun, living out her life at Les Oiseaux, a convent school at Westgate-on-Sea. In after years she corresponded with Edda and told him that his father had not wanted her to enter but had come to the station to see her off. She never saw him again. He was, she told Edda, quite the most gifted man she had ever known. But then she loved him.

Every year except the one Edgar went to India for the Coronation Durbar, Christmas was celebrated at Pantafon with a large party and at one of these Edgar dressed up as a ghost. He roamed about the house uttering sad wails and so frightened the butler's daughter that she had a fit and had to be taken to hospital. Giving concerts, singing and playing the piano were Edgar's greatest delights. One old lady remembered how when she was a girl he sat at the piano and sang Kipling's "Ford of Kabul River" with such pathos that she burst into tears and could recall, after half a century, every note of that beautiful voice. As one would expect from such a temperament, Edgar loved Wagner, and intensely enjoyed having the then famous opera singer, Marie Brema, staying in the house.

One day in the far future, this pleasure ground between the mountains and the sea would be left to Edda. But by then it had become a reproach, a white elephant, an empty shell of a house drained of life and joy and sold for less than one of Edgar's operatic guests would have been paid for a performance of a single night.

His son did not remember Pantafon as a pleasure ground. He acknowledged the beauty of its surroundings but was far happier in the fisherman's house in Sheringham. At what stage in his life his parents realized that although he was far in advance of other children in many ways, he was backward in others, we do not know. Today he would have diagnosed as having what is called 'the clumsy child syndrome', that is a form of dyspraxia or lack of muscular co-ordination and hurried off to Great Ormond Street Hospital. All his life he found it difficult to do up his shoe laces, knot his tie, turn door handles or lift a cup of tea. His hand was unsteady and in later years he found it hard to shave without cutting himself. He could not ride a horse, play any musical instrument, had no singing voice, was unable to dance or catch a ball without making a fool of himself. He was an anomaly at Pantafon, the son of the house, yet an outsider, a precocious child and yet a simpleton. It made no difference to Edgar that he loved the theatre, poetry and pictures and knew the names of all the flowers he brought home from his solitary walks. The child was odd, and his father was ashamed of him. Of all the many photographs, only two of Edda taken at Pantafon have survived. One was taken in the drawing-room. A fashionably dressed woman is sitting on the sofa, in the background a boy in long trousers can be seen with his head bent over a book.

Pantafon was a holiday home but then all the houses his parents lived in were holiday homes. Emmeline was a restless creature, often abroad, demanding more love than people can freely give, more happiness than the world can provide. She was always buying houses, selling them and building others. She never stayed tranquilly in one place save at the end, in exile in St Helena, and of her life there we know little.

The year of Queen Victoria's Diamond Jubilee was 1897. The actual date of her accession fell on a Sunday, so it was arranged that the public celebrations should be held on Tuesday, June 22. Edda was eight, the Queen seventy-eight and too lame to walk up the steps of St Paul's. Unlike the Golden Jubilee of ten years before, the festivities this time were intended to be a celebration of Empire. No European crowned heads were invited, much to the disappointment of the Kaiser and the relief of those who disliked and feared him. Instead, fifteen Colonial Prime Ministers had assembled, and each Colony had sent a detachment of troops, which meant the Colonial Procession was immensely long and showed a wonderful variety of different uniforms and races from the four corners of the globe. Before leaving Buckingham Palace the Queen had pressed an electric button which started a message telegraphed throughout the entire empire : "From my heart I thank my beloved people. May God bless them." They in their turn blessed her.

All expressions of mass emotion are catching. Nevertheless there was a genuine outpouring of loyalty and affection for the Queen who had reigned throughout the entire life of most of the spectators. By birth or adoption, they had won what Cecil Rhodes famously called the greatest prize in the lottery of life – the right to call themselves British subjects. The crowds were enormous, the cheers deafening. Here they were, in the greatest metropolis on earth, the heart of the Empire, and here she was, an old lady who on their behalf represented what they thought to be the strongest organized force for universal good in the world. But Kipling had already written "Recessional" and the next morning it would appear in *The Times*.

The route was six miles long and the sun shone all day, indeed for the last hour of the drive the Queen sheltered under a lace parasol. After the very long Colonial Procession came the gold and scarlet of the Royal Procession, led by a Captain of Life Guards, six feet eight inches tall. Relations, civil dignitaries, heads of European states followed in splendid uniforms, only the ambassador of the United States sat in his carriage wearing ordinary black evening dress. As Commander-in-Chief, Lord

Wolseley rode in front of the Queen's carriage, immediately behind it the Prince of Wales and the old Duke of Cambridge. The Queen sat in an open landau drawn by eight cream horses. With her was her daughter Princess Helena and the Princess of Wales, dressed in lilac. The Queen was wearing black silk, edged with grey satin and black lace, on her head a bonnet trimmed with white flowers. Edda was eagerly watching from a stand outside his mother's club. His books told him that all kings and queens wore gold crowns and carried the orb and sceptre. When he saw Victoria he burst out into a loud disappointed cry "Grandma! She looks just like Grandma!"

CHAPTER FIVE

A Coffin the Size
of a Child

Directly behind the gun carriage walked the German Kaiser, Wilhelm II, then just forty-two, who had measured his grandmother for her coffin. The Archduke Franz Ferdinand, to be murdered at Sarajevo in 1914, represented the Emperor. In the centre walked King Edward VII and at his side the Duke of Connaught, Victoria's second surviving son. The future Queen Mary's old uncle the Duke of Cambridge shuffled along behind these three, leaning heavily on the arm of his son from an early morganatic marriage.

It was taken for granted that Edda would follow his father at Harrow. In the September of 1897, therefore, when he was just nine, he was sent to a preparatory school at Elstree. It does not seem to have occurred to anyone that such a child was utterly unsuited to be thrown into the bearpit of conventional prep school boarding education as it was generally then and continued to be for many years to come. Sheringham was different. He had Nana, he was living in a house with ordinary people, he was free to go where he pleased in largely unspoilt countryside with no traffic, or fear of molestation. We do not have any details of what happened at Elstree because Edda refused to say much about it even to his children. Probably he was mercilessly bullied. His parents took him away after a single term.

In fact the débâcle was a blessing in disguise. It led in the end to a diversified education better suited to the kind of child Edda was. Edgar accepted that there was now no question of his son going to Harrow and before the guests assembled at Pantafon for the usual Christmas house party in 1897, he assured Edda that he would not ever be sent there. It was the only thing, Edda used to say in after years, that his father ever did for him. Edgar, however, was a great man for appearances. It is possible that his assurances were given less out of love for his child than fear that his school career would bring shame on the family name.

Under the circumstances, his parents' choice of a different kind of formal education was a good one. They wanted a small school with a high standard of teaching and were recommended to apply to an uncommon establishment run by the Revd the Marquis of Normanby. Lord Normanby was in Holy Orders and lived at Mulgrave Castle, Whitby, in Yorkshire. He was hard up and wishing to keep the Castle as his home, sensibly turned the place into a small but select establishment for the instruction of young boys. The school had a good reputation and was inspected annually by a Doctor of Divinity. His report of 1901, addressed to "My Lord Marquis", assured his lordship that the boys had acquitted themselves well in the classical languages together with French, and most creditably in Drill, which had concluded with an interesting illustration of the storming of a Boer fort.

The boys' caps and blazers had a coronet embroidered on them and Emmeline, who was no snob, objected to this. Being an Ingram, she wrote a strong letter to Lord Normanby and told him so, but being Lord Normanby, he paid no attention, so every holiday she confiscated the cap and blazer and they did not reappear until the term was about to start. Emmeline was very closely bound to Edda. She was Edda's "dearest and sweetest mother," he her "darling boy." Two poems have survived, written either at Pantafon or Mulgrave Castle when Edda was fourteen. One is called "The Lament of a Mother on her Son's Returning to School", the other "Farewell: To Mother on the Sad Occasion of My Parting from Her to Go Back to School." The first poem supposes Emmeline weeping at her loss and counting the hours until he returns home. The second, his devastation and grief at leaving her. "What is that love like a mother's," he asks, "in the whole course of life to be met?" To those of Watkin's children who never saw their grandmother and only heard her referred to in terms of hatred and opprobrium, these poems are as deeply sad as they are revealing.[1]

Edda was at Mulgrave Castle for nearly four years. He made no real friends and one suspects he only just survived which, considering his extreme oddness, was an achievement in itself. It was soon discovered that he was incapable of taking part in any game let alone an attack on an enemy fort. But nevertheless he was forced on to the playing fields and spent many an icy afternoon just running up and down by the side of the football pitch repeating Greek verbs and memorizing Latin constructions. He grew up to be one of those few people who genuinely enjoy being teased and to his children's jeers and accusations of being a swot and a prig, he would point out, grinning all over, that it was not he but the other boys who were wasting their time. This was true but it was not a point of view shared by his mother's sister Ada who did not understand how any child could show no interest in the things normal boys delighted in. Ada was closer to Emmerline than her other sisters. She was as forceful as Emmeline and a skilled and intrepid horsewoman. The children she knew exhibited no desire to learn Greek and Latin, would not spend hours reading history books, spout poetry by the yard, wander all day in the country with a Flora and, heavens above, actually talk about the Fathers of the Church.

Ada was married to the Lancashire and England cricketer A. N. Hornby, who was one of the few men who also played rugby football for England. He has been immortalized both in the history of cricket and literature. In cricket because he captained the famous Test Match played at the Oval in August 1882 when the Australians won by seven runs. It was their first win in this country and the victory led to the famous jibe about the death and cremation of English cricket whose ashes would be taken back to Australia. As for literature, Hornby was fortunate enough to be one of the subjects of some nostalgic lines written by Francis Thompson in his poem *At Lord's*:

> And I look through my tears on a soundless-clapping host,
> As the run-stealers flicker to and fro,
> To and fro: –
> O my Hornby and my Barlow long ago!

In those days cricket at this level was played by Gentlemen and Players. The Gentlemen were amateurs like Hornby, rich enough to play for pleasure. The Players were badly paid professionals who entered Lords through a separate gate. Ada used to insist upon Edda accompanying her to Lord's to watch the Eton and Harrow match and was horrified to see that after a few polite moments her nephew would bring out a book. She simply could not understand, she told her sister, how anyone in the world would rather read Gibbon than watch cricket.

Whatever the limitations of Lord Normanby's establishment, the school gave Edda an opportunity to witness a sight which given his love of history and the past, he was to cherish all his life. Normanby was not only in Holy Orders but a Canon of Windsor. This meant that he had to be in residence for part of each year and so the school moved into a house in the town for the spring term. Because of this they were allotted seats opposite the door of St George's Chapel for the funeral of Queen Victoria on February 2, 1901, and the experience made up for his disappointment of three years before.

Despite the long clinging to her own personal mourning, the Queen had disliked what she called the black gloom of most funerals and had given instructions that hers should be military and white. It had been intended to have the gun carriage pulled to St George's from Windsor station by cream horses. Unfortunately they had shied so violently while waiting that they had broken their traces and so had to be hastily replaced by blue-jackets taken from the Guard of Honour. The coffin was small, an onlooker remarked that it might have been that of a child. As we now know, according to Victoria's instructions, it was stuffed with family memorabilia which included a photograph of John Brown that had been placed in the Queen's left hand together with a lock of his hair.[2] The coffin was covered with a white pall with the Queen's coat of arms embroidered in gold on its four corners. The Royal Standard was thrown partially over the pall leaving a central space for the symbols of monarchy Edda so missed when the Queen was alive – the Imperial Crown, the Orb, the Sceptre and the Collar of the Garter.

Then, as Edda later described it, he "saw the great ones of the earth pass by" although he could not at that time have named them all. Directly behind the gun carriage walked the German Kaiser, Wilhelm II, then just forty-two, who had measured his grandmother for her coffin. The Archduke Franz Ferdinand, to be murdered at Sarajevo in 1914, represented the Emperor. In the centre walked King Edward VII and at his side the Duke of Connaught, Victoria's second surviving son. The future Queen Mary's old uncle the Duke of Cambridge shuffled along behind these three, leaning heavily on the arm of his son from a morganatic marriage.

Sir Edward died the same year as the Queen and was buried beside his first wife, his parents and his sister in the churchyard at Northenden. His son, now Sir Alfred Watkin, sold Rose Hill and Absalom's fine library as soon as he decently could. The house was bought by Manchester City Council and for a long time was used as a Juvenile Remand Home. One day, some seventy years later, a visiting probation officer noticed that the boys were fixing their dartboard over a large painting. It was taken down and discovered to be a work by the well-known American artist, Frederic Edwin Church, and sold for over two and half million dollars.

The Christmas of 1898 was the last Edda and Nana were to spend together. Soon afterwards she left with her gold watch to spend the rest of her life looking after another family and to travel to India and Constantinople. She was probably introduced to her new employers through Edgar who had met the family abroad. Their name was Babington-Smith. Sir Henry Babington-Smith was then private secretary to the Earl of Elgin, the Viceroy of India and had married Lord Elgin's daughter, Lady Elizabeth Bruce. They had nine children and Nana was well suited.

It is difficult to say what impression Nana made on Edda's life. That for a time she was a steadying influence on an extremely highly strung and volatile personality there can be no doubt. She was a strict moralist with high standards, knowing good from bad and making no bones about it.

In after years the Librarian of the Bodleian Library at Oxford told one of Edda's sons-in-law that of all his readers, Watkin was the most courteous. Nana must have played a part in this. This courtesy was not peculiar to him but shared by many of his generation and upbringing. One notices the politeness on both sides with which Watkin's and Churchill's fictional Dialogue of the Dead was conducted.[3]

Emmeline liked Sheringham. Pantafon was fun but remote. She had her flat in London. Edda was always so happy at Sheringham. She was still in touch with the Peggs and knew that the place was expanding at a great rate. In the last year of the old century she bought land overlooking the sea on the cliff at the east side of the town between Sheringham and the hamlet of Beeston Regis. She called the house Mount Felix but having built it decided that it was too small, sold it to the then well-known singer Ben Davis for a holiday home and built a far bigger house next to it. This she called Loudwater after the Ingram water mills at Rickmansworth. It was a large rather ugly brick house, since pulled down, and might now never have existed. It had no garden on the seaward side only a lawn leading to iron railings which marked the top of the cliff. The garden was at the front. It had conservatories for grapes and peaches and a fig trained on the wall. In this house Edda first met the girl who was to become his wife. When it was empty and derelict, Edda's children used to wander round outside peering in through the grimy windows, glimpsing the bare boards in the drawing room, the cupboard in the hall where their brother told them the champagne used to be kept, the high shelves in the kitchen, the spiders in the scullery sink, and to the sound of the incoming tide relentlessly eating its way along the coast, quickly steal the ripe figs to take home. Their mother may have found them a little bitter.

At the entrance to the drive there was a cottage originally intended for the gardener and his wife. In a year or two it was handed over to a chauffeur. Emmeline welcomed the arrival of the motor car and was one of the first in the family to buy one. She ordered a Daimler and employed a chauffeur whose name was Sharp. Edda, therefore, much to the astonishment of those who knew him in later life, was brought up with cars although he had no idea how they worked – only how they did not work, as he used to say. Punctures were frequent then. This he did not mind very much so long as he was left to read in peace out of the wind at the back. When he grew older his mother allowed Sharp to drive him all over Norfolk to visit the ancient churches he so loved. Paradoxically, the county which so quickly and so tenaciously adopted Protestantism had an immensely rich although grievously damaged heritage of medieval churches and Loudwater stood on the edge of a coast which could justly boast that it possessed more of them than any other shoreline in the whole of England. Edda would spend hours examining rood screens, fonts, remnants of painted glass, piscina, and the priest's stair up to the loft where the carved crucifix once stood, on either side the Virgin and St John. He could not understand why the waiting Sharp was rather surly each time he eventually emerged. Sharp should have joined him. He would have loved to have told him what everything was, when it was made, its purpose and all that was done for the worship of God in that church during the ages of faith.

In her own way, Emmeline was very good to Edda. She recognized that he was a most unusual child, gifted in a direction almost unknown to her family. She encouraged his interests, protected him from ridicule, made sure that he lived safely inside a membrane of affection and wealth which neither of them thought would ever break. She loved new experiences and movement and was determined that he should enjoy them too. When Edda was twelve she took him for a three-week sightseeing tour of Switzerland; he spent his fourteenth birthday in Venice where he wrote a short drama in verse about Pisani. When he was fifteen she hired a villa in Jerez for three months so that he could visit the places he so wished to see in Spain.

A year later, she decided that the time had come for him to make, as it were, a miniature grand tour of Italy and Greece. She chose Mr Dornford, a young Oxford-educated Church of England clergyman, to accompany him and the tour was planned to last four months. By now Edda was used to Church of England clergymen. Before he went to Spain he had spent nearly a year in the house of a Mr Rawnsley, the brother of Canon Rawnsley, one of the founders of the National Trust. Here he met the wife of another clergyman, Mrs Tatham, whose husband was Rector of Claxby in Lincolnshire.

Edda was then and continued throughout his life to be the sort of person many women, including his future wife, rushed forward to help. There was about him an absolutely natural innocence and helplessness about the things of this world. Unless he had a servant provided by his mother to look after him, he would forget to put on his tie, leave his shoelaces undone, lose his handkerchief and forget the time of meals or even in what house he was. Mrs Tatham was childless and took pity on him. She urged him to speak more slowly and less emphatically, to form his letters with care and not attempt to make his pen keep up with his mind, to be aware of the presence of other people and not to expect them to be interested in the subjects he was. She was a good influence and their friendship was one which would survive both Edda's change of religious allegiance and his marital troubles.

In the October of 1904 he set out for the Continent with Mr Dornford. Dornford worked out their itinerary, organized the hotel bookings, bought the tickets and knew the times of trains. In those days no passports were needed except for Russia which was considered barbaric for demanding them. The expedition was on the whole a great success. They visited all the places one should visit in Greece and for the first time Edda had contact with the Great Church of the East. Of course, he knew about the Great Church of the West but he still thought of it in a Protestant perspective, as the Roman Catholic Church, something very attractive but un-English and dangerous, whose spiritual riches could be enjoyed just as well within the confines of Anglicanism. His only complaint was that his tutor refused to stop for a cup of tea when they toured the plains of Marathon. This experience led him in later life to write at some length on the effect bodily fatigue has on aesthetic appreciation. After Corfu, Naples and Florence they spent Christmas in Rome where another difference arose. Edda wanted to go to Midnight Mass at St Peter's or S. Maria Maggiore but Dornford stood firm. In the end a compromise was reached. They attended a high church Anglican service in the Via del Babuino and returned to England in the January of 1905.

That summer Edda left home to spend almost a year with yet another private tutor, Mr Moss, the Rector of Bletsoe in Buckinghamshire who accommodated about six pupils in his country parsonage. It was here that Edda met the future historian Christopher Dawson, a boy just a little younger than himself.[4] Dawson was to become his greatest friend but the beginning of their long companionship was hardly auspicious. Dawson was then going through an adolescent phase of religious scepticism and advanced clever arguments against the existence of God and therefore the reality of any religious dimension whatsoever. At that stage in his life Watkin found it difficult to disagree with anyone without becoming violent. This was partly temperamental, partly because he had never been subjected to the discipline of a large school and partly because no one, not even Nana, had ever impressed upon him the necessity for self-control. His mother said and did exactly what she pleased and no one ever corrected her. He was born with a deeply religious nature and to hear someone put forward arguments against the existence of God was to him blasphemous. The conversation took place in the garden. As answer Watkin jumped up and thrust the deck chair's wooden canopy hard down over Dawson's head.

CHAPTER SIX

The City of Bells

How ludicrous it was to think of St Patrick as any sort of Protestant! How absurd to imagine that such a thin and narrow an interpretation of Christianity as Protestantism – the mere disjecta membra *of Catholicism – could ever have founded and built such a glorious place as Oxford!*

Despite this unfortunate beginning, Watkin and Christopher Dawson were to remain friends for life. However, although they shared the same interests, they were unalike both in character and background. Dawson's father, Henry, was an army officer, his mother, Mary Bevan, came from a distinguished and highly cultivated Welsh family. Her father was Vicar of Hay in Breconshire and Archdeacon of Brecon. Dawson was born in October 1889 at his mother's old home, Hay Castle, an Elizabethan house which took its name from the demolished Castle once on the site and at this time served as the vicarage.

It was Kilvert country and Dawson's early youth was spent in the world the diarist so wonderfully describes.[1] In a way it was an enclosed society of local clerical families and professional people often related to each other, a world of intermingling religious and social routine within the narrow confines of Anglicanism as it was then. But Hay is on the Marches, that land of contrasts which lies between England and Wales. On one side is Herefordshire, on the other the Welsh hills of Radnor Forest and the Black Mountains, ancient and mysterious places reaching far back beyond Christianity to other symbols and different myths to describe the meeting of earth and heaven. It was a fitting background for one who was to devote his life to the history and dynamics of culture. Dawson spent his most formative years here with his Welsh mother and her family, not moving to Yorkshire until he was seven when his father took early retirement.

Colonel Dawson was not in the least like the stereotyped army officer of that period. He was a man of wide interests and a great reader. "A delightful man," Watkin was later to say, "who loves books." While in the army he had formed a group for the study of Dante, his favourite poet, and in the long northern evenings his young son would pore over the three immense volumes of Botticelli's illustrations to *The Divine Comedy*.

Henry Dawson had inherited a property in the Yorkshire Dales between Burnsall and Bolton Abbey. He built a house, Hartlington Hall, to replace a former family home which had been pulled down. It was in a most beautiful position high on a hill with terraced gardens leading through wooded slopes to a stream in the valley below. Here Christopher continued to spend an idyllic childhood with his elder sister before he was sent away to school. "I got nothing from school," he wrote to Watkin in 1925, "little from Oxford, and less than nothing from the new post-Victorian urban culture, all my "culture" and my personal happiness came from that much-derided Victorian home life."

It was to Hartlington that Watkin would come after his friendship with Dawson was renewed at Oxford. They would bathe in the beck after the fashion of the Sheringham fisherboys, lie on the grass listening to the sound of falling water, picnic beneath the limestone crags and walk over the moors for ever talking and talking.

Their future publisher, Frank Sheed, used to point out how daunting it must have been for Mr Moss to have had to teach two such brilliant teenagers. In temperament the pair were unlike. Dawson was unusually shy and reserved, speaking freely only to a few of his closest friends. He was languid compared with Watkin and physically delicate, which was why he had left school at Winchester early and came to Bletsoe. This outward passivity and mild language, as Watkin came to realize, hid very deep feelings. On the surface Dawson was far more conventional than Watkin, who was full of energy and creativity and would talk to everyone and anybody whether they understood what he was saying or not. His mind, as it were, was set at a far higher rate than most people's. He thought so quickly that he found it difficult to express his ideas without stuttering nor impress their meaning on another person without moving his arms or legs.

The regime at the Rectory does not seem to have been either strict or intellectually demanding. In fact, they educated each other. The five or six boys were allowed to do more or less what they pleased and Dawson and Watkin spent long days walking together in the beechwoods and among the hills of the unspoilt Chilterns. Dawson introduced Watkin to Walter Pater. It became a craze with them both to seek out and to contemplate aesthetic impressions. They would stand for a long time looking at a sunset, watch the wind among the poplars and read choice passages from Ruskin aloud to each other. Bletsoe was a short intense interlude in their boyhood and one neither of them ever forgot. Watkin would never hear anyone sing "Pale Hands I Love" without thinking of Bletsoe, faint music from the drawing room and nights on the lawn with the evening light dying away across the valley.

The Christmas of 1905 was the last spent at Pantafon. Edgar and his son went together to church at Caernavon but Edgar's health was failing and the visitor's book comes to an end. That summer Watkin went to St Paul's School to prepare for Oxford, staying in his parent's London flat during term time.

As long as he could escape when he pleased, Watkin always enjoyed London with its theatres, museums and good company. What he hated was the dreary round of country house weekends where he was sometimes expected to change his clothes three times a day. Informal clothes were customary at breakfast, special garments worn for the afternoon field sports which good manners forced him to attend, then he had to change into formal clothes for dinner which meant a struggle with collar studs and bow ties. There was one visit, however, that was not boring. An unusual combination of circumstances was to lead to an invitation to stay at Lambeth Palace and a meeting with Archbishop Davidson.

The Ingram family in general, although violently against Roman Catholicism, were more or less only nominally Protestant. Grandma had been conventionally devout, she gave Edda a copy of the Book of Common Prayer, and went to church on Sundays. Nana had approved of a widely circulated book called *Peep of Day* written by the evangelical Mrs Mortimer. This was a re-telling of the Old and New Testaments in four volumes with pictures and made a tremendous impression on Edda. Mrs Mortimer had been a great friend of the later Cardinal Manning until "he ultimately arrived at such perverted ideas of religious truth." Strangely enough, she was buried at Upper Sheringham.

Watkin had a quick grasp of the implications of any intellectual position. He must have developed this faculty from an early age because when he was young he thought it absolutely extraordinary that the people he lived with expressed so little interest in the astonishing creed they claimed to believe. There was almost nothing in their behaviour or way of life that suggested it mattered in the least that God had become incarnate, had risen from the dead and offered them eternal life.

There are penalties for those who are not content to remain splashing in the shallows of religious commitment The mind may shrink from the surface implications of definite credal statements. When as a young child Edda was told about the Resurrection he thought immediately that it was too good to be true. With him a passionate reverence for God and things of the spirit existed side by side with a streak of scepticism and sharp, analytical intelligence.

He had long left the Protestant wing of the Church of England and when in London regularly attended Anglo-Catholic worship first at All Saints, Margaret Street, and then at St Mary Magdalen's, Munster Square.

But the so-called Modernist tendencies within the Anglican church alarmed him. If the Gospel miracles were not to be literally understood what then about the Virgin Conception and the Resurrection? What guarantee had he that the Church of England would continue to teach even the basic doctrines of Christianity?

It happened that as part of his tour abroad in 1904, Watkin and his tutor had visited Corfu. Here they had stayed with a friend of Emmeline's, Beatrice Cameron, a niece, Watkin thought, of the celebrated photographer.[2] She felt protective towards Watkin, understood his interests and kept up with him on her return to England. She had a friend who assisted with the domestic arrangements at Lambeth Palace and an appartment there. In Watkin's last year at St Pauls, Beatrice arranged for Edda and herself to spend the weekend at the Palace.

On Sunday morning Watkin was walking in the garden with Beatrice when they came across Archbishop Davidson who had just returned from preaching in the Abbey. He knew Beatrice well and before he left he had asked her if she would be kind enough to go out and buy him a Sunday paper. If he went himself, he had told her to Watkin's amusement, the Evangelicals would be outraged. An introduction was made and Watkin seized his opportunity. Being Watkin, he came straight to the point and poured out what was on his mind. In view of what was happening to New Testament criticism, how could he be certain that the Church of England would continue to hold on to the historic creeds? Davidson was patient and kind to this persistent schoolboy. But the subject was a delicate one. Davidson was himself finding it difficult to hold the ring between the Protestant, Catholic, and Modernist parties within the Anglican Church. But he evidently recognised the passionate sincerity of his questioner and after some discussion told him straightforwardly that the Church of England did not claim to give the kind of doctrinal guarantees Watkin was seeking. Nor did he believe that they should be given. If he wanted that kind of certainty, he must go to the Church of Rome.

This conversation was to influence Watkin considerably. It would remain in his mind all his life, to be recalled when Rome itself drifted into just those doctrinal uncertainties the Archbishop had considered to be part of the nature of Anglicanism.

Watkin went up to New College, Oxford, in the Michaelmas Term of 1907. Dr Spooner was then Warden, a man notorious for accidentally transposing the initial letter of words. He was supposed to have accused an undergraduate he was sending down of "deliberately tasting two worms." Watkin thought that many of what were called 'spoonerisms' were invented and that this affliction was greatly exaggerated. He intended to read *Literae Humaniores* or Greats, as it was known. This meant the study of Greek and Latin literature, ancient history and ancient and modern philosophy. The course lasted four years.

Unlike Dawson, he loved his years at Oxford, that city of bells, as he called it on his first evening. At no time in his life did he bother about class differences, or feel under an obligation to know the right people. He was at home with anyone who was at home with him. He did not care if a man was a public school 'hearty', an aristocrat or had come from a provincial grammar school. His insecurities were deep but they were never social. He gravitated naturally to those who shared his interests and here the trap was sprung.

He soon made friends with a man named Philip Fowke and with another named Eric Pontifex, or 'Ponty' as he was always called. Philip was the only child of a Mr Villiers Fowke of Saling Hall, Essex, a barrister who never practised. His wife, who had become a Roman Catholic, had died young and Philip had been brought up in that faith. Pontifex, also a Catholic, was one of the five sons of a convert Church of England clergyman. Watkin's Anglo-Catholicism was soon smelt out and he proved to be easy game. The Roman Catholic faith, he was swiftly reminded, was the faith that had created and sustained Europe. All the other Christian churches in the West depended upon it for their creeds, liturgy and architecture. How ludicrous it was to think of St Patrick as any sort of Protestant! How absurd to imagine that such a thin and narrow an interpretation of Christianity as Protestantism – the mere *disjecta membra* of Catholicism – could ever have founded and built such a glorious place as Oxford! Great Britain had been Roman Catholic, that is to say in communion in faith and worship with the successor of St Peter, for well over a thousand years. Protestants could justify their position only by vilifying their predecessors and calling them superstitious and idolatrous. It was obvious that they believed in Christianity on the authority of the Church of Rome, the very church they reviled. What could be more ridiculous than to have a Sovereign as Head of the Church and allow Parliament to decide what one should think about Almighty God? No wonder Anglicanism was falling apart.

All this was true. But it was by no means the whole truth and just the kind of polemic that Watkin came to detest. In the first flush of his conversion and later under pressure, Newman was capable of writing unpleasant things about Anglicanism. But in the depth of his spirit he continued to be attached to the Church of his baptism. Likewise, throughout his life Watkin remained grateful to the Church of England for all it had taught him. He never allowed it to be unfairly denigrated in his presence.

However, he realized that granted his understanding of Christianity, his position was untenable. He was acutely aware that the world was becoming more and more secular, that the supernatural was being driven into corners and that fewer and fewer educated people accepted that Christianity, or indeed religion at all, gave meaning to human existence. He recalled Archbishop Davidson and the garden at Lambeth. There was only one Church in the West capable of standing firm, the Roman Catholic Church, the single organization that had safeguarded Christian doctrine and religious experience down the ages.

Watkin learnt about the Benedictines at Downside from Pontifex whose brothers were being educated there. In July 1908 he went to Somerset alone and was received in the village church at Stratton-on-the-Fosse by Dom Ethelbert Horne. All converts were given conditional baptism in case the sacrament had not been carried out properly in the first instance. In those days even the Archbishop of Canterbury was theoretically considered to be but a doubtfully baptised layman.

Watkin travelled back to Sheringham "in a torment of fear," as he wrote later, "and in great misery as to how I should face mother." Yet bearing in mind her son's habits and disposition, his conversion could hardly have come as a surprise. Emmeline was now a widow.

Edgar had spent the Christmas of 1907 in a nursing home. In the spring of 1908 he returned to Loudwater only to die. North Norfolk is very cold at that time of year, and the house on its cliff faced directly seawards; there were fires in each room but no central heating. A wrapped up, shrunken Edgar tried to talk to his son. He asked him about his work, his friends and what he thought about life in general. Edda was awkward and silent. It was all too late, the gulf unbridgeable. His mind gone, Edgar died that June in the large bedroom overlooking the sea.

It is hard to say exactly what was wrong with him. His death certificate states that he died of partial dementia and a cerebral haemorrhage. But death certificates can be deliberately misleading. This one was signed by Dr Sumpter, the family doctor and friend. Edgar had been attended by male nurses from the Temperance Co-operative in Thayer Street, London. However, there is no evidence that he was a particularly heavy drinker nor did the certificate state damage to his liver. There are hints and indications but few hard facts about the details of Edgar's personal life.

What evidence we have suggests that he had had a young lover who was killed in the Boer War in 1900. Sir Edward got permission from the High Commissioner for him to go to Bloemfontein either to visit his mortally wounded friend or to visit his grave. All that remains is a scribbled reference to a last anguished kiss, two telegrams and an empty silver photograph frame. On top are his friend's initials and date of birth and death together with his own initials, both enclosed in a laurel wreath. At bottom are the words *Ave Atque Vale*.

The death certificate gives Edgar's occupation as "of independent means". He left £5. As his mental health deteriorated those he had once entertained so lavishly left him alone. At last Emmeline had him to herself. She buried him in the graveyard on the cliff by the old church at Beeston Regis. His grave is surmounted by a Celtic cross above his name, his dates and, at his request, the solitary inscription *Resurgam*. That is "I shall rise again."

The friendship with Christopher Dawson, not yet a Catholic, had been resumed when Watkin went up to Oxford and found that Dawson, a year his junior, was staying with a tutor to prepare for his matriculation. In 1908 Christopher went to Trinity College to read History and the two of them continued a companionship which was to endure to the end of Dawson's life. For the final two years at University they shared lodgings at 96, Holywell, where their landlady was a Mrs Knibbs.

We know this because Watkin kept a diary of well over a quarter of a million words in the eighteen months between January 1, 1911 and August 7, 1912. The diary owes its existence to the patience and loyalty of his old friend, Mrs Tatham, who urged him to undertake the task in order to get into the habit of writing slowly and legibly. It covers his last five terms at Oxford; his frequent expeditions, meals and discussions with Dawson; their final examinations; life at Sheringham; the accession of George V; a visit to Rome and the Holy Land and the time Watkin spent in Germany. It ends abruptly the day he meets his future wife.

Trains took the place of our buses and coaches. The network was extensive, the service frequent, and it provided an excellent system of luggage in advance. Only the poor carried things. A change of linen and books would be packed into what, even in old age, Watkin referred to as his "box". This box or suitcase would be put on an earlier train and be taken to its destination to be picked up by the traveller later in the day. But of course the porter had to be tipped.

All societies are servant societies and this one was a personal servant society. We know about Emmeline's chauffeur, Sharp. She had also a manservant called Alfred who used to shave Edda when he was at home, a personal maid called Lizzie and a number of cooks and gardeners. Dawson and Watkin rarely ate in Hall. Mrs Knibbs was expected to be prepared at all times to provide breakfast, lunch and dinner not solely for her two lodgers but for anyone they invited in. And it was she who had to bring to the table the whisky and claret which on one occasion made poor Philip Fowke very sick. At Loudwater champagne was produced at every opportunity, from formal dinner parties to complaints of mild fatigue. Emmeline was unconventional and lax but at Oxford chaperonage was very strict. It was only after intense persuasion that the mother of one of Edda's friends allowed him to accompany her fifteen year old daughter to hear the music and see the Chinese lanterns at the New College Ball in June 1911. Even so, she went up to Watkin's rooms to make sure that all was as it should be.

Not all his high church friends thought their theological position untenable. Two of Edda's old class mates from St Paul's stood their ground. One of them was King, who became an Anglican clergyman. The other was Peter Cook, who used to erect a flowery shrine in a corner of his room every January 30th in memory of the martyrdom of Charles I. Together with Philip Fowke, Pontifex and Watkin they formed the NCC, the letters perhaps standing for New College Catholics, since all its members did not equate Catholicism with its Roman variety. They were a small group which met regularly to discuss the mysteries of life and death. A photograph of 1910 has survived. There they all are, five young men staring with solemn eagerness into the future. Cork became Vicar of Gladstone's Hawarden. King volunteered to fight in the 1914 war and was the first to die; Watkin the last.

In many respects Oxford life was easygoing and casual. Watkin takes his essay to Rashdall at nine-fifteen in the evening and they discuss it together until almost half-past eleven. He mislays his logic paper for Mr Heath, strolls round to College, finds him there at a second attempt, and stays with him talking about metaphysics for an hour and a half. After success in the College races some tipsy undergraduates let off fireworks and make such a row one might think that "the Germans were bombarding Oxford." During the rag all the windows in the old quad were broken and doors and seats taken out and burnt. No one appears to be surprised. Next morning an army of carpenters and glaziers repair the damage and Dr Rashdall sends a disapproving letter to be pondered over during the vacation.

There was another marked difference between the present time and those days. The secularization of Catholicism had not begun. What separated religion from humanism remained absolutely clear. There is literally a world of difference between the *Dies Irae* and a modern Memorial Service. Nor had the Catholic liturgy yet been despoiled. The Mass was substantially the same as it had been in the Middle Ages. High Mass still existed and was sung in Latin on Sundays, Holy Days of Obligation and other feast days. Processions of the Blessed Sacrament with incense, candles and holy water took place at regular times during the Church's year. Sung Benediction was taken as a matter of course, Confessions were frequent, the faithful fasted after midnight before taking Holy Communion and received the Sacrament on their knees. Watkin and his friends Brandreth and Wilberforce, grandson of William, wore evening dress for the Corpus Christi procession and a modern Catholic would find much of their practice strange, although Wilberforce astonished Watkin by advocating women priests.

There were then two Catholic dons at Oxford. One was Francis de Zulueta, a future Regius Professor of Civil Law, later to be a friend of Watkin and his wife. The other a man who darts in and out of so many accounts of Oxford life both before and after the Great War, 'Sligger' Urquhart. It seems that the origin and meaning of his nickname is uncertain although Maurice Bowra maintained that it was a corruption of "the sleek one."[3] In this he was supported by Ronald Knox. He was the son of David Urquhart, the diplomat, traveller and Turkophile who had disputed publically with Watkin's great-grandfather, Absalom Watkin of Rose Hill, Manchester, about the rights and wrongs of the Crimean War.[4] Sligger was a Fellow of Balliol. "I cannot believe," Knox was later to write in the *Dublin Review,* "that anyone ever knew him without being somehow the better for it." A bachelor with private means, his kindness, commonsense and wide culture attracted undergraduates from all colleges to gather in his rooms in the garden quad at Balliol. He was famous for his reading parties. During the vacation he would take a small number of carefully chosen undergraduates to stay with him in England or Italy and to his chalet at Chamonix. He had once made a memorable ascent of Mont Blanc with Gertrude Bell.

Watkin did not belong to Sligger's circle and was never invited to any of the famous reading parties. It was true that he was a good looking youth and hard as it may be for anyone who knew him in later life to imagine, was dressed in expensive suits his mother had him measured for regularly. However, his unconventional demeanor, clumsy gestures, and quick stuttering speech together with utter indifference to cultivating the right people would have rendered him ineligible for the sexually ambiguous coterie drawn to those bachelor rooms over the west gate at Balliol.

In the past there had been a Catholic club at Oxford called "The Heretics". This club, whose purpose was to discuss the difficulties in Catholic belief or practice, had now been revived. Watkin attended its first meeting in Sligger's rooms. He was accompanied to the meeting by Father Joseph Rickaby, a Jesuit priest from what was later to be called Campion Hall, then known in Oxford as "Pope's Hall" from the name of its Master, Father Pope. It happened that Father Rickaby was one of two brothers, the children of a former butler of Lord Herries, who had sent the plainly clever boys to Stonyhurst to be educated with his own sons. They had both become distinguished Jesuits. Rickaby had been ordained priest together with that great poet born out of due time, Gerard Manley Hopkins. Watkin loved "dear old Joe" as he used to call him, to the end of his life and frequently acknowledged his influence. Not all his Superiors were so keen. Father Pope was a snobbish and rigorously correct American from St Louis who thought Father Rickaby's table manners owed more to his Yorkshire forebears than his father's profession as butler to a nobleman.

The subject under discussion was the ferocious reaction of Pope Pius X and the Roman curia to what is called "Modernism", a complex movement whose leader in England was Baron Friedrich von Hügel. Modernism is perhaps best described in the clumsy yet exact prose of the Baron himself. Writing to Maude Petre in 1918 about her proposed history of the movement, he pointed out that there were two distinct subject matters which could be described under the term "Modernism". "The one," he wrote, "is a permanent, never quite finished, always sooner or later, more or less, rebeginning set of attempts to express the old Faith and its permanent truths and helps – to interpret it according to what appears the best and most abiding elements in the philosophy and the scholarship and science of the later and latest times."[5] That sums up the movement as a whole and Watkin's position also. Von Hügel then went on to distinguish between this and the views of particular Modernists or groups of Modernists.

In 1907, both the attempt and these views, or a travesty of them as some would maintain, were condemned absolutely by the Pope in his decree *Lamentabili,* and his encyclical *Pascendi,* which famously stigmatized Modernism "as the synthesis of all the heresies." Draconian measures to suppress freedom of speech and written communication were taken three years later. An Anti-Modernist oath was imposed. On pain of dismissal, all clergy and others holding office in the Church had to take an oath affirming the propositions set out in *Pascendi.* Bishops were to set up Vigilance Committees in each diocese to examine exposures of unorthodox teaching and secret denunciations were encouraged. Basically, the entire matter depended upon the interpretation of Christian Revelation. How does God communicate to mankind, in what sense can the Bible be believed, can dogma remain substantially the same if its expression is culturally conditioned?

Diocesan censors were appointed to ensure that no publication which understood Revelation in a manner different from that now held by the Pope and Curia would be granted the *Imprimatur,* or permission to publish. Thomist scholasticism was declared to be the official philosophy of the Church and an end put to historical and scientific Biblical criticism.

Despite grave lapses, over the centuries the Roman Catholic Church had shown an enormous capacity to meet challenges and to integrate them into its theological and spiritual life. The Papacy had now taken new powers to impose, by threats and fear, what amounted to arrested development. The Church of Augustine, Aquinas and Bonaventure was in danger of contracting into a paranoid sect, as Tyrrell put it.

Those present that evening. knew the fate of of von Hügel's great friend, the brilliant,wayward Jesuit, Father Tyrrell, who was forbidden to celebrate Mass, deprived of the Sacraments and at the last even refused permission for a Catholic burial. The papal net was closely spun and widely cast. At the outset of his distinguished career the young Father Martindale had a breakdown after he was delated to Rome as a consequence of a book on St John's Gospel which had already been passed by the Censor.[6] As we shall see, the experience scarred him for life.

The majority of the Catholic laity were not directly effected by the measures taken to suppress Modernism. The shock for them lay in the future. On the whole, they believed what they were told to believe, prayed as they were told to pray, and accepted an autocratic papacy together with subservient bishops.

The people gathered at Balliol that February evening in 1911 were not arguing in the abstract. As intellectual leaders and future intellectual leaders, they were facing a problem which touched them all. Sligger opened the discussion and put forward the main objections to the Roman policy. Rickaby thought that this policy was aimed at France and Italy rather than England. The effect of Modernism, he said, had been to put the Church under martial law which would, like all martial law, hamper even the most law abiding. Watkin seems to have contributed nothing to the discussion. He was a new boy, received into the Church less than three years before. Yet we know from his diary that he had a grasp of what was essentially at stake and already a vision of the Church as it could be which would lead him to play a major part in the Catholic renaissance so falteringly attempted between the two wars.

On May 21, 1911, he had just returned with Dawson from a talk at the Newman Society by Belloc on the right of property. He had spoken himself and was ashamed at the speed and confusion of his delivery. Back at his digs after a very full day, he wrote a long entry in the diary, composed after midnight. "Surely," he wrote when he had almost finished, "we need a new Catholic revival. Our age like the Antonine is jaded and without enthusiasm. Yet we need no new creed, but only to have the same old faith brought home and made real to the world at large. Perhaps this will not be and the final apostasy may be at hand. Yet surely we need not adopt this attitude of despair. We may rather hope for a fresh Catholic revival like those of the thirteenth and fourteenth centuries. We need no teachers of a new gospel, religous, moral or economic, but a second St Francis to draw the ignorant and materialized masses to the faith, a second Aquinas to recast modern knowledge and thought acording to the fundamental canons of Catholic theology and philosophy and a new Dante to represent the modern world with all its new thoughts and its extended knowledge of the universe."[7]

For a short time his diary illumines the mind of an odd, complex but very gifted youth. But only part of that mind. Mrs Tatham would certainly read the diary, so would Edda's mother. The contrasts are marked. Intellectual brilliance exists side by side with transparency and an almost childlike innocence; spiritual profundity with naïvety verging on the credulous; a loving heart but one frequently oblivious to the reactions of others. "In some ways "I've always been an old man, in others never grown up," he was to write to one of his children many years later. Exceptional mental and physical energy are obvious, so is a remarkable memory and the capacity for abstract analysis which Dr Rashdall had recognized when he advised Watkin on coming up to concentrate on philosophy and history, not on the classical languages. Above all, one is struck by Watkin's overwhelming sense of the presence of God which exists side by side with intense appreciation of the natural world and love of life for its own sake. He has to express himself, he has to tell you what he has seen, what he is thinking and feeling. He was, of course young, but his energy was prodigious and to remain so until very old age. He climbed Snowdon when he was in his seventies and threatened to do so when he was eighty.

One fine morning in early February 1911 he took a train to Wantage with Dawson and walked up the Berkshire downs to the place where Hardy's Jude saw Oxford from a distance. They went on together for ten miles until they reached a village called Shefford where Dawson took the train back. Watkin walked on alone in the moonlight over the high downs for another sixteen miles then followed the railway line to Didcot station and so back to Oxford.

On a typical day in May that same year, he goes first to Mass and Holy Communion which he did every morning, has breakfast then reads three chapters of Greenidge's *Handbook of Greek Constitutional History*, his own notes on the *Hermocopia* and Aristotle's account of the revolution of 411 BC, and an account of Nerva's reign by the historian Bury, making extracts from it for his Roman chronology. He then bicycles with Christopher five miles to an inn at Stanton St John where they have lunch together under blue skies in an orchard by an apple tree.

On their return to Oxford Watkin reads four odes of Keats, part of *Endymion*, has an elocution lesson paid for by his mother in order to help him talk more slowly, then goes to Rosary and Benediction and comes home in the moonlight. He reads more Bury, a chapter of Pater's *Marius the Epicurean*, book four of Plato's *Republic*, canto seventeen of Dante's *Inferno*, and more of Greenidge. He then discusses the doctrine of hell at length with Dawson and finally writes his diary and his thoughts pour out. He recalls the names of some plants he saw on the walk, what he thinks about *Endymion*, and copies out a long passage from a friend about the difficulty of loving God and at the same time the beauty of the created world.

Why could not one combine them both? "Truly the light is sweet and a pleasant thing it is for the eyes to behold the sun," Mrs Mortimer had quoted from *Ecclesiastes* on the title page of his childhood book *The Peep of Day*. Whatever else of her work Watkin abandoned, this sentiment was entirely his. He loved life itself, swiming in the sea and feeling the sun on his skin, good food, wine and companionship. He loved the theatre, enjoyed being troubled by Ipsen and rendered impatient with the amusing superficialities of Shaw. The world was beautiful and beguiling and so were women. Philip Fowke was in love with Edda's first cousin, Gladys, the daughter of his Uncle Alfred, his dead father's brother. She had told

Edda that he would never love a woman enough to make a happy marriage. He was far too cerebral to win a bride. That remained to be seen.

When Watkin was received into the Roman Catholic Church he took "Aloysius" as his Confirmation name. St Aloysius Gonzaga was a sixteenth-century Italian and the patron of Catholic youth. Of noble birth, he became a Jesuit and, as a consequence of nursing its victims, died of the plague at the age of twenty-three. He was such a pure young man that, so the story goes, he hesitated to kiss even his mother. When he joined the Church Watkin sincerely imagined "that which is perfect has come." He used to refer to this early phase of his life as "Aloysian". He joined the Third Order of the Servites. The Servites, founded in the thirteenth century, are an order with particular concern for the poor. Those who belong to a Third Order are laymen or women who take no vows but under spiritual direction, dedicate themselves to leading a God-centred life in the world. They wear next the skin a scapular or small symbolic garment consisting of two strips of cloth joined across the shoulders and recite the Divine Office or part of it, every day.

That was not all. Probably at the suggestion of the Servites, Watkin belonged also to the Society of St Vincent de Paul, a lay organization which devoted itself to work among the poor. Watkin's particular task was to visit the old and the sick and to help the unemployed. He tried to get a job at Lucy's Oxford Iron Works for a man named Miller to whose daughter he had stood godfather and planned to help financially. The manager told him he had no job vacancies, he had to make the business pay for the sake of the shareholders. In his diary, Watkin lamented the "merciless and inevitable operation of that modern Juggernaut, the industrial machine" and went next day to the Cowley Steam Plough Works where he was equally unsuccessful. Miller hawked shoelaces in the street for a while then turned to begging.

There was no fear of this at Loudwater. In the late spring of 1911 Watkin went home for the vacation and stayed first with his mother in London. Emmeline was in bed with a cold and Edda dined in her bedroom and assisted her convalescence by reading sixty-two pages of a book dealing with the nature, knowledge and power of angels. The next day Sharp drove him alone to Norfolk. It took them three hours to reach Brandon in Suffolk which was not surprising since Edda insisted on an extended visit to an old church while Sharp was filling up with petrol. After Brandon the car failed to start, so Edda got out and joyfully stretched his legs for a mile. Sharp caught up with him but the engine soon failed again and botanizing all the way, Edda walked another joyful mile through a pretty wood. They continued stopping and starting until they reached Holt where they burst a tyre and Edda walked four and a half miles to Upper Sheringham. Here at last an exasperated Sharp picked him up and finally got him home.

CHAPTER SEVEN

Prophesying Doom

Albert brought out trays of iced champagne, they picnicked at Pretty Corner by the light of the car lamps and danced on the lawn to the music of a gramophone. In London Edda saw Melba's farewell performance in Gounod's Romeo and Juliet and was forced by Aunt Ada yet again to waste two days at Lord's. Yet beneath it all was a sense of unease. Every now and then the shadow of war crosses the pages of Watkin's diaries and the sun of that glorious summer is momentarily dimmed.

A t the end of the previous term Edda had taken a College examination called "Collections" and had come top of the list. He had won what was called the "scholars' prize", that is, got higher marks than those who had been awarded scholarships. He chose a leatherbound copy of Curtis's *Flora Londinensis* and his mother was delighted. She went round telling everyone about her brilliant son and foretold that he would do wonders in the world, of what nature she did not yet know.

Loudwater was full of people. Gladys was now permitted to be officially engaged to Philip Fowke but to the alarm of the parents on both sides, had already converted to Roman Catholicism. Pontifex arrived and so did Francis Birrell from next door where the Birrells had their holiday home. His father, Augustine Birrell, distinguished for the volumes of his civilized and amusing essays, was at this time Chief Secretary for Ireland in Asquith's cabinet.

To Lord Tennyson's initial disgust, Birrell had married the widow of the Laureate's younger son, Lionel and at his first interview with the poet was asked why he wished to intrude himself into the family. Birrell and his wife had two sons. One of these, Tony, was what was then called simple; he was a gentle creature much loved by his parents and all who knew him. The other son, Francis, later to own a bookshop and to live on the fringes of the Bloomsbury Group, was still at Cambridge and Edda thought him sarcastic and supercilious. It was the father who was to be his friend, never the son.

After Pontifex left, Gladys's brother Hugh arrived. He was one of the sons of Edgar's down-to-earth brother, Alfred. Much to his father's irritation, he claimed to be suffering from nervous exhaustion and had been advised by his doctor to take the then fashionable open air cure. Arrangements were therefore made for him to sleep outside in the summer-house. It was not long before Emmeline's sisters put in an appearance, Aunt Sissie, Aunt Daisy and the managing Aunt Ada. Sissie was the only one of the sisters to have no children. She and her husband Colonel Eyre-Williams had a house at Shiplake-on-Thames, a launch on the river and a place in Knightsbridge with a large garden where Edda had to sit that summer for many a boring hour entertaining those he considered to be fashionable fools. To hear the sisters talking was very amusing. A great deal of their conversation was taken up with describing confrontations with other people. "He contradicted me to my face – he dared to contradict me – and *"I – an Ingram."* This was accompanied by much tossing of heads and tapping of feet. It was an expression, constantly repeated, that cut into the mind and to have its own sharp resonances in the years to come. Much was said about their two brothers. Charles was prepared to make it up but William remained aloof. When he drew up his pedigree for the Royal College of Heralds, he omitted his sisters altogether.

The entire family had deplored Edda's conversion to Rome and at first none more than Emmeline. So angry was she that she instructed her solicitors, Cohen and Cohen, to send a threatening letter to Pontifex, in her opinion the agent and instigator of the whole thing. But she saw that she could not prevail and in time came to accept it as a fact of life. Her temperament was not in the least religious and few Catholics held out any hopes of her conversion. She did not believe, she did not disbelieve. It was her son's hobby, some would say his obsession. It was what he wanted, it made him happy, and on the whole she stood up very well to the long services Edda insisted on taking her to. Once, it was true, she was overcome by the incense and had to be helped out and on another occasion loudly complained that she could not be expected to kneel on a marble floor and demanded to be escorted to a more comfortable place usually reserved for the clergy. Two years before she had gone so far as to finance and accompany Edda and Christopher Dawson on a visit to Rome at Easter. Here they had met Father Carter, the parish priest of Sheringham, who arranged an audience with the Pope. What Emmeline made of St Pius X is not recorded but Dawson's reactions to Rome were interesting and proved a turning point in his life.[1]

Although, or perhaps because, his parents were Anglo-Catholics, Edda was the first Roman Catholic Christopher knew well. Strangely enough, before he went to Italy he had no notion of Catholicism as a living religion, he associated it entirely with the Middle Ages. His visit to Rome was therefore a revelation and it was here, on the steps of the Capitol, the place where Gibbon conceived the idea of writing *The Decline and Fall of the Roman Empire,* that he felt it was God's will that he should attempt to write a history of culture. Surrounded as he was by the ruins of a great civilization and the living monuments of another, he was already convinced that no culture could survive unless it continued to be fed by the spiritual springs that had given it life.

Emmeline was ambitious for Edda. His final examinations were in prospect and Loudwater was noisy. She made Sharp give up a room in his cottage so that her son could study there in peace. If he did well in his finals or "schools" as they are known at Oxford, she intended to give Father Carter a large sum to install the stained glass window he had so long desired for his church.

In the event, Edda went up early to do some reading before term started but he caught the wrong train from Norwich and found himself at Cambridge. After a long wait he got the train to Oxford via Bletchley and arrived there a good four hours after his box. After dinner he locked his door, took off his clothes and read Schopenhauer for a long time naked by the fire. What Mrs Tatham thought of all this we do not know. In after years he would often surprise people by taking off his shirt and stripping to the skin in front of a good blaze. He now spent almost as much time completing his translation of the sermons of Luis of Granada from the Spanish[2] as he did in revision and, like many emotionally insecure people, he seems from his diaries to have worried far more about his Oxford life passing and the prospect of saying farewell to old friends than he did about schools. No more solemn reminders from old Spooner about coming up on the right day, no more jokes with Brandreth about future dons having to put wires over the quad to prevent undergraduates landing there in private aeroplanes. Never again May morning by Magdalen Tower or the sound of Great Tom tolling over the city from Christ Church.

In early June he got up at 6.30 a.m. , had a swim in the baths at Merton College, went to Mass, and a little after nine walked with his friends Cork and King to the Examination Schools. Christopher sat his papers a week later. Edda says little about his examination questions. He spent almost his last day at Oxford cycling to Kingston Bagpuize to gather wild martagon lilies from a wood there to give to the remaining members of the NCC only to discover that his fears were justified. They had gone down already and their rooms were empty.

Towards the end of the month George V and Queen Mary were crowned and Edda went up to London for the occasion. He was met at Paddington by Gladys, her sister Hester and their mother, Edith. Sharp drove them all slowly back to Great Portland Street via Picadilly and Bond

Street so that they could see the decorations. Selfridges was brilliantly lit up, John Lewis conspicuously dark, in token, Watkin supposed, of its owner's republican sympathies. Next morning Sharp drove them very early to the Royal Societies Club in St James' Street to which Edda now belonged. Emmeline meanwhile had made her own way to Buckingham Palace where, totally regardless of what people thought, she climbed on to the railings and had a splendid view of the domestic side of things. This was before the alterations to the façade and she was able to see the royal guests starting out for Westminster, and the King, still in tweeds, walking from room to room, the little princes in sailor suits and the young Prince of Wales eyeing an enormous cake.[3]

At St James' Edda had brought with him Dante's *Purgatorio*, volume one of Ruskin's *Modern Painters*, and also his *Praeterita*, discovered in the Club library. These kept him going until the procession returned from the Abbey when he sat next to a man arrayed in full court dress and watched with pleasure the glass coach and the King and Queen wearing their crowns and carrying their sceptres. The dukes too were in state coaches, the lesser peers in cars. The procession was brought up by an old bus carrying the inscription "London and North Eastern Railway" bearing inside two Mayors in scarlet robes – a ludicrous sight which made the crowd clap and laugh uproariously. According to Watkin, the carriage of the German Crown Prince and Princess got the loudest applause.

Next morning they were up early again, this time to see the royal progress through London which they watched from the Daimler Supply Company in Piccadilly. Let us hope the long suffering Sharp was given a place there too. Kitchener, the man whose pointing finger before long Watkin was so to fear, rode beside the royal carriage. The Duke of Cambridge was no more but he would have been pleased to see his niece ride by as a crowned queen. Winston Churchill and his wife passed along the route in a carriage escorted by mounted police, to save him, Edda supposes, from the anger of loyal subjects. Churchill had crossed the floor and was now a member of Asquith's distinguished cabinet together with Lloyd George, Sir Edward Grey, Lord Morley and Birrell. Whether Watkin's comment refers to Churchill's uncharacteristic cutting of defence spending, his supposed responsibility for the use of troops against the striking miners at Tonypandy, or the part he played in the so-called battle of Sidney Street the previous January, is not clear.

After the Coronation Sharp drove them all up to Oxford for the New College Commemoration Ball. Edda made him stop en route at Dorchester Abbey but unfortunately inside it was all very high church and Aunt Edith nearly had a fit when she saw candles, crucifixes and Stations of the Cross and accused her nephew of luring her into a Popish building. The ball lasted until six in the morning and at the end all the company, but not of course Edda who could neither sing nor dance, bawled out the

Eton Boating Song followed by the national anthem. Edda gave a dinner party, as a symbolic gesture threw down his gown from the top of New College Tower and then departed for Erdington, a Benedictine Abbey near Birmingham.

He spent a week there more or less following their way of life and it is obvious that the monks hoped that he had a vocation to the priesthood. This slightly annoyed Edda. He would have liked to have been a priest but realized that he was not cut out for celibacy. For some time now his thoughts had been turning to marriage. He was still very immature emotionally. He cherished a romantic fantasy about a girl he refers to merely as 'J', whom he had met at a wedding. She was a Protestant. Was it practical to think about her, was it right? No one at Erdington seemed particularly interested in the sermons of Luis of Granada. He then went to visit the Oratory at Edgbaston and was taken to see Newman's room which, in the Victorian manner, had been kept exactly as it was at the time of death. Judging from the pictures and furnishings the Cardinal was not a man of good taste and the photographs of him spread out in an open album for visitors to look at were profoundly depressing. Rarely had Watkin seen a face of such intense sadness.

Perhaps it had been a mistake to have thrown down his gown from the top of the college tower or perhaps he had retrieved it, because in early August Watkin was summoned back to Oxford for his *viva voce* examination. He reached Oxford by steamer from Aunt Sissie's house at Shiplake, stayed in his stripped and deserted former rooms and was questioned in the Examination Schools on Philosophy for a short time only. Then he went to Yorkshire to visit Dawson.

Christopher met him at Grassington in the carriage and they drove back to Hartlington Hall by the upper road. In the valley below they could see Burnsall church where one day Dawson would lie together with his family. The more Watkin saw of the Dawsons and their house the more delightful they seemed. He was given the same oak-panelled and tapestry lined room as before. It had a plaque of the Madonna and Child and a crucifix above the fireplace. There were books everywhere. The weather was hot.

Colonel Dawson had built Hartlington Hall on a hill above the river Wharfe where a stream or beck, as it was called, over the centuries had cut a ravine through the limestone. It was a magical place, on one side the green hills, on the other the dark fells, with the beck running between and the constant sound of falling water, gentle in summer, a torrent in winter.

The next day the two of them lunched by the river and bathed in the deep pools of brown water and before returning to the house stopped to drink from a cold spring bursting out of the limestone. When they reached home they found that telegrams announcing their examination results had arrived. Watkin had a First, Dawson a Second. Next day a letter arrived from his "ever proud tutor" Alfred Zimmern together with one from a delighted Dr Spooner telling Edda that he had been awarded a better mark than all the scholars in the entire university and the highest of anyone in the College. Colonel and Mrs Dawson and Christopher's sister, Gwendoline, could not have been more warm or sincere in their congratulations and nor could Christopher himself. He had not tried for a First, very sensibly reading round the syllabus and concentrating on subjects which interested him. Nevertheless he minded, and Watkin, always diffident about his own achievements, felt awkward when letters and telegrams of congratulation poured in.

Two days before he left Hartlington Edda looked out of his window at night and saw over the opposite hill the two bright planets of Mars and Saturn together. Colonel Dawson told him that this conjunction of both planets in Aries signified war followed by pestilence for Britain, France, Germany and Russia.

In many ways it was a summer of roses and wine. Emmeline had bought a new Daimler and a de Dion runabout which to Sharp's displeasure the younger visitors borrowed to dash about the countryside. Philip Fowke had got his heart's desire. To his elderly father's disapproval, he and Gladys sat together in the summer-house feeding each other with ripe cherries.[4] Her brother Hugh spent his time flirting shamelessly with the Ben Davis girls next door, Albert brought out trays of iced champagne, they picnicked at Pretty Corner by the light of the car lamps and danced on the lawn to the music of a gramophone. In London Edda saw Melba's farewell performance in Gounod's *Romeo and Juliet* and was forced by Aunt Ada yet again to waste two days at Lord's. Yet beneath it all was a sense of unease. Every now and then the shadow of war crosses the pages of Watkin's diaries and the sun of that glorious summer is momentarily dimmed.

The crowd may have cheered the German Crown Prince but the general attitude towards Germany was ambivalent. The ties of blood and culture had been loosened by the Kaiser's bombast and expansionist claims. Then at the end of July came the Agadir crisis and German clamour for Moroccan territory. Augustine Birrell sat calmly on his lawn reading an old folio edition of *Paradise Lost* but during dinner at Loudwater war was discussed as imminent. It might be better to fight now, before Germany was ready.

It was expected that Edda would do something about a career but he dithered. It was not that he was idle. While still at Hartlington he had completed an article about Little Gidding which was accepted by the editor of the *Ampleforth Journal* and this, apart from a short poem in the *St Paul's* magazine, was his first venture into print. He was now engrossed in an essay on Catholicism as it was represented by Dante and Milton. To amuse himself and he hoped, his companions, he had also written a comic opera in two acts entitled *Fairyland*. This was based on Hugh's flirtation with the "fairies" as the Ben Davis girls next door were called. It included a German invasion of Sheringham and a chorus of boy scouts.

It had already been arranged for him to go in the autumn to Baden Baden to live with a schoolmaster's family in order to learn German, but what then? His mother wanted him to read for the Bar but he himself knew and others would soon have told him that this was unrealistic. He had the mind for it all right but neither the temperament nor manner. Mr Heath had suggested that he sat for a Fellowship at All Souls. He decided to ask Dr Rashdall's advice and was invited to stay for a weekend in Hereford where Rashdall was a residential Canon.

At the house he was greeted by Dr Rashdall's mother and his wife. Old Mrs Rashdall was very like her son to look at and his wife lively and amusing; without her, Watkin imagined, Rashdall would have turned into a fossil. In their turn, they saw an awkward, eager boy of twenty-two, slight, a little below average height, with speedwell blue eyes and thick dark hair. They were all very kind and hospitable but Rashdall told Edda that it was difficult to get a Fellowship by examination and advised him to take a further degree at a German university. He did not say that he himself had tried for an Oxford Fellowship twice and failed.

On the morning of his departure Edda suddenly decided that he wanted a long walk, so he sent his box ahead and started out to walk to Worcester, some thirty miles. This was the heart of the unspoilt England of dreams and childrens' books. The roads were almost deserted, the orchards heavy with fruit; not far from the Malvern Hills a farmer handed Edda an apple, a pear and a glass of milk over an old wall. He reached Worcester at half past seven, retrieved his box from the station and took it across the road to the Star Inn, next morning catching, amazingly, a through train to Sheringham.

Towards the end of September a tremendous gale blew along the coast. The sea in front of Loudwater was torn by the wind into huge foam-crested waves. Only those with knowledge of the sea, Watkin thought, could fitly appreciate the *Odyssey*. The wind howled against the window panes, tiles flew off the roof and at night Loudwater itself quivered and shook. Hugh's nightly refuge, the summer-house, was blown right down. Edda saw the deserted beach and was almost overwhelmed by nostalgia. The summer was over, the tents were gone, his friends dispersed, all life, happiness and laughter vanished.

On the evening of the first day of November, seen off by Philip Fowke and Pontifex, he left for the boat train and Baden Baden in the Black Forest. Before he left he added a codicil to his will. Thanks to Grandma, he had some money in his own right. In the previous May he had signed a deed by which he received £2,500 settlement money, quite a nice sum in the currency of the time. Perhaps he left some money to the church, perhaps back to his mother upon whom he was still emotionally and physically dependent. He went to her room every night before going to bed and sat with her sometimes for hours talking about books that could not have interested her in the slightest. She organized his life, and saw that he was shaved and properly dressed. He continued to eat his meals in her bedroom when she was ill, if he felt unwell she would call in the doctor immediately.

The boxes had of course gone ahead and Watkin was met at Baden by Herr Lentz who taught English, French and German at a local girls' school. Edda had a pleasant room and both Herr Lentz and his wife were very kind. There were three children in the family, two little girls, Gertrude and Gretchen and a little boy of six called Bube. There was only one servant and good Frau Lentz did much of the work. She was a republican and in the privacy of her home used to say "down with the Keiser" much to the agitation of her husband who feared she might be arrested. Watkin cared greatly for the children and they for him. He took them out for walks, bought them sweets, played card games, allowed them to stay in his room while he was reading and dressed up as a character called "Fairy Wonderful Sunshine" to make them laugh. As a child himself he had had few children about him; in the years to come he would have too many.

The Lentz's must have thought that they had a religious and botanical fanatic on their hands. He went to Mass daily, sometimes twice, visited on foot every church and monastery within twenty miles, disappeared with his knapsack for hours on end, reappearing in the dark , exhausted but still eager to show them his specimens. He loved the beautiful countryside, yet all the time he was homesick and letters from England intensified it. His mother had become an ardent suffragette and what was far more disturbing, had had dinner with 'J's' mother who had a grace and favour apartment at Hampton Court. Hugh had decided to become a Roman Catholic but was so terrified of telling his mother, Aunt Edith, that he had suffered a breakdown and been ordered to go on a voyage to Australia.

Edda wanted to get back and felt more and more homesick as Christmas approached. He could not see the Plough without remembering the sight of it high over the sea at Sheringham. Sheringham was the dearest of all the places in the world, scene of the happiest times of his life. He prayed that his last hours on earth might be spent there and that time would pass quickly before he saw it again. It did pass. On January 9, 1912, he came into Harwich by moonlight and before very long was falling asleep at Loudwater to the sound of the sea.

CHAPTER EIGHT

Joy

Among the guests was a couple from Aylsham, old friends of Fathers Carter and Squirrel. Their name was Shepheard and with them was their daughter, Helena. Edda was enchanted and before the afternoon was over determined to make her his wife. Here the diary ends abruptly. What he felt was not for the eyes either of Mrs Tatham or his mother.

Before a fortnight had passed Emmeline was busy making plans for a cruise to the Holy Land. She invited Father Carter, Edda's parish priest, to accompany them as her guest and immediately recruited him as her general agent and courier. He was sent off to Cambridge to see Mgr Barnes who was to lead the expedition, then to London to have a personal interview with Sir Henry Lunn about the exact position of their berths.

Watkin spent six weeks at home before the expedition started. There was no pressure on him to adopt a career. In any case, he had not completed his time in Germany, the Lentz's were expecting him back. The truth of the matter was that he had neither then nor at any time in his life, the slightest intention of taking ordinary paid employment. He wanted to write and he would write. From an early age Dawson had felt an urge to trace the history of culture and to show religion as its dynamic. Watkin's intentions were different and far more dangerous. He was convinced that Catholicism, that is the entire Christian drama, from the Fall of Man to the Return of Christ in Glory, if properly understood, provided an answer to the prevailing and ever encroaching secularism of which he was most painfully aware. It was useless, Protestant fashion, to cut off a limb here and a limb there in response to inconvenient scientific discoveries. The whole thing must be seen with different eyes. Any apologetic must be addressed not to the intellect alone but to life as it was actually lived, life which was at the present time cleverly but falsely interpreted by people like Bernard Shaw. He was convinced that he could present Christian truth to the outside world as something which science could in part clarify but not in its essence touch. He was too recent a convert to Catholicism, too good, too transparent, still too naïve to realize that the Church itself was part of the problem and that he was preparing to cross a minefield.

His first shock came in conversation with Father Carter. Thomas Carter was the son of a Liverpool architect and a most earnest and devout Catholic whose life revolved round his "mission" to Sheringham. He had pushed hard for the building of a church there and by his enthusiasm, preaching and adherence to the proper celebration of the Catholic liturgy, had increased his congregation at St Joseph's by leaps and bounds. But his mind was practical, not speculative, his theology restricted to what he had learnt in the seminary. He was delighted by Edda's conversion, still hoped for Emmeline's and at this very moment was seeing to the design and manufacture of the great window soon to be installed in his church in honour of her son's triumph at Oxford. However, when Edda told him what he hoped to do with his life, he looked grave and said that the laity should leave philosophy alone, for that path led to a risk of heresy. Watkin was surprised and horrified. Such an attitude amounted to fear of the truth and a fettering of the human mind utterly alien to Catholicism.

There was another priest in the district, a man of very different calibre and character, Harold Squirrel, the parish priest of Cromer and like Edda a lover of Dante. He had been born in Norwich and studied literature and art in Leipzig and Munich for eight years before being received into the Roman Catholic Church. He and Edda were very much together during those six weeks. It was winter and they trudged along the Norfolk coast sometimes in snow, often in rain and usually in a cutting wind. Once after dinner with Squirrel Edda walked in the moonlight back home through Sheringham woods. How much a part moonlight played in the life and literature of the past and what a dimension of seeing has been lost by the gradual spread of artificial light even in the country.

Sometimes the two walked to a place a few miles beyond Cromer known as "The Garden of Sleep". Here the tide had eaten away the cliff and a medieval church together with its burial ground had for years been slowly sliding into the sea. Only the tower and a few gravestones remained awaiting their turn on the edge of the cliff. In summer the whole place was a blaze of red poppies which covered the graves and stretched past the solitary tower to the fields beyond. As they spoke they watched together the falling snow gathering in the tower's wide cracks and in 1916, when Watkin returned alone, both the tower and its sleepers had gone.

Squirrel was very willing to talk about difficulties which Father Carter could not see. They spoke about the existence of hell which worried Watkin greatly, the development of doctrine, the Index and the fate of Father Tyrrell. In effect, Watkin was being given a warning quite as grave as Carter's, but for different reasons. Sophisticated himself, Squirrel recognised the fundamental innocence of Watkin's temperament. He was fond of Edda. He did not wish to see his life ruined by an inevitable clash with ecclesiastical authority. It was not the time for interpretive apologetics, he told him, the powers that be were on the defensive and the atmosphere unfavourable. This, as we know, and as Edda should have known, was to state the case mildly. But he was still at his Aloysian stage, a raw convert not yet ready to grasp by what ruthless methods the Papacy was crushing dissent from what amounted to a fundamentalist interpretation of Christianity.

Towards the middle of February Edda and his mother went to stay at Great Portland Street to prepare for their departure. He went with the Pontifexes to see *The Miracle*, which was produced at Olympia by C. B. Cochrane. This play, acted in mime and set to music, was to become famous after the War when Max Reinhardt gave Diana Cooper the part of the Madonna. Evelyn Waugh saw it in 1932 and until he became passionately devoted to Diana, judged it as full of blasphemy as an egg is full of meat.[1] Edda too had misgivings beforehand but thought not only was there nothing in it to offend, but that it was extraordinary beautiful and the sanctity and blessedness of the religious life was wonderfully displayed. Life was all rush. Edda read the whole of his comic opera *Fairyland* to an unusually patient Aunt Ada and in going to Harrods with his mother to buy some last-minute shirts and collars the day before they left, he saw with disquiet a man bearing an enormous placard bearing the message "Weep and howl ye gay and careless rich".

However, when Emmeline and Edda went to meet Father Carter at King's Cross in the afternoon they found that the poor man was suffering from a bad attack of flu. Emmeline was at her best when dealing with illness or animals. She drove to Lunn's office, explained the situation, stated that Edda should leave as arranged, that she and Carter would join the ship at Constantinople, and drove back to nurse the invalid.

Mgr Barnes was always known as 'the Mugger', although why is not certain. Edda introduced himself to him at Charing Cross, and was then on his own. Fortified by brandy and water he read Ward's life of Newman all the way to Calais and then got into the wrong train at the Gare de Lyons. Rescued in the nick of time, he was directed to a sleeper and read the *Purgatorio* until overcome by exhaustion. At Marseilles they were driven down to the docks by horse bus and boarded the *Dunottar Castle*. Invited to sit at the Mugger's table, he was introduced to his colleague, a Mgr O'Reilly who was closely attended throughout the entire voyage by a devout elderly female addressed as Miss Davies. The general feeling on board was that she was paying for him. There was a Mr Strickland, a Colonel Bowring and a Mrs Gilfoyle, the perfect setting for an Agatha Christie detective story; and how the later Watkin would have enjoyed reading it. Unfortunately the day was Friday which caused guilty flutters at the sight of any mention of meat on the menu but the Mugger made everything all right by assuring the Catholics on board that they were dispensed from abstinence, whether as pilgrims or seafarers no one seemed to know. Early Mass was said daily in the lounge and served by Edda. Everything was tiny, little toy candles and a small crucifix. The vestments were reversible, red on one side, white the other.

As they approached the straits between Sardinia and Corsica, Watkin thought of the becalmed and perplexed Newman writing "Lead Kindly Light" and after a church crawl at Naples was struck by the contrast between Latin and Teutonic Catholicism. Before they reached Piraeus the Mugger asked him to provide some notes on the contribution Athens had made to political history and philosophy for his lecture on our debt to that city. When it came to be delivered, Barnes was admirably succinct, explaining within an hour the importance of Athens in art, literature, politics, philosophy and religion. The occasion was, however, a little overcast by Miss Davies who pounced on the lecturer for suggesting that the Apostles may not have been fully cognizant of later and more exciting developments of doctrine.

When at last Athens was reached, Watkin had trouble avoiding her. She chattered incessantly and he thought that she would have preferred her parish church to the Parthenon. In her presence he felt nothing of the past, he saw merely stones. However, that night some of their party returned to the Acropolis to look at it by moonlight, something Edda had not done when he was there last. Escaping from Mgr O'Reilly and Miss Davies, he wandered alone round and about the Parthenon. Never before had he understood its real beauty and majesty. The pillars looked immense and as strong as the pillars in Egyptian temples. It was the great shrine of the human intellect, the temple of the Greek Madonna of Wisdom, as Ruskin had termed Athene.

At the end of the colonnade was a vast opening that widened upwards between two pillars and the marble floor gleamed in the moonlight that shone bright through the great doorway. He could hear a distant babble of voices from the city below, someone had said that they were holding an election. It was silent where he was. The noise below appeared futile compared with the abiding truth which had shaped the building and powerless to disturb its peace. He felt the awful majesty yet delicate beauty of the place, a sense of solemn, indefinable haunting, the presence of some mighty spirit. He realized with a shock how late it was and finding himself alone had to walk down at speed in order to catch up with the rest of the party and back to the ship.[2]

So they sailed on, round Sunium, past Lesbos towards Asia and the plains of Troy. Watkin barely mentions the fact that his mother and Carter were waiting for them on the quay at Constantinople. At last he could see the mosque of Sulieman, of Sultan Achmed and St Sophia where High Mass had been celebrated with the utmost magnificence for nearly a thousand years, with such magnificence indeed that the ambassadors from Russia thought that they beheld the ministry not of men but of angels.

Four days later they reached the Holy Land. They went to all the places devout pilgrims usually visit, Nazareth, Cana, the Sea of Galilee, Capharnaum, Bethlehem and Jerusalem, and Watkin describes them all in great detail. Yet, as he himself recognized with grief and guilt, something was missing in his response. He was setting his feet where Our Saviour trod, beholding the actual place where the Creator of all things was incarnate as our fellow human being but he had no imaginative realization of it. He thought that this was not because much of what was pointed out as authentic was plainly nothing of the kind. Perhaps it was that they had a mere eight days to see everything and the press of people spoilt the atmosphere, perhaps it was something deeper. They were all tired. The hospices they stayed at were often quite primitive and Father Carter, after securing a single room for Emmeline, had to share a room with Edda who got up at the crack of dawn to serve his Mass. Weakened maybe by flu, Carter fell ill just before they left. Emmeline summoned doctors and once back on the ship he had to be assisted to his berth. Here he remained for their entire time in Egypt and did not emerge until they were well on their way to Naples where after a visit to Pompeii, their cruise ended and they said goodbye to him and *Dunottar Castle* before going on to Rome.

It appears that some difficulty had arisen about Edda's return to Baden. Before they set out on their voyage, Dr Sumpter had written to Herr Lentz explaining that Edda was not in sufficiently good health to resume his studies quite yet. This was plainly untrue. Edda liked the Lentz's and cared for their children but it may be that he felt they were too *gemütlich* or perhaps too provincial, and in any case he wanted a wider experience of Germany. While he was in Rome he heard that Herr Lentz had, naturally enough, taken another pupil. He and his mother therefore decided to make a leisurely way back to Baden and find somewhere suitable for themselves.

On the night they left for Milan the *Titanic* went down. Contrary to rumour, poor Nes-Min was not on board. However, a friend of Emmeline's was, the fashionable couturier, Lucy Duff Gordon, who traded under the name of Lucile. She was the sister of the romantic novelist Elinor Glyn and appears twice in Edgar's Pantafon sketch-book, her dark hair over her shoulders. She and her husband, Sir Cosmo Duff Gordon, were to come in for a great deal of opprobrium because they escaped with only ten others in a lifeboat capable of holding forty people. Moreover, Sir Cosmo had unwisely given each crew member on board a

£5 draft on Coutts Bank.[3] This tale, often retold, remained in the children's imagination as one of the most vivid episodes connected with their father's past.

Edda had long wished to visit the famous Benedictine abbey of Beuron in Württemberg so he parted momentarily from his mother and went there alone. One of the monks heard that he was seeking somewhere to stay in Germany and advised him to apply to the parish priest of Neustadt, a small town in the Black Forest near Freiburg. Unfortunately when he got there he took an immediate dislike, even repulsion, to the parish priest whose countenance reminded him of Cruickshank's pictures of Wackford Squeers in *Nicholas Nickleby*. The poor man was very pleasant and anxious to have Watkin as a pupil. He showed him numerous testimonials, took him for a beautiful walk, gave him an evening meal and a bed in his presbytery for two nights, but not even all this and the discovery of a dear pussy on the stairs could overcome a dislike Edda knew to be irrational. He felt trapped. After breakfast some letters forwarded from Baden arrived. One of these was from Father Squirrel and another from one of his sisters who lived in Munich. Both of them strongly recommended a Prussian literary family, three ladies who lived on the Starnberger See, one of the Bavarian lakes not far from Munich. The cage door opened. Emmeline arrived to make sure that all was well, saw Edda and was then entertained by Father Rinkenburger, for such was his name, to a special lunch in anticipation of a fruitful relationship between master and pupil. She had to break the news of Edda's departure and the rest of the meal was eaten in an atmosphere heavy with reproach. Rinkenburger, whom Edda recognized to be a good man, was paid for his hospitality and the next step was to go to Baden to say goodbye to the Lentz's.

It was a joyful meeting on all sides. While Emmeline stayed at an hotel, Edda slept once again in his old room and wrote at his familiar table. He took the children for a walk to a meadow by a stream on the forest's edge, here Grete and Bube made a little house while he played ball with Trude. It was one of the happiest hours of his entire journey abroad, a happiness intensified a thousand fold, he wrote, by the presence of the three children playing so joyfully in the spring of their lives. On the evening before he left Frau Lentz cooked his favourite white beans, Herr Lentz discussed etymology and Edda dressed up again as Fairy Wonderful Sunshine. Next morning they all came out to say goodbye and the last sight Edda ever saw of them was little Bube standing in the middle of the road waving until the cab was out of sight. This is the last we see of them too. A single photograph has come to light, taken in 1926. A stout Frau Lentz is standing before a window with a grandchild in her arms. After that, silence. Did little Bube survive the Second War? Did Grete and Trude or their parents? We just do not know.

At Munich they had tea in Miss Squirrel's flat and met some of her friends together with Gräffin Bethury-Huc, one of the women who lived in the house where Edda had so impulsively determined to go. The rapport was instant and Emmeline was quickly won over by a poodle which ran across the floor to welcome her with roses in its mouth. Edda thought they were more like English people than most of the Germans he had known. There was nothing stiff, solemn or dull about them.

This impression was confirmed the following day when he went with his mother by train to Tulzing, a village about twenty miles from Munich and they saw the house where Edda hoped to stay for three months. It was named "Froh" which means joy and Edda thought he was in paradise. Froh looked over a meadow directly at the lake and Watkin's room had a balcony from where, in the distance, he could see the Bavarian Alps, still covered with snow. He was taken for a walk and found a new buttercup and a small purple anemone among the cowslips under the trees at the water's edge. He was in an ecstacy of delight spoilt only a little by the reflection that poor King Ludwig of Bavaria had drowned himself from the opposite shore. Emmeline soon settled terms and after a few more days spent in Munich together going to Strauss's *Salome* and seeing the sights from an electric car whose batteries occasionally failed; she left for England and he once more for Froh and its inhabitants.

These were three. Fraulein Steinbruch and Fraulein Servière, old friends who had retired from running a large girls' school in Leipzig and Gräffin Bethury-Huc, or Gräffin Hertha, as she asked Edda to call her. All three were agnostics, as was Father Squirrel's sister. Although no doubt warned, they may have been perplexed by Edda's lack of co-ordination. Gräffin Hertha took him out on the lake and mistakenly attempted to teach him to row but soon discovered, in her pupil's words, that she might as well try to teach a donkey to read. They may also have been puzzled by his extreme piety and obsession with church architecture and the liturgy. Too educated to deny the enormous part played by Catholicism in the making of European civilization, they rejected the belief that sustained it. Watkin thought this a delusion and the idea that ethics alone could produce a world of art, music and social justice was wishful thinking on the part of those who had rejected religion on understandable but inadequate grounds.

It was just these people he wished to reach. He was certain that there was a path between agnosticism on one hand and cowardly denial of the known truth on the other. Properly understood, Catholicism offered it. But when in the course of reading Schiller's *Maid of Orleans* Fraulein Steinbruck remarked that the crucifixion was a tragedy, Watkin was silent. He needed to think. One day he would answer her question and in print, but not yet.

In many ways he was very happy at Froh. His teachers were most conscientious. Every morning he had a long lesson in German, which was spoken all the time; there were wide-ranging discussions at dinner and interesting visitors came and went. Gräffin Hertha accompanied Edda on a walking tour from Garmisch in the Tyrol over the mountains to Imst and by train to Innsbruck. It must have been heavy going. He had in his knapsack a mackintosh, his breviary, a life of Oscar Wilde and a German guide to the Austrian alps, in his pockets a Dante, an alpine flora, the *Oxford Book of English Verse*, rolls and butter and bars of chocolate. As Edda had done in England, they sent their night things and sometimes their knapsacks on by train or motor bus to the place they were going to. The frontier between Germany and Austria was marked merely by a post on one side of the path painted in Bavarian colours, on the other in the Austrian black and yellow.

The churches in southern Germany opened the doors of his mind to something which was to play a very important part in his religious thought and in his books, a love of Baroque architecture and decoration. As yet the opening was barely a crack. He was still far too much under the influence of Ruskin and the Gothic school to appreciate what was under his nose and to his bitter regret in later life, he failed to visit the Baroque masterpieces then within his grasp.

The three women were very good to him. They arranged for him to see the Passion Play at Erl, which he did not altogether enjoy, and Wagner's *Götterdämmerung* and *Tristan und Isolde* in Munich, both of which he loved. But towards the end of his time there, he began to feel more and more homesick. It would soon be almost five months since he left England. Looking down from the tower of the Rathaus in Munich he saw the trams and multitudes of people below him moving like mechanical toys. But these comic little creatures were destined to endure for eternity while the majestic mountains that surrounded him would crumble into nothingness. What strange contrasts there were between outward appearance and reality. He longed to return to some of those comic little creatures, to see 'J', to see Dawson, his mother and Sheringham. If he *had* to die, let it be there.

He left Bavaria on July 17, 1912. Nothing is explicitly said but one feels that while his stay at Froh was intellectually stimulating, his heart remained with the Lentz family. He intended to visit Bruges en route home but unfortunately fell asleep on the train and passed Brussels where his boxes were taken out of the train so he had to stay in Bruges waiting for them far longer than he intended or those in England expected. He greeted the white cliffs of Dover with joy. A fleet of British warships was cruising along the coast. When he eventually arrived in Great Portland Street he found Emmeline very busy organizing the party she was going to give at Loudwater after the unveiling of the window she was presenting to Sheringham church in Edda's honour. Nevertheless, he kept her up until past two in the morning telling her about his adventures.

Sharp drove him down to Sheringham but because of two long stops at the abbey of Bury St Edmunds and then at Attleborough church they did not reach Loudwater until nightfall. Next day Emmeline arrived and took command of the social side of the celebrations that were to accompany the blessing of the new window for which the scaffolding was even now being erected. Edda had chosen a Jesse window or Jesse tree as it is sometimes called, a subject popular in the Middle Ages. It shows the descent of Jesus from King David and ends with the Virgin and Child. The design had been worked out by Dunstan Powell and the window made by the well-known firm of Hardman and Co. It is still there above Edda's name and the reason why his mother gave it.

They had a week to go. The invitations to the luncheon party to be held at Loudwater had long gone out, the presence of the clergy requested, together with old friends, certain members of the local congregation and important Catholics living in the district. Flowers arrived from Pantafon and were put in buckets out of the sun. Edda was not involved in the domestic side of things. He strolled among the workmen, went botanizing with his old friend Major Laffan and advised the Birrells to send their son Francis to Froh. Gladys arrived, so did Watkin's dear and respected friend Father Rickaby together with the Mugger.

On the day itself, August 7, owing to the press of clergy, no less than five Masses were said at St Joseph's, two of them served by Edda. At eleven o'clock the Bishop of Northampton entered the church vested in cope and mitre, accompanied by seven priests. The window was then unveiled and blessed, followed by High Mass *coram episcopo*. When that was over and the sermon preached by Father Rickaby, the clergy and servers left through the main door in solemn procession with Edda acting as cross bearer.

After that those who had been invited gathered for a splendid luncheon at Loudwater. Mgr O'Reilly together with Miss Davies and Mr Strickland represented the *Dunattor Castle*. Another bishop arrived just when the first course was being served. Among the guests was a couple from Aylsham, old friends of Fathers Carter and Squirrel. Their name was Shepheard and with them was their daughter, Helena. Edda was enchanted and before the afternoon was over determined to make her his wife. Here the diary ends abruptly. What he felt was not for the eyes either of Mrs Tatham or his mother.

CHAPTER NINE

I am the Master of My Own Life

The honeymoon was spent in Italy. It lasted five weeks and except for a week's rest at Sestri Levante on the Gulf of Genoa, probably at Helena's request, it was a vigorous tour later made more so by Edda's persistent seeking for a hermit whom someone had told him lived in a cave near Celano.

Helena was the eldest child and only daughter of Philip Candler Shepheard of Abbots Hall, Aylsham, a market town about twelve miles distant from Sheringham. His ancestors had farmed land between Bacton and Happisburgh on the North Norfolk coast for generations before coming inland at the end of the eighteenth century. Philip was, or appeared to be, a typical Norfolk gentleman of a certain type. He had, however, twice acted out of character.

After his first wife died he had become a Roman Catholic. This was not due to grief but conviction. Unusually for a convert, he was attracted to the Church through reading Cobbett's *Rural Rides,* an account of conditions in the countryside in the earlier years of the nineteenth century. Cobbett, no Catholic himself, persuaded Philip that the Catholic Church, which owned most of the land before the Reformation, had treated the rural poor far more humanely than its Protestant successor. Then, soon after his conversion, he had fallen in love, and obstinately pursued an Italian girl of exceptional beauty. She was Helena's mother and her name was Maria Pasqua.

Maria Pasqua had a most romantic and unusual history. She had been born in 1856 into a family of poor peasants from the Abruzzi in central Italy. Her father was an artists' model who daily plied for hire from the Spanish Steps in Rome. The beauty of his little girl attracted attention and he was advised that she would make a fortune as a child model in Paris. They journeyed on foot to Paris when she was six years old. She was an immediate success. When she was nine years old she was adopted by the Comtesse de Noailles, a childless English woman and a member of the Baring family and brought up as her daughter. Philip first caught sight of her when she was staying with friends at Bournemouth and after a long and troubled courtship, married her when she was twenty-five. He was then forty-two. Her story has been told elsewhere.[1]

Of all this Edda knew nothing. He saw a good looking, quiet and elderly Englishman, an elegantly dressed and far younger wife who spoke with an attractive French accent, and a slim girl with dark brown curly hair and eyes the colour of pansies. It had taken Philip three weeks to decide that he wanted to marry Maria Pasqua. It took Edda about three hours to decide that he wished to marry her daughter.

There was about all of them an air of old-fashioned courtesy as if they were survivors from another time or place. In a sense, this was so. Helena spoke the kind of old fashioned English which has almost died out. She said "crawss", "lorft", "Awstria", not "gurl" nor "gal", but something between the two. Philip had just resigned from his position as Chairman of the Bench of local Magistrates, he was now almost seventy-five, conceived therefore in the reign of William IV. Maria Pasqua had been brought up in the household and with the manners of a nomadic aristocrat, her daughter educated at a most expensive convent in London. It was not this that drew Edda to her. He would in time come to think that the convent had been in some ways an unfortunate influence upon his wife and children. It was her gentleness which attracted him, a steady, quiet passivity that suggested a temperament totally different from his mother's. Unexpected thoughts were running through his mind as they all sat there in a Victorian house on the edge of the North Sea talking so politely to carefully chosen guests over luncheon tables divided amongst the three reception rooms.

It is possible that Father Carter had long thought of a match between Edda and Helena. The Shepheards had played an important part in the renaissance of Catholicism in Norfolk. Philip's aunts had founded the Catholic church at Aylsham, Philip himself converted a small building in the grounds of his home, Abbots Hall, into a chapel and presented a crucifix and chalice to the fledgling church at Cromer. Although she looked younger, Helena was in fact thirty, six years older than Edda. She was called after her godmother, Helena de Noailles, and her name was pronounced in the old way with the stress on the second syllable, as the island of St Helena still is.

Living in an isolated house in the depth of the country she had met few suitable men and none of them had come up to her expectations. One of the first had been Piffie, the son of the poet Coventry Patmore, whose mother, the third Mrs Patmore, had been a friend of Maria Pasqua and anxious to make a match. The family's Protestant neighbours were wary of the Shepheards. They did not like that chapel in his grounds nor wish their sons to be lured into matrimony by an attractive half-Italian Papist whose altogether too lovely mother had had a singular past. Philip rarely entertained and Helena was bored by his shooting party friends. There was one man she liked who had a house in Norwich. He was a Catholic, a well-off dilettante named Percy Brooks and she went to his art exhibitions, the plays he produced and to his lectures in the Cathedral Close. Philip saw how fond she was of him and went off to make inquiries. One day he took Helena aside. He was afraid, he said, that Percy was not a man's man. But that, of course, was exactly what he was.

Very soon, perhaps the very evening of the luncheon party, Edda asked his mother if she would invite Helena to stay at Loudwater. She wrote to the Shepheards and obtained their consent. Not all the guests had left. Gladys and Edda's old New College friend Ponty were staying in the house but Edda was so serious and so plainly agitated that neither of them dared to tease him. Where now was the young man too cerebral to find a bride? A few days later, driven by Sharp, all three of them set out for Aylsham to fetch Helena.

They may have had some difficulty in finding the house. Abbots Hall lies off a narrow road between Erpingham and Aylsham. It was remote then and is so still. As a property, it was small by Norfolk standards, consisting of some four hundred acres of gardens, arable land, pasture and coverts for shooting. The River Bure ran through the grounds and near the gate a thatched barn faced a large pond. Sharp drove them up a tree lined drive and past a rookery. The house was Jacobean but it had long since lost its original windows and Philip had added a modern wing.

This was the place where Helena had been brought up together with her three brothers, Phil, Samuel and Martin. None of them was there. Phil was in the regular army and had returned to India after a long leave on the very day of the luncheon at Loudwater. Samuel had been unlucky in love and after qualifying as a doctor had in time honoured fashion gone to a remote place in South America as medical officer to a company working there. He was to bring home a new species of orchid which Kew named after him. Martin was dead. Born late in Maria Pasqua's life, ten years separated his birth from Helena's and only a little less from her brothers'. The most precious of all the children, he died of pneumonia when he was eleven and at school with the Jesuits at Beaumont.

Philip must have been puzzled by Watkin, Maria Pasqua less so. For all her eccentricities, Mme de Noailles had been a very cultivated woman. She knew Latin and Greek, was a patron of artists, writers, explorers, social reformers and had been herself an early feminist. If life at Abbots Hall was boring for Helena, her mother had felt the tedium more acutely and for longer. Edda's conversation was unusual. Sharp would have had tea in the kitchen, they in the drawing room by the fluted corner cupboards painted in blue and gold and the large looking glass which reflected the smooth lawns, the well-tended flower beds and the summer-house where Maria Pasqua loved to sit.

The routine was unchanging. After they had finished, Philip would get up and ask any new visitors whether they would care to see something of the property. He did not then know how much Edda loved gardens and the flowers which grew in them, how he enjoyed the walk by the orchard wall where last month the peaches and apricots had been ripe for picking and above all how excited he would become when he followed Philip and the others over the narrow road to the fifteenth-century farmhouse. In that building or its predecessor, their host explained, once lived some monks from the Abbey of Bury St Edmunds. It had been given to them originally by King John on condition that they kept enough bees to supply four wax candles to burn night and day before the martyr's shrine. Gladys and Ponty were impressed and this was just the sort of thing that Edda liked to hear. Secretly, he thought the farmhouse more interesting than the Hall. How wonderful that Mr Shepheard owned it, what a fortunate man he was. Philip was gratified. The fellow neither shot nor fished but he might do for his daughter.

It is uncertain how long Helena stayed at Loudwater, we know only that after a week she was engaged to be married. She told her children that because she was so quiet, Emmeline had not looked upon her as a likely bride for her son. This is hard to believe. Edda in love was as trans-parent as a plate glass window. They went to Mass together every morning at St Joseph's. On August 17, at Edda's request, a Mass was said by Father Carter for a private intention and throughout the service Helena heard low mutterings, and petitions for an answer to prayer. Later that morning he suggested that they should walk together along the cliff to Beeston church. So they did and all the way Helena heard Edda muttering "Will she take me? Will she take me?" under his breath. By the time they reached the thirteenth-century church porch, Helena had understood his intentions and acceded to them. Emmeline claimed to be dumbfounded but before long produced champagne and a fine emerald engagement ring.

Only those who read this book to the end will be able to judge if both of them made a terrible mistake. If Edda had wished to remain close to his mother, Helena was the last person he should have married. Although Helena looked very Italian, particularly when she was young, in character and temperament she was an Englishwoman and a Norfolk woman at that. She was exceedingly reserved and like many of her generation and background, considered it ill-mannered to show her feelings. She was upright, found social insincerity difficult, and was incapable of flattery or pretending to views she did not hold. But did Edda really wish to remain close to his mother? Knowing what actually happened, we can see that in one important respect his diaries were seriously misleading. Only once in all its hundreds of pages does he suggest any trouble between him and Emmeline. One day after lunch in Rome he uses "cruel language" to her. He is immediately "ashamed of my wicked temper and ingratitude for all her love" and they made it up directly. She would, of course, read the diary. She was his dear mother, he her grateful son. Hers was the stronger character. Watkin always found it difficult to disagree with people without working himself up and becoming agitated. He did not just resent her domination, he hated it. And since he was what he was, there was no middle way, nothing but a violent escape. Yet she was his dear mother, he her dear son and in that lay the tragedy of both their lives.

Outwardly conventional as Helena was, inwardly she was a most unusual and independently minded woman. Many, many years later, when she is in her eighties, in one of her weekly letters she reminds Edda that she has often thought people in mental homes were more interesting than those outside them. From the first she found Watkin's conversation intriguing. But from the first she pitied him. She could see that his family looked upon him affectionately but as a kind of freak, a clever child to be tolerated and protected. Yet at the same time he was neglected. Perhaps Albert had left. Edda's buttons needed sewing on, his tie was crooked, his shoes frequently unlaced. His helplessness appealed to her. She wanted to look after him and like many a woman before and since imagined that she could change him. Because it was not her nature, neither then nor at even more critical times in her life, did she make any attempt to make up to Emmeline. If she had said how how sorry she was to appear to deprive such a devoted mother of her only child but it was not a question of losing a son but gaining a daughter she might have won Emmeline's approval.

The reaction at Abbots Hall to the swift engagement must have been one of astonishment but at least Philip did not have to make inquiries. Evidently Helena was about to enjoy a more extravagant life than any to which she had been accustomed.

In October, Emmeline was driven over to Aylsham for what Philip always referred to as his "interview". She was amiable but came straight to the point. Everything had happened too quickly. They should wait for a year. Philip agreed. Now about the wedding expenses. £50 Philip thought would be enough. No, no, £150 and she had some ideas of her own. Very well, let it be £150 and £100 for the linen and trousseau. Emmeline then raised the matter of the marriage settlement. In those days few people of Watkin's and Helena's background got married without a settlement and Philip would certainly never have expected his daughter to marry without one. If she were widowed with children she must have something to support her. It was usual for both families to contribute. Emmeline was prepared to settle sufficient capital to produce £200 a year and to give them her house at Bexhill and all the furniture in it. Philip undertook to contribute £1000.

It is impossible to say at what stage things started to go seriously wrong. We know for certain that at one point early on Emmeline announced that the nuptials should be celebrated at Brompton Oratory, the occasion would be subsidised by her and turn out to be the wedding of the year. She went so far as to buy material for Helena's wedding dress, yards of beautiful cream satin hand- embroidered with gold and silver flowers or perhaps ears of wheat. Helena's youngest daughter was married in what was intended to be its petticoat.

However, sometime between her interview with Philip and the New Year she turned violently against the whole thing. Perhaps she realized that she would never again be the most important person in Edda's life. The evening talks and the eating of meals from a tray in her bedroom were at an end. Her son was determinedly and tactlessly in love, and incapable of pretending that he did not wish to spend every hour with Helena. Emmeline got into a temper whenever the wedding was so much as mentioned. Edda departed from Loudwater, took rooms in Oxford and left his early youth behind him. Events forced him to take the initiative and to assume responsibility for his own life. He would marry whom he pleased. He defied his mother – and she an Ingram.

At the end of January 1913 Philip received an abrupt and discourteous letter from Emmeline. Edda must earn his living before she could fix any date for his marriage to Mr Shepheard's daughter. Besides, the delay would "give you and your wife time (as I hear that you both say that you cannot afford to buy your daughter a proper *trousseau, linen,* and wedding breakfast or reception) to put by a little money to do the thing properly." She was, she continued, in no hurry to part with her son who was too young to undertake the responsibility of married life. The wedding should not be hurried on. She is sure that he does not wish to part from his daughter and she understands that Helena does not much like leaving her mother.[2]

One wonders who was her informant. Philip was not a man to be either flustered or bullied. Two days later he wrote a brief and dignified answer. He intended to carry out all the undertakings he had made at their interview including his consent to the marriage taking place this coming October. He did, however, agree that Mr Watkin should have some occupation.

In the June of this year, perhaps under pressure from Philip or one of his mother's emissaries, Edda enrolled as a pupil at the Inner Temple. He had, however, no intention of practicing at the Bar or taking up any legal work. In this respect he was as obstinate as his mother. He wanted to write and he would write. His families were to be supported, in a fashion, not by his books, not by Emmeline, nor his rich Watkin cousins but by the rescue of a few of those numerous trusts drawn up by Grandma. The handing over of the baby had paid off but not in the way his mother had imagined.

Emmeline's letter was but the first of a barrage of letters to Philip from her solicitors Cohen and Cohen. To each Philip replied calmly reiterating that he would do what he had undertaken to do. Edda told him that he did not know how much of his inheritance was tied up but he would see that the whole matter was legally clarified after his marriage. If he alienated his mother further she might disinherit him altogether in order to make it impossible for him to marry Helena. She was "wildly eager" to get him under her thumb. Years of resentment piled up into defiance. She and Cohen must understand that he was master of his own life, capable and determined to look after himself . He would not be bullied by the power of her purse. The time to make peace was after the marriage. He had set £130 as the outside limit for furnishing the entire house, £100 for furniture, £30 for linen and utensils and had been helped in this by a furniture dealer. He was anxious that on their return from the honeymoon, Helena should go into her own home, not lodgings. The fact is that when Watkin put his mind to it he could be just as practical as anyone else.

In early August, Emmeline fired her final shot. Unless the wedding was postponed she would put nothing into the marriage settlement. Edda responded by putting in himself £2000 worth of stock. The completed settlement is an enormous document of four folio parchment pages copied out by hand in the offices of Philip's solicitors Purdy and Holly from Aylsham Market Place. It has five wax seals, one by each signature. The practice of substituting miserable circles of red paper for wax seals did not come in until after the War which was so soon to break out. The settlement was brought to Abbot's Hall on September 30. Among the signatures are the two trustees, Helena's brother Samuel, and Colonel Dawson, Christopher's father, as the other. In three days time Edda and Helena were married.

It was not the wedding of the year. Emmeline of course was not present, nor Sissie, Ada or Daisy, nor Philip and Gladys or Hugh Watkin. The ceremony was performed by Father Squirrel at Cromer church early in the morning of October 3, 1913. Helena wore a blue dress. Her father gave her away, Christopher Dawson was best man, Maria Pasqua and Samuel Shepheard the only other witnesses. At Edda's request, inside the wedding ring was inscribed "May our love be sanctified by the love of Christ." After the Nuptial Mass they had a small reception at the presbytery next door. All of them had been fasting since midnight. Father Carter played no part in the proceedings. Emmeline was his patron, not Edda; the last thing he wanted was to offend her. On the afternoon of the wedding Samuel left for London, first to see the girl who had rejected him, then to make arrangements to attend a course at the School of Tropical Medicine.

His intention was to leave England and take up a post in Ghana, then called the Gold Coast.

No alteration in her financial prospects would have deterred Helena once she had committed herself to marrying Watkin, but Emmeline was right about one thing. She was utterly devoted to her mother and dreaded leaving her. The honeymoon was spent in Italy. It lasted five weeks and except for a week's rest at Sestri Levante on the Gulf of Genoa, probably at Helena's request, it was a vigorous tour, later made more so by Edda's persistent seeking for a hermit whom someone had told him lived in a cave near Celano. They went to Turin and Rome where they had an audience with Pope Pius X who was looking, Edda wrote to Philip Shepheard, very tired and ill.

Afterwards, when the children came, someone, perhaps Father Carter, obtained a certificate from his successor. This certificate, under a photograph of Pope Benedict XV raising his hand in blessing, gave the family, humbly prostrate at His Holiness's feet, the Apostolic Blessing together with a Plenary Indulgence to be obtained under certain conditions at the hour of death. It was placed on the chimney-piece in the nursery and closely scrutinized by the children as they dressed and undressed in front of the coal fire in the Norfolk winter.

After a visit to Venice, Edda and Helena did what they could to explore the Abruzzi for Maria Pasqua's sake. She remembered no names only mountains, almond blossom, goats and the feel of small stones under bare feet. At the beginning of the last century and indeed until very much later, the Abruzzi was still wild and little visited. It is surprising how far Edda and Helena were able to go by motor coach and trains. They visited Celano, Scanno, Sulmona and Sora and saw the headdresses and aprons striped in yellow and red and green which Maria Pasqua so loved. Every day of their honeymoon Helena sent her mother a picture postcard. Maria Pasqua tied them together with pink ribbon and this is how they were found, wrapped in tissue paper in an empty house over seventy years later. Edda took his pocket Dante with him and to Helena's secret dismay and to the surprise of their fellow passengers, used to quote from it in a loud sing-song voice as they travelled along.

The rented house Edda had got ready for his wife was a pleasant one in Chalfont Road, Oxford. When Watkin left Loudwater after the quarrel with Emmeline he settled down to write the book he had long had in mind and in defiance of the warnings of Fathers Carter and Squirrel was determined to attempt. Whatever they said, he remained convinced that Catholicism could be presented in such a way as to make an intelligent challenge to the prevailing secularism. He called his book *Some Thoughts on Catholic Apologetics: A Plea for Interpretation* and now in the first months of his married life, he started to correct the proofs.

Despite its sometimes clumsy structure and tedious genuflections in the direction of ecclesiastical authority, the book is surprisingly bold for the time it was written and contains within it the germ of much he was to develop more fully and more cogently in later life. It is a short book of some 140 pages and like all his work, closely argued. He recognizes that the civilization whose political and social fabric rested essentially on Christian belief had broken down, that the Church of Constantine had served its purpose and was now dissolved. Unlike many Catholics of the time he does not confine his hopes to the survival of a faithful remnant, an isolated minority clinging to past structures.

He believed that religion is part of humanity's very nature, that the flood of unbelief was slowly abating and that the collapse of one phase of Christian history would be eventually succeeded, not by a restoration of what went before, but by a different kind or type of Christian victory. Before this happens, there may well be a period of moral, intellectual and social anarchy but there must be no retreat into the citadel. Catholics must prepare themselves for changed circumstances by being ready to present their faith in terms understood by the modern mind.

His intention is not to go through the creeds item by item. His purpose is to show a fruitful approach to the whole question of religious belief, to discuss basic philosophical and theological attitudes and ways of interpreting Christian dogma so that people could give it their assent with intellectual integrity. He wishes to remove the incrustations of outmoded philosophical or scientific thought which of necessity surround dogmatic formulations.

Watkin is saying, in effect, that the substance of doctrine is one thing, its expression another. When he goes on to urge theologians "to keep all the windows open through which the thought of man looks upon reality," he is anticipating words yet to be spoken.

In order for interpretive apologetics to be effective, Christians must not confine themselves to learned books few will read. To deepen and understand their own creed Catholics must worthily perform the sacred drama of the liturgy, to engage with unbelievers; they must be open to solid scientific discoveries, make use of all forms of communication, popular journalism, plays which reflect the tensions, choices and dilemmas of real life, write sacred opera, and engage in any activity to show that Christianity is far from a mere survival from a credulous age.

The book is wide ranging and full of those penetrating perceptions which were to distinguish the best of Watkin's work throughout his life. Towards the end he comes to a subject which is to him the heart of the matter. He is writing about the attraction of Pantheism. The aspect of Catholicism which corresponds to the truth in Pantheism is, he thinks, neither its most obvious aspect nor, in the contemporary Church, its most popular. It is its mystical aspect, the aspect least known and realized among Catholics themselves. Nature mystics, as he called them, have a direct apprehension of God present in nature but they may interpret their experience of the Divine immanent in material nature as the experience of the Divinity of that material nature and are so misled into Pantheism. This nature mysticism should be valued and accepted for what it is, the apprehension of the presence of God in nature, but the experience should not be misunderstood and confused with the higher value and deeper truth of supernatural mysticism. Mysticism falsely interpreted favours Pantheism; mysticism truly interpreted will be Catholicism's best and most powerful apologetic. This was to be Watkin's core message as far as his philosophical and theological work was concerned and the subject of his next book.

Throughout his literary life Watkin always scrupulously acknowledged those who had helped him either in print or in conversation, a generosity not always reciprocated. Here, in his first book, he refers among others to Christopher Dawson. In January 1914 Dawson was received into the Roman Catholic Church at St Aloysius church in Oxford with Watkin as his sponsor.[3] Dawson was to spend fourteen years on research, writing essays, and articles, pursuing what he described as his isolated studies before his first book was published. Watkin's publishers were the Manresa Press in conjunction with Herder. The date given is 1915. By then the world was a different place.

1 William Ingram and his sister Emmeline when young at their home, Mount Felix, Walton-on-Thames. This house, designed by Barry for Lord Tankerville, was where Watkin was taken as a baby to live with his grandmother.

2 Statue of E. I. Watkin's grandfather, Herbert Ingram, by the church at Boston, Lincolnshire.

3 Edgar Watkin and Emmeline Ingram before they were married, 1887.

4 Grandma with her little charge aged four months.

5 A drawing of Watkin aged three by his father, Edgar Watkin.

6 Photograph of Sir Edward Watkin.

7 Photograph of Sir William Ingram.

8 The Opening of the Watkin Path, September, 1892. *Back row standing, left to right:* Emmeline and Edgar Watkin; Herbert Gladstone, W. E. Gladstone's son, Home Secretary in 1910, First Governor General of the Union of South Africa; Alfred Watkin, Sir Edward's son; Lord Armistead, the Lord Lieutenant of Caernarvonshire; Gladstone's daughter, Mary Drew; Lloyd George, then Liberal Member for Caenarvon. *Seated in front:* W. E. Gladstone, Mrs Gladstone. Article *Gladstone, Lloyd George and the Gladstone Rock by C. J. Williams*, reprinted from the *Caernarvonshire Historical Society Transactions,* 1999.

9 Sir Edward's Chalet built at the foot on Snowdon in 1891. It was constructed of corrugated iron. The picture is reproduced in C. J. Williams's article where the author points out that at least six servants are watching the photographer at work and a dining room table can be seen behind the shuttered windows.

10 Pantafon, Llanberis, Caernarvonshire, was one of Watkin's homes as a boy. Three hundred feet up, it had fine views of the mountains on one side and the sea the other. It had twelve bedrooms, a lake and nearly sixty acres of land. It is now three separate houses.

11 Hornby captained England at the famous test match played at the Oval in 1882 when for the first time in England, Australia won by seven runs. This victory led to the jibe about the death and cremation of English cricket whose ashes would be taken back to Australia. Hornby was one of the few men who also played rugby football for England.

12 Sketch by Edgar Watkin of Lucille Duff Gordon at Pantafon as a young woman. She and her husband Sir Cosmo Duff Gordon were on the *Titanic* and came in for much opprobrium since they escaped with only ten others in a lifeboat capable of holding forty people.

13 Watkin and Dawson as boys at Bletsoe Rectory, Bedfordshire, 1905. Dawson in *front row on the ground left*; Watkin in *front row on the ground, right*.

14 New College Catholics, Oxford, 1908. *Standing, left to right*: King; Watkin. *Sitting left to right*: Philip Fowke, Cork, Eric Pontifex. King became an Anglican clergyman. He joined the army as a combatant in the First War and was killed. Philip Fowke married Watkin's first cousin, Gladys Watkin. Cork became vicar of Gladstone's Hawarden. Pontifex became a monk of Downside and took the name of Dunstan.

15 Abbots Hall, Aylsham, Norfolk. Helena Shepheard's old home.

16 Portrait of Maria Pasqua in 1863 by Henriette Browne. It is entitled *A Greek Captive*. Courtesy of the Tate Gallery it is now on loan to the National Gallery.

17 Claughton Pellew and John Nash "rushing into the sea" in Norfolk, 1912. From Ronald Bylthe's *First Friends. Paul and Bunty, John and Christine – and Carrington* (Viking, 1999)

18 Helena and Christopher, Sheringham, 1918.

19 St Mary's, Sheringham, 1928. Watkin is sitting in the garden. The house was rendered a creamy blue

CHAPTER TEN

Dulce Et Decorum Est

To believe in the love of God despite all contrary experiences is the hardest and most essential act of faith.

The slaughter on the Western Front during the 1914–1918 war has left an indelible mark on the minds of the descendants of those who took part in it. Many of them remember where their grandparents, great-uncles and their cousins fell. Names like the Somme, Arras, Paschendaele, Ypres, toll in the minds of those not born when these battles were fought. And they ask how was it that such a thing could happen and what madness drove people to accept ten or even twenty thousand casualties in a single day.

Bertrand Russell walked the streets round Trafalgar Square on the night Lord Grey committed Great Britain to fight in defence of Belgium. He observed the cheering crowds with disgust. The whole thing was utter and unspeakable folly. He never "believed anything so frightful could happen."[1] Yet he was the man who in the name of what he called civilized government had vigorously supported Britain's part in the Boer War. One forgets, perhaps, the instability of the human mind and how long it takes for the dust of the dead to settle. The majority of the upper middle class went to war as a matter of course. They had been educated as leaders, to accept personal sacrifice for the general good, and not to question the excellence of the present social structure and the part they were expected to play within it. Nor was this attitude confined to flannelled fools. It was shared, for the most part, by artists, writers, and poets.

"Thou careless awake! Thou peacemaker, fight!" the Poet Laureate, Robert Bridges, wrote for *The Times* four days after war was declared. "Stand, England, for honour and God guard the right!" In the first week of the war, thirty thousand men a day came forward to enlist. Some did so for economic reasons, most because they were obeying the herd instinct. The Empire had dominated the globe for as long as they could remember. It was outrageous of the German Kaiser to challenge our supremacy.

As soon as he heard that war had been declared, Helena's brother Samuel left the Gold Coast and set out for England. He enlisted as a doctor in the Middlesex Regiment. Helena's father, who had been a medical practitioner before he married money, immediately offered his services to the government. Phil of course, was already in the army. Philip Fowke had been appointed British Consul in Seoul, Korea; he and Gladys were told to stay at their post. Watkin's relations behaved as one would expect and some of them far better. Gladys's brother, the flirtatious Hugh, volunteered and survived the war only later to endure the loss of his son, John Watkin, MC, who was to die of wounds at Dunkirk. Hugh's elder brother, Teddy, employed in the family's cotton business in Manchester, joined the Welch Fusiliers and was so severely wounded in 1915 that he was permanently disabled.

The outbreak of war changed Emmeline's life. She ceased to be a sad widow lamenting the behaviour of an ungrateful son. It would be unfair to say that she enjoyed the conflict. Many of her own family were killed or wounded and she was the first person to feel for those who had lost their children. But she was an intensely active woman, a born organizer and the war gave her an opportunity she was quick to seize. She soon made up her quarrel with Edda and Helena, and once more the doors of Great Portland Street and Loudwater were opened to them. She would have allowed them to go to Pantafon but Helena shrank from being in charge of such a large establishment and in any case neither of them wished to live in so remote a place.

Emmeline volunteered immediately to help to prepare bandages in the surgical branch of Queen Mary's Needlework Guild in Cavendish Square and before long was the recipient of a Certificate of Merit issued from St James's Palace. She took a course in First Aid and passed the examinations, but her supreme achievement was the part she played in the success of a superior canteen in Paris called "A Corner of Blighty".[2] Its founder and manager, Miss Lily Butler, persuaded the French government to lease some palatial premises in the Place Vendôme. Here, under the patronage of the British Ambassador and Lady Bertie, Allied Forces were invited to come and enjoy, free of charge, splendid teas, writing rooms, concerts and a library. Cigarettes were provided on the house and tours of Paris and tickets to theatres arranged. The Prince of Wales visited it three times and so did the Duke of Connaught. How it was all funded is not clear. In 1917 Emmeline arrived with her maid, Lizzie Wilson, and they stayed in an hotel in the Rue de la Paix. Wearing a striped yellow and blue apron, Emmeline managed the kitchen, waited at table and did everything she could to entertain "the boys".

One of these "boys" could have been Sharp, who, like his former employer, was given a chance to come into his own. There was to be no more hanging about medieval churches in an east wind. He enlisted almost at once and according to a newspaper report, because of "his thorough knowledge of automobiles and his excellent capabilities as a driver" he had the honour of being chosen to take to the Front an ambulance presented to the Forces by the King. He ended up as a sergeant and the holder of the Military Medal for "conspicuous bravery and devotion to duty as driver of an ambulance car under heavy hostile shell fire." We never hear of him again, perhaps he retired to his native Wiltshire.

From beginning to end Emmeline had no doubts about the justice of the war. It was otherwise with Edda.

When he was a small boy he thought that human life was divided up into three phases: Bible Times, which were exciting and often frightening; History Times, which were exciting too and full of great deeds accomplished by famous people; Modern Times, which were dull because nothing ever happened. He tells us[3] that he was in Oxford on the afternoon of Sunday, August 2, 1914, and walking by the river. In the distance the spires and domes of the city stood out against the sky, the river's edge was brilliant with the gold and red of the purple loosestrife. That evening, back at home with Helena, he heard the shout of a newspaper boy. At first indistinguishable, the sound grew nearer and louder and louder. France had mobilized.

As soon as war was declared, Watkin sat down to write a book which was completed in a few weeks and published the next month by the Catholic Truth Society. It was called *A Little Book of Comfort in Time of War*. A disaster, he wrote, had come upon the human race, a disaster whose magnitude had yet to be realized. When he did realize its magnitude, his attitude was to change. In August 1914, however, he thought our cause was just and our actions courageous. It is a small book of a little over a hundred pages and it would not be of much help to counsellors today because its message is almost entirely religious. Without God there are palliatives, but no abiding consolation. Watkin was one of the early popularizers of Julian of Norwich. He recalls her words about love. Before God made us "He loved us . . . and in this Love hath done all His works and in this Love hath made all things profitable to us and in this Love our life is everlasting. In our making we had a beginning but the Love wherein He made us was in Him without beginning: in which Love we had our beginning."

These words, Watkin says, contain the quintessence of the Christian revelation of God and are the sole philosophy of the universe that can permanently satisfy the soul of humanity. To believe in the love of God despite all contrary experiences is the hardest and most essential act of faith. This is Watkin's understanding at its best, but when he comes to the particular, to war as it actually is, one feels he brings with him not only too much of his lingering Aloysian baggage, but a certain unreality, the consequence of compassion without experience.

In February 1915 Helena's brother Phil came to stay with them at Chalfont Road. This was the first, and as it turned out, the last time he was to meet Edda. They got on together very well indeed. Phil was Helena's favourite brother. Edda had found Samuel difficult to talk to. They could not discuss country sports because Watkin took part in none and he thought his brother-in-law despised him for it. The soldier was the gentler of the two. He was a good shot and he too loved country pursuits, but he was well read both in poetry and prose and he and Edda took to each other at once.

Phil was in fact on embarkation leave. After bidding goodbye to Helena and Edda he went to spend the rest of his leave at Abbots Hall. Maria Pasqua hated the war. She was not English, she was not French, she thought her native countrymen were exceedingly foolish to involve themselves in a conflict that was no business of theirs and could result only in misery, bloodshed and sons torn away from their mothers. Phil loved his old home. He was now thirty, a handsome man like his brother. He had planned to retire from the army when he reached the rank of major and come home to help his father run the estate. Now he walked round with Maria Pasqua and in his heart said farewell to the old farmhouse across the lane, to the river, the beehives, the walled garden and the flint tower of Banningham church in the far distance. He told his mother that he had had a happy life but the best of it was over. He did not tell her that for years he had loved the wife of a fellow officer stationed in India and she him, and that their parting had been grievous.[4]

He was not sent to France but to Gallipoli. He was in the First Battalion of the Essex Regiment, part of the famous 29th Division composed of regular soldiers of the imperial overseas garrison, organized by Kitchener. Some of his letters to Helena survive. The last, dated May 17, was scribbled in pencil on a scrap of squared paper. They had just come for a day's rest after seventeen days in the firing line but there were shells coming over at that very moment. He didn't know how he had escaped. He had had his rifle shot out of his hand and bullets through his clothes. The landing had been very bad. There was barbed wire in the water. He did not know how one could get through such a time and the sights he has seen. He has had to bury several RCs. German officers come into the trench at night and shout "Essex this way" or "all officers wanted on the right." They got caught once but not again. The food was good and plentiful. He is certain that it is all of their prayers that were keeping him [safe]. He was killed three weeks later.[5]

After Passchendaele in 1917, the war artist Paul Nash was to write that "evil and the incarnate fiend alone can be master of this war and no glimmer of God's hand can be seen anywhere."[6] Thousands lost their religious faith after what they had experienced at the Front. To believe in God despite evidence to the contrary, as Watkin had pointed out, is the hardest and most essential act of faith.

The blow fell at a bad time for Helena who was then in a nursing home near her mother-in-law in Great Portland Street. She had now been married for nearly two years and as yet there was no sign of a baby. She feared that she had some gynaecological trouble that might make it impossible for her to conceive. She consulted a London specialist who told her that she had an inverted womb and should have an operation to correct it.

Emmeline sprang into action, declared that she would pay for the most skilful surgeon in London and the operation should be performed in the best nursing home in the kingdom. Things had regained their rightful proportion: she was again the benefactor, her son and his wife the grateful recipients.

In January 1916, about six months after Phil's death, voluntary military recruitment was ended and unmarried men between the ages of eighteen and forty-one were compelled to serve. More were killed than came, so that in April of that year compulsion was extended to married men as well. In deference to what remained of the liberal conscience, tribunals were set up to allow objectors to military service to state their case.

With most interesting exceptions, the nation as a whole was in the grip of an illusion that it was fighting for its life, that the Germans and their allies were fiends out to destroy every decent thing that civilized people had believed in over the centuries. Kipling's wife Carrie wrote to her mother about Belgian children arriving in England with their hands cut off and a captured German soldier found to have a woman's hand in his pocket with the rings still on it. Watkin thought it was as if great crowds of people had been cast suddenly under a spell or swallowed a strange draught which obliterated good feeling and rational judgement.

"If the only way to protect adequately an English babe is to kill a German babe," the Reverend H. D. A. Major, Principal of Ripon Hall, Cuddesdon, wrote in 1917, "then it is the duty of our authorities, however repugnant, to do it. More particularly is this so when we reflect that the innocent German babe will in all probability grow up to be a killer of babies himself."[7] But not only Germans grow up to be baby killers. Before we condemn Mr Major, we should remember that as far as is known, not a single Roman Catholic bishop in Great Britain spoke out at the time against the bombing of Hamburg, Dresden, Hiroshima or Nagasaki. The plain fact is that war corrupts and coarsens morality, and for most people it was abhorrent to witness spineless intellectuals like Bertrand Russell and Lytton Strachey bleating their way out of defending their country while thousands of better men were being killed day after day. "In my opinion," an army major told a Quaker who refused to put on army uniform, "conscientious objection is just another name for arrant cowardice." Many endured brutal treatment, some spent years in solitary confinement, others were sent to labour camps.

Like many others, Watkin had begun the war thinking that we had a just cause and that the conflict would soon be resolved. As the casualties increased and he saw that people on both sides were actually accepting the daily butchery, his views changed. His attitude to the Catholic Church altered too.

Although, as von Hügel was to perceive later, Aloysius was not entirely dead, Watkin's former naïve trust in all things Catholic was shattered. He saw the majority of bishops and priests on both sides acting as recruiting sergeants not for God but for Caesar. Henceforward he looked upon the institutional church as the earthen vessel, the fallible, often foolish, and sometimes devious container of the spiritual truths by which he lived. But he did live by them. The Roman Catholic Church remained for him the most precious source of prayer and the guardian of Christian revelation. It was just because of this conviction that he struggled for so long to disentangle Catholicism not only from its structural abuses but from its fixed and inflexible manner of presenting those doctrines upon whose credibility its existence depended.

He did, however, regret not having the courage to declare himself to be a conscientious objector. Helena was against it. She was far less in favour of the war than most people but she felt it was better to leave things alone. Edda's disabilities were obvious, no one in his senses would let him anywhere near a rifle. If he announced himself to be a 'conchie', as they were then called, the stress and strain of the proceedings against him and their consequences might cause a mental breakdown. She was certainly right, but Edda felt that his decision was streaked with dishonour. And he felt this more acutely because his friend the artist Claughton Pellew had come out as a conscientious objector, been before a tribunal and suffered accordingly.

Pellew had been at the Slade together with Carrington and Paul Nash. Pellew, Paul wrote later in his autobiography, *Outline*, was the "first creature of a truly poetic mind" he had ever met. They spent a holiday in Norfolk together and Pellew fired his feelings for nature, taught him to look at the individual beauty of trees, hayricks and stooks of corn. Moreover, it was Pellew who on another holiday in Norfolk, transformed the life of Paul's brother John by convincing him that he too was an artist.

Edda admired both Claughton and his work and foretold a splendid future for him. In 1913 Pellew became a Catholic. This separated him from his former friends at the Slade most of whom looked upon his action with utter incredulity and bewilderment. The chasm between the gifted shallowness of many of his contemporaries and those who insisted upon the reality of a metaphysic, was too great to bridge. Bertrand Russell, still searching for a God he knew did not exist, was painfully aware of it. He hated "the Bloomsbury crew with all their sneers at anything that has live feeling in it." The centre of him, he wrote to Constance Malleson, was always and eternally a terrible pain, "a searching for something beyond what the world contains, something transfigured and infinite – the beatific vision – God." He was haunted, he told Lady Ottoline Morell: "some ghost from some extra-mundane region seems always trying to tell me something that I am to report to the world, but I cannot understand the message . . . I feel I shall find the truth on my deathbed and be surrounded by people too stupid to understand . . . "[8]

He was never to understand the message. Nor, in his lifetime, did Pellew achieve the success that Watkin had predicted. Soon after his conversion the war came and with it ill-treatment and solitary confinement, his subsqent withdrawal to live an isolated life in Norfolk with his wife, Carrington's friend the artist, Kechie Tennent. His output was small. The beauty of his engravings and etchings have only recently been recognized and exhibitions of his work mounted.

Many of his letters to Edda and Helena from prison have survived as a terrible witness to what can happen to human beings even in a country with such a long tradition of freedom as Britain when church and state combine to crush dissent.

The Military Service Act of 1916 had allowed exemption from military service for three reasons: absolute exemption on medical grounds; qualified exemption which meant forcible service in what was called the Non-Combatant Corps which was sent to France to serve behind the lines; exemption on condition of taking up work of national importance like factory work or farming. Claughton Pellew was what was called an "absolutist". That is, he refused on principle to accept any form of war service whatsoever.

He was now twenty-six. Edda and Helena were among his strongest supporters and in the early summer of 1916 he came to stay with them for a month in Chalfont Road before he was arrested and held at the detention centre at Cowley Barracks, Oxford.

Not all objectors were treated in the same way. In 1916 Bertrand Russell was forty-one and therefore not yet liable for military service. As a consequence, however, of his passionate anti-conscription activities, he was summoned for "impeding recruiting and discipline." The case was heard before the Lord Mayor at the Mansion House and Russell declared in his defence that " the noblest thing in man is the spiritual force which enables him to stand firm against the whole world in obedience to his own sense of right." To its shame Trinity College, Cambridge, deprived him of his lectureship. Russell did eventually go to Brixton prison where he paid extra for a large cell furnished by his sister-in-law and decorated with flowers from Garsington. He was supplied with *The Times* daily, allowed books for the continuance of his work and had his bed made and his cell cleaned out by a fellow prisoner for sixpence a day.[9]

What Claughton Pellew went through was very different. Under the Act all those who were called up were regarded as soldiers and under military discipline. After arrest at Oxford he was taken before "a pompous and [self]important magistrate" then spent three days alone in a police cell sleeping on boards under a blanket alive with bugs. It was his first experience of what he later told Helena was the slow death of solitary confinement. On the third day he was escorted through the streets of Oxford between a sergeant and a private who informed him that the army intended to break the hearts of people like him. Later he was taken to the barracks of the Dorset Regiment at Weymouth where he refused to put on khaki uniform or to march. He was therefore court-martialled and sent to Dorchester prison. He was then imprisoned at Winchester from where he was taken in handcuffs to Wormwood Scrubs in order to appear before a tribunal. He was sent to to Wakefield prison, to Scotland and finally to a penal settlement on Dartmoor. At times he was subjected to brutality. Khaki uniform was put on him by force, at Weymouth barracks the soldiers stripped him naked and ran him up and down the room beating his body with knotted wet towels. He realized that people in the mass behave so very much worse than individuals and told Edda that he both saw and experienced many acts of goodness. Of all his sufferings, he said that solitary confinement was the worst, while he was at Wakefield prison four men went mad. He was sustained by his faith and never lost hope. He told Helena that at night he escaped and in his dreams returned to them both in their garden at Oxford. He was allowed to keep the Keats she had given him and the prayer book Edda had sent.[10]

Surprisingly, considering the mounting casualties and the continuence of war fever, as time went on conditions improved. Perhaps, as Pellew remarked at the beginning, the government really did not know what to do with them. In Scotland he was employed as a hospital cook and it seems, even granted leave to see his mother. When in prison he met the typographer, Stanley Morison, also a conscientious objector, who told him he was in correspondence with Watkin. Morison was not an absolutist; he was given early release because he agreed to work on a farm. Watkin was also in touch with the typographer and founder of the Pelican Press, Francis Meynell, later Sir Francis, the youngest son of Wilfred Meynell, Manager of the Catholic publishers, Burns and Oates, and his wife the poet Alice Meynell. Francis too was a consciencious objector. He was arrested in 1916 and went on a hunger and thirst strike before being released "as unlikely to become an efficient soldier."

Both Francis's parents supported the war and made haste to disassociate themselves publicly from the stand taken by their son.[11] On the whole, Watkin was isolated. The majority of writers and artists were not with him. It was *trahison de clercs* on an extended scale, comparable only to the widespread political correctness of our own times which insidiously, in the name of social equality and compassion, undermines an order of values and denies the known truth.

"I feel as strongly as ever about the madness of war," Siegfried Sassoon wrote not long before his death. "And the 1914 war seems to be more insane the further it recedes into history." Such a view then was generally considered outrageous and it took courage openly to support it.

Baron von Hügel became a naturalized British citizen on the outbreak of war. He believed whole-heartedly in the conflict, invested in War Loans, criticized the Pope's neutrality and maintained that the nation should hold out "till victory is ours." He expressed some of his views in a short collection of his periodic pieces published in 1916 as *The German Soul,* of which indeed he had a good share. He detaches himself from judging the morality of the present conflict by pointing to the Gospel Christ as one who, first and foremost, concentrated on the profound reality of God and the proximity of the arrival of His Kingdom in the light of which our earthly conduct must gradually be conformed. Opposite his title page the Baron quotes an instruction to his novices from a medieval German Franciscan friar: "Let a man continually paint in his heart Thine image, O Lord Jesus, of Thee, eternal sunshine, how Thou didst always bear Thyself with a gentle, genial and benign earnestness." In the year the book came out, over one million three hundred thousand were slaughtered on the Somme.

To G. K. Chesterton, the war was a crusade, the most genuine and popular movement since the Chartist rising. He relished the ironical humour of those about to die in the trenches and rejected out of hand any suggestions for a compromise peace. Gilbert Murray, a pacifist who in the early days of August had signed a petition for British neutrality, was soon referring to "the strange, deep gladness of war" and adding his voice to those who so successfully made out that a serving soldier's life was one of open air, good food and cameraderie. As time went on, this kind of trash appealed less and less to the men who were actually doing the fighting. "A blind God," Raymond Asquith wrote to his wife, "butts about the world with a pair of delicately malignant antennae to detect whatever is fit to live and with an iron hoof to stamp it into the dust . . . " The war, he agreed with his wife, was utterly senseless, yet with what courage and *sang froid* he gave his life away.

In 1916, the year Asquith was killed, Meynell and Morison founded "The Guild of the Pope's Peace". Pius X had died in 1914 to be succeeded by a Genoese papal diplomat who took the name of Benedict XV. The war ruined his pontificate. He was appalled by the conflict, convinced that it could be resolved by diplomatic means and used most solemn words to condemn the continuation of the slaughter. "In the Holy Name of God," he announced in 1915, "in the Name of Our Heavenly Father and Lord, by the blessed Blood of Jesus, we conjure you to put an end, once and for all to this awful carnage which has already been dishonouring Europe for a year." In words addressed to the entire Catholic world he implored the heads of government to hold a conference to achieve a just and lasting settlement and meantime to declare a truce.

The Guild of the Pope's Peace was formed to print and distribute Benedict's appeals to both sides to stop the fighting. But the Catholic world preferred to listen to Lloyd George, Kitchener and the Kaiser rather than the man they claimed to be the Vicar of Christ on earth. Where now was the respect for every utterance from the Holy Father that Watkin had heard so much about from his zealous Oxford friends? Thou Art Peter and Upon this Rock and the pity they felt for those poor Protestants who had no living authority but the so- called Archbishop of Canterbury who deluded himself into believing he was the successor of St Augustine. When it came to the point, the majority of Roman Catholics would obey the state, not the church. One day Pope Pius X11 would know this and in despair keep quiet. As Meynell remarked wryly in his autobiography, he doubted whether propaganda ever had such fine printing to so little effect.

The Guild had a committee of seven which included Morison, Watkin and two priests, Father Squirrel and Father Kent, OHC. Meynell was honorary secretary and designed its publications two of which, through a Swiss priest, Watkin managed to get into the hands of Cardinal Gasparri, Benedict's Secretary of State. He also compiled a book of prayer taken from liturgical sources. This, entitled *A Little Book of Prayers for Peace,* was printed by the Oxford University Press in seventeenth century Fell type. A few were printed on linen-rag paper and bound in vellum. These are now rare. The Catholic Repository at Oxford refused to stock copies although the book bore the *Imprimatur.* Praying for peace was unpatriotic, almost treasonable, and might somehow be connected with the Gunpowder Plot.

In 1917 Benedict XV suggested terms towards a negotiated peace, these included an agreement to waive compensation for war damage and were not therefore popular with the British and French. A commentator has since described the Pope's plan as "the loftiest and most far-sighted peace document which has been written and one which corresponded to the common feeling of the people."[12] Meynell printed the proposals as a pamphlet. Watkin spent hours outside Westminster Cathedral after Mass thrusting them into unwilling hands. The proposals were ignored by the Catholic hierarchy and in this country the Bishop of Clifton went so far as to publicly denounce the members of the Guild. Kipling agreed with him. From early life trained and shaped for sacrifice, in 1915 his only son had been killed at the Battle of Loos aged eighteen. All compromise was betrayal. His genius fled, Kipling wrote a poor poem entitled *Cockcrow*.

But how was Watkin to escape Pellew's fate? He was now twenty-eight and living at Oxford awaiting the summons in a most dreadful state of agitation which Helena's calmness was quite unable to soothe. It was to be like that always. In a strange way her very steadiness acted as a stimulant to increase his agitation. The less she spoke, the more excited he became. Helena very rarely interfered in other people's lives even when perhaps she should have done. However, Edda was so distraught that for once she acted. Both of them knew the Colonel in command at Cowley so she made an appointment to see him. He remembered Watkin and assured her that although it was nothing to do with him, her husband would not be conscripted if he were the last man in England.

On June 22, 1916, Watkin went to Mass at the Franciscan Friary at Cowley before going on to the barracks. At that time he was keeping a short diary he called *Impressions*. He describes how the friars gave him breakfast after Mass and the whole atmosphere was one of goodness and tranquility which sustained him for his coming ordeal. He spent a long morning waiting in the barracks feeling he was caught in an iron system of servitude which snatched people out of this life and buried them. No one seemed human, they were slaves of a huge machine, the very trees in the barracks grew in a confined and formal fashion like the trees of a toy Noah's Ark.

At last the moment arrived and he was examined. The doctors, he wrote, seemed angry that he had so poor a physique without any serious illness or defect. More likely they were exceedingly puzzled. Watkin always had excellent physical health. The first time he went into hospital was his last, when he was aged ninety-two. His hearing and eyesight were unusually good. Yet his hands were unsteady, his grasp was weak, his limbs unco-ordinated, his whole body and spirit filled with a kind of uncontrolled energy it is difficult to describe. The doctors retired behind a curtain and consulted together for ten minutes. The fellow literally didn't know his right hand from his left. Whatever was wrong it was obvious that he could never be taught to hold a rifle or march in step. Watkin was put in the category for sedentary work at home. "Oh the joy of walking out of the barrack gates," he wrote, "free once more of the earth and sky – free to live, to be a human being. But poor Pellew is still suffering, still fighting alone in his glorious warfare against military tyranny."

Christopher Dawson did not share Watkin's views about the war. His temperament was more cautious and his outlook in some ways more conventional. His father was a professional soldier. Not for nothing did he describe himself as a Roman and Watkin a Greek. From boyhood he had suffered ill-health which was why he had left school at Winchester after little more than a year. He was physically weak, short-sighted and had a delicate chest and very soon was classed as grade III. He was relieved. His wife was later to say that what he dreaded most was not being sent to the trenches but being allocated administrative office work in the army and so be unable to continue his studies.

This shows how remote the real war, the one actually being fought, was to the consciousness of the majority of people at home. "Come and die," Rupert Brooke wrote to John Drinkwater in 1914. "It'll be great fun." As we now know, and few in England did, the actual experience was very different. It is not likely that Dawson could have endured the mud, blood, filth and animal slaughter of the trenches for a single day. In our own times, with obstinately intrusive media, trench warfare of that kind could not have continued for so long.

Towards the end of July, Watkin and Helena spent ten days at Hartlington. The battle of the Somme had begun on July 1. The soldiers who were sent there formed part of the biggest volunteer army in our history. Many, however, were poorly trained and the majority not even twenty-one. It has been estimated that nearly twenty thousand were lost on the first day. The furthest British advance was twelve kilometres.

Hartlington was at its loveliest. Christopher's sister Gwendoline was there and on the feast of St Mary Magdalen played and sang Edda's favourite hymn from the Office "Mary Weep Not" to its medieval plain-chant melody. Throughout her life she remained faithful to her parent's interpretation of Anglicanism and was to become a most affectionate friend of Helena. Christopher and Edda bathed in the beck, climbed the hills and lay on the grass in the sunshine. Yet all the time Watkin was oppressed by the slaughter in France and haunted by Pellew. There was no earth and sky for him alone in his cell, peered at every quarter of an hour through a hole in the steel door.

Dawson was preparing to get married. One evening years ago at Oxford when they were dining together, Christopher showed Edda a photograph of a beautiful girl dressed as Joan of Arc for a pageant. Her name was Valery Mills. Dawson fell in love with the photograph and then with the possessor of the beautiful face. Valery was one of the three daughters of an architect. Her mother had been recently widowed and was struggling to support her family on a small income. Valery had no money to speak of, Christopher was dependent upon a not over-generous allowance from his father and had as yet adopted no profession. Moreover, neither of Christopher's parents wished their son to marry a Roman Catholic and Valery's mother feared that Christopher's health was too delicate for him to undertake such a commitment. The pair got engaged despite these objections although they were not able to marry until three years later by which time Dawson himself had become a Catholic.

A week after Edda and Helena left Hartlington Christopher came to

Chalfont Road, as Watkin put it "to spend his last bachelor days with us." He was run down, Watkin noticed, and in consequence depressed. In other words, like many a bridegroom, let alone someone as shy as Dawson, he looked upon the actual wedding as something of an ordeal. It was celebrated quietly at Chipping Campden in Gloucestershire on August 9. Mrs Mills was renting the Woolstapler's Hall, where the reception was held. It was "a lovely medieval house," Watkin wrote, "rambling, ill-arranged and full of the dear past – my golden age. The bride was lovely. She was dressed in grey with a necklace of green stones. Happiness made beautiful eyes doubly beautiful." He acted as what he amusingly calls "pro-best man" and for some reason the registrar would keep on mistaking him for the groom. There was a sung nuptial mass and he and Helena were the only guests not members of both families.

If the war had hastened Christopher and Valery's marriage it was the cause and occasion for one which, in some quarters, was far less welcome.

CHAPTER ELEVEN

A Season of Good Will

"The mystics," Watkin tells us, "are but the advance guard of the army of the elect. They are the spies who have gone on ahead and entered before death the promised land, to report somewhat of its bliss to their fellow travellers in the desert. For proof of their journey and vision they bring back a cluster of grapes such as never grew in the vineyards of Egypt."

A week after Dawson's wedding Edda and Helena went up to London to see Emmeline. They found her "radiantly happy with news long suspected. I am very glad for her sake," Edda wrote in his *Impressions*. She was engaged to be married to Major, later Lieutenant-Colonel, Sam Heakes, OBE. Heakes was a mining engineer from Toronto, now serving as an officer in the Canadian contingent of the Seaforth Highlanders, of which he was chief field cashier. The significance of his civilian profession together with his wartime duties was not lost on the Ingram family and the jokes made at his expense were no less amusing because they were true.

Emmeline was sixty-six, Heakes in his forties. Where they first met is unknown. "A Corner of Blighty" was much patronized by Canadian officers on leave in Paris but the friendship must have started before Lily Butler founded her famous establishment. The engagement indeed was no surprise. That June both Emmeline and Sam had stayed at Chalfont Road. Edda records the fact briefly in *Impressions* before going on to discuss electricity as a possible illustration of the mystery of the Blessed Trinity. He had nothing whatsoever in common with Sam Heakes but always maintained that he was a good natured if not a clever man.

He was clever enough, however, to catch Emmeline and they were married at Holy Trinity, Marylebone, on March 16 of the following year. Sam, who was quite good looking, wore the Seaforth kilt and the *Daily Mirror* published a photograph of them walking arm in arm under the swords of the guard of honour after the ceremony. Emmeline's sisters rallied to her side. Annie was there together with Sissie, and of course, the redoubtable Ada. Emmeline gave Pantafon as her address. Why Edda and Helena were not present is uncertain because Watkin's good wishes were entirely sincere. Indeed, had they played their cards wisely the marriage might not have been altogether a bad thing. But they did not grasp the elementary rules of the game.

Edda and Helena were happy in their Oxford house although, until old age, there was no such thing as a tranquil Edda. Safe from the call-up, he was now agitating about his investments. He refused to put money into any business connected with the war effort. He was constantly writing to his stockbroker instructing him to move this, that or the other shares, but to his increased distress and Helena's relief, he found it impossible. Everything, either directly or remotely, was connected with the continuation of the war.

Looking back now when all is over and cannot be undone, one can see that probably those years at Oxford were the happiest of their marriage. There were as yet no children to destroy Edda's peace and drain his bank account. The material, educational and psychological distance between the rich and the poor remained huge. Wages were low, so servants were cheap. Even the lower middle class employed servants and the rest of society in ascending order would simply never have dreamed of doing without them. The widespread demise of the servant society was not foreseen by educated middle class women whose reforming activities in fact depended upon its continuance.

Helena never cooked nor did she clean the house or take sole charge of her own children. She employed people in order to be released from those tasks which would have prevented her from living the life she had been educated and trained to perform. She kept Edda as quiet as she was able, she ordered the meals, entertained, painted, gardened, corrected her husband's typescript where she could, and after the children came, was always there to help and encourage them. Such was the custom for people of her background and it was a way of life not to be despised.

Watkin had a wide circle of friends both within and without the university. Both his former tutors Heath and Alfred Zimmern, who was now working for the government, urged him to try either for a tutorship or a Fellowship at All Souls. Francis de Zulueta, however, told Helena that in his opinion, her husband was too eccentric to be accepted even at Oxford. Watkin does not seem to have worried very much. He was happy as things were. They enjoyed the company of Father Maturin, the Catholic University Chaplain, who was later to go down in the *Lusitania*. Maturin was suceeded as Chaplain by the Mugger, who, Ronald Knox said, had brought with him to Oxford the sofa on which his father had proposed marriage to his mother. Percy Brooks, Helena's old flame from Norfolk days, came to stay with them and as they had done in the May before Pellew's arrest, they enjoyed dinner in the garden, read poetry together by candlelight and listened to the wind in the poplars.

They were not to spend much longer in Chalfont Road. Towards the end of 1917 Watkin was directed to war work and he accepted a post teaching philosophy at the Oratory School, Hagley Road, Birmingham. He was releasing someone to fight or otherwise directly to assist the war effort; Pellew would not have approved. Helena, however, persuaded him to go quietly and they left Oxford for Birmingham in late December taking with them all the furniture from Emmeline's house in Bexhill. In a burst of generosity just before her second marriage, Emmeline had told Helena that if she hired a removal van she could take away all the contents she wanted from the Bexhill house. Helena had the sense to act quickly.

Both Edda and Helena loved their Oxford garden with its lilies and its lilac, the cherry blossom and the pear trees. On the morning of their departure for Birmingham grief overcame Edda. To Helena's dismay and the irritation of the removal men, he sat down on a packing case, started to write a poem, and refused to stir until it was completed. He called it "A Farewell to my Garden" and it was later included in his book of verse called *Poplar Leaves*. It is a charming, sad little poem, telling us that he was glad it was winter, for had it been spring or summertime, he could not have left without tears.

The Oratory School at Birmingham had been fashioned out of a row of private houses and looked like Kipling's Imperial Services College at Westward Ho!, only without the sea. One cannot imagine that Watkin was a very successful teacher: he spoke too fast and tended to think people more intelligent than they actually were. The best surgeon in England had operated to some purpose because that winter Helena conceived. Unfortunately, she miscarried and this may have been the reason why neither of them had been present at Emmeline's wedding. "You have," Edda would tell his children very much later, "a little brother or sister in limbo." This puzzled them very much and when inquiries were made about the biological and theological aspects of this event, Watkin just raised his eyebrows, waved his arms and shook his head. Helena conceived again and towards the end of February 1918, she gave birth to a son, Christopher Paul. He was one of the very few people who claim to be able to remember the sensation of life in the womb and the shock of being born. Perhaps it was more of a shock for Helena. The birth was prolonged and the baby was eventually delivered with forceps while Edda, in a dreadful state of agitation, was serving Mass in the Oratory church for the safety of mother and child. Maria Pasqua came to stay with Helena and acted as proxy for the absent godparents, Samuel Shepheard, Helena's surviving brother, and Valery Dawson.

Emmeline was delighted that the child was a boy although she did not like the name Christopher and always referred to him as Paul. So pleased was she to have a grandson that she told them that as soon as they could get away from Edgbaston they could all come and live rent free at Loudwater. Furthermore, she would pay for *Poplar Leaves* to be published. This, a small volume of some eighty pages, was dedicated to Edda's old friend, Mrs Tatham. To gratify his mother he printed her name above a poem she particularly liked.

Helena missed her own mother greatly and the return to Norfolk seemed under the circumstances a sensible thing to do. When they left they brought another person with them besides Christopher. Her name was Harriet Latimer, "Hetty" to the children's parents, " Nanny" to them. The daughter of a farmer, she had wished to train as a teacher but her family could not afford the money. She went instead into domestic service and was house parlourmaid to the Mayor of Birmingham before she came to Helena in the same capacity. Before long it became clear that her real vocation lay in looking after Christopher and she became the family nanny for many years, caring for them in good times and bad until in the end she was called back to nurse her sick father.

Sheringham was the same and yet not the same. The days of the lamp lighters and the muffin men were over, the old flint cottages stood incongruously side by side with modern villas, cafés and boarding houses. Public lavatories had been built on the promenade. Loudwater too was different. Edda was no longer a boy but a married man with a child and about to become a father for the second time. The Ben Davis family had left, Hugh Watkin was married, Philip and Gladys still abroad, Alfred had gone and so had Sharp; only the now widowed Augustine Birrell remained at The Pightle and the Pegg family with their fishing boats and profitable lodgings. The world itself had changed.

The years between had not been kind to Augustine Birrell, whose political career had ended in catastrophe. In many ways he was far too civilized to go into politics, even in those days, when the government was run by cultivated men. His gifts were literary, his temperament what now would be termed laid back. As Chief Secretary for Ireland he depended upon the advice of the Irish leader in the House of Commons, John Redmond, who in 1914 had pledged the support of the people of Ireland for the war with Germany. The situation had been misjudged. At Easter 1916, Sinn Fein, in collusion with Germany, rose up in armed rebellion and this at the very height of the war. Birrell visited Ireland at once and on his return accepted responsibility in an eloquent and moving resignation speech in the House. "I say sorrowfully that I made an untrue estimate of this Sinn Fein movement." He went on to describe his feelings as he "stood amid the smoking ruins of Dublin, surrounded with my own ruins in mind and thought."[1] He did not seek re-election in 1918 but shared his time between his house in Chelsea and the Pightle where he and Edda enjoyed each other's company. It was here that Watkin came round in 1920 and lamented the slow sale of his book, *The Philosophy of Mysticism*. Did he think, Birrell wrote later from Chelsea, that it would have a Pickwickian sale? The subject was caviar to the general. Time would give it the success it deserved.[2]

The Philosophy of Mysticism was Watkin's first important book and although in later life he lamented its shortcomings, it expressed themes which were fundamental to his entire work. It is original, vigorous, crammed with ideas, insights and learning, full of references to music, poetry, literature and art. But like his speech, the writing was ill-disciplined and the book would have been greatly improved by severe cutting and an index. Copies are now scarce. It included two most interesting appendixes on the nature mysticism of Richard Jefferies and the mystical interpretation of Scripture, together with an Epilogue in praise of God composed by himself which many later readers and one contemporary reviewer suggested was so fine that it should be printed and distributed separately.

His purpose, Watkin tells us, is not to teach people to be mystics. As an outsider, a non-mystic, his concern is the theoretical aspect of the matter, with mysticism as a theory or science. The mystic claims that he has found a reality of infinite value. It is therefore important to find out if there is any justification for this claim and if this should prove to be the case, to learn something of the nature of that reality. The evidence must be considered, the witnesses examined, the truth about God given in these experiences studied, for they are the underpinning of all dogmatic theology.

"The mystics," Watkin tells us, "are but the advance guard of the army of the elect. They are the spies who have gone on ahead and entered before death the promised land, to report somewhat of its bliss to their fellow travellers in the desert. For proof of their journey and vision they bring back a cluster of grapes such as never grew in the vineyards of Egypt." We notice that he refers to the mystics as being "but the advance guard." One of the reasons for the originality of his book was pointed out by the well-known writer on prayer, Dom John Chapman, later Abbot of Downside. "As for Watkin," he wrote to a correspondent in 1920, "I think he . . . has made a very good attempt at uniting the mystical way with ordinary Christian life. But it is a first attempt, he has no precursors really and hence not always quite convincing."[3]

Watkin is arguing that despite superficial differences in the religious experience of different people, the path to God is one of underlying unity. All who are saved tread the mystic way to union with God, the few here, in this world, the many hereafter. The ordinary soul in a state of grace does not go through those stages of union described by the mystics, but the general principles remain the same for both. In the next world, purgatory, that is the purification of the will from adherence to finite things, takes the place of that purgation and union with God that the mystics tell us they experience in this. Watkin bases his analysis and his conclusions primarily on the evidence of two Spanish mystics, St John of the Cross and the Carmelite nun, Mother Cecilia of the Nativity.

The book is dedicated to his mother. Although she probably could not understand much of it, Emmeline was so proud of her son's achievement that she paid for a number of press-cutting agencies to send Watkin reviews. This is why many have survived. As Birrell had pointed out, the book was not on a popular subject and it was hard to read. One is astonished by the number, seriousness and length of the reviews both here and in the United States and the amount of notice it attracted in the secular papers. The *New Statesman* gave it a long and appreciative review. The reading public may have been considerably smaller than it is today but it was very much better informed and intelligent, as were the literary editors.

The Catholic press fell into two camps. One camp were alarmed by Watkin's originality, suspicious because there was no *Imprimatur* and rendered uneasy by the author's whole approach. The Jesuit periodical *The Month* complained of excessive boldness, the popular Catholic paper *The Universe* dismissed the book as merely a running commentary on St John of the Cross with some non-Catholic writers thrown in. An American reviewer was shocked that Watkin could link the mystic raptures of St John of the Cross with a passage from Wagner's *Tristan*. Another complained at length because the author had the temerity to state openly that he did not believe in the physical fires of hell, even though we had the strong words of Our Lord in the Gospels. The doctrine that the wicked burn for ever in material fire prepared for the devil and his angels was a doctrine no Catholic could deny.

All this was nothing, however, compared with the most wounding review of all, that of Dean Inge, written for the *Times Literary Supplement*.[4] Inge was, of course, a notorious anti-Catholic but he was deservedly a much respected writer and to make matters worse, some of his criticism was just. Watkin claimed to be a student of mystical philosophy Inge pointed out, yet he attributed to Plotinus a letter which in fact was composed not by Plotinus at all but was a mere compilation of his views put together by a popular writer named R. A. Vaughan. Inge then went on to pick out some of the remaining Aloysian elements in Watkin's thought in reference to the visions of St Vincent Ferrer, apparitions at Lourdes, and the restoration of Malchus's ear. " Mr Watkin's work," he ended, "is written exclusively for his co-religionists, others will not find it worth while to study it." This was perverse and unworthy of Inge as anyone reading the book must agree. What the Dean was really objecting to was Watkin's identification of Christianity with Roman Catholicism.

By no means all reviewers agreed with Inge. *The Irish Independent* thought Watkin had written a highly original, delightful and wonderful book. *The Manchester Guardian* gave it a long review both in its daily and weekly number. The writer was sharp enough to pick up Watkin's warning not to make "a false identification of the Catholic faith with a superficial, often childish understanding of it." This was a lesson Inge could have learnt with profit. *The Tablet* confidently recommended it as that rare achievement, an interesting book on a profound subject, while the Provincial of the Dominicans thought the first part was "magnificent", the "most original contribution to the restatement of the Faith in terms of modern English since the days of Newman."

Watkin had come among them but he had not come among them unmuzzled. He had started this book as long ago as 1916 but after it was finished months and months were taken up with an acrimonious dispute with the Catholic censor. It would be a mistake to think of the censors merely as ignorant bigots. They were not ignorant but very well versed in a certain kind of theology which was later to be called by its opponents "seminary theology" or "Denzinger theology" after the reference book of that name. It was an approach which equated revelation with what was said about it in Conciliar decrees, encyclicals and so on, in effect an ecclesiastical fundamentalism as unenlightened as the scriptural fundamentalism still maintained by some Protestants and unfortunately largely subscribed to by Catholics themselves. Newman rightly described this attitude "as narrowing the terms of Catholicity" and notoriously suffered from it. "I know, anyhow," he wrote in a famous letter to Henry Wilberforce in 1868, "however honest are my thoughts, and earnest my endeavours to keep rigidly within the lines of Catholic doctrine . . . I shall be fighting *under the lash* which does not tend to produce vigorous efforts in the battle, or to inspire either courage or presence of mind."

The censors would not have thought of themselves as bigots. As clerics most of them lived in an enclosed world with playgrounds of their own making. They could not go to the theatre nor read books on the Index except as part of their job, and feared both liberal Protestantism and secular society in general. They were like Communist officials, only probably more sincere. Under the direction of the Papal Curia they acted to prevent the spread of Modernism whose infiltration they believed would bring the whole edifice tumbling down and to an extent they were right. Their interpretation of Christianity could not without conflict exist side by side with those who thought that like Jesus, they had come not to destroy the law but to fulfill it.

As Newman pointed out, it was not easy to break "that formidable conspiracy which is in action against the theological liberty of Catholics." The censor's report on *The Philosophy of Mysticism* still exists, crumpled, dog-eared and covered with Watkin's sometimes angry marginal comments.[5] It is an authentic and telling illustration of an attitude of mind which dominated the Catholic Church for so many years and was in the end to prove so deeply damaging. The *Imprimatur* could not be granted. Watkin's criticism of the Church is a sign of heresy. Catholics are expected to deny the evolution of the human body, to believe in the physical fires of hell, and that baptized babies and young children have to endure purgatory. The report demonstrates what an enormous gulf existed between the censor's interpretation of Christianity and that of the world of educated, informed secularists who would have found his remarks ludicrous. Nor would his attitude have been in the least helpful to numbers of people who were by no means without a religious sense but could find no credible faith to attach it to.

Watkin offered to omit some of his statements and to modify others but it was all to no purpose. From now on he was under suspicion as an untamed spirit. Nor did his annotated file gather dust. Seven years later, when Sheed and Ward were interested in reprinting his book, a discourteous letter addressed to Watkin arrived from the Westminster Diocesan Council of Censorship. It could have come from Moscow, East Berlin or Beijing. No, the book ought not to have the *Imprimatur*. Nor could any remaindered copies be sold in a Catholic bookshop. "The question simply is this:" the letter said. "Is a Catholic publisher allowed *to sell* in a Catholic bookshop a book which he is not allowed by the Catholic Authorities to publish? I think you had better drop the matter. It is not likely that any sort of permission would be given by the Authorities to sell the book as it stands."[6]

Dawson thought that the censors deserved a good dose of castor oil. Indeed, one wonders how educated, liberal minded English Catholics ever allowed themselves to be bullied in that way. The frequent Protestant gibe that they were priest-ridden had a good deal of truth in it. For his part, Watkin was thankful that he did not live in a theocracy and found secular publishers, Grant Richards in England and Harcourt, Brace in America.

Helena had not long settled in Loudwater before she became pregnant again. For a short time before the birth Edda moved into the nursery. Christopher remembered that his father would get up very early in the morning to go to Mass and always obsessively modest, would glance anxiously in his direction before dressing himself slowly all the while chanting to himself lines from Coleridge's *Kubla Khan*. In January 1920, Helena gave birth to a daughter in the same room overlooking the sea where Edgar had died and where during the war, she had watched a burning Zeppelin plunge into the water. The baby was brought into the world by Dr Sumpter who had seen Edgar out of it and must have been one of the few people who knew the real cause of his death.

The child was named Perpetua after a saint whose name in those days was recalled every time Mass was celebrated. Emmeline was disappointed that Helena had had a girl. She came down from London to see what was going on, gave one look inside the pram and turned away. All her attention was fixed on the boy she called Paul. The arrangements at Loudwater were not altogether satisfactory. Emmeline and Sam stayed there whenever they felt inclined and with the exception of Nanny, the servants did not know who exactly was mistress of the house. The situation was soon to be resolved.

The year wore on, Christopher was nearly nearly three and Perpetua eleven months when Christmas approached. Emmeline and Sam spent it with the family at Loudwater and on Christmas Day itself Edda, perhaps emboldened by a glass or two of champagne, brought up the subject of money. He did not ask for any, that would have been straightforward. After all, his household had increased, and any request would have been quite natural. Instead some deep-seated resentment, some almost uncontrollable urge to get the better of his mother, made him refer to one of the trusts Grandma had made in his favour.

Many years later Christopher maintained that with the best of intentions Emmeline had got her solicitor to put the reversion of one of Edda's trusts on by a further generation. Moreover, in order to increase the income of the trust, between them they had taken money out and put it into equities instead of gilt-edged securities, which was then illegal.[7] Whether Christopher was right or not, we shall never know. Presumably he got information along these lines from Helena, at that age even he could hardly recall conversations of that nature.

Emmeline was furious. There was a great deal of stamping, shouting and throwing things about on both sides, after which she and Sam left for London. Angry letters were exchanged but neither party would give in. In January, Helena conceived her third child and when spring came Emmeline wrote from Great Portland Street and ordered them out of her house.

Edda and Helena, Nanny and the two children left Loudwater forever in March 1921 and rented a house not far away in Cliff Road. Here Helena's third child, Teresa, was to be born. She was so small that her head fitted into the palm of her mother's hand and so delicate that Sumpter decreed that she should be given only goat's milk. Edda went every day to fetch it from two women who tethered their goats on Beeston Hill.

Before Teresa's birth there had been one final attempt at a reconciliation with Emmeline which Christopher later recalled in vivid detail.[8] It was probably Helena, at her wit's end, who persuaded a reluctant and obstinate Edda to meet his mother when she returned to Sheringham and at least try to put matters right. It may have been Hetty who suggested that he should take Emmeline's beloved grandson along as well.

They walked up to Loudwater together, Christopher clutching his father's hand. When they got there they were shown upstairs and the door of Emmeline's bedroom opened. She bent down and said to him in a sad voice, "Paul, this is your wicked grandmother." She and Edda then went down into the drawing room leaving Christopher alone with the maid. He got restive and asked to go down to see his father. As they went down the stairs they heard an almighty row going on, shouting and yelling, and the word "trust" which Christopher understood as "crust". It was once more Ingram against Ingram, not in the law courts but in an ordinary house within the sound of the sea. In distress, Christopher ran towards the door but the maid drew him back telling him that they were "just talking." Eventually the door opened and Edda rushed out. He seized Christopher's hand and dragged him off in the direction of Cliff Road.

Mother and son were not to meet again for ten years and by then Edda's hair was white.

CHAPTER TWELVE

Thirteen Vicarage Gate

Von Hügel was now seventy-one, in poor health and with little over a year to live. He had a great deal of work of his own on hand and although he had a secretary, his personal and professional correspondence was a heavy burden. If anything could have demonstrated his largeness of heart, it was his treatment of Watkin.

Watkin was able to detach himself from his surroundings to an unusual degree. The most fruitful period of his life was when his domestic affairs were at their most turbulent. In his last fretful years at Loudwater he was wrestling with the censor, finding a publisher for the *Philosophy of Mysticism* and had already started to translate from the French Halévy's *History of the English People in the Nineteeth Century* for Ernest Benn. He was also completing two long essays for a symposium published by Longmans entitled *God and the Supernatural*. This book was intended to be the Roman Catholic reply to a publication called *Foundations: A Statement of Christian Belief in Terms of Modern Thought*, published in 1912 by a group of Anglo-Catholic scholars and theologians. It was in fact a successor to *Lux Mundi*, an earlier collection of essays whose publication in 1889 marks a turning point in the history of High Anglicanism. Some indeed would call it a *volte face*. Newman was so dismayed by *Lux Mundi* that he declared it to be "The end of Tractarianism. They are giving up everything."

As Dawson pointed out in his *Spirit of the Oxford Movement*, the real religious issue in the nineteenth century was "was not whether High Church or Low Church should prevail in the Church of England but whether the Christian religion should preserve its spiritual identity or whether it should be transformed by the spirit of the age and absorbed into the secularized culture of the modern world." This was true. The early leaders of the Oxford Movement had stood solidly behind the dogmatic principle, for supernaturalism against rationalism, authority against religious liberalism. But one must ask if in a wider sense the successors of the Tractarians had, as Dawson suggests, really betrayed their former principles.

The Roman Catholic Church had withdrawn from the fray. Anglo-Catholicism could likewise retreat behind the barricades or it could openly discuss those challenges to Christian belief with which the modern world so relentlessly confronted it. Christianity owes its whole being to the Great Church of the East and the Great Church of the West, yet it was those communities on the Protestant side of the Reformation divide who by default had the courage and integrity to attempt to build the edifice anew.

Lux Mundi was edited by Charles Gore, then Principal of Pusey House, later Bishop of Oxford. It was an attempt to interpret the Catholic creed for an age of profound intellectual and social transformation. The essayists believed, as indeed did Watkin himself, that if the Christian faith were to be explained reasonably, it would be accepted, or at least considered, by sensible and open minded people. To do this, they had to a certain extent to allow theological liberalism to enter a party hitherto united against it.

The authors recognized the progressive revelation of God, the savagery of the early history of Israel and its gradual climb to ethical monotheism. What distressed some people and gave welcome relief to others, was the partial extension of this approach to the New Testament. Gore, in his essay on Inspiration, suggested that Christ's human knowledge was limited by the conditions of the world he lived in. That was as far as he went. He accepted that the Old Testament presented "a most unspiritual appearance" and was a mixture of folklore, legend, poetry and profound religious insights, but did not apply this critical approach to the New Testament as a whole. He made a distinction between what he called liberal Catholicism and theological liberalism. The former was good and necessary, the latter dangerous and led to infidelity. For him, and others of his school, the Gospels remained dependable historical accounts of what actually happened.

However, the door had opened and the New Testament was increasingly scutinized by theologians, historians, philosophers, linguists and experts on mystical experience. Accordingly, *Foundations*, a book from the same stable as *Lux Mundi,* was published twenty years later. This book is plainly indebted to various strands in the work of some Roman Catholic Modernists now thrust underground by papal fiat. In its discussion of the Resurrection and the historicity of the Gospels, some of the contributors went far further than Gore's "liberal Catholics". So far indeed that many Anglicans refused to accept it as Catholic at all.

One of these was Ronald Knox who had recently been dismissed as private tutor to the young Harold Macmillan for allegedly Roman tendencies. Knox was then at Oxford, newly ordained as an Anglican priest and much in the company of the coming generation of Church of England theologians. Everyone in that circle knew that *Foundations* was being prepared and Knox was convinced that the real threat to Anglicanism came not from its Protestant wing but its Modernist. He published one of his most amusing lampoons, *Absalom and Abitofhell,* a poem in the manner of Dryden, which mocked what he considered to be the inconsistencies and assumptions of the contributors. The form was light-hearted but the intention serious, and in 1913, in response to the urging of others, while still an Anglican, Knox attempted a refutation of *Foundations* which he called *Some Loose Stones.* Despite its witty title and engaging style, the book was not altogether convincing. Therefore, with the object of providing, he hoped, a more solid foundation for Christian belief along traditional lines, in 1919 Father Cuthbert, the Franciscan Principal of Grosseteste Hall, Oxford, gathered together a group of Catholics to contribute to a symposium for this purpose.

He chose his essayists from the new generation of Catholic writers. Knox, now a Roman Catholic, wrote the Introduction which Father Cuthbert told Watkin he did not care for very much.[1] Father C. C. Martindale contributed three essays, Father Martin D'Arcy one, Father Cuthbert himself two, Watkin two and Christopher Dawson one. The majority of the contributors were Oxford men and converts from Anglicanism in one or other of its forms. Father Cuthbert chose *God and the Supernatural: A Catholic Statement of the Christian Faith* as its full title.

By Catholic was meant Roman Catholic. When Ronald Knox was received into the Church in 1917, he said that one of his first reflections was "now I belong to the same Church as Judas Iscariot."[2] Until the Second Vatican Council the Roman Church identified itself with the one Church founded by Christ. The Eastern Church was in an anomalous position. It was in schism, not heresy; its orders were valid, although not to be resorted to unless in danger of death. Anglicans, however, were undeniably on the wrong side of the Reformation fence. They could take as much or as little from Rome as they pleased but were not considered to be fully part of the Christian communion; their orders were doubtful and *communicatio in sacris* was forbidden. In Newman's opinion, and he recognized it to be only an opinion, a Catholic might attend family prayers in a Protestant household provided he took in his hands a crucifix or a devotional book like *The Garden of the Soul* and kept to his own prayers. This was practised in the case of Catholic servants.

The book was not intended to be controversial and was so only by implication. As Father Cuthbert wrote to Watkin and repeated in his Preface, the intention was "to present the ordinary educated non-Catholic with an exposition of Catholicism – both of faith and action – as a *dynamic force* in life."

God and the Supernatural is interesting for many reasons, not least for the high calibre of its contributors. It included Dawson's first publication. Dawson may have been a slow starter but he had known what he wanted to write about since he was a young man. He had spent the years since leaving Oxford studying world civilizations in preparation for his projected history of human culture. Watkin's opinion about the book's contents had been sought early on and his suggestions circulated to the group who were planning it. He was determined to include Dawson, who accepted the invitation to contribute an essay he called *The Nature and Destiny of Man*. It is a good paper, different from the mannered style of Knox and Chesterton, and the overture to his future work.

Watkin's essays were two: *The Problem of Evil* and *The Church as the Mystical Body of Christ*. He had been given the first subject very late in the day since the person originally chosen pleaded illness. Perhaps he just could not face such a difficult assignment. In 1933, in his chapter on Julian of Norwich in *The English Way*, Watkin was to remark that "the problem of evil is the riddle of the universe."[3] He starts his essay here by welcoming fashionable modern pessimism because it forces those who believe in an all-loving and omnipotent God to face the powerful challenge to Christian theism that existence of evil raises. He insists that it must be stated at once that there is no adequate solution to this problem, only partial, converging indications of an answer. It is useless to pretend that evil is an illusion, or that it is the result of human sin when we know that suffering existed for millions of years before humankind lived on earth. Nor, when we consider the suffering of children, the insane, animals or perhaps even of plants, can we maintain it is always of direct moral value to the sufferer. Neither can the burden be lightened by the consideration that the Godhead shares in the pain of His creation. Such a god would not be the transcendent God of Christianity.

In 1804, after his brother's tragic loss at sea, William Wordsworth wrote a letter to his patron, Sir George Beaumont. "Would it be a blasphemy," he asked, "to say that upon the supposition of the thinking principle being destroyed by death, however inferior we may be to the great Cause and ruler of things, we *have more of love* in our nature then he has?"

In Watkin's eyes this would be a blasphemy whether or not the thinking principle survived death. In his essay he argues that from the philosophical point of view, evil is an unreality, not a mere absence of good but absence of due good, therefore a privation, its power to infect and destroy grounded not in evil as evil, but in the good thing or person in which that evil adheres. Evil as such is powerless. Only in virtue of something good to which it belongs is it a force of attraction or destruction. People never sin for the sake of evil, only for the sake of some good. Even wanton cruelty is a perversion of the desire to exercise power, in itself good, and the infection of national or class hatred depends upon positive instincts like love and loyalty. The evil lies in the limitations themselves, such as blindness to the good in other groups or plain ignorance.

Once we admit evil as a positive entity we have to accept either that there is a radical dualism in the constitution of reality, a bad principle opposed to the good God, as the Manicheans held, or that evil is a reflection and participation of the single ultimate Reality, a reflection of one aspect of the Divine Nature. This would be a denial of the goodness of God and therefore of any theism of religious value.

The metaphysical unreality of evil, however, does not prevent it from being in the ordinary sense very real indeed, a bitter reality marring on every side the positively good universe. Pain and grief, suffering altogether, whether physical or mental, are obviously quite other than mere privation of pleasure or joy. Watkin is of course, in this book, treating evil on the supposition that the full Catholic and Christian faith is true. In that context he discusses the nature of suffering, its creative and redemptive aspects, the forms of evil, sin and free will, purgatory and hell as he then understood them. Much of what he says about the fundamental purpose of evil being a struggle in and through human solidarity was to form the basis of his later work in this field and to be the subject matter of his second essay, entitled *The Mystical Body of Christ*.

From beginning to end, Watkin argues, our salvation is a progressive incorporation into a supernatural society of human souls. We are not self-contained, isolated individuals but part of an organic whole. We cannot therefore pray alone. The very fact of our union with God means that we are united with all other souls in union with Him. This fundamental doctrine of Christianity is the same doctrine taught by St Paul and has hardly developed since. It does though need exposition, clarification and extension in other directions which Watkin goes on to do. The reviewer in the *Times Literary Supplement* thought Watkin's two essays the finest and strongest in the book. They also caught the attention of von Hügel.

"How thankful we were to get the Baron safely underground," Helena would sometimes remark, much to the puzzlement of her children. She meant that his friends and admirers were relieved to get him buried at Downside with full rites of the Catholic Church. Clement Webb, who knew von Hügel well and wrote the entry on him in the *Dictionary of National Biography*, suggested that, to a greater extent than he realized, the Baron escaped ecclesiastical censure because of his social position.

Tyrrell could be broken on the wheel of the Roman machine to the lamentations of a few devoted disciples but the public destruction of von Hügel was quite another matter. He has been called the "pope" of the Modernist movement and he was certainly one of its leaders. Tyrrell's disciple, Maude Petre, describes von Hügel as its "arch-leader". He was what perhaps would be called today the web-master of the European movement, he searched Modernists out, read their books, introduced one to another, stiffened their resolve against ecclesiastical interference and got their work reviewed in influential publications. He was Tyrrell's greatest friend. Yet he never risked refusal by applying for the *Imprimatur* for any of his books. Abbot Chapman of Downside had the honesty to admit that it probably would not have been granted had he applied.

There was an ambiguity about von Hügel, what Maude Petre called a temporizing quality, which has led others to describe him as the Erasmus of the movement. Ill, old and fearful for his English pension, Erasmus shrugged off what Thomas More died for. The Baron never abandoned nor watered down the central tenets of his faith.

He stood by what were then considered advanced views about the historicity and interpretation of the Bible, but as Clement Webb and others have pointed out, became increasingly uneasy about the subjective or immanentist strain in Modernism. He was repelled by opinions which led to a denial of the objective, full reality of God postulated by adoration, which he considered to be the essence of religion. He has been accused of being preoccupied with metaphysics and obsessed with transcendence.

Watkin recognized this position immediately because it reflected his own views. "I have always considered von Hügel," he wtote in 1969 to a scholar who wished to consult some of the Baron's letters to him, "as an historical but *not* a philosophical modernist. This, I'm sure, was the radical reason why he did not follow his friends into open revolt."[4] The Baron was also not unlike Watkin in his deep attachment to the Roman Catholic Church. Alfred Fawkes, a Modernist who reverted to Anglicanism but chose to be buried by the side of Father Tyrrell at Storrington, drew attention to this aspect of von Hügel in a letter to Loisy after the Baron's death. "He seemed to me to feel strongly that the Roman Catholic Church was the main current of the spiritual experience and life of mankind; and that, in comparison with this, the excesses of the Papacy and the breach with knowledge were secondary – and would, probably, be temporary."[5] In his calmer moments, this was Watkin's own view throughout his life.

Watkin must earlier have sent the Baron his previous book, *The Philosophy of Mysticism*, because in August 1921, he received a long letter from Vicarage Gate which had taken von Hügel two days to complete. He apologizes for the long delay in acknowledging Watkin's book which was due to pressure of work and the over-stimulated condition of his brain, from which he had always suffered. This meant sleepless nights and "saddening breaks" in his day's toil. He agrees with the appreciative review of Watkin's essays in the *Times Literary Supplement*. He was in fact to refer to them favourably in the Preface to the second impression of his *Mystical Element of Religion*. As for *The Philosophy of Mysticism*, which he has not yet finished reading, he praises Watkin's learning which was both wide and deep and his reverent love of his subject. The book was "rich in information, in thought, in conviction." Having said all this at some length, the Baron goes on to make a most interesting comment. He perceives, he says, "a doubleness" in Watkin's thought. He saw two people "a devout lay brother, perhaps, even a pious altar boy which stands side by side and is sometimes curiously mingled with your quite other, beautifully comprehensive, delicately Catholic current . . . "[6] He was recognizing, of course, the Aloysian strain in Watkin's approach, the ambiguity present in his own, and the one which is patently apparent in the thought of Newman. This "doubleness" is surely the consequence of deeply religious temperaments allied to minds which cannot yet reconcile the known historical, scientific and moral facts with an intuitive grasp of the underlying truth of Christian revelation.

Newman said that he believed in the Flying House of Loretto with the same conviction that that he believed in the existence of "a new planet called Neptune."[7] After all, He who floated the Ark and enclosed within it all living things, who sustained thousands for forty years in a sterile wilderness, who transported Elias and keeps him hidden to the end "could do this wonder also." Quite so. No Ark, no Resurrection, no Flying House, no Ascension. Both Pusey and Keble refused to face the factual difficulties scientific scholarship presented to traditional Christian belief. In this, Newman differed from them. His "inexhaustible mutability" was due to his spasmodic recognition of the difficulty in accepting Christian revelation in the form it has come down to us and his acute awareness of the consequences of rejecting it. "Phaeton has got into the chariot of the sun," as he wrote inimitably in the *Apologia*, "we alas, can only look on and watch him down the steep of heaven." This ambiguity, this doubleness, was also apparent in Tyrrell which was why he was so amusingly concious of it in von Hügel. "The Baron has just gone," he wrote famously to a friend. "Wonderful man! Nothing is true; but the sum total of nothings is sublime."[8]

Christopher Dawson has sometimes been referred to as "Culture Dawson" because of his persistent and wonderfully worked out theme that religion is the soul of culture and despite superficial appearances to the contrary, any society that has lost its spiritual roots is in fact dying. Watkin's soubriquet was less complimentary. It was 'Slogger'. In old age Harman Grisewood told the author that he remembered Watkin and his conversation vividly. As a young man he had listened to it in the hope that he might attain something of Watkin's perceptiveness and breadth of view, so needful in the post-war world of Joyce and Lawrence, Stravinsky and Diaghilev, which was rushing in upon his generation of ill-prepared counter-reformation Catholics.[9] Why Watkin was called 'Slogger', Grisewood could not recall; he was so brilliant and found easy what most people found difficult. The clue may lie in an amusing remark made by the philosopher Dom Iltyd Trethowan, a monk of Downside. "Watkin," he said, "is the kind of man who never takes yes for an answer." This was true. Once he got hold of a good point in an argument, Watkin would drive it home, leaping up from his chair and emphasizing each syllable by thumping his closed fist on an open hand. Nor, in his relentless search for God, was he backward in pursuing people he thought could help him.

Having entered von Hügel's orbit he felt that it would not be presumptuous to write and ask for guidance. He was troubled by difficulties which the very writing of his last two essays had brought to the forefront of his mind. He received an answer to his plainly very long letter in early October 1923. Von Hügel's controversial years were over. He had, to use his own expression, "fallen back upon his central light." He was now seventy-one, in poor health and with little over a year to live. He had a great deal of work of his own on hand and although he had a secretary, his personal and professional correspondence was a heavy burden. If anything could have demonstrated his largeness of heart, it was his treatment of Watkin. His answer, dictated to his secretary, runs to more than thirteen pages. He had read Watkin's important statement about his theological and biblical difficulties and invited him to stay the night so that they could discuss the problems raised.

The Baron is meticulous about the arrangements. Watkin should come in time for lunch, they would talk in the afternoon of that day. After dinner Watkin would be taken to the cinema because, for the sake of his health, he himself must play Patience then go to bed early. The next morning would be spent in further discussion, lunch would follow and Watkin would then leave. In the meantime he would prepare his answers. He goes on to give Watkin some advice "learnt by and for myself through years of pain and trouble." Some of it was wide of the mark.

He fears that Watkin has no paid profession. He must take up some vigorous non-religious activities. He feared too that he was not married which was a pity. He should take up walking, gardening, excavation of Roman remains or rubbing church brasses – "everything, anything that is decent." As for religion, Watkin should quietly, unlearnedly, unbookishly, concentrate upon his faith which was, as it were, the egg from which he can hatch a new zest. *Pectus facit theologium.* Let him take the Holy Eucharist with as few "dogmatic involvements" as possible. He can believe in the Real Presence whilst evading being bothered by transubstantiation.

At the appointed time he arrived at Vicarage Gate and after lunch they spoke together about what von Hügel called Watkin's metaphysical difficulties. For this discussion, the Baron had prepared eight pages of notes in his own hand which he gave to Watkin before he left. From this only do we know the nature of Watkin's problems.[10]

The first matter they discussed was human immortality, a difficulty which was to remain with Watkin until the last. He had an imaginative or psychological horror of physical dissolution, "to lie," as Shakespeare has it, "in cold obstruction and to rot." He hated funerals, morbid hymns, and the Victorian panoply of death. When in the Holy Land he refused to enter Lazarus's tomb with the other pilgrims. He had ceased to believe in the possibility of eternal torment, either physical or spiritual, yet in some strange way, perhaps because of his Protestant background, he was haunted by what his rational understanding of God could not accept. He had too honest a mind to evade those passages of the Gospels which present us with a threatening Christ and this was an obstacle to his devotion. As we know, he had a tenacious love of life for its own sake. What he really feared was annihilation. *Shall Thy wondrous works be known in the dark: and Thy righteousness in the land where all things are forgotten?* Anaesthetics were a form of annihilation and he had such an intense fear of undergoing the experience he would rather let his teeth fall out than have them extracted under gas by the dentist.

This fear was strengthened by rational objections. As he told von Hügel, it was "terribly hard" to believe in survival because everything seemed to point to the complete dependence of the psychological life on the physical. The independent existence of the soul seemed inconceivable. To this the Baron answered that he himself had for some years come to hold immortality as a secondary, derivative conviction. The proofs for it are insufficient to meet the three or four objections Watkin had brought forward. Its truth derives solidly only from our belief in and our experience of God, our relation to His reality. But it is secondary. We know as a fact that there have lived deeply religious "adoration-full" souls who had no belief in immortality, that is, a consciousness after bodily death at least equal to that experienced before. The psalmists are almost entirely without such a belief, they explicitly exclude it, yet how "unshaken, unclouded, all permeating is their faith and love of God!" We must not drop immortality but it must never be taken separately or before or on the same level as God, always together with God and as inferior to our faith in Him.

The Christian outlook and temper, von Hügel continued, required an abiding union of soul and body as definitely as in any modern psychology. He then went on to assert that the early Church held that the soul did not cease to exist as a distinct entity at the body's death but that it slumbered until it informed its corresponding body at the resurrection. Watkin was surprised. He did not think this was the view of the early Church but did not presume to question his host.[11]

Their conversation continued throughout the afternoon, the Baron making a careful distinction between existence and consciousness. He "refused to deny as impossible" that the soul could exist after the cessation of consciousness although he admitted that this was not conformable with other doctrines and Catholic practices. Watkin's faith, like his own, should be strengthened by the body and spirit teaching of the sacramental system, and the deeply Catholic doctrine of the natural and the supernatural. Limbo, he thought, in answer to another of Watkin's difficulties, could be extended to include barbarous and utterly rudimentary souls which some have thought to be the majority of the human race.

Their conversation ended with a discussion about the General Resurrection and the Last Day in connection with our modern knowledge of the universe. Von Hügel thought that Einstein had not proved the universe to be limited, but he had at least made that position tenable. All of the universe which we can observe bears the marks of having a beginning. He could not, the Baron said, picture to himself a sheer end or a sheer beginning, but he could believe in both "as truths dimly traceable on the horizons of my outlook."

One wonders who was present at dinner, whether Lady Mary, so perplexed by her husband's views, shared it with them; which person was assigned to accompany Watkin to the cinema and what film he saw. The Baron's written resumé of the following morning's talk is far more scanty than the previous afternoon's. We catch only brief snatches of their discussion, which started with the virginity of Mary. Von Hügel, held that the brethren referred to in the Gospels were Joseph's children by a previous marriage. They then spoke of the Real Presence in the Eucharist and finally what concerned Watkin most, the divinity of Jesus. Two scribbled notes are interesting. One, typical of the Baron, on the importance of the "fringe" on the margin of our knowledge, the other that sheer Christocentricism was not Catholic. Watkin left after lunch and they never saw each other again.

Watkin, however, never forgot von Hügel's kindness, and some twenty-two years after their meeting, he contributed an appreciation of the Baron in a series called "Retrospect" for the Church of England paper *The Guardian*.[12] From the mass of spiritual perceptions contained in the Baron's work, Watkin picked out a few dominating insights. The first was his insistence that adoration is the essence of religion. God is the supreme Reality, the source of all value, wholly other, yet intimately present. This insistence, Watkin points out, is security against the insidious error which confounds religion with ethics, and replaces the worship of God with the loving service of our fellowmen. Von Hügel combined this central insight about God's transcendent Being and our consequent dependence upon Him, with vigorous commitment and appreciation of this world and activity within it. He may not have been able clearly to state the relationship between the revealed doctrines taught by the Church and what seemed to be the results of critical Biblical scholarship, he may indeed have accepted these conclusions too easily, but nothing could detract from his stature as a profound religious philosopher, a teacher whose thought, like

Elijah's cake and water, sustains the human spirit through the desert to the Mount of God.

CHAPTER THIRTEEN

The Blue House

The house was rendered and painted blue, a creamy mid-blue mixed by Edda himself, the colour, he said, of Our Lady and contemplation. He called the house St Mary's and above the porch, in a special niche, placed a wooden statue of the Blessed Virgin, an exact copy of the one above the porch at the church along the coast at Happisburgh which for some reason had survived the Reformation.

When Watkin left London that afternoon in 1923 he did not return to the rented house in Cliff Road. In order to stimulate employment and encourage the provision of homes fit for heroes, the government had initiated a scheme by which anyone who built a new house could apply for a grant of £250. In after years his children would tease their father mercilessly about his reward for gallant war service. He would point out that there were no conditions attached and he would have been a fool not to accept such an offer which, after all, they too had profited from. Although £250 was worth very considerably more than it is today, nevertheless he must have added some money of his own to build even the modest house he did.

If the occasion demanded it Watkin was far more capable in practical matters than people assumed. Before his marriage he had outmanoeuvred his mother and acted in a reasonable and practical way to ensure that he and Helena started life together in some comfort. Now he bought a plot of land at Sheringham at the top of Avenue South near Beeston Hill and designed the house with the help of a local builder. Helena very sensibly suggested that it should be built with an extra large loft space which could be converted into bedrooms should the family increase still further. Downstairs there was a hall, drawing room, study and kitchen. On the next floor was a nursery, a night nursery, where the latest baby slept with Nanny, and their parent's bedroom. Above that were three small bedrooms created out of the space so thoughtfully devised by Helena.

Since the dining room had been sacrificed to their father's study, all meals were eaten from a large round table in the drawing room. Here, when the children had left the nursery, much of their life was spent. The younger ones wrote, painted and cut out pictures on the table carefully covered with an oil-cloth. The three elder played board-games on the rug in front of the fire. This became a sacred space for a game called "Sorry", enjoyed for hours on end. In this room they acted plays, read on the sofa, listened to agitated conversations between their parents and loud discussions between their father and his visitors about religion, art, literature and politics. There were few criticisms of Roman Catholicism to which they were strangers. They knew all about the League of Nations Union, appalling people called Stalin, Mussolini, and Hitler and the disgraceful behaviour of Pope Pius XI. None of this affected their faith in the least. It was just part of a world that was fundamentally uncertain and dangerous.

Helena never cooked. Whenever possible she avoided employing Catholic servants because they had to go to Mass on Sundays and that interfered with the preparation of the lunch. She and Edda gave few dinner parties for much the same reason. Most cooks were local and wanted to return home at night. So they entertained at midday instead and had a small meal in the evening, often cooked by Hetty.

Hetty was a Protestant but when the children were small or Helena ill, she would walk with them to Mass and stay throughout the service. She shared the night nursery with the youngest of the family and so as not to disturb the child, instead of lighting the gas, undressed by candlelight. Before getting into bed she would kneel down and say her prayers, a memory that was etched deeply into the minds of all her charges.

Sport or games of any kind were never the subject of conversation. With one exception, the children were educated in all that matters just by being there. The exception was music. There was no piano in the house. Helena was tone deaf. Edda was not tone deaf but had a defective ear and could not sing in tune, nor could any of his daughters. The only one who had inherited any of the family's musical gifts was Christopher. However, they had a large wooden gramophone and when he was in the mood Edda would wind it up and play some of his collection of records, a curious mixture of bits of Wagner, melancholy renderings of poems from the *Shropshire Lad* and snatches of music-hall songs. His favourite was "Daisy, Daisy". He would jump up, wave an arm in approximate time to the music and join in with gusto "Give me your answer, do. I'm half-crazy, all for the love of you."

During the thirties, a wireless was introduced. Encased in brown leather, it was placed on a table near the window, the large accumulator on the carpet at its side. The bird cage was covered and they sat solemnly round to listen to the first broadcast, which happened to be *Romeo and Juliet*. Helena did the mending. Edda sat with his eyes closed murmuring unintelligibly but interrupting every now and then with "Clapping. They're clapping" or when loud rumbles overcame the actors' voices, "Nothing to do with the play. Atmospherics. Only atmospherics."

When they first moved, Oscar Wilde's former lover, Lord Alfred Douglas, lived in a rented house opposite. Much later, the children asked if their father had called on him. He sighed, shook his head and answered in the whisper he reserved for such conversations. "No. In those days . . . Their mother . . ." But he wished he had. So did they.

The house was rendered and painted blue, a creamy mid-blue mixed by Edda himself, the colour, he said, of Our Lady and contemplation. He called the house St Mary's and above the porch, in a special niche, placed a wooden statue of the Blessed Virgin, an exact copy of the one above the porch at the church along the coast at Happisburgh which for some reason had survived the Reformation. Red and yellow roses climbed up the house and the small garden was designed by Watkin in such a way as to surprise and please with its unexpectedness.

The apparent size of a garden can be doubled if it is divided by hedges of such height and shape as to suggest a further garden on the other side. This idea Watkin had borrowed from engravings and survivals of seventeeth- and eighteenth-century Baroque gardens which he so loved and was to write about later. He devised a minute orchard consisting of three apple trees, an enclosed garden for Helena with the beds divided up by brick paths, curved flower borders, a lawn for the children, a summer-house and a piece of rough ground by the lane which ran down to the sea. Here were the beehives, the childrens' plots, a swing and the bonfire.

Steps led down from the garden gate to the road and it was here that the organ-grinder took up his post. Edda used to hate seeing the monkey in his little red jacket shivering in the bitter east wind. He would rush out to give the man money to buy a thicker coat which, as Helena would dryly remark, only encouraged the owner to continue his profession.

It was a sunny house, a place of laughter, confusion, grief and joy, obstinately loved and painfully abandoned. Today neither house nor garden bear any resemblance to the place where Helena's fourth child, Catherine Mary, was born in June 1923. Birrell wrote on Garsington notepaper to congratulate Edda and insisted on being present at the baptism. After the birth Helena had in fact a bad haemorrhage and Dr Sumpter warned her that another baby might be fatal. She, or Edda, paid no attention to this and the following year she conceived again. Perhaps it was because of this warning that Christopher and Perpetua were sent away for two months beforehand to stay with Aunt Ada. It may be that while deploring Edda's folly and Emmeline's obtinacy, Ada felt sorry for the children. Neither Edda nor Helena had any notion of preparing them for the birth of another baby but in that small house, Perpetua must either have overheard or sensed that something was going to happen. She was devoted to her mother and after saying goodbye rushed back and begged Helena to tell her that nothing was wrong.

Ada lived in a large house in Nantwich called Parkfield and it was particularly good of her to have them just then because her husband, A. N. Hornby, old and crippled from a hunting accident, had to be pushed along the corridors in a wheelchair. He was to die in the winter of 1925 and Father Rickaby, reading about the funeral in the paper, was touched by a photograph of Hornby's two hunters "looking wistfully over the park fence as the hearse passed." The cricketer was one of Rickaby's boyhood heroes and he was astonished to find that the former Captain of England had been married to Watkin's aunt.

Towards the end of July that year Christopher and Perpetua were fooling about in the billiard room when Ada came in with a telegram in her hand. "That stupid woman," she said, "has had another daughter." Sumpter's gloomy predictions had not been fulfilled. Nothing went wrong, the birth was normal. But Helena was forty-three and this was to be her last child. She had been less worried by the fear of death than what the baby's name would be. Edda threatened to consult his missal and the feasts of Saints Apollinaris and St Pantaleon were uncomfortably close. Fortunately, so was St Mary Magdalen.

Ada herself had had four sons. One died of an illness in South Africa, another of wounds during the War. A third son, John Hornby, was to become one of the main actors in a tragedy which, widely publicized, shocked all who read about it.

Jack had rebelled against his background and after leaving Harrow lived for years as a hunter, trapper and trader in the north of Canada. He returned to fight in the war, was wounded, awarded the Military Cross for gallantry and hero-worshipped by his young cousin Edgar, the son of Colonel and Mrs Christian of Bron Dirion, Caernarvonshire. When Hornby returned home for his father's funeral in 1925, he persuaded Edgar's parents to allow their son, who had just left school, to join him on an expedition he was planning to make to the Barren Grounds, the desolate Arctic and sub-Arctic tundra to the far north of Canada. The expedition was reckless, badly prepared and ended in tragedy. Jack was determined to live off the country but that year the caribou never came. He, Edgar and a man named Harold Adlard whom they had recruited at Edmonton, slowly died of starvation in the log cabin they had built by the side of the Thelon river. Edgar was the last to die and left his diary together with letters to his parents among the cold ashes of the stove.

The diary is a remarkable document and caused quite a sensation when it was published by John Murray under the title of *Unflinching* in 1937.[1] After the others had died and the bodies, wrapped in blankets, were dragged outside to be left in the snow, Edgar remained in the hut for a month alone. He kept himself alive by digging up bits of frozen animals, boiling bones and strips of leather. When he knew that the end was coming, he climbed into his bunk and covered his head. There he was found by a group of prospectors in July 1928. Ada died before the fate of the three men was known.

Before the expedition left, Ada brought Jack to St Mary's to say goodbye. There was a strong likeness between the two cousins, so different in their desires. Perpetua was nearly six. To the dismay of Watkin, who agonized enough over Father Christmas, Jack took her on his knee and assured her that mermaids existed. He knew because he had seen them. But how could parents teach children about a world they did not see if they lied about a world they did?

W. G. Ward once observed that when a Protestant met a Catholic in controversy "it is like a civilized man meeting a barbarian."[2] This was a gross exaggeration as any one who has read Bishop Ullathorne's autobiography will testify. Nevertheless, it was true that the Catholic clergy and laity were educated, not badly, but in an increasingly different way from their Protestant and secular contemporaries. Ward's son, Wilfred, the author of a life of Newman which is one of the finest biographies of a period rich in that art, agreed with his father in this respect although his approach was utterly different.

Wilfred recognized that since the triumph of the Protestant Reformation and the imposition of the Penal Laws, English Catholics had been living in what he called a state of siege. He believed that the time had come to venture out of the fortress, abandon the siege mentality and meet a largely agnostic society on its own ground. He pursued this policy when he followed his father as editor of the *Dublin Review,* a scholarly Catholic Quarterly owned by the publishers Burns and Oates, opening its pages to contributors of far more varied opinions than W. G. Ward would ever have tolerated. This was to pave the way for the Catholic intellectual revival of the nineteen twenties and thirties and the brilliant editorship of one of his successors, Algar Thorold.

To the distress of their families, four sons of Anglican bishops converted to the Church of Rome before and soon after the Great War. Algar Thorold was the first. He was the only son of the Bishop of Rochester, later Winchester, and caused a moderate sensation in 1884 when he became a Catholic while still an undergraduate at Oxford. The second was the later novelist Robert Hugh Benson, the youngest son of E. W. Benson, Archbishop of Canterbury and father of an odd and gifted family about whom much has been most entertainingly written. Fortunately, the Archbishop did not live to witness the disgrace. Seven years before his son's reception in 1903, he died on his knees when visiting Mr Gladstone at Hawarden leaving on his dressing table the draft of a letter to *The Times* protesting against the Papal Bull which had just condemned Anglican Orders as "absolutely null and utterly void". The

third convert was Ronald Knox, son of E. A. Knox, the evangelical Bishop
of Manchester, who suffered much from the Romish tendencies of two of
his sons. Ronnie's rosary could be heard clinking at family prayers and
made the terrier growl. "Between ourselves, Winnie," the Bishop
remarked to his daughter, "I cannot understand what it is that the dear
boys see in the Blessed Virgin Mary."[3] The fourth convert was
Christopher Hollis, son of the later suffragan Bishop of Taunton.

All these men were exceptionally gifted in their different ways.
Thorold's mother was the sister of the famous Victorian politician, journalist and wit, Henry Labouchere, whose life he wrote. Thorold had
joined the Foreign Office, was a member of the Peace Delegation in Paris
and acted as Second Secretary at our Embassy there. He was, as Watkin
was later to write, a mystic, a philosopher, a man of the world and a brilliant and amusing conversationalist. This combination of spiritual
profundity with breadth of human interest made him one of the most
congenial of all Watkin's friends. Nor was the relationship one-sided.
Thorold appreciated what he called Watkin's "mordant dialectic" and
still more his contribution to the success of the *Dublin Review* of which
Thorold was editor from 1926 to 1934.

"The *Dublin* has received a certain standing," he wrote to Watkin early
on, "and it is principally to you that I feel inestimably grateful." He more
or less let Watkin have his head, assuring him that he owed him far too
much both intellectually and spiritually to think of interfering with his
work. Towards the end of Thorold's life, when Watkin thanked him for
giving him the opportunity to write so many reviews and articles, Thorold
replied that on the contrary, without Watkin he would never have been
able to edit the paper as he wanted to while Watkin's genius would surely
have surfaced in the long run. Early on, Thorold had asked to be introduced to Dawson whose articles in *The Sociological Review* had interested
him. In time Dawson himself was to become a distinguished editor of the
Dublin.

When Watkin introduced him to Thorold, Dawson was living in the
West Country employed by what was to become Exeter University, and
lecturing, as he told Watkin, once a week on comparative religion to half
a dozen spinsters and a retired sea captain. He had a wife and children to
support and his father's allowance was not generous.

At one point indeed Thorold jokingly told Watkin that unless the
Colonel died soon, Dawson and his family would be forced to live abroad.
This fate was spared them. The good Colonel died in 1933 and Dawson
inherited both money, Hartlington and that year an opportunity to be
appointed to the vacant Chair of Philosophy and the History of Religion
at the University of Leeds. He was turned down. What was in question
was not the applicant's widely attested scholarship but his religion.

Perhaps we do not sufficiently realize what a gulf exists between the way in which Catholics and Protestants perceive each other's faith. When the Catholic priest Edmund Campion said at his trial for treason that in condemning him his Elizabethan judges were condemning all their own ancestors, he was speaking the plain truth. That Dawson was perhaps turned down as Professor of Philosophy and Religion largely because he belonged to the Church whose beliefs and structures had created the very civilization he was employed to teach is ironical. It displays the same kind of blindness and inner contradiction which exists when Christians despise Jews upon whose religion they depend.

Some other factor however might have led to the rejection. Whilst supporting Dawson's application for the post, Dean Inge wrote to him that his own distrust "of Catholic scholars is almost as great as Dr Coulton's but honestly I believe you are quite straight."[4] Unfortunately it is true that in their zeal to propagate and defend the true faith, some Catholic scholars and publicists were not quite straight, they did doctor the facts and deny the known truth, an attitude which infuriated Watkin who took great pleasure in unmasking it.

In the event, the failure at Leeds may have been fortunate because it meant that Dawson could get on with his own work without interruption. A year later, when he was nearly forty, he published his first book, *The Age of the Gods: A Study in the Origins of Culture in Prehistoric Europe and the Ancient East*. Not printed, but in his own hand, in Latin on the flyleaf, Dawson dedicated his book to Watkin who had corrected the type-script and proofs, compiled the index and devised the detailed chapter headings. The tone is elegiac and harks back to their boyhood at the Rectory. The author dedicates the first fruits of his labour to E.I.W., his one very close friend with whom in the fields of Bletsoe he first learnt to know the Great Mother and the Theandrican Bread.

This refers not only to Watkin's early influence but to the subject matter of his book, which was an examination of the social and religious life of ancient societies, the foundation of ideas and even technologies upon which our later cultures rested. It was intended to be the first of a contin-uing series on the history of culture to be called *The Life of Civilizations*, as it were a Christian counter-blast to H. G. Wells' secular version. The project was never carried through in that form but would be triumphantly achieved through Dawson's long series of books and studies of various cultures at the most important point of their development.

Unlike Watkin, Dawson belonged both in temperament and back-ground to the Anglican establishment and like Ronald Knox, might have found more personal happiness in his life had he been able to remain there. Watkin had made him a Catholic and helped him into print but he was never really at home in the Roman Church and thought that his work was insufficiently appreciated. That was why he depended so much on Watkin's companionship, criticism and knowledge; "my leader and my friend," as he once wrote to him. He had nothing in common, he said, with people like Douglas Woodruff and Christopher Hollis.

Nor had he much in common with what is thought of as the school of Chesterton and Belloc. He was in some respects an isolated figure and felt this to be so. "Conversation is more than bread and meat to me," he wrote to Watkin in 1956, "I cannot exist without it." Yet, he went on, he was forced to do so and that was far and away the greatest drawback to his conversion. As a Catholic he never expected to get a good job or prosper in material ways, "but I never realized it would mean living in an intellectual vacuum without intellectual or spiritual contact with one's fellows and I shall never get accustomed to it, if I live to be a hundred." Three years after this despondent letter he was appointed as the first occupant of the Chair in Roman Catholic Studies at Harvard University.

It was not intellectual but financial vacuums that worried Watkin. He had a very large amount of work on hand besides the *Dublin* but was finding it increasingly difficult to make ends meet. Rates of pay were pretty meagre. In 1926 Thorold paid ten shillings for a page of about four hundred words, then in 1928 when the paper was in financial difficulties, this was reduced to five shillings for an article of ten pages and upwards unless it reached twenty pages when the piece would be divided between two issues.

The Babington Smiths were living at Loudwater. Lady Elizabeth was now a widow. One of her nine children was just leaving Cambridge, the youngest was too young when her father died even to remember him. Nana used to come round to St Mary's to see Edda. What they said to each other we cannot tell but the conversation must have been painful on both sides. Nana was now living in the very house from which he had been expelled. Emmeline was not dead, but lost. Pantafon was let, Loudwater was let, Mount Felix a dim memory. The rich gifted boy she used to boast about was living in reduced circumstances with a half-Italian wife and more children than he could support.

Some profound psychological damage must long ago have happened to result in Edda's violent and implacable hatred of his mother. It is easy to say that he really loved her very much, so much indeed that he was able to escape her domination only by total rejection. It is too simple to point out that as a tiny baby he was handed over to an old lady and looked after by strangers, that his father was more interested in his boy friends than his son, that he was born with brilliant intellectual gifts together with physical and temperamental difficulties from the consequences of which his mother protected him with her money and devouring affection. These things are true, but they are not sufficient to account for the depth, persistence and undeviating hostility of an unusually loving nature. It was not until their father was dead and they read his early diaries that the children realized that the lane where he took them primrosing every spring was the very place where he and his mother used to gather them when he was a little boy. Nor did they know that the Carlsbad plums in their wooden box he insisted on having every Christmas were the same as those he used to give her for her birthday. But perhaps that particular lane was the best place to gather primroses and he just happened to like Carlsbad plums. The relationship between them lies beyond analysis. There was an untamed, unbalanced element in his inheritance that drove him to act against his own interests.

One of the people to perceive this early, although he knew little of Watkin's background, was Father Martindale. At one time he and Watkin had got together to publicize the work of the Russian writer, Solovyev, in whom Watkin was then particularly interested. Watkin was to do the literary work, Martindale to lecture. Unfortunately they fell out and some rather angry letters were exchanged. It seems that for some reason or another Watkin lost his temper with his publisher and demanded the return of his manuscript. Martindale, who had had to type out Watkin's bad handwriting himself, wasted weeks of work. Martindale accused Watkin of having no sense of the appropriate; he was already suspected of being a sub-modernist and the very fact that he had written a book on a new apologetic was enough to make people ask if the old apologetic was not good enough. "The world is full of tragedies rather like your own," he wrote, "but though you once deprecated my suggesting that your temperament was responsible for a lot of your distresses, I am forced to say it simply *is*." It runs away with him, and then he "may get desperate and do things that wouldn't occur to anyone else." This was only too true but it was not the end of the story. They always kept up with each other's work and as an old man Martindale was to tell Watkin that he was the only reviewer to get the point of his last book.

Edda's quarrel with his mother meant a long-drawn out struggle with comparative poverty, the constant stress of attempting to provide for five children, a nanny and servants to help an increasingly invalid wife. It was not the luxury of his youth which he regretted but the loss of the financial security which made possible the continuation of the work he knew he was capable of doing. His uncle William Ingram had bought the island of Little Tobago to secure a fitting environment for his specially imported birds of paradise. This was superfluity indeed and may have lurked at the back of Watkin's mind and added to the bitterness of his own situation. Birrell was fond of him and in 1926 when for some reason peace between him and his mother appeared possible, implored Edda to put his pride in his pocket and effect a complete reconciliation. But he did nothing. Whereupon Emmeline took Sam off to Salt Lake City to investigate the Mormons whose religion she found to be far more exciting than Roman Catholicism.

CHAPTER FOURTEEN

Making Waves

Some people have looked back on the Catholic literary and religious revival of the nineteen twenties and thirties of the last century as a golden age. Others have gone to the opposite extreme and regarded its achievements as the ephemeral products of a small, almost incestuous, rather snobbish group of ultramontanes with Fascist leanings.

When Emmeline allowed Edda and the family to live at Loudwater, Helena was absolutely delighted. She would be back in Norfolk, close to her parents, able to visit her old home as often as she pleased. Their move to St Mary's made no difference. Aylsham was about twelve miles distant and was an exciting expedition for the children. Christopher, Perpetua and Teresa would bicycle over and were very superior about the whole thing. Helena and the younger children would go by train from Sheringham station to Aylsham where they would be met by Samuel in his car and be driven the few miles to Abbots Hall. Philip Shepheard was eighty by the end of the War and Samuel decided to retire from medicine and remain at home to look after his parents and take some of the responsibility for the running of the property.

To Christopher, Abbots Hall was paradise. His grandfather would take him about, cross the lane to show him the cows, tell him what crops they were growing, and explain the original purpose of the many brick outbuildings, survivors of a self-sufficient economy, which in those days still clustered round the house. He was given the freedom of the orchards and kitchen garden and nothing was said when he was found smoking behind the raspberry canes. The River Bure ran through the grounds and Philip taught Christopher how to fish, just as he had Phil, Samuel and Martin.

Although the younger children looked forward to going there, the visit was something of an ordeal. Maria Pasqua remained beautiful, and this they took for granted and never spoke about. She was also just a little formidable in the sense that she expected a high standard of good manners. She felt soft to touch but kissed them remotely almost as if they came from another planet. Her Italian was long lost. She spoke English in a clear voice with a slight French accent and would sometimes slip into French when talking to their mother. Samuel was handsome, with a bluff, downright manner which concealed his shyness and they were frightened of him.

At lunch in the panelled dining room conversation was subdued. They were expected to sit up straight, to eat everything on their plate and afterwards the two younger children were accompanied up the oak staircase by a maid and told to rest on beds prepared for them. In the shadows on the sides of the staircase were photographs of their grandmother's portraits painted in Paris when she was a little girl not much older than they were. Of this they had no imaginative realization. They were more interested in themselves than in their grandmother. It was the moment that counted, the maid, the stairs, the conversation drifting up from the hall below. Glad to be together, but hating their banishment, they lay in silence, watching the wasps slowly crawl up the window-pane and waiting for the frenzied barking from the kennels as feeding time for their uncle's hounds grew nearer.

Edda did not often join them. He preferred to walk there by himself. He would begin by taking the cliff path or go along the beach according to the state of the tide and eventually turn inwards towards Aylsham and the great sweep of the flat fields and wide skies. Sometimes he would arrive unexpectedly when Philip was out and would be shown into the drawing room where Maria Pasqua would give him a glass of dark, nutty sherry and put on the gramophone. If Philip came in he would ask Edda what he was writing and try to remain attentive to what he could not understand.

Watkin was in fact very busy indeed.

Some people have looked back on the Catholic literary and religious revival of the nineteen twenties and thirties of the last century as a golden age. Others have gone to the opposite extreme and regarded its achievements as the ephemeral products of a small, almost incestuous, rather snobbish group of ultramontanes with Fascist leanings. It is true that most of the moving spirits behind this revival were upper class and knew each other. Granted the more rigid social structures of the time and the small size of the educated Catholic community, this was natural enough. It is absurd to call people snobbish because they enjoy the company of those they have been brought up with and whose interests they share. In his *A Spiritual Aeneid* Ronald Knox lists some of arguments he brought forward then both for and against going over to Rome. He had reminded himself that although his fellow priests would not be married, on the other hand they would be very much more vulgar. This was true. It is also true that this period has been overshadowed by the brilliance of Chesterton and Belloc who, in their different ways, like Ronald Knox, on the surface suggested a kind of Catholicism that has not stood the test of time. One day Knox would recognize this himself.

In June 1928, Algar Thorold wrote a letter to Watkin about his rather critical review of Knox's *The Belief of Catholics* with which he agreed. Thorold refers to a m/s note of von Hügel's which runs: "Nothing to be got by cleverness – Knox and Chesterton." Yet, Thorold continues, he fancies that Knox is better than his intellectual attitude would lead one to suppose. "The truth is that [Knox] is a morbidly shy man and has constructed an impenetrable mask of epigrams and sophistry through which to look at the world. If people like that sort of thing and if it is likely to help them save their souls, why let them have it!"

Perhaps it was Frank and Maisie Sheed's over-estimation of Chesterton as a Roman Catholic apologist that led their son, Wilfred Sheed in his *A Memoir With Parents* to dismiss Chesterton as a serious thinker. It is true, however, that Chesterton the poet, the author of *Ubi Ecclesia* and *Holy of Holies*, the novelist, the critic, the artist, is in a different class from the Catholic controversialist who imagined he had freed himself from Anglican ambiguities forever and fought street battles with Dean Inge about the wickedness of divorce and the horror of birth control.

The majority of the writers who contributed to this Catholic renaissance were, like the bishops, ultramontanes, in the sense that they accepted the centralization of the Church, and had an almost automatic respect for the Pope and the decrees of the Roman Curia. Watkin was convinced that there were as many different approaches to authority as there were other ways of understanding scripture and dogma. In this he was in a minority, but by no means alone. In his autobiography Bede Griffiths pays tribute to both Watkin and Dawson: Watkin for enabling him to see the possibilities of a synthesis between science and philosophy, Dawson for enlarging his knowledge and helping him to understand the relationship of Christianity to other cultures. He often thinks of Watkin, he wrote from India in 1984, and realizes how much he owes to him. His books made an impression on him that he can never forget, they opened the way to a Catholic philosophy beyond the limits of Thomism.

In the nature of things, Catholicism, unlike Protestantism, cannot be insular although Catholics under pressure and in particular circumstances can be isolated. The revival of the twenties and thirties brought the work of writers like Maritain, Gilson, Péguy, Karl Adam and Peter Wust into the general stream of educated Catholic consciousness. This was largely the work of Frank Sheed and his wife Maisie to whom the entire revival owed an enormous debt.

Maisie was a granddaughter of W. G. Ward, "Ideal" Ward, and the daughter of Wilfred. Her mother was a niece of the Duke of Norfolk and in certain circles it was a matter of some surprise when in 1925 she married the Australian, Frank Sheed, the lawyer son of a Presbyterian Marxist of Irish extraction. Their very differences added to the richness of their marriage. In some ways Frank Sheed's approach to Catholicism was that of a lawyer. The Catholic religion was a logical, coherent system of creeds, sacraments, ethical rules revealed by God, the whole enclosed within the net of a single, visible, infallible Church, at its head a Pope who was prevented by the Holy Spirit from teaching error. It was this confidence that made the breakdown of the system after the Second Vatican Council, which he had at first so warmly embraced, not only painful, but profoundly perplexing. His faith, however, was more deeply rooted than his apologetics.

Sheed came from an unsophisticated background and, as he himself was to write later, like most Catholics then he "so innocently saw the Church and its prospects," not foreseeing the explosion of thirty years in the future. These years between the two world wars were to him a blissful Catholic summer unimaginable to what he called the "twilight Catholics" of the post-conciliar generation.[1]

Maisie, on the contrary, should have foreseen the explosion. Her father, Wilfred, in the words of his grandson, the novelist Wilfred Sheed, died of cancer and melancholy after the condemnation of Modernism by Pope St Pius X.[2] She knew the whole sorry story from inside and described it in her book *Insurrection Versus Resurrection,* whose uninviting title obscures a work of much interest and considerable ambivalence. Whatever the inconsistencies of hers and her father's position at this most difficult period, of one thing Maisie was certain. In her own words "the Catholic mind had lost touch with its own depth." This was well said. She also believed that it was simply untrue that no Catholic could continue to think and remain in the Church. That, however, depended on *what* they were thinking.

In September 1911, Lord Hugh Cecil (Lord Quickswood) wrote an interesting letter to Wilfred Ward. "I dispute with you," he said, "because I think it very important that Roman Catholics should realize the fate that is fast overtaking them. They live emphatically in a fool's paradise . . . " Earlier in that same letter he had written that Modernism and its derivatives "are an amalgam of truth and falsehood, which is of all things the most formidable type of onslaught – the lie that is half a truth. The blunt contradiction, the rigid suppression, and the general campaign against independence of thought which are the weapons of ultramontanism, are utterly useless in such a conflict . . . Fr Parsons and the Duke of Alva are equally out of date. The consequence is a failure on the part of Rome quite as extensive as at the original reformation and . . . even more fundamental and penetrating."[3]

In 1926 Frank and Maisie threw themselves heart and soul into forming and extending the Catholic Evidence Guild, an idea first thought of by the New Zealander, Vernon Charles Redwood in 1919, who was impatient with the absurd notions of Roman Catholicism prevalent in England at the time. Well-instructed lay men and women should go into the market place, explain the Faith as it really was and be ready to answer objections. Such a venture suited Frank Sheed's temperament and legal background and Maisie's enthusiasm and organizing ability. After a considerable period of training and testing, the volunteers were sent out not to London alone but to many other cities. The soap-box was little more than a step-ladder with a sloping top and a crucifix mounted on a short pole. The London market place was Hyde Park Corner, Hampstead Heath or a care-fully selected site in some busy street.

Philip Fowke was a volunteer and eventually Secretary of the Guild. Helena would have died rather than speak in public but she accompanied him at his first talk at Hyde Park Corner to give him moral support. The object was to gather a crowd, to be provocative, invite heckling, to stick to the outlines of the Catholic faith and know your stuff, question and answer fashion, from the existence of God to the robust certainties of death, judgement, hell and heaven, or more commonly, purgatory, limbo and indulgences. The attitude of the speakers towards Protestants was far from ecumenical. The Guild relished the story of an English monk who recognizing an Anglican clergyman "celebrating Mass" at Lourdes threw him bodily off the altar.[4] The CEG, as it was known, plainly then was not an approach which suited everyone. Nevertheless it was brave and consci-entious and as long as the Catholic faith lasted in that form, did a considerable amount of good.

That same year Frank and Maisie founded their publishing firm, Sheed and Ward. The "Ward" was originally intended to be Maisie's brother, Leo, but he became a priest and she took his place. This may have been fortunate, Leo was not cut out to be a successful publisher. Eventually he became a missionary in Japan and died on his way back to England in the dark days of 1941. An old friend of Edda and Helena, he admired Watkin's first book, *Some Thoughts on Catholic Apologetics*, and was extremely keen on the *Philosophy of Mysticism* which he passed on to Frank and Maisie who were even more enthusiastic and had plans to reissue the remaindered copies. These hopes were dashed by the severity of the Censor's report. Leo thought this proof that Watkin was called to do great work for the glory of God.

Sheed's choice of Tom Burns as his first manager and right-hand man was inspired. Until he began to have doubts about the value of that approach, Burns had been a frequent speaker for the Catholic Evidence Guild, an apostolate he kept to himself, as something quite apart from his job in the City and his exceedingly active social life. He had had no actual experience of publishing but knew a fair amount about it and cherished a connection with that world through his great-uncle, James Burns, an Anglican publisher who had followed his friend Newman into the Church. As a result he lost his livelihood but Newman gave him the copyright of his novel *Loss and Gain* together with some other works and he set up on his own under the imprint of Burns, Oates and Washbourne, which at some time acquired the double-edged distinction of being designated "Publishers to the Holy See". Tom hunted down promising authors, he was convivial, energetic, and a conscientious editor who managed the production and publicity as well.

Watkin was a maddening contributor to any paper or publishing house. He tended to write at greater length than required and would make extensive and costly changes to his text when it was already in proof. His handwriting was almost illegible which meant that his work had to be sent out to an expensive typist. Eventually he got a machine of his own and managed to type by using both index fingers to jab very hard and very slowly on the keys. This he did to the accompaniment of a low, moaning sound rather like that made by a solitary tiger roaming the jungle. Owing to the force of his fingers, the paper was punctured by holes at each full stop. The lines somehow jumped all over the page, the words ran into each other or split apart, capitals and lower-case letters got jumbled up while the whole was covered with innumerable corrections marked from A to Z in an almost indecipherable hand. An exasperated member of the staff at Sheed and Ward who did not like him anyway and thought that Sheed vastly over estimated his authors, complained that Watkin once submitted a reader's report which he had typed out without noticing that there was no ribbon in the machine. This Watkin had sent in with an accompaning letter suggesting that since there were indentations on the paper, the report could be easily read if held up to the light.

Eventually the machine was abandoned and Watkin reverted to his fountain pen. His contributions to the *Downside Review* would then arrive written on scrap paper, scattered with insertions and qualifications, the lines crossed like a Victorian letter. However one of its patient editors, Dom Daniel Rees, remarked that despite appearances, they were the most careful, courteous and discerning of all the reviews he received and revealed a most intimate and detailed knowledge of the whole sweep of the history of Christian spirituality.

Tom Burns hunted down authors not solely for the sake of his employer's list but for himself. An ardent Catholic, he was yet a seeker, one who was unhappy with certain aspects of the presentation of Catholicism in England. In his own words at that time he looked on the Church "as almost an obstacle to faith" and was thoroughly disenchanted with many of its outward aspects.[5] He was in his mid-twenties and Watkin came into his life at what he called "a providential moment."

When Watkin walked into Sheed and Ward carrying a carpet bag full of books Tom knew at once that he was no ordinary person. He walked on his toes, negotiating the space between them by tacking backwards and forwards in a strange manner and even when at rest, emphasizing the points he was making with movements of his arms, legs, hands and feet, while his sky blue eyes "would shine or darken with his thought and sparkle with his cackling laughter."

To some of Sheed's staff Watkin was felt to be a great nuisance, to others a figure of fun. With a mixture of alarm and amusement they would describe the extraordinary way he crossed the busy road outside the office. Shrugging off any assistance, he would run a little way to the left, start to cross, draw back, then run a little way to the right, draw back, look both ways and make a dash for it.

Once when he was walking up Ludgate Hill towards St Paul's with the writer and translator Jimmy Oliver, one of his shoes fell off. He was talking so vehemently that he did not notice and Oliver, then a young man, did not like to draw attention to such a trifle. After a time, however, he thought that matters could not go on as they were, nervously pointed out what was amiss and suggested that they turned back. Still talking, Watkin did so, reached the shoe, slipped his foot in into it and without interruption continued his reflections on the massive simplicity of St Augustine. It was neither his absent-mindedness nor his learning that endeared him to Oliver but his transparent nature and total lack of pretension.

To Tom Burns he provided the detachment that he badly needed. Tom wanted someone to point out that much that he felt was wrong with the Church was not of its essence but the consequence of abuses which could be corrected. Watkin summed it all up under the single name "ecclesiastical materialism" and freed Tom from what until then he had thought was an obligatory outlook.

In May 1928, while still working at Sheed and Ward, Burns published the first number of a review he called *Order*. At its masthead was a quotation from Aquinas: "those are called wise who put things in their right order and control them well." The poet and artist David Jones designed and cut a wood engraving for the cover – a unicorn prancing in an enclosed garden.

David Jones was Dawson's great friend and one would have thought he would have been Watkin's too. This was not the case. The words and rubric of the Mass were to weave in and out of David Jones's two great poems and both he and Watkin were devastated by its dismantling after the Second Vatican Council. But much as Watkin was in sympathy with Jones's approach, like his own rooted in the past, he disliked and therefore failed to appreciate the modernist movement in poetry. Poetry may not, frequently should not, be understood immediately, but it ought not to be so obscured by a private vision that the reader has to struggle with footnotes to grasp what the writer means.

Dawson once brought David Jones to St Mary's. They had tea outside, for some reason by the bee hives in the patch of ground close to the lane that led to the sea. Watkin was a little withdrawn, frightened perhaps that he was expected to comment on their visitor's work. Jones got on much better with Helena.

The artist's proofs of his original engraving on the cover of *Order*, signed and mounted, could be obtained from the Editor at the price of ten shillings and sixpence. All the contributors, except presumably David Jones, were anonymous. The periodical itself was published under a monomark address. To such mean measures had Catholicism been reduced.

As a frequent visitor to Tom's house in London where he met congenial people like Bernard Wall, later editor of *The Colosseum*, Alec Dru and Harman Grisewood, the son of his old friends Colonel and Mrs Grisewood from Oxford days, Watkin was concerned with the venture from its very beginnning and overflowed with ideas and advice. He could not, Tom wrote, sufficiently express his gratitude for all the help he had given. As a matter of course editors flatter their best contributors but in this case Burns was sincere. Watkin dared to say what others were thinking whether the establishment welcomed it or not.

The leading article was written by him and entitled unsurprisingly *Ecclesiastical Materialism*. Catholics, Watkin argued, frequently hear denunciations from the pulpit against the materialism of an age that sets a higher value on the needs of the body than the welfare of the soul. But why are the faithful never warned against its more insidious counterpart, the ecclesiastical materialism which in practice values the body, the visible, institutional Church, more than its soul, the invisible communion of all souls in a state of grace, as if the soul existed for the sake of the institutional Church and not the other way about? Of course, since the Catholic Church is not Erastian, this is never professed as doctrine but it is revealed by value judgements and general attitudes.

It would not be too much to say, Watkin maintained, that apart from the vices of individuals, every abuse which has stained the face of Church history is an example of ecclesiastical materialism. The medieval Church trusted in the arm of the state to compel an exterior conformity. It could not compel interior assent with the result that when the state exchanged the role of protector to that of persecutor, a large part of the Church collapsed like a pack of cards. We owe the survival of Catholicism in England today not to the materialism which issued papal bulls and launched invasions, but to the faith of the martyrs whose sole weapon was prayer, preaching and suffering.

Only too often the Kingdom of God, the invisible Communion of

Saints, is treated as simply identical with external advancement. Success is measured by the number of converts, particularly the rich and powerful; concordats favourable to the status of the clergy in various countries necessarily regarded as a triumph for God's cause; fear of scandal results in historical window-dressing in which in the cause of exterior seemliness, *suppressio veri* amounts to *suggestio falsi.*

When English Catholics go on sniping at Anglicans and lamenting the doctrinal shortcomings of Protestantism and overlook the devotion and self-sacrificing goodness which marks so many Protestants, and indicates a living membership of Christ that no intellectual error can destroy, we are guilty of ecclesiastical materialism. Those who think like that in fact set a higher value on the body of the Church to which Protestants do not belong, than the soul to which they do.

Watkin's hard-hitting piece was written with a tumbling release of thoughts, at last enabled to be freely expressed. He was later to develop his theme with more discrimination and sobriety in his book *The Catholic Centre.* Dawson wrote to say that he expected daily to hear that his friend had been excommunicated.

Watkin's article was followed by a piece written by Eric Gill called Repository Art, an article on modern methods of religious education, some book reviews and finally Burn's *bête noire,* the contemporary Catholic press, in particular *The Tablet,* a paper which in time he would come to edit himself.

Order, to quote Tom, "had a bombshell effect." Ronnie Knox, Catholic chaplain to the undergraduates at Oxford, advised his flock not to read it. Perhaps he felt the advancing shadow of that destructive spirit which had undermined his faith in Anglicanism. The first number sold two thousand copies in two weeks, a success which proved costly because only five hundred copies were printed originally and the broken-up type had to be re-set and a new edition prepared. Dawson wrote articles in the following three numbers, one of these on the psychology of sex. His first contribution was entitled *Civilization and Order,* an essay which encapsulates in a short space his central argument that behind every great civilization there exists a spiritual order. He developed this theme in his seminal book *Progress and Religion,* to be published by Sheed a year later.

Burns closed his review down after only four numbers. His reasons are not altogether plain. Perhaps he was uncertain whether the unicorn had muddied the waters or cleansed them. He may have thought that Sheed and Ward's next venture would achieve his ends in a different, less provocative and ephemeral way. This was to launch and edit together with Dawson an excellent series of short books called *Essays in Order.* The intention was to widen English Catholic consciousness by introducing readers to contemporary European thought and the new generation of English Catholic writers. Dawson suggested the contributors, Burns hunted them down, saw to the contracts and acted as travelling salesman. David Jones engraved another unicorn rampant for the covers and inside each copy was a quotation Jones had found from John of Hesse, a priest who had written his account of a pilgrimage to Jerusalem at the end of the fifteenth century. The allegory expresses much of what those writers and artists who were involved in the Catholic renaissance were trying to achieve:

> Near the fields of Helyon there is a river called Marah, the water of which is very bitter, into which Moses struck his staff and made the water sweet, so that the Children of Israel might drink. And even in our times, it is said, venomous animals poison this water after the setting of the sun, so that the good animals cannot drink of it. But in the morning, comes the Unicorn and dips his horn into the stream, driving the poison from it so that the good animals can drink there during the day.

The series included writers like Maritain, Berdyaev, von Hildebrand and Ida Coudenhove; Watkin translated and wrote the Introduction to *Crisis in the West* by Peter Wust who became a lifelong friend. Herbert Read and Dawson wrote books specially for the series as did Watkin, who called his *The Bow in the Clouds* from the chapter in Genesis where God makes a covenant with Noah after the Flood: "Behold I will set my bow in the clouds . . . "

This "profound and beautiful essay", as Evelyn Underhill referred to it in the *Spectator,* was well received and the most popular of Watkin's philosophical books. A revised edition was published by Sheed and Ward in 1954. No *Imprimatur* was applied for but only the *Clergy Review* questioned its orthodoxy.

Its subject matter is metaphysics, that is the nature of ultimate reality as experienced by man. The modern rejection of metaphysics has produced an intellectual anarchy which leaves society without a principle of unification; until it finds one, it will disintegrate as surely as the body when its life principle has departed. Philosophy, for Watkin, was clarified commonsense. "A re-assertion of the metaphysical order of being, " he wrote, "is the most urgent need of the present day. On that order depends, in the last resort, the entire order of human life, theological and practical, individual and social."

Watkin argues that this metaphysical order is revealed in the varieties of human experience and that human experience itself is integrated by that order. Man is not merely the highest achievement of biological life, King of the Animals, nor is the human spirit just a shadow or by-product of physical life. The true order of being is exactly the reverse.

Watkin's subtitle is "an essay towards the integration of experience". In other words, an attempt to make sense of human experience, to examine the truth, meaning, and therefore the value of what we see, feel and know of the mysterious world we live in. "What is matter? We do not know. Or life? Another cloud. Closer still – our own nature. What is the soul? How is it united to the body? Clouds. And above us – God is hidden in the 'cloud of unknowing'." Like the Lady of Shalott, we are half sick of shadows. Watkin is as full of "eager thoughts" as Wordsworth was on the night he climbed Snowdon.

This world is beautiful and full of good things, but since we are spirits we crave a sure knowledge of truth, a permanent, satisfying good. However, not all is dark. In the same way as the rainbow refracts the light of the sun, God's presence in the world does in fact manifest itself through the obscurity of our human experience.

Watkin follows this theme throughout his short book. Each chapter is given a colour of the rainbow starting from ultra-violet, imperceptible to the human eye, which Watkin uses as a symbol of elementary matter whose effects are known but of whose nature we are ignorant. Violet, the first visible colour, illustrates the most obvious ordering of experience, the positive sciences; blue stands for metaphysics, its nature and scope, an important essay which sustains his whole argument. Green represents biological life; yellow, a blend of the green of nature; and the red of religion represents art which occupies the frontier between biological and spiritual life.

Watkin's choice of orange, a blend of yellow and red, as a symbol for sex caused a little disquiet in some quarters for its outspokeness. He has placed it above art and below the red that represents supernatural love. Sex is not simply the culmination of biological life. Whether recognized or not, at its best it aspires beyond the biological level towards the highest plane of spirit, like a flame which, fed on the fuel of earth, rises towards the sky. Moreover, it is the best reflection, on the natural plane, of the spiritual union and fecundity in which the spiritual life culminates. While the Victorians lied about sex and pretended that it did not exist, the pendulum has swung in the opposite direction and sex now absorbs all other values. There is no department of human life where commonsense and a sane application of metaphysical principles is so necessary.

Watkin did not of course, like the artist Stanley Spencer, consider sex to be the essence of religion. He did argue, however, that after religious, sexual experience is undoubtedly the most intense and most ecstatic of all forms of human experience. History has shown us that a strong suscepti- bility to sex indicates a very favourable predisposition to mystical spirituality. Moreover, the psychological experiences which accompany sex show a remarkable correspondence with those which accompany mystical prayer. The Freudians therefore maintain that sex is the substance, religion the shadow, that the union of the spirit with God as described by the mystics is but a projection of unsatisfied sexuality on to another plane. To accept this, Watkin points out, would be to surrender his entire thesis. There is but one soul in man, one psychical energy that is the substratum and matter of all its activities. The difference lies in the purpose for which this energy is employed. Religion, like any other form of activity, will simply give that energy a particular direction and mode. Thus the spiritual activity of the soul in prayer differs from its biological activity in sex not by its matter, the vital energy employed, but the form imposed upon it. Sexual union, the biological shadow of the spiritual and mystical union of mystical prayer, reflects that union but is simply a reflection, a shadow, not the other way about. The illusion lies not with those who regard spiritual union with God as humanity's highest, noblest and truest life but with those for whom biological life is the sole reality and its sexual flower the highest good. D. H. Lawrence was a man of profound religious capacity and need, his tragedy the vain attempt to find the substance in the shadow, the light in its reflection.

Orange is followed by a discussion about religion, represented by red and finally by ultra-red, which Watkin wanted to call infra-red but was overruled by Sheed. Infra-red represents mysticism. This, Watkin says, is no odd, accidental ornament of religion, a rare, quasi-miraculous gift like prophecy or healing. It is deplorable that mysticism is widely regarded with suspicion as something with which ordinary people should have no concern. On the contrary, it is organically connected with our normal supernatural life, that is God's own life in the soul, usually called sanctifying grace. If the beatific vision of God is the flower, mystical prayer, that is the conscious or unconscious intuition of God present and active in the soul (by no means confined to Christians), is its bud here and now on earth.

Watkin started his journey up the ladder of human experience from the lowest rung to the highest, from the ultra-violet of primal energy about whose nature science can tell us nothing but whose effects are harnessed for our purposes, to infra-red where the visible red passes into the invisible, experienced also only in its effects. This is because the knowledge of God expressed in conceptual theology passes into mystical apprehension beyond image and beyond concept. We know *that* God is, not *what* he is. "Thought fails in adoration and adoration is dumb."

The Bow in the Clouds is far more important than its length suggests. It was, as it were, the blueprint for Watkin's most valuable work, *A Philosophy of Form*, to be published some time later.

Almost ten years after the great row that led to his expulsion from Loudwater, Edda and his mother met again. How this happened, and by whose agency the reconciliation was achieved, we do not know. Christopher had accompanied his father on the failed peace mission of 1921 as a pledge of Ingram immortality. Now he was twelve and in 1930 an invitation to stay in London with his grandmother was accepted. Edda took him there but what mother and son said to each other is not recorded.

We do know, from Christopher's account, that the London visit was a great success. Sam Heakes, he remembered, behaved like a warm-hearted child. His mouth was full of gold teeth and he smoked through a telescopic cigarette holder. On a sideboard Emmeline kept a crystal ball covered with a black velvet cloth. Both of them consulted it regularly. Sharp was no more but Christopher travelled about London in his grandmother's or Aunt Sissie's chauffeur driven cars, was allowed to buy, within reason, what he pleased at Harrods and taken to the coast to visit the surviving Ingram brother, Charles. He enjoyed it all enormously and hoped it would last forever. In her turn, Emmeline wrote to say that Paul, as she continued to call him, was a very good companion and enclosed a term's fees for his prep school. The grandson could achieve what his father could or would not, and time was short.

In March 1930 Emmeline and Sam set out once more for America. From Boston she sent another cheque for Christopher's school fees together with £50 for the coal bill at St Mary's out of which Edda was to buy a new suit. From New York she sends love to all, together with a pair of socks for Edda and kisses to the children. She and Sam had had a glimpse of the Graf Zeppelin, it looked like a large white sausage though some people said it reminded them of the Madonna. Sam had seen Paul's face in their crystal ball and his grandmother wrote to tell him that she would pay for his riding lessons for three months. From Quebec she tells Edda that she is selling Sam's house for him and intends to join him at Aurora, Toronto, to see his sister who was married to a clergyman there. One wonders what they made of her. Soon she will be home and introduced to her grandchildren, "they may not like me, but I shall only laugh whether they take a fancy to me or not."

This sad sentence comes from the last extant letter from Emmeline. The children had no chance to take a fancy to her because they never met. Almost immediately on the return from North America, Emmeline and Edda quarrelled again. The following year he wrote her a letter telling her that she was mistaken if she imagined that her money would buy her a front seat in heaven. Helena implored him not to send it but he rushed out and posted it in the box not far from the house. Between the posting and its collection he became calmer and Helena suggested that he might ask the postman to return it to him on the pretext that it was wrongly addressed. Perpetua, now eleven, was eager to go with him. Together they waited in the road, Edda muttering wildly and in the distance, the screech of geese from the Common. At last the postman arrived, opened the box and despite Perpetua's pleas and Watkin's increasingly violent expostulations, stoutly refused to surrender His Majesty's Mail. Emmeline wrote her final will in 1932 and in 1933 set off with Sam to live on the Island of St Helena. The children understood there was nothing left now but the workhouse.

CHAPTER FIFTEEN

Kicking Into Touch

Although Elie Halévy rejected both the Judaism and Christianity of his forebears and became an agnostic, he had a keen interest in religion and appreciation of its force. The problem which interested him more than any other was the relative importance of the part played by material and spiritual forces in shaping British society. The emphasis on the power of religion, but not its truth, led him to formulate the famous Halévy thesis, namely that the influence of dissenting Protestant preachers helped to save industrial England from the revolution predicted by Marx.

Philip Shepheard celebrated his ninety-fourth birthday with a shooting party. After that he gradually faded away and died early in the morning on the last day of December 1932. He was buried with his family in the churchyard at Erpingham, a village close to Aylsham, not far from the house where he was born. Edda and Helena went to the funeral and Christopher was the cross-bearer. As they stood at the bottom of the stairs at Abbots Hall and watched the coffin slowly carried down, he looked across at his grandmother. Her expression was enigmatic. After the funeral she told Helena that she wished never to see her again.

Of all the things which had happened and were to happen to Helena, Maria Pasqua's rejection was the most painful. It came as a terrible shock. From childhood she had shared her mother's dreams about her return to Italy, the land of warmth and light, singing and laughter, of mountains and wild places, of vineyards and orchards where apricots and peaches grew. Together they had banded against her father and his stuffy ways, together pored over patterns from Paris, laughed at the old-fashioned Norwich shops and the sensible shoes from Stead and Simpson. Now *le vieux*, as she called her husband, was dead; *la déliverance* had come but the bird was too crippled to fly.

Philip's death, Helena thought, had unhinged her mother's mind. It was not until she heard about the provisions of her father's will that she slowly began to grasp something, but never all, of what must have happened behind the scenes. By co-incidence Philip Shepheard wrote his final will in May 1932, one month before Emmeline wrote hers. The contents of Emmeline's will were of course as yet unknown, but the provisions of Philip's soon came to light. It may be that after Phil was killed, thinking that Helena had married a rich man, he had once left the entire estate to Samuel in trust during Maria Pasqua's lifetime. When, however, it became evident that Edda's expecations from Emmeline were in doubt he altered his will without telling Samuel. He wished to do what was best for his daughter and her children. He therefore left the property in trust, equally between Samuel and Helena, the amount in the trust to be decided by its value at the time of his death. It would not be much. The times were bad. He had been told that value of land was as low as £25 an acre. Pasqua, as he always called her, would have the income of the trust during her life and the contents of the house absolutely. On Helena's death the capital in her share of the trust would be divided among her children.

Samuel thought the provisions of his father's will outrageous. He had been born at Abbots Hall and expected to die there. His whole life was bound up with his old home. To remain there, he and his mother would have to sell some of the more valuable contents of the house, a few cottages and part of the land itself. And all to pay Helena what was his by natural right. She was the cause of it all, a grasping woman who must have come over whining to their father about a foolish husband, a tyrannical mother-in-law and five children with mouths to feed.

So it was that he worked upon Maria Pasqua and dissolved those ties of love and longing that had bound mother and daughter together for over fifty years. Helena went over to Abbots Hall and rang the bell. The house parlourmaid came to the door and refused her admittance. If it had been us, her children told her, we would have got in through a window. But Helena would only shake her head.

Although the children grieved for their mother's sadness, in fact their exclusion from Abbots Hall came as no particular surprise. All of them, from the oldest to the youngest, walked not gently but warily through the minefield that was their world. Only two of them would ever see Maria Pasqua again. Samuel drove over frequently to visit his sister and the three eldest children used to bicycle across country to join the meet of the Bure Valley Otter Hounds of which their uncle was Master. Nothing was ever said about money but every Christmas he would come to St Mary's and give them ten shillings each from their grandmother, which they thought a fortune He now wore a monocle and was a wonderful subject for imitation. But the pheasant and partridge which in season used to be sent so regularly by their grandfather ceased altogether.

They did not, as they feared, have to go to the workhouse but their lives were an odd mixture of poverty and riches. They had a nanny, they had local servants to cook and clean, their mother continued to receive catalogues from Marshall and Snelgrove, the Army and Navy and Swan and Edgar, but her only extravagence was French coffee which arrived in a tall striped tin from Harrods. Until it wore down completely, their father used a shaving brush encased in silver inscribed with the family crest, and took cuff-links and collar studs from leather covered boxes with crested silver shields set in the lids.

Once the children found his old top hat in the hall cupboard. They seized on it joyfully and after trying it on and making faces asked their father if they could play with it in the garden where they kicked it about like a football. Hearing excited shouts, he came out to join them and after many vain attempts to make contact eventually kicked it into a flower bed. He cared nothing for the trappings of his past. All he wanted was a measure of financial security, enough to live on so that he could continue writing and support his family.

When the Birmingham doctor who had helped Christopher into the world came to say goodbye to Helena before she left for Loudwater after the war, he told her that the boy ought to be brought up like a cabbage. This was wise, useless advice; it applied to all the children and most of all to Watkin himself. A great many of his troubles were caused by the peculiarities of his temperament. His mind moved so fast and was rarely at rest. From whatever cause, nervous anxiety was part of his nature. He almost never referred to his childhood unless asked directly but in old age he wrote to one of his children that the shock he must have had at the outset of his life, "a mother's love replaced with life with my grandmother, in effect by a nurse chosen by her, though *later* mother did love me", had made him subject to fears that the state of the world had fostered.

It was not only the state of the world, it was the constant struggle to make ends meet. The more violently agitated he became over his mother, the bank manager, the stupidity of the clergy and all the ideas flooding into his brain which he wished to get down on paper at once, the more tired and ill Helena became. Only on winter nights did they hear the sound of the sea. Instead the children would fall asleep to the rising and falling of their father's voice – Mussolini, his wicked mother, the bishops, Abyssinia, eternal punishment, Soviet Russia, Germany and another war which would annihilate them all. This they thought very likely. Their mother suffered from asthma and frequent bronchitis, and spent much time in bed. It was her way of coping with an impossible situation but Dr Sumpter was not cheap.

In the kind of house they were both used to, Edda and Helena would have had separate bedrooms. This was impossible at St Mary's. Watkin would get so agitated that he would stamp violently on the floor. When one of his children was very young and still sharing the night nursery with

Nanny, something happened that she never forgot. Half-asleep, from next door she heard shouting and turned over in bed. Then there was a tap on the door, it opened and the gas light from the landing showed her mother standing there. She was in her nightdress.

"Hetty," she said in a voice quite unlike her usual manner, "Hetty. I cannot bear it." Hetty turned on her elbow and reached out to light the candle. "O, Madam," she said. "Sit down." The child put the bedclothes over her head, heard no more and at the time told nobody.

Education was not cheap either. Fortunately there was a small convent at Sheringham run by nuns belonging to what was then called the Institute of the Blessed Virgin Mary. The school was intended for children of the upper classes who for one reason or another were unsuited to usual boarding education. All the family, including Christopher, attended it in their early years. They went daily, walking there with Nanny at first, by themselves when they got older. At a later stage, a secular mistress wearing a cap and gown was introduced to teach the older children but the school was never academic nor, by Catholic standards, particularly strict.

When Christopher was born Emmeline wanted to put him down for Eton. Watkin was still in his Aloysian stage and prevented her. That was a good thing, because as Helena pointed out, there was no guarantee that the payments would be kept up. Watkin's objections were different. Eton, despite the personal holiness of its unfortunate founder, its dedication to Our Lady and the beauty of its chapel, was no longer Catholic. His future therefore still undecided, Christopher left the convent when he was eight and went to a small boys' preparatory school across the lane from St Mary's.

After the war Philip and Gladys Fowke returned home on leave from Korea. They had two children, Francis and Catherine. Edda was delighted to have Gladys back again, Helena dismayed to find how faded was her beautiful red hair. In 1928 she died at Sheringham after a miscarriage. Dr Sumpter was away, another doctor was summoned who, according to Helena, bungled the case and her death was unnecessary. Philip was inconsolable. He resigned from the Consular Service in order to be with the children in England and never married again. Of all Watkin's relations he was the most loyal and remained at his side when almost all but he had fled. He now undertook to pay Christopher's fees at Stonyhurst. Edda refused. He did not approve of Jesuit education. In the end, through Fowke's kindness, Christopher was sent to the Dominicans at Laxton, the only Catholic public school which did not have that detested organ of militarism – an Officers' Training Corps.

During all this time, in fact from the eve of the First World War until after the end of the Second, on top of all his other work, Watkin was gradually translating the seven volumes of Elie Halévy's *A History of the English People in the Nineteenth Century*. The first volume of the History,

England in 1815, was published in France 1912. By what chance, fortunate for both author and translator, it came into Watkin's hands we do not know, only that he was commissioned by Halévy's English publisher, Fisher Unwin, to undertake a work which was not to be actually published until 1924. We can only guess at the obstacles which prevented its publication for over ten years. What is certain is that during this time, despairing of his work ever seeing the light, Watkin threw his unfinished translation into the waste-paper basket. From there it was rescued by Helena who put it out of harm's way in the airing cupboard.

Halévy's father, Ludovic, was the playwright and novelist who together with Meilhac had written the libretti for Bizet's *Carmen* and for Offenbach's best known operettas. Although Elie Halévy rejected both the Judaism and Christianity of his forebears and became an agnostic, he had a keen interest in religion and appreciation of its force. The problem which interested him more than any other was the relative importance of the part played by material and spiritual forces in shaping British society. The emphasis on the power of religion, but not its truth, led him to formulate the famous Halévy thesis, namely that the influence of dissenting Protestant preachers helped to save industrial England from the revolution predicted by Marx.

To our eyes, the method of work was both laborious and amateur. Neither of them employed a secretary, both wrote handwritten letters about the numerous problems which arose from a book of such meticulous scholarship. Quotations from English sources translated by Halévy into French had to be traced by Watkin and quoted back again in the original English; newly researched information was integrated into the text and added by Watkin, who was paid £65 a volume. Halévy was exceedingly pleased with Watkin's work, delighted, he said, to have chanced upon such a translator. He was in for a surprise.

The History was not written in chronological order. The French edition of what was to be the fifth volume, *Imperialism and the Rise of Labour 1895-1905* arrived for translation in the autumn of 1927. However, Watkin wrote to its author that the pleasure with which he looked forward to his task was clouded by a difficulty. The book contained certain judgements on Christianity and Catholicism which he would have to translate while being in entire disagreement with them. He was, he wrote, referring to the implications of Halévy's remarks on the Catholic revival, especially in the Introduction.

What was in question was not solely the recent Catholic revival but the earlier nineteeth-century revival of Catholic forms of Christianity, both Roman and Anglican, in response to the decline of an Evangelical Protestantism which depended upon a literal acceptance of the Bible. Watkin agreed with Halévy that the revival had been accompanied by a far deeper movement of alienation from Christianity but he could not accept that "the Catholic revival is the euthanasia of the Christian religion and that the Catholic movement is a phenomenon of senile decay motivated by intellectual timidity and moral weariness."[1] Of course, as a liberal, he fully recognized Halévy's right to express his beliefs but he disliked very much even to appear to approve views so radically opposed to his deepest convictions. Would Halévy object to a translator's note expressly disclaiming any agreement with them?

This was typical Watkin but hardly the usual relationship between author and translator. Dawson had never heard of anyone doing this before, but did not see why not. Halévy behaved very well and replied from London almost at once. His tone is one of ironic detachment. He had no objection to Watkin disclaiming responsibility for certain passages in his book so long as they were not polemical. Watkin must belong to that most interesting sub-species of the Catholic church, the Liberal Catholic, to him "a living paradox, an unfathomable mystery."

Only part of Watkin's reply has been found, unfortunately too late to be included in their published correspondence. This is a pity, because even in its truncated form, it states his position, and the position of those few like him, very clearly. As for the practical matter between them, they are in agreement. Of *course* he had never thought of adding any polemical note. That would have amounted to using Halévy's book as a vehicle for ideas Halévy believed to be false, not to speak of the fact that any adequate discussion of the points Halévy raises would require pages of closely packed argument.

"I am not particularly fond of the title Liberal Catholic," he goes on. "It is so vague. However, if it means a Catholic who accepts the Liberal doctrine – hardly if ever carried out in any Catholic country – of perfect religious toleration, a really free church in a free state, I will not disclaim it. If further it means a Catholic who believes that Catholic truth is so vast that for its full intellectual statement it requires all the truth freely discovered by any branch of science, I would also call myself a Liberal Catholic. But only in the sense that St Thomas Aquinas is a typical Liberal Catholic."

"Only one point in your letter surprised me a little," Watkin went on, "your words ' the passages of my book which have *shocked* your orthodoxy.' The implication ascribes to me a state of feeling I do not possess. While profoundly disagreeing with the rationalist philosophy which is I gather your own, I am not blind to the number and weight of the arguments by which it is supported. For myself I believe it is based on too narrow an interpretation of the facts of human experience, too strictly confined to certain, no doubt more obvious, levels and aspects of that experience to be finally . . . " The rest of the letter is lost.[2]

Still in London, Halévy replied at once. The formula 'A free church in a free state' does not make for liberty if it means a church free from all kinds of state control but also free to control everything and everybody and free to define where the spiritual ends. "Catholicism does not make for liberty and that is why I remain an impenitent enemy of Catholicism." Watkin's position struck him as slightly absurd. His conscience allowed him to translate a book which would be actively instrumental in spreading the knowledge of it throughout the English-speaking world, yet he informs readers that parts of it hurt his conscience.

Watkin too answered by return of post. He had not made himself understood. What he objected to were but a few sentences in a book for which as a whole he had the greatest admiration and which would be of much value to the student of modern history. His position was not absurd. Had the History been wholly or even primarily concerned with religion, he would have declined to translate it. But there is nothing in Halévy's religious position with which any intelligent student is not already perfectly familiar. As a matter of personal self-respect all he wanted was to make it clear that Halévy's position was not his. It is neither possible nor desirable to suppress honest expressions of belief or disbelief. The remedy against error is to teach the truth. He had no fear of rationalist arguments, Halévy should have no fear of Catholic.

So far, so good. Watkin now came to a matter he clearly felt keenly about and which underlay all his remarks about toleration. He thought Halévy was in a false position. If he really believed in freedom and toler-ance how could he support a Government which had expelled most of the religious orders, both men and women, closed schools and prohibited members of religious orders from teaching? His tone becomes more excited. What was really painful about Halévy's letter was his plain avowal "that he did not believe in toleration or religious liberty. In England we have, *on the whole*, 'a free church in a free state' since no man is penalized for not being an Anglican. . . To me it is an elementary prin-ciple of liberty that all religions – Catholic, Protestant, Unitarian, also secularist bodies such as the Rationalist Association – have an intrinsic and inalienable right, prior to the state, to spread their creeds by all peace-able means, so long as no one is *compelled* to see or hear what offends his conscience." No adherent of any creed whatsoever, Watkin goes on, has the right to use force directly or indirectly to interfere with the religious convictions of an adult. It is because France has never accepted this prin-ciple and the English have that in France politics and religion are necessarily intermixed. He was, he had to admit, *shocked* to find Halévy defending intolerance. "Why are you afraid of the Catholic Church? You are so sure she is on her deathbed. Why violate a fundamental principle of liberty to hasten by murder the inevitable end?"

Halévy wrote a short letter from France in reply. What induced Watkin to think that he did not believe in toleration or religious liberty? In any case, he goes on to explain that Watkin has misunderstood the state of affairs in France. A more worldly man would have let the matter drop. But Watkin was not called 'Slogger' for nothing. The fact remained, he answered, in France members of religious orders are "legally deprived of the intrinsic right of men and women to live together and practise any mode of life which does not interfere with the liberty of others." He concluded that Halévy did not accept absolute religious toleration and freedom of conscience when he objected to the formula 'A free Church in a free state' and expressed belief in state control of the church. He was glad he was not a French elector. If he voted for the Right he would be voting for an odious militarism, if for the Left, against religious liberty.

Halévy had now either to meet the challenge or refuse it on the justifiable plea of pressure of work. He met it in a letter of nearly ten pages. There was no state monopoly of teaching. Not all the religious orders were outlawed, only contemplative and teaching orders. He admitted that there was no plausible justification for this. It was passed in the throes of the Dreyfus Affair. For Halévy, the Dreyfus Affair was in fact a personal and sensitive issue. He had himself joined his brother Daniel Halévy, Proust, Jacques Bizet and others in getting signatures for the 'Petition of the Intellectuals' which demanded a revision of the case. Watkin, he went on, had called him a persecutor and enemy of liberty because he did not accept the formula 'a free church in a free state.' In Catholic countries that meant 'a free church in an unfree state', a very different thing from free *churches* within a free state, the situation in Protestant England.

So the correspondence continued, Watkin suggesting that Halévy hates the Church because his eyes are fixed on the wrong aspects of Catholicism, on its intolerance, occasional credulity, the behavour of the anti-Dreyfusards and so on. He himself judges it by Dante, Aquinas, Michelangelo and in our day by Solovyov and von Hügel. His History "is so splendid in its impartial treatment of historical parties and movements – only when I turn to the pages where you deal with Catholics and Irish (Catholics) I feel a different spirit, the spirit of that bitter warfare waged so long on the Continent between the secularist and the Catholic. It is against the war spirit that I plead as much when it appears in the field of thought as in the field of national rivalry." Halévy, Watkin ends, must not think he is saying this with any wish to be impertinent. "I think you would not have written to me at such length if you had objected to my expressing my feeling – very deep – on this subject."

Halévy answered that he never dreamed of calling or thinking Watkin impertinent. On the contrary, his letters interested him very much. "I find in them something candid, English (and if I may so so without offending you) un-Roman, which I like." Their discussion then turned to an examination of Pope Benedict's conduct during the last war about which Halévy disagreed with Watkin, before coming back to the matter in hand. Halévy had called Kipling the son of a *fonctionnaire* in India but, Watkin asked, wasn't he the son of an artist and curator of a museum?

Their collaboration proceeded smoothly and when in 1934 another difficulty arose, they were of one mind. Halévy had not been flattering about King Edward VII. When he came to the King's death, he made some observations about the number of Edward's mistresses. His publishers, now Ernest Benn, took fright and asked Watkin to omit the passages. Watkin refused so they were excised in London. Watkin restored them when he came to read the proofs and Halévy was pleased. They could do no more, it was a silent protest made by them both against censorship. As the thirties wore on and the international scene darkened, Halévy grew more and more despondent. While they were working on volume six, *The Rule of Democracy*, Hitler became Chancellor of Germany. "The future of Europe, our future," Halévy wrote, "is too gloomy for words." How long would Austria be able to resist the impact of Teutonic delirium?

Halévy died in 1937. He lived neither to see his country collapse before the Teutonic delirium nor to complete his great work. The issue that had started the entire correspondence was never mentioned again. Watkin took Halévy's advice and did not publish any personal disavowal of his statements about religion. However, in 1949, over ten years after Halévy's death when a revised and completed edition of the *History* came out, what he had wished to say all that time ago was said at last. "I must point out," he wrote in his Translator's Note, "in justice to my personal convictions, that I cannot accept M. Halévy's theological judgements. His religious standpoint is not mine. By descent and upbringing I belong to the Liberal tradition of freedom of which M. Halévy is the sympathetic historian, by religious belief to the Catholic 'Reaction' of which Newman was the outstanding English representative. Are they, I cannot refrain from asking myself, irreconcilable? Is a synthesis embracing what is true in both traditions impossible? Was not their mutual hostility the tragedy of the nineteenth century? However that may be, they are both confronted today by a common foe, the despotism of the totalitarian state. In opposition to its tyranny M. Halévy and myself would stand side by side."

CHAPTER SIXTEEN

The Mark of the Beast

Watkin detested totalitarianism, whether Fascist or Communist. Its claims, he wrote, amounted to the very deification of the state which had found expression as Caesar worship when Christianity first entered the world and was condemned by St John as worship of the Beast. The totalitarian state is the Beast, he wrote to a correspondent, "whether it is frankly atheist as in Russia or uses the holy things of God for its services as in Fascist Italy. To compromise with it as the Pope and the Italian hierarchy have done is to betray the cause of God to His worst enemies."

By descent and upbringing Watkin most certainly belonged to the Liberal tradition. His grandfather, Herbert Ingram, spent time, money and forethought in helping those less successful than himself as did Absalom Watkin and his son, Sir Edward. Four of Watkin's close relations stood as Liberal Members of Parliament. The days when Edda could give freely to the poor were long gone but not the impulse behind them. His undergraduate lament against "the merciless and inevitable operation of that modern Juggernaut, the industrial machine" remained unabated together, as he made plain to Halévy, with his passionate defence of the rights of the individual against what he judged to be the illegitimate demands of church or state. If the state ordered him to go to Mass, then it was his plain duty *not* to go. He denied the right of the state to compel people to fight in national wars or even to insist upon compulsory education which, in his opinion, sooner or later is used as an instrument to impose state ideology. In this he was proved right as state control of textbooks, teachers and syllabuses in Russia, Italy and Germany was to demonstrate. He believed, no doubt too optimistically, that if parents were prevented from using their children as wage earners and if education were completely free, there would be only a very small number of illiterates.

When the *New Statesman* reviewed Watkin's *The Philosophy of Mysticism*, it picked out a passage for especial praise. "The poverty of the East-end slum, " Watkin had remarked, "is not that of Nazareth or of the saints but an abomination to be abhorred by all good men." He considered that probably the balance between state tyranny on one hand and anarchy on the other was obtained better in nineteenth century England than in any other country, but that there was far too little governmental interference in the economic sphere where the strong were allowed to oppress the weak. This injustice had been, to an extent, redressed by the Liberal Party.

In 1924, therefore, he wrote to Augustine Birrell asking him to be President of the Sheringham Liberal Association. Birrell was now in his seventies and lived mostly in London. His reply was not encouraging. He was too old. Watkin persisted. No, Birrell replied, he did not wish to be an ornamental figurehead. It would be a hard job to get the dry bones to live in Norfolk. Watkin was undeterred and part of an address of his delivered to a political meeting at Sheringham during the General Election of 1929 survives. He did not in fact think very much of the Liberal Party as it actually existed but he had to fight for it all the same. It was, he reminded the electors, not merely an intermediate between Tory and Labour. It was the traditional party of free political thinking and a rallying point for anyone who wished to escape from the poisonous atmosphere of class warfare. The Tories were so bound by vested interest that it was impossible for them to reform the present system. Nor were the Labour Party free, entangled as it was with a Socialist doctrine which would in time reduce everyone to servants of the state. Freedom requires private property, private property limited by the good of society in the same way as personal freedom was limited.

It was all to no purpose. The dry bones could not live in Norfolk or anywhere else. As a united, identifiable political party, Liberalism was dead. As an influence it was indestructible as the failure both of old Toryism and Labour dogmatism has shown.

Watkin detested totalitarianism, whether Fascist or Communist. Its claims, he wrote, amounted to the very deification of the state which had found expression as Caesar worship when Christianity first entered the world and was condemned by St John as worship of the Beast. The totalitarian state is the Beast, he wrote to a correspondent, "whether it is frankly atheist as in Russia or uses the holy things of God for its services as in Fascist Italy. To compromise with it as the Pope and the Italian hierarchy have done is to betray the cause of God to His worst enemies."

As a younger man Watkin, like St Bonaventure, found it difficult to disagree with others about fundamental matters without becoming agitated and sometimes losing his temper. In later years he learnt to keep quiet and say nothing rather than make a scene, but the time was not yet.

The stubborn, dishonest, self-blinding of the left wing intelligentsia to the known horrors of the Stalinist regime infuriated him. The extent of Stalin's atrocities was not fully revealed until the archives were opened up after the collapse of Communism but quite enough was then known to expose the regime for what it was, a ruthless, murderous dictatorship which had already cost the lives of hundreds of thousands of innocent men and women. Yet people like H. G. Wells, Shaw and the Webbs trotted off to Russia and came back mouthing inanities. This psychological blindness remains to this day. People can be put in prison for denying the Holocaust but not for denying Russia's numerically even more dreadful crimes against humanity.

Hitler learned how to systematically exterminate people from Stalin, who was an extreme racist and anti-Semite. Persecution of the Jews most particularly agitated Watkin. Once, after a lunch at St Mary's at which the children were present, some Catholic visitors made persistent derogatory remarks about Jews. "Remember," he said to their discomfiture, "there's a Jew in the tabernacle." It seemed to him that anti-Semitism was a form of blasphemy and he pursued his argument with the disquieting logic which so irritated his opponents. If, as Catholic orthodoxy teaches, the Second Person of the Blessed Trinity, in virtue of his personal union with the human nature of Jesus, was born and was crucified, it follows that the second Person of the Blessed Trinity is a Jew. Did the Germans propose to expel the Divine Jew from their churches?

When Catherine was very young she said that she felt sorry for the devil because everyone was so nasty about him and to her parents' amusement asked if she could invite him to tea. She was quite sure that a little kindness would soften his heart. The years passed and then it happened that the daughter of an old friend of the family fell in love with a German SS officer and married him. He came to St Mary's and after he had left Watkin turned to Catherine and said "Now you *have* had the devil to tea."

He was later to suggest that the Pope should ask all German Catholics to wear the star of David. Didn't priests refer every day in their Mass to "our father Abraham", he would call out angrily to Helena. Ironically, in the last months of his life Pius XI was to make, not indeed the same suggestion, but precisely the same point. We know this because an exiled priest called Luigi Sturzo had the wit to publish the pope's speech in a Belgian newspaper.

In the nineteenth century the Papal States had been taken over by the secular powers and absorbed into the Kingdom of Italy. In 1870 Rome itself was lost. In his *Reminiscences,* Maisie Ward's father Wilfred, then studying for the priesthood, gives a vivid picture of life at the English College in Rome during the last years of Pope Pius IX. No Cardinal's carriages, he wrote, no public processions, the high altar of St Peter's completely disused, the Jesuits expelled from the Gesu, Piedmontese soldiers all over the place. While a dying Pope was shut up in the Apostolic Palace, the students made rude gestures at the carriage of King Victor Emmanuel as he drove by. They looked upon him simply as a brigand. Over forty years were to pass before in 1929, the Lateran Treaty and the Concordat with Mussolini settled the Roman Question for good and ill with the Pope retaining sovereignty over a state about the size of London's St James' Park.

The Pope's sovereignty is primarily spiritual but the spirit expresses itself through the flesh and the flesh is subject to the desires of mortal men. The problems brought to the surface by the disappearance of the historic states of the Church can never be satisfactorily resolved. The Pope must live somewhere and since he cannot be under the thumb of any secular power that somewhere must be an independent sovereign state. Probably, in the existing circumstances, the Lateran Treaties were the best compromise that could be obtained. The wings of both autocrats were clipped.

The treaties followed, in fact, the policies that Pope Pius X1 and his Secretary of State, Pacelli, had been pursuing in international affairs for many years. The papacy could allow democratic political parties either to develop naturally without unnecessary interference, it could attempt to control these parties, or it could influence events by itself negotiating directly with powerful rulers. Unfortunately for the future of Italy and in the event for almost the entire world, the course it chose was the last. It was concluded that the Church could gain far greater influence in public life from negotiating agreements with powerful governments than it could from supporting democratic parties whose very democracy rendered them less effective. This policy had caused the exile and even threatened the life of a man who was to become one of Watkin's most valued friends, Don Luigi Sturzo. In 1919 Sturzo had launched what has been described as one of the most interesting and most noble political experiments between the wars.

Sturzo was a Sicilian priest whose early life was devoted to active social and political work in southern Italy. At the end of the first war he launched his Partitio Popolari or Popular Party and was elected its General Secretary. No man was more loved by his supporters or more hated by the Fascist leaders. The party was non-confessional but inspired by Christian principles and represented Italian political Catholicism in much the same way as would the centre party in Germany. It stood for democracy, both central and local, agrarian reform, extension of the social services, disarmament and free enterprise directed along the lines indicated by Leo XIII's encyclical *Rerum Novarum*.

The programme appealed to the electorate and by 1921 the Popular Party had the largest number of deputies in the Senate after the Socialists. But Sturzo and his party stood between Mussolini and his ambitions. A moderate, democratic, centre party was doomed. The Duce was busy ingratiating himself with the Vatican, which was determined to play the game in its own way and get the best deal it could from the Fascists. After the Fascist march on Rome in 1922, under Vatican pressure, Sturzo resigned from the direction of the party, which was subsequently disbanded. In 1924 all priests were forbidden to belong to any political party. Catholic Action, a lay organization founded by Pius XI to apply Christian principles to community life, had to be confined to clerically dominated social and charitable organizations "outside every political party and in direct dependence upon the Church hierarchy for the dissemination of Catholic principles."[1] So was the natural opposition of democratic centre parties to dictatorship fatally weakened and the way cleared first for Mussolini and then for Hitler. The Duce boasted that he had bundled out Sturzo "neck and crop". In danger from the secret police and other Fascist toughs, Sturzo went into exile in London to be the not altogether welcome guest of the official Catholic community who came under pressure from Rome to force him to abjure active politics.

This "diminutive and dynamic" man as Tom Burns called him, did nothing of the sort. "I am convinced," Watkin wrote later to Sturzo, "that the totalitarian state is the most dangerous peril at present facing mankind." So Sturzo had long perceived. Like Watkin, he believed that Communism, together with Fascism, whether Italian or German, were all part of the same evil since they denied the freedom of the individual to act according to his conscience. He was to give the rest of his life to fighting the totalitarian state through his books on philosophy and sociology, his journalism, lectures and the network of free people he tried to establish throughout Europe.[2]

He was enabled to do this through the devotion and generosity of two friends of Watkin, Barbara Barclay Carter and Cicely Marshall, with whom he lived until he left for America in 1940. Barbara was a fluent Italian speaker, a novelist, a Dante scholar and the leading light of the Catholic feminist organization called St Joan's Social and Political Alliance which Edda persuaded a not very enthusiastic Helena to join. He found Barbara attractive, which indeed she was.

Watkin first met Sturzo at Miss Marshall's house in London in 1927 and wrote to her immediately afterwards from Aunt Sissie's flat in Thurlow Place to say he counted the meeting with Sturzo among the privileges of his life. "I have met men devoted to prayer and the love of God and usually found them either uninterested in the political and social improvement of mankind or definitely reactionary in their sympathies and again [I have met] liberals (in the wider sense of the term) full of zeal for the social service of man and for political liberty but indifferent if not hostile to religion." The combination of both activities in Don Sturzo was all the more welcome since it was embodied in such a remarkable and charming personality. "How well one understands Don Sturzo's hold over his party and how unspeakably tragic that a movement led by such a man has been destroyed by the brute violence of a Mussolini. If only the British public understood what it meant when Italy lost Don Sturzo and was subject to the Fascist regime instead."[3]

Few Catholics among whom Watkin moved were particularly interested in Sturzo. In 1930 Thorold turned down an article for the *Dublin* by Sturzo on Nationalism and Internationalism. He was a nationalist, he told Watkin, and had no sympathy with the League of Nations.

In the spring of 1930 Sturzo asked Watkin if he knew of any English Catholic beside himself who would like to take part in a "Societé Internationale de Culture" he was forming as a defence against dictatorship. The obvious person was Dawson. But Dawson did not in fact share Watkin's politics or his out and out denunciation of Mussolini and Fascism. By background and character he was as conservative as Watkin was liberal. His friend Dawson, Watkin replied to Sturzo, was just the man, he would give him Dawson's address but he feared that he was "not sufficiently democratic in his sympathies." This is by no means to suggest that Dawson supported Fascism in all its aspects. When he spoke at an international conference in Rome in 1932, he used the occasion to plead against racial hatred, an unwelcome subject for many of his listeners.

Yet in those days he was far more sympathetic to Fascism than Watkin. When in 1936 Watkin reviewed Dawson's *Religion and the Modern State* he defended his friend against the charge of Fascism and stated that the difference of opinion between them was one of emphasis. It was more than that. Dawson was not a man to stick his head over the parapet. For Watkin, the passionate liberal, political freedom was an indispensable condition of spiritual liberty.

Dawson's attitude was not unusual although opinions differed. The enlightened and civilized Bernard Wall was also at first tepid in his opposition to Fascism. Like some other Catholics, he still had faith in Mussolini's so-called corporatism, that is mixed unions of employers and workers which in reality served to bring labour under the control of the state. Barbara Barclay Carter, who saw Fascists under every bed, complained bitterly that both the Dominican periodical *Blackfriars* and the *Catholic Herald* were Fascist and pointed out that Dawson's disciple, Jimmy Oliver, had used Bernard Wall's *Colosseum* to argue that Fascism, French Royalism and Nazism were simply "a return to morality."[4] In the year Sturzo fled to London, Belloc met Mussolini and commended him along the lines that he stood for order and a punctual railway network. Chesterton's reaction, although more nuanced, was favourable for more or less the same reasons. Most British Catholic writers between the wars admired certain aspects of Italian and even German Fascism, at any rate their opposition was muted.[5] The reasons are obvious and partly psychological. In contrast to the Church of England, Catholicism was itself an

The Mark of the Beast

authoritarian regime and proud of being so. Democracy and liberalism had failed to produce a just society. Socialism led to Communism which was the real enemy. The Pope himself had legitimized the Fascist regime in Italy, his bishops crawled to it.

It is easy to mock ambivalent attitudes when all is known, when the consequences of certain actions are clearly perceived and what was hidden or glossed over comes out into the light of day. Watkin's utter loathing of Stalin, Mussolini and Hitler together with his contempt for papal appeasement and the attitude of the majority of Catholic bishops and clergy towards the Fascist dictators were the product of his temperament as well as his intelligence. He was a free spirit. His friend Michael de la Bédoyère was in a very different position.[6]

Bédoyère was the nephew and then the son-in-law of Algar Thorold. So he had both Labouchere and Thorold blood in his veins and his career showed it. When Watkin first came across him he was at Stonyhurst studying to be a Jesuit. In that capacity in 1928 he wrote his first article for the *Dublin* which he entitled "Religion as Adventure". It was to remain so throughout its author's life. Bédoyère soon realized he had no vocation to the priesthood and in 1930 married Catherine Thorold before joining the staff of the *Catholic Herald*.

The *Catholic Herald* had been founded and edited by an Irish newspaper proprietor named Charles Diamond.[7] Diamond, known as 'rough Diamond' by some and the 'Catholic Harmsworth' by others, was a rich and pugnacious individualist, a man of definite but not always consistent views. Once a Member of Parliament and Home ruler, he had also, in his journalistic capacity, served six months in Pentonville Prison for incitement to murder. Not a man to make friends easily, for some reason he took Watkin to his heart as soon as they met and asked him to contribute regularly to his paper. Unfortunately he fell mortally ill in the spring of 1934. From his death bed he sent Watkin his "love and greetings and please would he go on with the fight for liberty." He hoped that Watkin's deep wisdom and calm reasoning would do more to further the cause than his own "tempestuous and violent attacks." To most people Watkin would have appeared anything but calm; however his writing was very much more temperate and measured than his conversation.

For a few months after Diamond's death there was great doubt about his paper's future. Barbara Barclay Carter visited the office and reported that Watkin was regarded with enormous respect and would probably be the next editor. This was not a position he would have wanted nor would he have been suitable. In fact, as Diamond's confidential secretary, Mary Bottrill, made plain, Diamond, who had complete faith in Watkin's judgement, wanted him not as editor but to play a large part on an editorial board which he hoped would run the paper along the same lines as himself. Bédoyère now set about finding people with money to buy the paper and invest in it. Such people were found, a Chairman and a Managing Director were appointed, Bédoyère was made editor. He tripled the circulation of the paper but from first to last, his position was a difficult one.

Very soon after his appointment he wrote a revealing letter to Watkin whose article for the paper had to be toned down. His Directors wanted to be all things to all men. They suspected Watkin's violent anti-Fascist views and the uncompromising way in which he stated them. "My own future on the paper is very precarious," he wrote, "because I am sure sooner or later to come up against them in some vital point. . . . The real trouble is the absolute impossibility of lay initiative in England at the present time. The Bishops will not allow the slightest *risk* without withdrawing their support and I am afraid that the new owners are very anxious for that full support. The paper, I am afraid, is likely to go the way of all Catholic efforts, either to sheer subservience and success or to opposition and failure. It is very disappointing but I am hanging on for the present in the hope that all is not yet lost." But for the time being it was.

Letters on the Abyssinian question, about which it must be said Bédoyère himself held equivocal views, were being printed in the correspondence pages. Watkin's letter on the subject, Bédoyère wrote, had reached his office "at the same time as one from the Apostolic Delegate pretty well demanding that we should finish the correspondence. In a paper like this I have to accept that. I have written to Godfrey the following sentence: 'May I be allowed respectfully to say to Your Grace that I myself feel terribly, as a Catholic, this policy of concealing awkward and difficult questions which continue to trouble consciences.'"

Bédoyère left the paper that year and did not return as Editor until 1936; by then Italy had actually invaded Ethiopia, or Abyssinia as it was then called. His problems were more acute than ever, but perhaps this time he faced them with more resignation. In reply to what may have been a letter of reproof from Watkin he protested that he was *all* in favour of complete freedom to criticize Pope and bishops on serious grounds but the Papacy sees international questions differently from most of us. "I honestly feel that full criticism of Italy can only justly come from those who intend to reform their own colonial arrangements. I think history will take a very different view of contemporary events." History did.

One of the few people who spoke out was the novelist Compton Mackenzie. His reasons were the same as Watkin's. As one who believes in the Catholic faith, he declared at an anti-Fascist meeting, "I detest this tendency to deify the state . . . there are no words to condemn sufficiently this damnable false nationalism which is sweeping the world."[8]

Because it failed so miserably in the end, the achievements of the League of Nations Union are often forgotten and the entire enterprise is sometimes surrounded by a faint air of ridicule. This is unjust. Although appalled by the disproportionate response to aggression and the vindictive peace terms, Watkin was not blind to the fact that in 1914 Germany had betrayed trust and violated the law of nations. With Sturzo, he was seeking a legal and moral organ "which would be inspired by the idea of the common good identical for all states, that is for mankind." However, it was mankind that was the problem.

The Covenant of the League might pledge its signatories to accept arbitration, to disarm and to support each other against unprovoked aggression, its social and juridical organizations at Geneva and The Hague might work tirelessly for the good of humanity, but in the end, as well we know, it was to fail. From the first Watkin foresaw that the League would not succeed in its main objective because none of the member states was prepared to sacrifice an iota of its national sovereignty.

Despite this, he supported the League energetically both in London and in Sheringham, urging Helena, who was too tired, and his children, who were too bored, to attend its fund-raising whist drives, bazaars and informative lectures. But the political will was not there. When Mussolini invaded Abyssinia in 1935, collective security gave way to *realpolitik*. No one, except the British Trades Union Congress, was prepared to risk war in order to restrain widely shared imperial ambitions. Evelyn Waugh, who like Belloc had been impressed by Mussolini, thought that the Abyssinians were barbarous and it was Italy's duty to conquer them. Anthony Eden tried to buy off Mussolini by suggesting a partition of the country, France gave Italy more or less a free hand. For a while economic sanctions were applied but not an embargo on oil; Italian troops continued to pour into Eritrea and Somaliland. Poison gas was used and the Emperor Haile Selassie fled to London. In June 1936 sanctions were withdrawn altogether.

In the first month of the invasion, *Punch* published a cartoon drawn by Bernard Partridge. It showed Mussolini arrayed in the armour of a Roman soldier, beneath a satirical caption which quoted a verse from Macaulay's *Lays of Ancient Rome*. Above the picture Watkin has written: "This is the man worshipped by Pope Pius XI and the Italian clergy. The man whom the Pope prefers to the living God."

At heart, despite what had happened in the Great War, Watkin found it hard to believe that the papacy could behave as badly as it did. The contrast in his mind and soul between the Church as the mystical body of Christ, the one organization whose teaching and liturgy could uniquely unite us to God, and how it acted in concrete circumstances, drove him to states of agitation and distress difficult to live with.

Pius XI never denounced the conquest of Abyssinia or the means by which it was accomplished. He maintained strict neutrality. Although Watkin would not have agreed, the Pope was bound to do so. It has been pointed out that Leo XIII did not condemn the Boer War, nor did Benedict XV condemn Germany's violation of Belgian neutrality. However, the Pope is not only Supreme Pontiff but Primate of Italy. He could and should have sternly rebuked those bloodthirsty members of his episcopate who rushed to burn incense on the imperial altar.

The Bishop of Cremona blessed regimental flags and evoked the blessing of God "upon these soldiers who, on African soil, will conquer new and fertile lands for the Italian genius . . . ." Cardinal Schuster of Milan hoped that the war would smooth the way for the Gospel, the Bishop of Civilta Castellana prayed that God would grant victory to Italian arms and gave his blessing on the King and Duce. The Bishop of Terracina spoke on the wireless and informed Mussolini that Italy was Fascist and the hearts of all Italians beat together at one with his. A cutting from *The Times* informs us that the Bishop went went down in a submarine and celebrated Mass under the sea before he made the broadcast. At the side of the report Watkin has written words absolutely typical of him at his most agitated: "We have *no* king but Caesar. Canon Law forbids the Blessed Sacrament to be taken into a brothel but Mass may be said in a murder machine."

Later, on the eve of the Second World War, he made a more balanced and sober assessment. Faith and Christ's Church are pure gold, he wrote, the people who represent them in this world are the alloy. But, as von Hügel had pointed out, gold without alloy is unusable.

CHAPTER SEVENTEEN

Bordering on Genius

A Philosophy of Form came out early in 1935. Helena and Edda walked down to Bertram A. Watts, the local stationer and bookseller to admire a display of it in the window under a notice "Local Author". It is doubtful if he sold many copies to the inhabitants of Sheringham. The book was dedicated to Perpetua which was rather unfortunate just then because Helena had received a letter from Reverend Mother Archer-Shee informing her that Perpetua's behaviour had recently been so bad that the nuns thought it best for her to remain at home for a term.

At lunch time on New Year's Day 1934, a telegram arrived for Hetty summoning her back home to look after her ill mother. She left St Mary's that afternoon for Warwickshire where she remained until the end of her life, looking after first her mother, then her widowed father and after that her brother.

Her departure was a terrible blow for the entire family. She had cared for all five children since their birth, helping Helena to give them their bottles after the monthly nurse had left, bathing them, dressing them, ironing their clothes, carrying up food from the kitchen to the nursery, sitting there patiently mending while they played with their bricks on the floor. It was she who pushed the pram along the Cromer Road to West Runton and in summer accompanied them to those daily visits to the beach with bucket and spade, thermos flasks and boring jam sandwiches.

Helena remained as the heart of their home, always present and always calm. But her life became much more troubled. Hetty had known Edda since Birmingham days and accepted the fact that he was a learned eccentric whose violent outbursts, however exhausting for her mistress, had nothing to do with her. It was otherwise with the ordinary servants who were becoming increasingly hard to get. Some complained that Mr Watkin's agitations kept them awake at night, they were quite frightened and their mother had told them to give in their notice. Helena's asthma grew worse, her bronchitis more frequent. Leaving Edda's peculiarities on one side, many servants found it difficult to work for a woman so often in bed and whose children, when they were there in the holidays, rushed about so independently for ever arguing and contradicting each other.

A long time ago at Abbots Hall, when Maria Pasqua was yet a young married woman, she and Philip entertained a Jesuit for the night. This visit was to have far-reaching consequences for Helena and her children. He had come to say Mass in the little chapel in the grounds and before he left Philip asked him about a good convent school for his daughter. The priest knew the very thing, the Convent of the Sacred Heart, Roehampton, just next door to Manresa House where he had done part of his training.

The convent at Roehampton was probably the richest, perhaps the most select and certainly the most snobbish of all the Catholic boarding schools in the British Isles. It may be the most written about. It was to make an indelible impression upon Antonia White and be the inspiration for her first and best novel *Frost in May*.

One of Edda's children was to accept Roehampton and maintain that she was happy there. When she read *Frost in May*, she did not recognize it as the school she knew. One was to reject Roehampton altogether as the most horrible place on earth. Two, like their mother, were to remain deeply ambivalent but drawn back to it again and again. So was Antonia. "We are still conscious of all we have experienced since we left Roehampton," she wrote in old age, "yet in one sense we have never left it and never will so long as we have life and memory."[1]

There are no female Jesuits as such but the Society of the Sacred Heart was founded by a French woman under the direction of her Jesuit brother, and was the equivalent. It was not a school for free spirits but the strictest of the teaching orders and among the first to disintegrate in the aftermath of the Second Vatican Council. Its purpose was to train children of the upper class to be good and informed Catholic wives and mothers, the leaders of society wherever they happened to be.

Academic standards were for the most part high. The nuns who taught Watkin's children were by no means the softly spoken Irish peasants of popular imagination but distinguished women many of whom had degrees from Oxford and Cambridge. The curriculum included philosophy, political theory and logic among much else, and was far wider and more stimulating than most public schools at that period. More importantly, Catholic education had not yet lost its nerve. There was no surrender to secularism. The children were offered an entirely different view of humanity and its destiny.

This was achieved at a price. A manual circulated among Jesuit schools at the turn of the twentieth century advised their priests not "to let the boys know anything of your past history. Be among them as though you had dropped from the clouds."[2] This attitude, combined with the customary upper class aloofness practised by the nuns, gave the impression of coldness and lack of humanity which for many years terrified some of Edda's children as once it had done their mother. He certainly thought that the system had crushed Helena's natural spontaneity.

Although the nuns were mostly English, they had inherited from their French origins a conviction that discipline depended upon constant and close supervision, careful monitoring of conversation, censorship of correspondence and general snooping. Tougher spirits had their own way of confronting life. Lady Ottoline Morrell's daughter, Julian, was sent a rope ladder by Dorothy Brett but escaped after two terms by more conventional channels.[3] Vivian Leigh survived although she got into trouble when she was discovered pushing a pink object rather like a rubber rolling pin up and down her stomach in an attempt to reduce her puppy fat. Her mother had sent it to her.[4]

As things were Edda could not possibly have afforded the fees for Roehampton even if he had wanted to. That his daughters were able to go there at all was due to the kindness of Helena's childhood friend, Winifred Archer- Shee, then Reverend Mother. Winifred was the sister of George Archer-Shee, the "Winslow Boy" of Terence Rattigan's famous play who, as a cadet at Osborne in 1908, was falsely accused of stealing a five shilling postal order, expelled and finally vindicated by his patent honesty and the oratory of Carson. George Archer-Shee was killed at the First Battle of Ypres in 1914.

Perpetua and Teresa went to Roehampton when Perpetua was nine and Teresa was seven. Teresa was a very unusual child, beautiful to look at, with dark hair, deep blue eyes and a heart-shaped face. When she was small she was so intensely happy that Helena felt anxious for her.[5]

But when she went to Roehampton, she was so homesick and cried so bitterly that the nuns thought it best for her to sleep in the infirmary so that they could keep a closer eye on her. Afterwards she was befriended by the kind hearted Sonia Brownell, later to marry George Orwell on his deathbed and to be the model for the defiant Julia in his novel *Nineteen Eighty-Four*. It is ironical that Roehampton should have influenced a book that exposed the evils and absurdities of all systems which attempt to instill implicit obedience, to control every thought and feeling.

In some respects, the Watkin children were far better informed than most of their contemporaries but at the same time grossly ignorant of the things that mattered to most girls of their own age. They knew the names of no film stars or tennis players. Even Norwich was remote to them let alone London. They had never heard of Bertram Mills Circus, Covent Garden or Drury Lane, Claridges or the Dorchester. The grandest restaurant they had been to was Jessops in Cromer where they kept their hands on their laps and wondered how to eat the meringues with a double-pronged fork.

At school the children kept their home life to themselves as did most of their companions. In fact, there was little time for ordinary conversation. No one was allowed to talk in the dormitories nor in the school corridors, special friendships were discouraged and sisters met only once a week. To the Watkin family this prevailing reticence, so alien to their volatile and excitable temperaments, proved a blessing. They were only too pleased to have been dropped from the clouds.

Soon Aunt Sissie invaded their new world. She was aware that her great-nieces were incarcerated in a Roman Catholic convent. How she surmounted the barricades is uncertain but her chauffeur-driven car arrived with her personal maid, and Perpetua and Teresa were swept off to tea at Thurlow Place. Not long afterwards an enormous parcel of goodies arrived from Harrods. It caused the children more confusion than pleasure.

Poor Aunt Sissie. A lonely widow, she was among the gentlest of the Ingram sisters. She was entranced when she first saw Teresa and wanted the child to live with her in exchange for paying the school fees. The offer was refused. She now fell victim to a confidence trickster. Where she met him no one knows, but a man who called himself Major Impey ingratiated himself into her household with such success that before long she entrusted him with the management of her business affairs. The family were suspicious, but she had no children to keep a watchful eye on their inheritance. Her strong minded sister Ada was dead. Emmeline would have pounced but she was far away in St Helena and nobody bothered to consult the army lists. Once, after a dinner in London where Impey was present, Helena acted quite out of character and told him that they all hoped that he was playing straight with the old lady. Of course he was not and he ended up in the dock at the Central Criminal Court convicted of embezzling about a million pounds of Aunt Sissie's money in today's values. The *Daily Mirror* published a photograph of a bent old lady, dressed like a charwoman, being helped along the pavement to give evidence at the Old Bailey. She was not ruined. Dainty, her chauffeur, accompanied by Alice her maid, still came to Roehampton to fetch the children to Thurlow Place and she died under the delusion that she was the richest woman in London.

When one is a child, love, however deep, seems as nothing compared with the respect of one's contemporaries. Edda's children were uneasy when their father appeared in the parlour. The parlour was the music room of the original eighteenth-century house; it was very beautiful with large windows looking out over the terrace. One of Edda's children rejoiced during the war when she heard it had been destroyed by bombs. Relations or accredited friends were allowed to visit on Sunday afternoons and expected to go to solemn Benediction afterwards. A nun sat in front of the grand piano to make sure that all was in order and that no undeclared books or boxes of chocolates were handed over.

Someone, perhaps Nana, perhaps Mrs Tatham, had trained Edda to greet people in a certain way and repeat a polite formula before he started to speak as nature had made him. Edda was in fact not indifferent to other people's feelings. He just did not perceive them. Unless told that something was wrong, he assumed that everyone he met wanted to discuss the world with the same zest as he did. He would stand up with a hunched, bowing motion, inquire about health, a good journey, and when appropriate the well-being of relations before asking, at great speed, what the visitor thought about Germany's reoccupation of the Rhineland, Aldous Huxley's latest novel or a very interesting interpretation of the Emperor Charles V's pre-emptive funeral service.

The children would see him as soon as they opened the parlour door, a lonely figure in shabby clothes, staring out of the window at the statue of the Sacred Heart on the terrace, a battered trilby and a book on the chair beside him. The room was decorated in pale green and gold; it smelt of scent, furs and floor polish, of money, worldliness and the good manners which dictated that the children dropped a short curtsey to the nun in charge. "Oh, there you are," Watkin would say a little too loudly. Then repeating "there you are, there you are," in a low satisfied hum he would venture cautiously across the parquet floor, hands in front of him, as if he were skating across a lake.

This particular time, the years between the publication of *The Bow in the Clouds* and the end of the Second World War, were the most prolific period of Watkin's life as a writer. In 1935 Tom Burns left Sheed and Ward not altogether sorrowfully to take charge of the religious side of Longmans. Early in 1936 Cardinal Hinsley restored the Catholic weekly, *The Tablet*, to lay ownership with Douglas Woodruff as editor and Tom Burns as one of the directors. Watkin's wide knowledge of history and religion, and his ability to translate from Spanish, French and German as well as the classical languages, made him a valuable contributor to an international journal. Tom, who had a genius for networking, wrote to Watkin at once to secure his services for the paper, asking him to work exclusively for *The Tablet* and no other Catholic weekly.

Watkin had the power of intense concentration. Once in the world of the mind, very little else impinged upon his consciousness. When his study was being cleaned, he would bring his work into the drawing room and write on his knee while children were running in and out or food was carried to the table. In fact he seemed to like background noise so long as it remained in the background and he had no responsibility for it. He used to write with his study door open, unheeding the sound of numberless feet clumping up and down the uncarpeted stairs. To the surprise of many he liked to write and think to the sound of broadcast dance music "as a cocktail to stimulate my nerves" and in his major work, *A Philosophy of Form*, he used this habit to illustrate the direct effect inferior art has on the emotions.

In 1928, after reading one article by Watkin on Santayana and another on Bremond, Algar Thorold had urged Watkin to write a book on philosophy. He did not know of any living thinker in Europe so well qualified as Watkin. He owed it to God and man. "If the Catholic intellectual renaissance of our day is to be more than a reaction of anti-war fatigue it must find its own philosophical expression, not necessarily anti-Thomist – *non alia sed aliter.*" That is, the same truths but expressed differently. Watkin followed his advice.

A Philosophy of Form was first published in 1935, a second edition came out in 1937 and a third in 1950. It is a development of his *Bow in the Clouds* – an outline of an apologetic based on religious experience the work of "original insight" which helped the young Bede Griffiths to see the possibilities of a synthesis between modern science and traditional Christian philosophy. It was widely and favourably reviewed both at the time and in the 1950's, even by those who had reservations about its methodology.

Despite the book's fascinating excursions into numerous subjects like the nature of art, sexuality, psychical phenomena, poetry and politics, it must be admitted that *A Philosophy of Form* does not make easy reading. "Watkin's mind begins where most people's ends," Bédoyère remarked as part of a puff in the *Catholic Herald*. Watkin had been trained in philosophy and logic, his arguments are so closely reasoned that a layman would find them difficult to follow. He begins by establishing a philosophical position and then applies its principles to important aspects of human experience. An achievement, in one critic's opinion, of great erudition and versatility but especially of such keen power of intellectual insight and analysis as to border on genius.

From the start reviewers were faced by a difficult task. The book covered such a wide range of subjects, it was too rich, too original, too profound to be dealt with in a short space. The vehicle was carrying, one complained, too heavy a load but no original book had come out of modern England that could stand by its side. It was the work of a master, the philosopher and theologian Father Martin D'Arcy remarked, "who swears by no master; modern, ancient or medieval."[6]

The philosophy both expounded and applied by Watkin is the eternally valid system of metaphysics, alone adequate to the entire breadth, height and depth of human experience without denying it or explaining it away. This is the abiding philosophy, the *philosophia perennis,* descending "from Plato (or was it Socrates?) modified by Aristotle for better and for worse and continued through Plotinus, Boethius, 'Dionysius', Scotus,

Erigena, Anselm, Bonaventura, Albert and Thomas Aquinas to Wust and Lossky among contemporary philosophers." However, this was very far from being yet another book on Thomist philosophy. Watkin differs from Aquinas in several important respects as more hidebound reviewers were swift to point out.

It was the very reason why others found his work so liberating. Watkin went beyond Thomism, Bede Griffiths wrote, opened his mind to St Bonaventure and others and "developed what interested me most, a theory of intellectual *intuition*. This gave me the clue which I was seeking and enabled me to work out a system of philosophy which really satisfied me."[7]

Two fundamental beliefs unite all thinkers who adhere to this tradition. First, that the chief end of human life is not action but contemplation, secondly, that since true knowledge of external reality is attainable by our senses and our understanding, we can accept the reliability of our organs of knowledge. Watkin is therefore making a direct challenge to, among others, the positivists, logical or otherwise, the so-called empiricists of the school of Russell and Ayer who insist that the sole objective truth attainable is truth susceptible in principle to scientific proof and that experience more remote from sensible objects, like ethical or aesthetic perceptions, is purely subjective with no ascertainable foundation in objective fact. In other words, since metaphysics are concerned with facts beyond the sphere of scientific examination, it has no part in philosophy.

It is from this strait-jacket Watkin would free us. On the contrary, he argues, there are degrees and kinds of created being, energy-objects determined by the Form which informs their metaphysical matter. These are the object of human experience and contemplation upwards from the gross matter of material objects studied by the sciences to the intellectual and spiritual beings studied by metaphysics.

He therefore begins with a detailed examination of the knowing process and the concept of Form in metaphysics. He concludes that knowledge of objects comes from two factors which are distinguishable in thought but not in fact. "Not even sense perception is exclusively sensible, a mere aggregate of sense data – sensations of sound, light, colour, touch – could not of itself construct an object." Our perceptions of sensible objects are then not purely sensible but need as well intuition to discover what their nature is.

This nature is constituted by its Form, which gives the book its title. In ordinary speech form usually refers to shape or outline. In philosophical terminology it means that everything we experience, whether physical or mental, has an intelligable form or character, a chair or a horse has the quality of chairness or horseness. The matter is that which makes what we perceive a unique thing, a particular chair or horse.

Our perception of this or that form, whether physical or metaphysical, in fact the entire fabric of our knowledge and consequently of our action, is founded on contemplation. When most people think of contemplation they restrict its meaning to a mental pondering on aesthetic or religious experience. For Watkin it is a focused, deliberate intellectual apprehension or intuition of form, that is the nature of created being: "a view of what *is*, not a desire that this or that should be."

Thorold thought that in the same way as Newman called his book on faith and reason *An Essay in Aid of a Grammar of Assent*, so Watkin's book might be called *An Essay in Aid of a Grammar of Contemplation*. What is remarkable about the book is its breadth as well as its depth. Watkin is no ivory tower philosopher, he wants us to act, but not to act mindlessly. But before we can act we must make sense of our experience. If we cannot, the world is no more than a mere kaleidoscope of accidental, unrelated happenings. "A structure of active achievement, individual or social, which lacks this foundation is but an imposing sham, doomed to collapse. For we cannot profitably handle objects whose nature is unknown."

Today this warning against mindless activism is more urgently needed than ever. The state cannot educate human beings unless there is a measure of agreement about their nature and destiny. Applied science, valuable though it is, is not the most significant part of our learning. In a plea for a greater realization of the importance of the humanities, Sir Colin Lucas, former Vice-Chancellor of Oxford University, recently pointed out that the core function of universities "is to seek and defend the first principles that underpin the true nature of things."[8] This was precisely what Watkin was trying to do.

As his arguments develop, Watkin applies them to a wide range of human experience which include natural theology, sociology, politics, ethics, aesthetics, literature, history, and psychology. A glance at the index alone reveals the extent of his investigation.

Since the book is concerned with the hierarchy of being, degrees of reality, there must be ultimate reality. If not, Watkin's thesis falls to the ground, all our experiences in the end come to nothing. Some of his readers considered his final chapter on religious contemplation, placed as it is on the ladder of being next to aesthetic experience, to be the finest in the book. It is, Watkin says, because we do not contemplate, cultivate an interior, organic view of religious truth, that it seems unreal in contrast with the obvious realities of secular experience. Contemplate and it is the latter which will seem unreal in contrast with the reality of God and His self-communication to the souls of man.

A Philosophy of Form came out early in 1935. Helena and Edda walked down to Bertram A. Watts, the local stationer and bookseller to admire a display of it in the window under a notice "Local Author". It is doubtful if he sold many copies to the inhabitants of Sheringham. The book was dedicated to Perpetua which was rather unfortunate just then because Helena had received a letter from Reverend Mother Archer-Shee informing her that Perpetua's behaviour had recently been so bad that the nuns thought it best for her to remain at home for a term.

Perhaps it is true to say that of all Edda and Helena's children, Perpetua was by nature the most conventional and least unusually sensitive. She was the only one who, after the first homesick years, was happy at Roehampton. Physically, and to a certain extent mentally, she grew up more quickly than her sisters and brother. Her judgements were shrewd but she was not at all academic and during this stage in her life did not share her father's interests in the least. She minded his eccentricities even more than the others and was continually embarrassed and ashamed by his behaviour. Far deeper than that, she felt rejected.

As a very young child her father adored her. One of her first memories was of him trying trying to dress her and getting every garment on back to front. Before the arrival of the others he used frequently to take her and Teresa for walks in the woods as once he had taken Gertrude, Gretchen and little Bube through the forests at Baden. He would tell them stories, recite poetry, show them the wild flowers and together they would pick primroses in the spring. Then the scene darkened. Fairy Wonderful Sunshine retreated behind the clouds of the world as it was, not as Edda had hoped it would be.

There were too many children to support, too many books to be written, too many women to flirt with, too many controversies to engage in, too many dictators to be shouted about in his bedroom at night. There were also too many doctor's bills to be paid and bank managers to be pacified with furious letters passing between Sheringham, America and St Helena. The walks in the woods and by the sea were occasional and her place taken by others.

"I must grow up quickly," Perpetua wrote in a childish hand in the first diary she kept, "so that I can write stories and save us from the work-house." From an early age she felt responsible for the family and it may be that Helena depended too much upon her. She was not only the eldest but by far the most practical of them all. She would help her mother plan meals, do the shopping and visit the registry office in an attempt to find maids. For all that, she remained an uncertain, insecure adolescent out to make trouble. At school she talked in the study room, refused to go to classes or to mend her stockings and hid under beds to pinch the nun's ankles when she carried in the holy water stoup at night.

Helena looked upon Perpetua's banishment as an expulsion and was both shocked and distressed. There were enough tensions in that household already. Emmeline, who had a life interest in Pantafon, had let it to people she knew called McDowell. Mrs McDowell realized that the house belonged to Watkin and felt sorry for the children. In 1932 therefore she invited both Perpetua and Teresa to stay with her and saw to it that they had a good time at their father's old home. Rumours of trouble had reached Edgar Christian's parents, Colonel Christian and his wife Cousin Marguerite, at Bron Dirion. They also invited the two children to stay and Perpetua began to look upon Marguerite as her second mother.

All this, however, had been unsettling. Perpetua had seen Pantafon, rowed on the lake, explored the gardens and admired the beauty of Snowdonia. It was a reminder of everything Edda had thrown away. Christopher boasted that he had twisted his grandmother round his little finger. His sister lamented her father's folly. There was talk of letting St Mary's. But where would they go? It might really be to the workhouse. If he was so poor why couldn't he get a job? Why did he have to write books which no ordinary person would want to read and be for ever agitated about mystical union, the immortality of the soul, the League of Nations and someone called Oswald Mosely? She began to torment Edda. Good hearted teasing turned into deliberate provocation.

At meal times she would start the conversation by announcing that she had just read a most interesting article in the *Catholic Herald* reporting the Holy Father's address to Ugandan missionaries. Everyone present knew that she had little idea where Uganda was and that the *Catholic Herald* was the last paper she would want to read. But not Edda. "The Holy Father?" he would answer in incredulous tones. "Pius XI is *not* the Holy Father. Not – not – not." Perpetua would look sanctimonious and continue to poke through the bars. "The Holy Father said -" Edda would bang the table and start to shout. "He's the Pope but *not* the Holy Father. How could a Holy Father encourage God-denying people like Hitler and Mussolini?" So it would continue, louder and louder, Helena vainly trying to keep the peace, until Perpetua would burst into tears, call Edda a madman and rush from the room.

Yet she was his eldest daughter, united in an affection nothing that was to happen in the future could really dissolve. When she returned to school, she told him how sorry she was for her dark moods and he assured her that everything was forgotten. Of all his children she was the one who would in the end give him the most practical help as he stumbled his way through the world.

CHAPTER EIGHTEEN

There Are No Rules

He meant that years of reading and observation had showed him that human beings are frequently inconsistent both in their behaviour and in their opinions. We cannot, therefore, say with certainty that such and such a person would not have acted in a particular way because there are no dependable rules upon which we can rely to make such a judgement.

In the spring of 1935, still banished from Roehampton, Perpetua went to see Christopher at Laxton. They were near in age and very close. Christopher was in his last year. Perpetua stayed at a guest-house and that evening went to the school play and next morning for a walk with her brother and three of his friends, ending up at the "Golden Bull". Here they assured the barmaid that they were all over eighteen, smoked cigarettes, drank sherry, played darts and had what Perpetua described as marvellous fun before the boys had to return to school and go into retreat.

Christopher was not a success at Laxton either on the playing fields or classroom. That the Dominicans did not recognize his intellectual ability was not their fault. He was, as he realized only late in his life, a disturbed child. He made himself unpopular by proclaiming that the Catholic liturgy was wasted on the majority of the clergy and given the chance they would ditch it. In this he was proved right. He cared little about the curriculum and spent most of his free time cycling about the countryside looking at old churches and getting permission to play their organs.

He shared his father's interests but not his temperament. In this respect they were totally unlike. Christopher had none of Watkin's innocence and transparency, his unconscious peculiarities of speech and gesture and his complete lack of social snobbishness. When King George V celebrated his Silver Jubilee in May of this year, Watkin joined in the local festivities, dancing, or rather holding hands and jumping up and down, with everyone else in the street before taking the children off to a fish and chips supper. It was not an occasion Christopher would ever have spontaneously enjoyed.

At this time he felt antagonistic towards his father, an antagonism which increased as events developed. His School Certificate results were mediocre and the authorities did not think it worthwhile for him to remain at Laxton. He had to earn his living somehow but had no idea how to set about it. Frank Sheed, who remained very fond of Watkin to the end of his life, suggested that Christopher should find digs in London and come to work at Sheed and Ward.

This he did and was set to work immediately on the second edition of his father's *A Philosophy of Form* which he called, to the amusement of everyone in the office, "A Form of Philosophy". In fact Watkin was busy on another book, not published by Sheed but by the Unicorn Press in its "Christian Challenge" series. It was a short book called *Theism, Agnosticism and Atheism,* dedicated to his unappreciative son. Watkin, the *Manchester Guardian* reviewer remarked, was a man to be reckoned with. "There is an entirely new flavour in his thought which is stimulating. It is some time since I met a book which excited me so much or so agreeably." The author, he went on, was disarming in his frankness.

This is true. Watkin divides his book into four chapters: The Contemporary Situation; the Metaphysical Proofs of Theism; the Proof from Man's Need of God; the Proof of Theism from Religious Experience. His analysis of the contemporary situation is his longest chapter and is remarkable for its depth and honesty. He starts by quoting the Archbishop of Westminster's tribute to King George V who had just died. The King was "as fearless in the profession of faith in God as in his attitude towards the difficulties and perils of his high responsibility. Such a manifestation was almost unique in these days." In what other age in history, Watkin asks, would it have required courage in a ruler to profess his faith in God? In what other epoch would it be "almost unique" to manifest confidence in Divine Providence? History knows of none. The annals of Christendom from Constantine to the nineteenth century have produced many rulers who did not love God, not one who did not believe in Him.

Any serious investigation would show that the vast majority of Britons, far from believing in Christianity, do not believe in God with any clearness or conviction. This widespread atheism or agnosticism is not due to contemporary moral depravity. Religious insight is one thing, ethical insight another. A number of canonized saints have accepted what we now perceive to be immoral. This is because the relation between religion and ethics lies deeper than external and naturally human morality. It consists in a fundamental determination of the will towards God and our fellow-men in Him.

As his book progresses, Watkin sets out to consider all the facts, to face any criticism that freethinkers could make and to state his opponents' arguments absolutely fairly. He leads him, the *Manchester Guardian* reviewer continued, "through all the difficulties of philosophical discussion, brings the reader to the point where thought can reach no further and having shown him the inadequacies of the metaphysical criticisms of theism, confronts him with the solid weight of Christian experience, challenging him to neglect it at the peril of his intellectual integrity."

The Catholic censor uncoiled himself. A letter arrived at St Mary's inquiring in dry tones whether Watkin's book had been granted the *Imprimatur* and if so by whom. Of course it had not been granted and the Catholic Truth Society Library refused to stock it. Saints were not expected to have blind spots nor was the evidential value of religious experience to be so plainly spelled out. Those in authority were wary of religious experience, partly because it might conflict with dogmatic definitions, partly because it was associated with Quietism and partly because it was connected in their minds with the extravagancies of certain Protestant sects. The authorities who read the manuscript of Wilfred Ward's biography of Newman had strongly advised him to play down the Cardinal's own account of his boyhood conversion.

When Maisie Ward arrived at this point in her life of her father, she wrote to ask Watkin's advice and published in her book part of his reply. The error, Watkin said, came from confounding experience with mere feeling. This experience, Watkin wrote, "is not feeling, but a function of the profound intellect. If a man accepts the Catholic Church as teaching a divine revelation, his faith is an obscure intuition of God. And this I submit is religious experience, not indeed of the individual dogmas, but of God in and through the organic system to which these dogmas belong. My hope indeed in my *Philosophy of Form* was to outline an apologetic based on religious experience which should be not emotional, subjective and immanental like the Modernist, but intellectual, objective and transcendent."[1]

Reverend Mother Archer-Shee's treatment of Perpetua turned out to be the right one. From the beginning Helena made it plain that if Perpetua was not at school then she must help in the house. This Perpetua conscientiously did but she became bored, missed her friends and was glad to be back at school. The nuns welcomed her affectionately and to her mother's joy Perpetua became a reformed character, first a Child of Mary and in time a Blue Ribbon which in Sacred Heart language meant a prefect. Catherine was now at Roehampton as well. It was a well-intentioned but bad mistake to send her there. She was not a child who ever should have been sent to any boarding school, still less to one with such rigid structures. She had a most affectionate nature, loved her parents and her cat and clung to her home. She could not understand why the nuns were so cold and remote or why she saw so little of her sisters. Moreover, she was left-handed and badly dyslexic, a condition then barely recognized. Her reading, handwriting and spelling were far below the standard of most children of eleven. She was quite mistakenly considered stupid and felt discouraged and hopeless.

Her release came suddenly. In the first week of December 1935 she developed a bad stomach ache and went to the infirmary. The nurse gave her a dose of castor oil and sent her back to her class. Her appendix ruptured and when she reached the hospital of St John and St Elizabeth the surgeon doubted if he could operate in time to save her life. Helena and Edda came up to London by train and much to Catherine's disquiet when she leard about it later, discussed whether she should be buried at Roehampton or her body taken back to Sheringham.

The nuns were extremely distressed and did their best with prayer and practical help. They had Magdalen to stay at the convent so that she should not be left by herself at home and later Perpetua in order that Catherine should have one of the family with her at Christmas. But the child did not forget. When her life still hung in the balance and she lay in hospital forbidden to swallow even a drop of water, Helena sat by her bed and asked if there was anything in all the world she could do for her. Yes, Catherine whispered, promise to take me away from Roehampton. So when she was fully recovered Catherine returned to St Mary's Convent in Sheringham.

In an account of his early life written many years later, Christopher maintained that although he continued to practise his faith externally he had in fact ceased to believe in it since he was a small boy at St Mary's Convent. However, when he was sixteen and still at Laxton he had a sudden flash of illumination "and saw in a moment – a moment that has never left me since – that the next world was so much more *real* than this world that you could not put them together."[2] While he was still at Sheed and Ward's he met Dom Bruno Hicks, Abbot of Downside, and was accepted by the monastery as a postulant. In the January of 1936, just before his eighteenth birthday, accompanied by a delighted Edda, he arrived at Downside without ever having seen the place or knowing anyone there. It was, he wrote in old age, the best thing he ever did.

Watkin often used to say "there are no rules." By this he did not mean that there are no commandments, that no moral guidance exists or no perception of good and evil conduct in the human heart. He meant that years of reading and observation had showed him that human beings are frequently inconsistent both in their behaviour and in their opinions. We cannot, therefore, say with certainty that such and such a person would not have acted in a particular way because there are no dependable rules upon which we can rely to make such a judgement. We are left only with probabilities. This observation applied to himself. Martindale had put his finger on it years before when in the course of their quarrel over Solovyev, he had warned Watkin not to let his temperament run away with him, not to get desperate and "do things that would not occur to anyone else."

Watkin was now desperate and did things which perhaps Father Martindale had not then in mind.

He was desperate financially. His *A Philosophy of Form* had been a *succes d'estime* but did not bring in money. Nor did his book on theism and atheism, nor did the numerous articles he wrote for various publications. Above all things he wanted financial security, not to continue living from hand to mouth, fearing that at any moment the cliff would crumble and they would all fall into the sea. Someone, perhaps Edda himself, perhaps Helena or Perpetua, had an idea which they hoped might save them yet. The beaches along the coast were strewn with cornelians, onyx, topaz, crystals and moss agates. They were always picking them up. A firm in Cornwall, it was discovered, specialized in polishing and mounting semi-precious stones as rings, brooches, necklaces and pendants. In the summer of 1935 they started an enterprise which they called "Sheringham Gems" and very pretty they were. A table was set up outside the back gate to attract visitors who walked along the lane leading to the sea. Edda and the children hunted for stones along the shore, Helena or Perpetua sold them from the table where the jewellery was set out and later from a shop they rented in the town for thirty shillings a week. The trade was seasonal but money trickled in and they did quite well in the time that was left to them.

That was not to be long. Watkin was desperate emotionally as well as financially and had been for some years. The more wildly agitated he got about his wicked mother, the international situation, the stupidity and spiritual blindness of the ecclesiastical authorities, the more ill Helena became and the longer she spent in bed. Watkin wanted companionship and sexual fulfillment, life was for living. He passionately denied that this world was, or should be, a vale of tears.

He first met Zoë Ella Bowen in 1934. She had an unfortunate background. Her mother was an artist and evidently of some ability because she exhibited her work a number of times at the Royal Academy. But she was a selfish woman who wanted to look after neither her baby nor her young husband. They divorced and Zoë lived with her grandmother and great aunt in England while her mother settled permanently in the South of France. When Watkin met Zoë she was thirty, full of all the energy Helena lacked, a vigorous walker, tall, well-built, red complexioned, round-faced with dark curly hair and a deep, almost masculine, voice. She dressed in bright colours, wore gipsy earrings, sandals and scarves and carried about embroidered and beaded bags. She was spirited, lonely and frantic to escape from the house near the Common where she lived with the old ladies. Perpetua used to tease her father about his girl friends but when she laughed at Zoë he was furious.

The liaison was embarrassing for Edda's family although he did not seem to think it was anyone's business but his own. His indifference to the neighbours' opinions was absolute. "N-e-i-g-h-b-o-u-r-s," he would say, throwing his head back and imitating a sheep, "n-e-i-g-h-b-o-u-r-s." In the beginning Helena rarely referred to Zoë and when she did she smiled. Her children were too young to be charitable and protested loudly when they saw their mother helping to prepare the picnic basket Edda and Zoë took to the beach.

Christopher, who felt the attachment most keenly as an insult to his mother, made up witty and amusing verses about Zoë's name and appearance. The others pretended not to see the pair when they came across them on the road or beach. Both Watkin's and Helena's family were well known not only in the district but in the county. The news reached Aylsham and Samuel's manner became even more bluff and breezy. At Sheringham the ticket collector on the station had once been an indoor servant at Loudwater, the friendly engine driver who took Watkin's half-delighted, half-frightened children into his cab had been Emmeline's chauffeur. The Babington-Smiths had left Loudwater. Nana was dead and spared any wounding talk about her brilliant charge. The local gossips fed on the behaviour of their distinguished local author whose books, so they understood, 'were all about the Roman Catholic religion.'

Once during the time Perpetua was exiled from Roehampton, as a joke, she invited Zoë to tea at St Mary's. Edda was in London, Helena spending the day in Norwich; Magdalen was the only child at home. Perpetua gave the maid instructions to make sandwiches and to bring in the silver teapot. Zoë arrived wearing a jade green knitted coat and skirt. Perpetua was ostentatiously polite, their guest was clearly uncomfortable and spoke at length in her deep voice about her experiences in the South of France and at Marlow in Buckinghamshire. No child today can possibly be as ignorant of sex as Magdalen then was. Zoë was the undoubted enemy but Magdalen had no idea of the meaning of the word mistress in that context, only a confused sense that she and Perpetua were doing something wrong and that the person they had lured to the house in order to mock was as unhappy as they were.

Zoë does not seem to have had friends at Sheringham who might have advised her not to get involved with a middle-aged man with a family. Nor, until there was a child on the way and exposure inevitable, did she take her grandmother and great aunt into her confidence. They were old fashioned and straitlaced and to their credit when they were told what was going on did their best to help her.

In October 1936, when all her children and Edda were away and Catherine a boarder at the convent, which was as full of gossip as the town itself, Helena received a letter from Zoë. It was a pitiful letter, full of contrition for what she had done, admiration for Helena, explanations about her previous love affairs and all the young men drifting away, how much she loved Edward, as she always called him, and would not let him go. Helena asked her to come and see her at St Mary's.

Winifred Archer-Shee would never have been such a close friend of Helena if she had not realized that the quiet and reserved exterior hid a woman of great strength of character. What the two said to each other in that almost empty house can be gathered from the angry, truculent, defiant letters Zoë wrote to Helena after her return home. These Helena never showed her children. They were found in strange circumstances at Abbots Hall nearly forty years later and read in an hotel room at Cromer.

It had been, Zoë wrote, a long, painful, terrible interview between mistress and wife but at least they knew where each other stood. She absolutely refused to be discarded and given an allowance. Her baby needed a father's love all the more because it would be illegitimate. She adores Edward, he adores her and had written her over four hundred letters. Helena must learn to share her husband. Helena did not answer. Nor did she reply to two other wild letters which declared that Helena was trying to break her by encouraging gossip but she refused to be driven away and intended to stay in Sheringham just as long as it suited her. This she did, causing embarrassment and distress as her pregnancy became more obvious.

Zoë was self-centred and obstinate but essentially a good-hearted woman. That was her tragedy. She knew what she had done and would have to live with that knowledge until the end of her life. For her sake and the child's Helena was quite willing to give Edda a divorce but the priests she consulted told her that to do so would threaten the sacrament of marriage and encourage sinful behaviour. This undermined Zoë's hopes of happiness from the start. She longed to be a respectable married woman and indeed always called herself "Mrs Watkin", but like T. E. Lawrence's mother, dreaded exposure. Moreover, she was a sincere and practising Anglican and deeply minded living in sin. When in after years divorce became easier and the matter was raised again, Watkin refused to have anything to do with it. He could not, he would not, ever say that he was not married to Helena.

She was aware of Zoë's position. Never, not even in the months to come when things were at their worst, did she speak against Zoë, or more importantly for the children, against their father. What he was doing was wrong but he was a genius and simply could not be judged like an ordinary person. When she tried to discuss their situation, Edda would get uncontrollably agitated. She could not get him to see that the idea of him living for six months with her and six months with Zoë simply would not work. A number of his relations, Edda maintained, kept mistresses and remained with their wives. But they were very rich, Helena would point out, and able to manage things discreetly.

At the begining of 1937 Watkin rented a house for Zoë at Hunstanton, a seaside town further up the coast, the place where Rebecca West had lived with her illegitimate son by H. G.Wells. He remained as energetic as ever, travelling between Zoë at Hunstanton and Helena at Sheringham, going up to London, attending meetings, correcting the proofs of Dawson's *Religion and the Modern State* and completing his own *Men and Tendencies*, a far more interesting and lively book than its dreary title suggests.

It consisted of a collection of essays, some already printed but now revised and extended, others completely new. Four of these essays are on the philosophers: Bertrand Russell, Santayana, Peter Wust and Plotinus. These are given the most detailed treatment. There are three essays on contemporary literary figures: H. G.Wells, Galsworthy, and Aldous Huxley. There is an essay on Havelock Ellis, another on Haldane, three essays which examine the origins and principles of the totalitarian state, and a careful and interesting analysis of the philosophy of Karl Marx. Watkin ends with a chapter entitled Peace and War, a timely discussion of the morality and practical consequences of modern warfare. A stimulating book, one reviewer wrote, of astonishing erudition so skilfully woven into the author's arguments that the reader does not feel overwhelmed by a flood of undigested facts.

In February news reached them that Emmeline and Sam were on their way back to England. Emmeline was now eighty-five and as her solicitor informed Edda, very ill. He had arranged for them to live in a service flat in Jermyn Street. Emmeline refused all medical assistance so a doctor disguised as a waiter was sent up to have a look at her. Nothing could be done.

Watkin saw her twice. The first time she whispered, "Edda, it's all been so sad." He saw her once more. The whole subject was very painful to him. When he was almost ninety he mentioned it in a letter to Perpetua. His mother had deprived him of a great deal of what should have been his "but on *many occasions* she had been very loving to me. I must and I hope I do *now* remember those. Thank God, we parted on her death bed with a last affectionate goodbye, though expressed by gesture since she could not speak."

She died on March 5 and was buried in the same grave as Edgar near the cliffs at Beeston church. Sam was not present and Catherine was the only one of the children there. When she got back to the convent, the nuns questioned her and told her that since, on her own admission, she had said the Our Father aloud she had taken part in a Protestant service and must immediately go to Confession.

She had left a disconsolate house. The solicitor who had attended the funeral had just informed her parents that Emmeline had left everything to Colonel Heakes and should he die before her, to the Government. The blow, although not altogether unexpected, was nevertheless a heavy one and could not have come at a worse time.

Zoë gave birth to the baby towards the end of March and a fortnight later fifteen of Emmeline's cabin trunks arrived at St Mary's. They were forwarded by the solicitor as Sam did not want them. Edda was with Zoë and anyway not in the least interested, so the task of unpacking them fell to Helena and Perpetua for the most part. The weather was good on the whole so the trunks were left in the garden, the one selected dragged into the hall, its contents examined, sorted, taken back into the garden and another dragged inside. No one had any idea what they would find. And what they did find was strange.

Trunk after trunk was filled with curtains and new linen sheets from Harrods. On each was pinned a notice in Emmeline's writing "For Heaven." Emmeline had been impressed by Salt Lake City and its Mormons and according to Chrisopher before she left for St Helena had expected hourly the Elect to be wafted up to heaven in the manner described by St Paul in his letter to the Thessalonians. She had, therefore, spent huge sums at Harrods to furnish her heavenly home. No one, not Edda, nor Sissie, had realized how confused her mind had become.

Each trunk had its own surprises. In one were Russian sables and ermine wraps. In another diamond and sapphire rings, diamond pendants, bracelets, pearl necklaces and an attractive diamond parrot with a ruby eye. They found the crystal ball in which Sam had once seen Christopher's face and in yet another trunk a heavy piece of silk embroidered with gold and silver thread, at its side a length of ivory satin. Helena immediately recognized these as the material her mother-in-law had bought for the grand wedding that never was. The brocade was given to the Church to be made into a cope. One of Helena's children was married in the satin petticoat.

It is too late to establish with any degree of certainty who persuaded Helena that her best course of action was to leave Edda without telling him beforehand. Most likely it was Perpetua. As the daughter now living at home, it was she who minded the gossip most, was just then hostile to her father and wanted to spare her mother any further trouble and humiliation. It was therefore decided that they should pack up clothes and personal belongings, send them on to an address ahead and then secretly leave the house. The others, even Christopher, were neither told nor consulted. Teresa and Magdalen left for the summer term at Roehampton with no idea that they were leaving their home for ever. Emmeline's trunks were a godsend. Edda showed no interest in them or their contents. He was the easiest of people to deceive. There were trunks everywhere, clothes everywhere, strange objects strewn about in all the rooms, but he remained quietly writing in his study.

Catherine was still at the convent. She came home at the weekends and had to be told. Once Edda arrived from Hunstanton unexpectedly when Helena and Perpetua had made arrangements for the carrier to call. Catherine was told to ask her father if he would like a walk in the woods. They went off together, Watkin repeating, as he always did at that time of year "Loveliest of trees, the cherry now, wearing white for Eastertide." She wanted to tell him what was happening, that they were all going, that he would be left, they would never again see the cherry trees in bloom. It was the most unhappy walk of her entire life.

The sister of a local friend kept a guest house at Epsom and they intended to stay there for the present. Christopher was told of their new address. A letter arrived back saying that he was leaving Downside and would come home at once. Hardly had they received it when another followed enclosing one from his novice master, Dom Leander Donovan, explaining that he had persuaded Christopher that it would be best for his mother if he remained where he was. Father Leander was a most saintly man who many years later was to bring comfort and calm to Watkin on his deathbed.

April 25 was the last day they spent at St Mary's. Perpetua was liable to occasional panic attacks. Now stressed, exhausted and facing the finality of what they were doing, she momentarily gave way under the strain. She truly loved her father and only last Christmas when she was alone in France he had written to tell her that thought and affection united people more closely than space. Desperation made her cruel. She forbade Catherine to leave behind some chocolate which she had bought out of her pocket money for her father to find after they had gone.

In those days the Walls icecream salesman gave all his customers a card with "W" on it which they placed in a front window if they wished him to call. When he knocked at lunch time Perpetua was convinced that her father had returned. She started to scream and hid behind the sofa. When night fell she got more and more hysterical, telling Helena and Catherine that she knew for certain that her father would arrive suddenly and cut their throats when he saw that they were about to leave him. Catherine became terrified. She had betrayed him that afternoon in the woods. He would know it and come for her. Helena was absolutely calm and told them both that it was utter and complete nonsense. All three of them, however, slept in her bedroom that night. Two days later Edda did come back and did find the house empty.

CHAPTER NINETEEN

Only Connect

"What use is life to any of us," he wrote to Barbara Barclay Carter in his usual uninhibited manner, "if there is no God and no communion with Him? To kill painlessly would be an act of virtue, to allow a baby to be born alive a crime. The sooner the human race were extinct and its long tale of meaningless agony closed the better."

There were those who thought that Watkin had got what he deserved and Helena was absolutely right to leave him. There were others who thought that if she had stayed quietly at St Mary's, Edda would have soon tired of Zoë and life would have continued as before. Things did not turn out like that.

Edda came to Roehampton and his children sat upright in the convent parlour as he told them that whatever happened in the future he had no intention of leaving them. The outside world was celebrating the Coronation of King George VI and Queen Elizabeth. About this time Helena received a letter from the Reverend Mother of the convent at Sheringham. The scandal was too great, she wrote, to allow Catherine to return to the school.

Helena met Edda in London and they discussed terms for a legal separation. The children learned with a mixture of dismay and amusement that their Uncle Samuel had reluctantly agreed to act as their guardian in the event of their mother's death. No one knew where money was to come from. Frantic efforts were made to persuade Sam Heakes to come to some agreement before he left the country. Helena saw him, Edda saw him, Philip Fowke saw him, solicitors saw him, but he smiled and smiled, smoked his cigarettes and said nothing to the purpose. In despair, Edda turned to his closest relation on earth, his father's brother, Alfred Watkin, Fowke's father-in-law, a rich man and a former High Sheriff of Cheshire. No support was forthcoming. His nephew had been a fool to spit out the silver spoon he was born with. So the Colonel, who must have endured much in his time, set sail for Canada to share his inheritance with his sister, the wife of a well-known clergyman, the Reverend Percy Soanes of Aurora, Ontario.

The family spent the first summer without their father in a rented house by the sea at Felpham in Sussex and Helena took in a Swedish girl as a paying guest. Edda hoped they would be happy there. It was, he wrote, the place which inspired some of Blake's finest work, Milton's ghost came and talked to him also the ghost of a flea. This was encouraging but perhaps even more so the fact that one of Grandma's famous settlements was somehow salvaged and Edda was enabled to do what he had suggested to Helena in the first place. Property was far cheaper in those days. He bought a house of her own choosing for Helena, and another for himself and Zoë. Gradually it became the accepted thing that he would spend about half the year with his first family and half the year with his second.

Helena's choice was sensible. It was a house on the edge of Dorking in Surrey with a good view of Box Hill and yet within a short walking distance from the station. It was not exactly Helena's milieu and her brother referred to it contemptuously as suburbia but it suited them well enough. Perpetua liked it better than St Mary's. It was called "Fairmead" and Helena's children were very flattered when, later on, one of their boy friends referred to it as "Fair Maidens". Their mother was amused but she had all the Victorian distaste for vanity. If before going out her children asked her if they looked all right, she would tell them that they would pass in a crowd with a push.

Edda, when he came, did not stay with them but in a house nearby owned by a kindly widow who gave him bed and breakfast. Helena's health improved, her asthma attacks became less frequent, and her bronchitis diminished. She loved Edda deeply and missed him when he left. When they were apart they wrote to each other every week. But, as she admitted to her children, he was the most tiring man on earth to live with. Zoë had probably saved Helena's life, certainly made it a happier one. She remained delicate and lacked stamina but ceased to be an invalid.

St Mary's had to be emptied of furniture and put up for sale. Helena asked Perpetua to meet her father at the house to divide the contents between them. We do not know what they said to each other when they met, only that Edda asked for almost nothing. He took his library, the dining room table, a few prints and the portrait of his father standing before a darkened window at Pantafon. All else, including a charming pastel of his mother as a little girl at Mount Felix, he left for Helena.

Now that Pantafon was Edda's he could have given it to Helena or allowed her and their children to live there at the termination of the present lease. But all the reasons which prevented their settling there before still prevailed except that Emmeline could no longer drive them out.

For all her faults, Zoë was not in the least acquisitive. She was greedy for love, not objects, and accepted that Edda would bring her little in the way of worldly goods. The Separation Settlement, and it was small enough, gave Helena a larger income than anything Edda and Zoë had between them. After her experiences at Sheringham Zoë was determined to live in a larger place where she hoped no one would discover her history. They chose to live at Torquay in a pleasant semi-detached house on the outskirts of the town. But she was poor, isolated and uneasy, psychologically worlds apart from Helena. It would enter no one's head to think of her in connection with Pantafon.

The approach of Christmas 1937 presented Helena with a dilemma. Edda wanted to see his children, she wanted to see her mother. An old friend of her youth, Dorothy Charlton, now Dorothy Cafferata, had invited them all to spend Christmas with her and her husband at Stiffkey Old Hall in Norfolk. The Old Hall had been designed and lived in by Sir Nicholas Bacon, Keeper of the Great Seal in the time of Queen Elizabeth I. It stood close to the Rectory whose now illegal incumbent was the Reverend Harold Davidson, a highly eccentric man who had been defrocked for immorality. Despite this, he arrived from London to conduct the service every Sunday. The scandal was great and Edda's children had felt sorry for him. In 1937 he was mauled to death by a lion with whom he was sharing a circus act at Skegness.

The Cafferata's had no children of their own and had been particularly kind to Edda's and Helena's. Louis bought the younger ones expensive sweets to take back to school, Dorothy gave Perpetua her cast-off clothes. Both drove them about the countryside and frequently had them to stay at Stiffkey. But this time no one except Perpetua really wanted to go. Helena feared being patronised and dreaded being the subject of pity. Her younger children were still too bewildered and disorientated to express an opinion either way.

Dorothy worked hard to give them all a good time. She was accustomed to hiring a small coach to take the village children to the Christmas pantomime at Norwich. When she heard that neither Catherine nor Magdalen had ever been to one, she drove them over there at the last moment and bought them tickets. They did not enjoy it. Dorothy produced an expensive frock for Perpetua and an invitation to the local hunt ball but at the last moment Perpetua was overcome by shyness and refused to go. In Dorothy's mind they were all very literary and so she invited Henry Williamson, who was farming near by to come to tea together with his wife and children, but the only book of his anyone had read was *Tarka the Otter*. This was an unfortunate subject for a family whose uncle spent much of his free time trying to kill them.

Deeply as he would have disagreed with many of Williamson's opinions, things would have been completely different if Watkin had been present. Williamson was a gifted, prolific writer, a lover and observer of nature, deeply influenced by the man Watkin was so interested in, Richard Jefferies, author of *The Story of My Heart*. Scarred by his experiences as a young man in the First War, appalled at the growing prospect of history repeating itself, like others at this time, Williamson supported Oswald Moseley and had hopes that Hitler was building a better Germany.

If Dorothy did not understand Williamson, she had even less time for Watkin whose behaviour had been almost as bad as Mr Davidson's. Marriage is an uncertain haven. Dorothy had converted one of the rooms at the Old Hall into a chapel and the Bishop had given permission for the Blessed Sacrament to be reserved there. Every night and morning she and the servants, and any Catholic visitors, would gather for prayers. Louis was never present. Dorothy would announce the recitation of yet another decade of the rosary this time for the intention that the Master, as she referred to her husband, would once again share her bedroom. This would send Perpetua into fits of silent laughter but Helena would look grave and composed. It was doubtful if she was praying along the same lines.

Watkin was still at Hunstanton with Zoë and determined not to let go of his wife and children. He met Helena and Perpetua at the nearby town of Wells-next-the Sea and spent the day with them there, the others did the same the following week. It was a failure. Watkin wished to give them lunch but he could not afford very much. Louis dropped them at a café entrance in his Humber Snipe and their father came forward eagerly to meet them. But he was out of context, a strange figure in a shabby restaurant trying to elicit a response that could not just then be given. He was pleased because he had received a kind letter from Christopher. His sisters thought his Novice Master had dictated it. Uncle Samuel came over to lunch but to Helena's great disappointment pointedly did not invite her over to Abbots Hall.

Their last expedition was to drive to Sheringham and to make one final tour of the empty St Mary's. After that they went to solemn Benediction at St Joseph's church, and then met Canon Carter at the presbytery to say goodbye.

Carter may have been, indeed was, a narrow seminary theologian but he did not deserve to be included in Christopher's lofty anti-clericalism. The liturgy of the Western Church had not yet been dismantled but in many parishes it was very badly celebrated. Only too frequently the priest performed his part at the altar while the congregation drowned his voice with the singing of generally third-rate devotional English hymns. Carter, on the contrary, every Sunday celebrated a sung Mass with the Asperges, holy water, incense, the correct vestments and ritual gestures in a manner that would astonish most Catholics today. He had no choir and the whole congregation joined in the Latin plainsong.

He was now a tired old man with a bad heart and when the time came for them to say goodbye he wept. As a young priest he had said Mass in the little chapel at Aylsham founded and endowed by Helena's aunts Charlotte and Betty Shepheard; he had known Edda when he was still Aloysius, a fervent convert bent on explaining Catholicism to the rest of the world, had benefited greatly from Emmeline's largesse, had hopes that she too might be converted and baptized each one of Helena's daughters. But what had it all come to? Scandal, adultery, an illegitimate child and a deserted house. He died the following year and is buried by the church door.

The international situation was becoming more and more threatening and people's minds were being prepared for war. The League of Nations had failed to curb the ambitions of Japan, Italy and Germany. The first German concentration camp had already been established at Dachau and the Jews deprived of citizenship. Dorothy sat in the vast cavern of her drawing room at Stiffkey wrestling with a printed list from the Civil Defence telling her how to help others in the event of an attack by different kinds of poison gas. She would concentrate on the list, close her eyes, repeat it quietly, then hand it over to Perpetua for interrogation like a child confronted with the catechism. Mustard gas, tear gas, definition, symptoms and remedy. One effect, it appeared, was loss of civilian morale, a new word to all present.

Mussolini had written that Fascism meant "everything is in the State and nothing human or spiritual exists, far less has value, outside the State." For Watkin, both Fascism and Communism, far from being alternatives, were but other names for tyranny of the worst kind, what Luigi Sturzo indeed designated as a form of pantheism, to be resisted whether the trains ran on time or not. The Spanish Civil War, which broke out in the summer of 1936, therefore presented them both with a difficult choice.

For most English Catholics the issue was clear. Franco represented law and order, Catholicism, civilization itself; the Communists or Reds as they were called, a militant atheism which would destroy Europe and was manifesting itself by appalling atrocities against the clergy. One should not over-simplify, but it is probably true to say that the majority of Watkin's fellow writers thought more or less along the same lines.[1] Chesterton died before the war started but he had seen the coming conflict in black and white terms. Belloc thought in the same way, as did Sheed, Ronald Knox, Evelyn Waugh, Douglas Jerrold, who had played an important part in flying Franco from the Canaries in a British chartered aircraft, Tom Burns, Douglas Woodruff, and probably Bédoyère, although his sympathies were not always easy to unravel.

It was said that Cardinal Hinsley had a photograph of Franco on his desk and at Roehampton, as at many convents, prayers were said regularly for the success of his arms. It is true that given the propaganda from both sides, the balance of atrocities was difficult to judge. It is, however, undoubted that there was a strong element of sheer hatred of religion among the government forces and literally thousands of priests, monks and nuns, including a number of bishops, were murdered in a cruel and horrible manner; nuns were frequently raped and churches burnt or vandalized. Statues of the Virgin were subject to insult and mockery, the Blessed Sacrament itself profaned. On this matter, a fair-minded liberal atheist had good reason to be on Franco's side.

The General's opponents, however, were blinded in a different direction. In fact, although many of their supporters did not recogize it, the Communist element among the so-called Reds stood for a far greater tyranny than Franco's Fascists ever did. Vanessa Bell's elder son, Julian, threw his life away for the sake of a self-blinded idealism as did Julian Cornford, the gifted son of Watkin's friend, Frances. The civilized liberal humanist E. M. Forster, who thought of himself as a progressive, had no difficulty in taking the side of the Reds. "Only connect," he was to write. "Live in fragments no longer." But he did not connect. We hear of no protest from a man who owed his Cambridge education to a member of the Evangelical Clapham Sect and the glories of King's to Roman Catholicism.

Sturzo, still an exile in England, certainly did not see the war as a crusade. In his book *Politics and Morality* he was at pains to point out the number of diverse, indeed conflicting elements among the supporters of each side of the struggle. "I leave it to God," he wrote to Watkin in October, 1936, "to decide about victory and defeat in this atrocious civil war in Spain. What is of interest to me (and this is why I write) is that the Church is not believed to be on the side of the rebels and doesn't get tied up with them in victory."

That was not altogether Watkin's view. He was acutely conscious of the dilemma he faced. His hatred of war was in conflict with the most powerful and deepest conviction of his life, the threat to which caused him as a boy at Bletsoe to lose his temper with the youthful Dawson and to push the canopy of the deck chair over his head. This conviction was that God exists and that the purpose of human life is union with Him now and for all eternity. "What use is life to any of us," he wrote to Barbara Barclay Carter in his usual uninhibited manner,[2] "if there is no God and no communion with Him? To kill painlessly would be an act of virtue, to allow a baby to be born alive a crime. The sooner the human race were extinct and its long tale of meaningless agony closed the better." He refused to accept the moral equivalence of both sides. Whatever the balance of atrocities, the Reds stood for militant atheism and blasphemy, Franco stood for the support of religion and the worship of God. National autonomy was not worth a single innocent life and in so far as Franco was fighting for Spanish nationalism Watkin had no sympathy for him whatsoever; it was precisely the millions of lives sacrificed for national ends which made the war of 1914 so unspeakably wicked. Out of personal weakness and want of courage, he finishes his letter to Barbara, "I couldn't help preferring my life to the destruction and defilement of the churches here [but] I know quite well that it would be a far less evil that I should be murdered than the Mass suppressed and the Church outraged. It must be so, since God is infinitely more than man."

Watkin is in effect saying that war for a religious end is justified but for national, secular ends alone is totally wrong. He makes the same point in a letter to Sturzo. Even in the face of aggression in 1914 the Allies were wrong to fight what he called "other national herds" in order that their particular national herds should keep power, wealth and prestige. That millions of men, women and children were slaughtered in order to prevent Belgium from being a dependency of Germany was evil. But it is not evil to support a man who, however mixed his motives, is preventing atheism and blasphemy being forced upon a people and little children deprived of the knowledge of God. He adds, typically Watkin, not to speak of saving great works of art from wanton destruction.

The reference to 1914 must have struck home with Sturzo. Whether Watkin knew it or not, Sturzo had supported Italy's entry into the war on the side of the Allies. He had, however, changed his views. He now denied the legitimacy of recourse to war as a means of settling disputes between nations. On Christmas Day 1937, he wrote to Watkin and told him that during the night he had been thinking a great deal about Watkin's work on mystical philosophy. As for the Spanish question: If Jesus Christ had wanted an armed defence of religion he would have given adequate teaching on the subject. What texts we have suggest the contrary. If war is to be authorized to resist anti-religious persecutions we should have permanent war almost everywhere in the Christian world. Those who accept war being waged in their names for religious goals lower themselves to the human mundane level and restrict their own mission to the national and party level.

It had gone against the grain for Watkin to support Franco, which is why his letters are so agitated and intense. He feared that even if Franco were victorious the Church would be reduced to a most unhealthy dependence upon the state as the sole bulwark against Red atheism and in that atmosphere it would be impossible to convert the hearts and minds of their opponents, which was the only way forward. However, he had been forced to defend violence as a necessary evil in defence of the only cause that really mattered to him. It was better to have another Fascist Italy than another Soviet Russia.

In March 1937, Bernard Wall, the editor of *Colosseum*, published a symposium on war and peace and invited various contributors to express their views. Watkin argues, as one would expect, that modern international wars produce more evil than good. He believed that considerations of honour were the main reason why the majority turned against pacifism. "The supposition," he writes, "that any foreign power could annex and hold Great Britain is absurd." It was not to be so absurd in 1940. The Dominican, Father Gerald Vann, argued that a future war would bring anarchy and revolution, the collapse of culture and religion for victor and vanquished alike. Eric Gill wrote brusquely. "War has become impossible and that is simply that." He did, however, think that national defence was justified in certain conditions and circumstances. The Anglican Maurice Reckitt's main point is that we have to rid ourselves of the idea that Christians have to accept war as a normal part of their earthly obligation. Bédoyère feels that the honest answer to the questions raised is simply that he does not know but goes on to discuss them with his usual energy. Douglas Jerrold argued the case for war on Catholic principles.

Dawson, in a long and interesting article, discusses historical aspects of war and pacifism. If there is an European war in the near future it will not be a capitalist war for markets but a war of creeds for the possession of men's minds. Our task is not to abolish war or to set up a cosmopolitan superstate but how to effect a reconciliation here and now between the rivalries and animosities of the existing national states. War is not only the work of man. "It is also willed by God as the punishment of sin and as the instrument by which Divine Justice performs its inscrutable judgements."

We know what was to happen, the contributors did not. One reads the multitude of opinions expressed at this time with a mixture of superiority, sadness and above all, perplexity, as people still searching for an answer.

In Dostoyevsky's *The Brothers Karamazov* Ivan challenges Alyosha to say whether God should have created the world with the object of making us happy in the end but at the certain cost of the torture and death of one single baby. No, Alyosha answers. The same challenge, on a less profound level, faced a large part of humanity now. How many babies could be sacrificed, not in order to preserve national sovereignty alone, but those civilized values so painfully arrived at down the centuries. Was there any consistent position between absolute pacifism and total war?

CHAPTER TWENTY

To Reckon in Centuries
and Plan for Eternity

*The mood was very different from what it had been in
1914. The British Empire extended even further now but
there was little complacency, none of the easy confidence
of that long ago summer, rather a sense of dread.*

In April 1936 Watkin agreed to become President of a newly formed
peace society named *Pax*. This society would one day merge with the
world-wide organization *Pax Christi*. If any single person could be said
to be its founder, it was Watkin.

Its origins were curious. After Bédoyère's departure from the *Catholic
Herald,* he was succeeded as editor by Donald Attwater, the scholarly
hagiographer who among much else assisted Father Thurston to revise the
twelve volumes of Butler's *Lives of the Saints*. On March 13, 1936, a letter
appeared in the *Herald* above the pseudonym "Keladon". Its author
announced that in the light of natural reason, Catholics should refuse to
bear arms because the evil attendant upon national wars was, in modern
times, greater than any good that could emerge. Watkin seized his opportunity and wrote up at once. He attacked the *Herald*'s previous stand on
disarmament and stated that in the conditions of modern warfare all
Catholics should be conscientious objectors although an armed international police force was acceptable. Before his letter was even printed he
had one from Attwater.[1] He was glad to receive Watkin's letter because
he himself was "Keladon"! He had resigned from the editorship because
the directors were not happy with his views but he had got his own letter
in first. By the same post came a letter from Bédoyère telling Watkin that
after much soul-searching he had accepted a request from the *Herald*'s
owners and directors to return as editor. There were difficulties but a
compromise had been arrived at and he couldn't afford to lose the offer.

Other letters appeared supporting both "Keladon" and Watkin and on April 10 Watkin wrote to suggest that a Catholic league should be formed, joined by all who believed that a future war would be race suicide. Another correspondent, Hugo Yardley, asked anyone interested in Catholic pacifism to get in touch with him.

Three people responded. They were Christian Lucas, (later Hardie) like her sister Barbara, Bernard Wall's wife, a granddaughter of Alice Meynell. The two others were a Miss Ouwerkerk and a young man named Alban Evans. It is to him that we owe detailed reports of the early years of the movement. It was he who thought of the name Pax, became Secretary and drew up prayers for the group to recite. In 1938 he became a Dominican novice and in time was ordained priest and known as Father Illtud Evans. His letters are among the most enthusiastic, interesting and informative of all the correspondence Watkin received. These four people met and decided to ask Watkin to draft a statement of principles for the formation of a Society to promote Catholic pacifism. But what was Catholic pacifism? On what principles was this Society to act and what were its aims? Moreover, what in this context did the word "Catholic" mean? Roman Catholic, Anglo-Catholic or plain Christian?

Attwater, now free from the *Herald*, told Watkin that he understood the whole project was more or less revolving round him. But although he accepted the position as President, Watkin was overburdened with his own work, tormented by his financial position and his domestic difficulties. Moreover, he lived far from London. The formation of the Society involved him in constant correspondence and demands upon his time. At Cambridge the organizer of the von Hügel Society, a new Society which was being founded in memory of the Baron's brother Anatole, asked him to address its first meeting. The subject was to be peace and war, a matter which haunted minds.

The mood was very different from what it had been in 1914. The British Empire extended even further now but there was little complacency, none of the easy confidence of that long ago summer, rather a sense of dread. At the top, counsels were divided and a reluctance to fight yet again was strong in all classes and many parts of the world. Through the *Herald* Watkin heard from America, Italy and Switzerland and he drew up an analysis of the principles behind traditional Catholic teaching on a just war and its application to the present situation, which was read together with a paper from Attwater at a meeting of *Pax* at the end of May.[2]

The story of *Pax: An Association for the Promotion of Peace* is a microcosm of the history of much human endeavour, a tale of frustrated goodness. Its principles were revised at least six times. The word "Catholic" was dropped. In one way it is sad to go over the correspondence its foundation engendered. So much hope, so little achieved. When war came no British Catholic bishop came out against conscription or the plainly immoral methods by which the Allied victory was eventually secured. Sadly, Attwater's son, Robin, in the RAF , was to be killed in action aged twenty.

However, *Pax*'s efforts were not in vain as its later history was to demonstrate. It was founded on the conviction that human beings are all one, that there are limits to what the state can command from an individual. But the hope that if war came the Catholic Church as an institution would stand by its own teaching was unrealistic. Modern warfare, however just the cause, inevitably means the indiscriminate slaughter of innocent people and is quite obviously not in accord with either the Christian Gospels or the official teaching of the Church. Described as "a crime against God and man" it was to be subject of the single anathema uttered by the Second Vatican Council.[3]

In the twelfth century Pope Paschal II wished to cut the sinews which bound church and state by renouncing all ecclesiastical property derived from the secular power since the time of Charlemagne. Henceforth the Church should be maintained by tithes and voluntary offerings. He and his cardinals were hurried off to prison. Paschal's radical proposal was as impractical at that time as the adoption of pacifism by any twentieth-century pontiff.

In the nineteen-twenties and thirties for a number of complex reasons, frequently rehearsed, the Catholic Church did not free itself from its historical ties to the state and unequivocally assert the supremacy of God over Caesar. It is true that in the final years of his pontificate Pius XI made increasingly uncompromising attacks upon Nazi ideology. These included his 1937 encyclical, *Mit brennender Sorge*, which condemned Nazi treatment of the Catholic Church and in the last year of his life he made outspoken attacks on racism. In peace time the Vatican had a network of informants throughout the world and knew perfectly well what was going on in Germany, Austria and on its own doorstep. The Roman Catholic Church was the only international organization left with sufficient power, knowledge and reach capable of standing in Hitler's path. If it had acted then, the ovens of Auschwitz might never have been fired. Neither the encyclical nor general attacks on racism were an adequate response to the actual situation. Probably Pius's encyclical against birth control, *Casti connubii*, had more influence than *Mit brennender Sorge*. Obsessed with politics and the Lateran Treaty, the Pope neither condemned Hitler nor his entourage by name nor was there a detailed, explicit condemnation of what was happening to the race to which Our Lord himself belonged.

The well-known remark of Sir D'Arcy Osborne, the British Minister at the Vatican before, after and during the Second World War, probably states the position best. "Not only," he wrote, "is the attitude of the Vatican supranational and universal . . . it is also, so to speak, outside of time . . . They reckon in centuries and plan for eternity and this inevitably renders their policy inscrutable, confusing and on occasion reprehensible to practical and time-conditioned minds."[4]

So was the way opened to what in retrospect came to be seen by many as one of the greatest scandals in Christian history. When war broke out it was too late to change course. After the conclusion of the Concordat of 1933, the German episcopate as a body approved the Nazi regime and in 1939 gave their undivided support for the war effort. The Papacy was not prepared to risk schism, persecution and widespread apostasy by insisting that any German bishop who encouraged his flock to fight for Hitler should be deprived of his office and any Catholic who took part in the systematic persecution of the Jews was guilty of grave sin. The mission of the Church is to save souls *in whatever circumstances.*

Many of the Catholic community in Great Britain were confused and uncertain. At the end of April 1936, probably under pressure, Bédoyère closed his letter pages to further discussion about *Pax*: "If it has the right spirit" he wrote, " it will make its own way." In his turn the editor of *The Tablet*, Douglas Woodruff, wrote a lengthy and interesting letter to Watkin lamenting that he was heading the movement. He was sorry both on personal grounds and as one who disagreed fundamentally with the position *Pax* had taken up. The personal grounds were of course that he found himself in difficulties. According to their agreement, Watkin's reviews for the paper were still anonymous but as editor Woodruff had to take responsibility for them. The paper's editorial policy on the question of duty in war, he said, was not in harmony with his. In future Watkin would be sent for review only books which did not deal with those issues.

To an extent the ghost of Guy Fawkes still haunted English consciousness. It must not be thought for one moment that Catholics would hesitate to fight for king and country. Had not Catholics sheltered Charles II after Cromwell's victory at Worcester and the gallant Jane Lane carried the crown of England in her hands when the king, disguised as a servant, rode pillion behind her to make his escape from Charmouth? Why should *Pax* claim to be a Catholic organization when its literature had not been passed by the diocesan censor?

Moreover, having the *right* to be a conscientious objector was not the same thing as having a *duty* to be one, as its promoters implied.

Cardinal Hinsley, the Archbishop of Westminster, had condemned both Fascism and Nazism outspokenly. However, he shared these anxieties about the formation of *Pax* and a letter requiring clarification arrived from his secretary. His Grace was concerned lest any Catholic organization should form "wrong consciences" in this matter. In particular, he was worried about a proposed paragraph in the statement sent to him which said that one of the objects of the Association was "to give practical support and professional help to those of any nationality who at any time come into collision with the civil or military authorities on account of conscientious refusal of military service." This was the point of the Archbishop's letter, the central difficulty, the sensitive nerve. It was circulated to the Committee together with a reply, drawn up by Watkin, for approval and comment. A copy of this reply, dated October 18, 1936, still exists in Helena's handwriting. It is three pages long, skilfully argued, and uses traditional Catholic teaching on conscientious objection in defence of *Pax*'s position.

After the war broke out in 1939 Hinsley forbade the distribution of *Pax* pamphlets outside Westminster Cathedral or any other church in his diocese. In 1943, when the conflict worsened and consciences hardened, the Cardinal died and his successor, Archbishop Griffin, asked all Catholic priests to resign from an Association that had no authorization from the Church. In the spring of 1944 Bishop Parker of Northampton in a Pastoral Letter warned congregations to be beware of being led astray by false teachers who erroneously attempted to convince others that modern warfare was alien to Christian morality. To join the Forces was to do the will of God, to disobey lawful authority mortal sin. This was something deeper than lingering memories of the Armada or Guy Fawkes. The German bishops were making precisely the same point.

On March 13, 1938, to the initial approval of Cardinal Innitzer, Hitler marched into Vienna and Austria was incorporated into greater Germany. In that month Joseph Kennedy was appointed American Ambassador to the Court of St James. Three of his daughters Eunice, Patricia and Jean, were to be sent to Roehampton.

In the autumn of 1938 the Czechoslovakian crisis began. Perpetua had just started a secretarial course in London. Her diary at this time is full of fear and foreboding. She had had to listen since childhood to Watkin's violent denunciations of the three dictators – Stalin, Mussolini and Hitler – and now she prepared for the worst. She saw trenches being dug in the London parks. The next day gas masks began to be distributed and the Fleet was mobilized.

Before the Munich Agreement had been arrived at, Watkin came up to London for a meeting of *Pax*. He had lunch with Perpetua and went to Roehampton to see Teresa and Magdalen. They rather dreaded his coming. He might get angry, raise his voice and jump up and down in the parlour, and they would die of shame. Almost no wirelesses or newspapers were allowed in the school but some news was given and rumours abounded, bits and pieces from parents in the know, gossip from embassies or, some proclaimed, Buckingham Palace.

When their father arrived he was surprisingly calm. The weather was good. They walked up and down on the terrace, past the statue of the Sacred Heart and the white pillared façade of the eighteenth-century ballroom and the chapel above where the nuns prayed so silently before the Blessed Sacrament day after day. Almost exactly two years later incendiary bombs would reduce it to rubble. Watkin said that we could not save Czechoslavakia without war for which neither Britain nor France was prepared. Chamberlain was doing what he could. But it was only a postponement.

His two daughters were amazed by their father's quiet manner although the reason was not far to seek. He had already explained what he felt in a letter to the ever anxious Perpetua.

He could not pretend that we were not in great danger. When world calamities threaten we must return to first principles. Do we, or do we not, believe that the world was created by a good God? We believe that it is and if so we must be sure that His Will will be done. All these evils drive us back to God. There are times when we have to become what the psalmist describes as "a dumb animal with thee," in other words to submit to see nothing and put one's will into His hands to guide us. Then we shall find what follows is true: "Thou hast held fast my right hand." Also this attitude – the very *essence* of prayer – helps our suffering fellow men. It may not be able to stop war but it will act as a *force* against war, to over-come the evil of it and make it in the end serve God's eternal kingdom of souls and to maintain that peace which even war cannot take away since it belongs to a higher order. "It is only of late that I have come to any practical sense of these things. I have known them for years in theory but *could* not attempt to live by them."

After that Christmas, spent at Stiffkey, the family returned home without their mother. The strain of the visit, above all her grief at not being invited to Abbots Hall, had made her ill. She had set her heart on seeing Maria Pasqua again. As the time for going back to Dorking approached she developed a severe attack of asthma and had to be left behind in Dorothy Cafferata's care. She did not, however, despair of seeing her mother and in the spring of 1939 she seized an opportunity. After Catherine's experiences, the family were on the alert for any early signs of a defective appendix. Perpetua had already had hers out before they had left Sheringham and Magdalen's was removed, probably need-lessly, in the winter of 1938. The following spring Helena wrote to Samuel and explained that she and Magdalen were going to spend a week at Cromer for the child's convalescence. Could they both come over to Aylsham? Yes, he said, their mother would receive them. So Helena and Magdalen went to Cromer and eventually were met at Aylsham station by Samuel and driven to Abbots Hall. Magdalen was the last of the chil-dren to see their grandmother alive.

It was a sticky lunch. Maria Pasqua sat at what was now the head of the table opposite Philip Shepheard's empty chair. Magdalen looked at her eyebrows because Helena had told her that her mother once used to smooth them with black vaseline. Conversation was difficult. Samuel mixed Maria Pasqua a glass of Sanatogen which she drank in delicate sips while his beloved terrier, Daisy, shuffled about on the boards close to the window. There was no sound from the kennels but the child knew that Thor, the bloodhound, would be aware of visitors and pulling at his chain. Edda's name was never mentioned and Dorking was a foreign country.

One day towards the end of June Samuel telephoned Helena and told her that their mother had not long to live. Helena left for Norfolk at once and remained at Abbots Hall until the end. Maria Pasqua was very weak and in bed. She greeted Helena as if she had just come in from a long walk and their years of separation had never been. The past to her then was not her married life, not even her experiences with the Comtesse de Noailles, but Italy, the sun and the dancing and the snow-capped mountains of the Abruzzi. She died, holding Helena's hand, on July 14. She had wanted to be buried in Rome but if that were not possible, in the same grave as her little son Martin at Egham. Her coffin was made on the estate and carried into the cemetery at Englefield Green by four men who had worked at Aylsham for many years. Perpetua was present with her mother and Samuel.

Helena was heartbroken. Nor was her grief lessened by learning of the terms of her mother's will. Everything had been left to Samuel, including the jewellery. She minded this deeply, not for the sake of the money although she needed it, but because she felt it to be the final rejection. When she came to write her own will she resolutely refused to make any distinction between her daughters, however reasonable, because she knew how hurtful discrimination could be.

In one of the letters Zoë wrote to Helena after their meeting at St Mary's, Zoë expressed a hope that what had happened would not ruin Watkin's career as a writer. It was not ruined, but undoubtedly damaged, although one should not exaggerate. In those days other people's lives were not subject to the unremitting probing so many now have to endure. Nevertheless, his reputation suffered. He could not become one of those approved Catholic figures wheeled out whenever some scandal occurred or an Anglican bishop made a particularly foolish doctrinal statement. Had he been an actor, a novelist or a sculptor, it would not have mattered so much. But although his work was far-ranging, it fell into the religious category and his way of life laid him open to the charge of insincerity or at the least, of not practising what he preached.

His real friends were distressed at what had happened but ignored it. His behaviour made no difference to his personal or professional relations with Frank and Maisie Sheed. They were fond of him but naturally this was mixed with an element of self-interest. He was among their most distinguished authors and his advice was invaluable. Maisie frequently called upon him for assistance in her work. She writes in 1937 when she knows he is living at Hunstanton with Zoë and thanks him "again and again" for his criticisms of her life of Wilfred Ward of which she will make the fullest use. After the war, when she was completing *The Young Mr Newman,* she had made use of *all* his suggestions. "I shall never cease to wonder that you should have been able to send me twenty-five foolscap pages almost by return, filling the gaps I've left in my writing. Your learning always fills me with amazement, admiration and just a touch of envy."

No one who had actually met Watkin could think of him as a bad man. Peculiar, unpredictable, a little mad even, but transparently good. There is nothing in his extant correspondence to suggest that there was the slightest diminution in any of his friendships, personal or professional, nor is there any mention of the plight he had got himself into. However, he may have destroyed some more personal letters. His former mentor, Mrs Tatham, is suspiciously silent, so are Squirrel, Barbara Barclay-Carter, Evelyn Underhill and Kechie and Claughton Pellew.

Not every outsider was charitable. A pious Catholic woman from Sheringham, whose name was not revealed, called on Watkin's parish priest and told him about the situation, adding that to give such a noto-rious sinner Holy Communion would be a cause of scandal. Most reluctantly, the priest had to explain to Watkin what he had already accepted. It must be said that the Catholic clergy as a whole, from the beginning to the end, were exceedingly kind to Edda.

On the purely practical level there were difficulties too. It became increasingly hard to make ends meet. He and Zoë led a Spartan life but as Helena had once pointed out, it was expensive to maintain two house-holds. Watkin lived now even further from London than before, fares were costly and so was accommodation. He had to keep up contacts with publishers, travel to various places to lecture and what he valued more than anything else, keep in touch with his friends.

There was another penalty. As we have seen, those officials who guarded the purity of Catholic doctrine as it was then presented were already suspicious of the direction his thought was taking. Nor did they like his unremitting attacks upon Mussolini and Hitler. Until it entered the war as our gallant ally, it was of course meritorious to criticise the ungodly Soviet Union but Italy was a Catholic country and so were large parts of Germany. The implications of Watkin's attitude were unsettling. Information about his private life lent weight to their original suspicions. It might be even more difficult than in the past to obtain the *Imprimatur.*

During these years, quite undeterred by his domestic troubles, Watkin was in fact writing what would prove to be one of his most popular and successful books, *The Catholic Centre,* first published in 1939. It was widely read and reprinted on wartime paper in 1943. If any single book of his can be said to herald the Second Vatican Council it would be this one.

Watkin argues that we find in Catholic Christianity the *via media,* the centre, both in the Church's dogmatic teaching and the philosophy which underpins it. This he develops and explains. However, as often practised and understood, Catholicism has only too often failed to occupy this centre. There was an urgent need for reform both in religious thought and practice. But this reformation can only be a return to Catholic truth. It must not be a going out of Catholic truth but rather a coming into it by means of a deeper, interior understanding of the faith.

It is this book which contained his oft-quoted injunction "Come in or go out." He means that the alternatives for us today are either a far deeper understanding of Catholicism or an exit from it. Seen on the surface Catholic dogma and devotions "seem a distracting complex of diverse truths and objects of worship." Viewed from within, however, the many are seen as one, parts of a single organic body of truth. Doctrines like the Atonement, redemption by the Precious Blood and the Communion of Saints will then no longer appear incredible or even distasteful.

Watkin helps us towards an interior understanding of these truths and to those put off by the externals of Catholicism; he enlarges upon much of what he said in Tom Burn's short-lived publication *Order*. Most of the abuses that have littered the history of Catholicism have been due to ecclesiastical materialism, a perversion which places a higher value on the body, the institutional church, than its soul, its inner life and meaning. But the fact that the these abuses flourish is no more an argument for discarding the Church than the fact that green fly infest rose bushes is a reason for dispensing with roses.

The movement for reform is widely felt but unless at its very centre there is a mystical revival, a revival of contemplative life, the movement will fail. "For the windows will not be opened and the new plant will wither in the poisonous atmosphere of ecclesiastical materialism." The contemplative vocation is for everybody, in a hostile world it will soon be impossible to maintain a genuine Catholic religion without it.

It must be remembered that this was written long before the Second Vatican Council and long before Karl Rahner was to remark that "the Christian of the future will be a mystic or he, or she, will not exist at all." By this Watkin (and Rahner) meant the practice of interior prayer, the prayer of adoration, making direct contact with the transcendent God . Contemplation bestows inner understanding which penetrates below the letter of the entire Catholic programme of Masses, ceremonies, sacraments, prayers and scripture to the underlying spiritual reality, which is their true significance. Someone who practices it, Watkin wrote, "will not abandon the Faith for any difficulties to which he has no conceptual solution nor for any scandals however grave."

It is a mistake to imagine that the Second Vatican Council came like a bolt from the blue. The ground was prepared but not sufficiently. Many people found Watkin's book both refreshing and helpful. "If the task of converting England, my own South Africa or any other country devolved upon me," a correspondent wrote in a published letter from Cape Town, "I think I should begin by placing a copy of *The Catholic Centre* by Mr E. I. Watkin in the hands of every Catholic capable of digesting it. It is a book which enables the disillusioned convert to get a grip on the Faith and go on hoping."

It was remarked at the time that there were two kinds of Catholics, the G. K. Chesterton type for whom everything in the Church's garden was lovely and the E. I. Watkin type whose loyalty was more critical and profound. *The Catholic Centre* was a corrective to the then prevalent over-confident, cocksure Catholicism whose collapse in the aftermath of the Second Vatican Council was to lead to catastrophic defections from the faith. Someone who was a young convert at the time pointed out later in his life that the book revealed to him "a new vision of the Church as the *rightful* place for all truth which may yet be partially held and lived out in many instances better outside her frontiers than within them."[5]

This outlook was not altogether shared by the censor although it must be admitted that his comments were phrased in a more courteous manner than usual. Naturally, he did not like Watkin's catalogue of abuses, however gently stated. He could, with an effort, accept Watkin's under-standing of Catholic doctrine but he did not want to hear about liturgical decadence, over-centralized authority, and far too great an emphasis on the value of external membership of the Church. Before he would grant the *Imprimatur* he insisted upon various excisions and devised a carefully worded formula to be printed in front of the text: "This book is the fruit of much personal meditation upon the truths of the Catholic Religion, and a humble attempt to elucidate some of its mysteries, so far as this has been given to one finite mind. *Credo ut intelligam.* There is, of necessity, in this book much that is speculative, much that is personal and here and there I may seem to depart from the common explanation. Further, I sometimes say hard things about the actions of Church officials, because the heavenly treasure is borne in earthen vessels. But I wish to disclaim in advance any idea of the criticising the Church as such. The Catholic Church is the pillar and ground of the Truth and our Infallible Teacher. To her judgement I willingly submit all that is written here."

Watkin spent the last two weeks before the war with Helena in Surrey. Christopher used to say that his father was the only person he had ever met who literally wrung his hands. Now the worst was about to happen, however, he remained quiet and resigned. Perpetua had taken a job as a secretary at St John and St Elizabeth's Hospital in London and spent her weekends with him and the others walking over Box Hill. They looked for orchids and visited Meredith's home, Flint Cottage. Watkin quoted the lines "Lovely are the curves of the white owl sweeping," from the poet's *Love in the Valley* and stayed tranquil.

Perpetua, on the contrary, was full of apprehension. A few months before, the BBC had broadcast a programme about the deaths in the Canadian Arctic of her cousins Edgar Christian, Jack Hornby and their companion, Harold Adlard. Colonel Christian had hoped that his son's example might inspire the rising generation with courage, loyalty and endurance. Perpetua hoped so too and in the event was to show some of these qualities herself. In her diary she recounts step by step by step the countdown to war as perceived from the outside by a girl of nineteen who knew little about the diplomatic manoeuvres going on in high places.

By August 25 no more children were admitted to the Hospital. The next day those left were taken for treatment elsewhere and a little over twenty people remained in the entire building. The windows were everywhere blacked out and the evacuation of all children from London began. On September 1 German troops crossed the Polish frontier and on September 3, war was declared. By then Watkin had left for home and Helena went on adding to her store of candles. They were so scarce, she said, last time round.

CHAPTER TWENTY-ONE

Our Armies are Broken, the Saints are Dead

If the Nazis were in power in England there would be no religion, no freedom, we would all be like dogs without teeth and with our tongues removed – attached to the Nazi leash, not even able to speak.

Three days after the declaration of war, Perpetua wrote an impassioned letter to her father. She utterly disagreed with his view about welcoming peace at any price. He of *all* people should object to Hitler's price. Unless we were prepared to allow the whole of Europe to become the tools of Nazism, we had no alternative but to fight. We are not fighting for our Empire, she wrote, or because we are frightened that Germany will get more powerful than we are or out of hate for the Germans. She has never come across any hatred of the German people, only horror at the wickedness of Nazism and a desire to speak to Hitler in the only language that he understands. If the Nazis were in power in England there would be no religion, no freedom, we would all be like dogs without teeth and with our tongues removed – attached to the Nazi leash, not even able to speak.

He has had most of his life, she continued, his loves and his children. She and thousands more have had none of these things yet are willing to fight and to suffer against Nazism. The man she loves is going out to France in a few months and with him goes everything that counts for her. We spoke soft words into the mouth of a gun for a long while but a gun can only answer with bullets. She has not his gift for expressing herself but she knows that peace will come only when Nazism is exterminated. If only he were nearer. She does not love him the less because they disagree.

Watkin gives the reply one would expect. He is up against one of the most powerful of human instincts – the instinct that divides men into herds against other herds. Sovereign states are as much an anachronism as the states of the Anglo-Saxon heptarchy. The last war was fought to keep the world safe from Kaiser Wilhelm and it led to his replacement by a far worse tyrant. This war may end in such mutual exhaustion that Stalin would be left supreme to make Europe safe for tyrannical and atheistic communism.

This, in its way, was prophetic. Yet Watkin is a man of his time, the child who witnessed Queen Victoria's Diamond Jubilee and stood outside the door of St George's Chapel at Windsor when her body was carried in. He found it hard to believe that Great Britain could be conquered by Germany and thought that if we had only kept quiet Hitler would have left us alone. The utmost which would have happened would have been the loss of power and influence in Europe and Asia and a falling back to the status of a second-rate power. Would we be any the worse for that? Is not Holland a far happier place than England?

Substitute Denmark for Holland and it is what Bertrand Russell was arguing in his wild and inconsistent book written, he was to say later, with conscious insincerity, *Which Way for Peace?* Russell urged disarmament, the end of Churchill and warmongering, abandonment of our colonies, perpetual neutrality, and turning ourselves into a defenceless country like Denmark which Hitler would have no motive to attack. The Germans were essentially civilized people, even if they did invade Britain life would not be so bad provided we did not provoke them.

Russell did not believe this any more than Watkin who may have been guilty of political naïvety but had no illusions about what would happen if the country were conquered by Germany. But his hope lay elsewhere in a dimension of being that Russell understood very well and had once deeply appreciated but could not accept.[1] The philosophy that he had adopted did not admit the existence of any reality which did not lie within the competence of scientific proof. Nor would it have fitted in with his way of life. "Put not your trust in princes," Watkin reminded Perpetua. Had he hope only in this world he would despair but in the depth of the soul – far beyond the rise and fall of kingdoms – he feels not despair but the peace of God's Power and Presence.

Russell was lecturing in the United States in 1940 and as the German army carried all before it in Europe, his fine theories melted away. He loved England and the idea of permanent exile in America appalled him. "I try to remain a pacifist," he wrote to a friend, "but the thought of Hitler and Stalin triumphant is hard to bear."[2]

In the summer of 1940 he gave up the struggle, publicly retracted pacifism and announced that if he were of military age he would be fighting. He and Philip Mumford resigned as sponsors of the Peace Pledge Union and took over six hundred people with them. These included Rose

Macaulay, A. A. Milne, Maude Royden, Ellen Wilkinson and C. C. Joad who had proposed the famous "King and Country" debate at Oxford in 1933.Vera Brittain remained steadfast in her pacifism and so did Watkin's friend, the well-known Anglican spiritual writer, Evelyn Underhill, whom Thorold had once wickedly referred to as a nice old *female* clergyman.

In 1932 she had got in touch with Watkin as "a great admirer of his writing" in order to ask him to contribute an article on the problem of suffering for the *Spectator*. Most of her quasi-pacifist friends, she wrote in December 1939, are more warlike, apparently feeling that "the only way to combat sin in others is to commit sin ourselves." The attitude of the Anglican bishops, she added, was disappointing. This must have amused Watkin who in his turn had no expectations whatsoever from those who were actually in communion with the See of Peter.

As the conflict worsened, she pointed out yet again that so many of her fellow pacifists seemed to think that Hitler's wickedness justified participation in the war and when we have won it, would be pacifists again. But committing sin to cure sin is neither Christianity nor commonsense. "Perhaps we have reached a level of collective sinfulness in which we *cannot* do right." During our darkest hour in 1941, she wrote that, as horror piled upon horror, it became more and more clear that one cannot fight evil with evil. "We are witnessing Armageddon without knowing what Armageddon really means, so we have not the 'material' for forming a considered judgement on what one's own action can and should be. But to adhere to the eternal God and to help others to steady their lives in the same way must always be right." She had not much time left to help others. Two months later she died from acute asthma. Perhaps she knew that she had not long to live because she signed her letter not with her customary more formal ending but "yours always".

Bédoyère, as intelligently unpredictable as ever, hovered between apprehension, hope and pessimistic detachment. There will be no war, he wrote in the *Catholic Herald* on the last day of 1938, and three months before war actually broke out declared that the enemies of Germany were not concerned to curb Hitler's aggression but to destroy Germany for imperialist, economic and so called ideological motives. As the war progressed, however, he too retreated into a kind of conformity. He printed a letter from a priest who suggested that Catholics should refuse to participate in the wholesale slaughter of their fellow Christians but wrote a sharp editorial comment at the bottom telling his correspondent not to be more Catholic than the Pope who had blessed all Catholics "who did their duty by their country." Being Bédoyère, the doubt remained. In view, he added, of the extreme difficulty of applying the Church's moral teaching on a just war to the complexities of the world situation, the presumption appears to be that it is right for us to follow the Pope's counsel.

Don Luigi Sturzo, who had a bad heart, left for the United States when the bombing intensified in the September of 1940. He spent six difficult years without the constant support of Barbara Barclay Carter and Cecily Marshall but despite ill-health, exile and lack of contacts, he continued valiantly to write on politics and sociology. In 1945 the Italian government tried to make amends by publicly thanking him for his "noble activity carried out with such humane equanimity and disinterested wisdom . . . " In 1946 he returned at last to Italy. His travelling companions from New York to Naples were two Jews from Trieste, father and son, who helped him daily to set up his portable altar so that he could celebrate Mass.

Nevertheless, his position was a difficult one. His views on the morality of modern warfare should logically have led him to pacifism. Earlier, he had denied the legitimacy of war as a means of settling disputes between nations. In 1938 both in his *Pax* pamphlet and his book *Politics and Morality,* he had argued that we must put morality before the interests of any nation, Church or class. The end, therefore, never justifies the means. No one, he had written, can maintain that massacres of the innocent, or killing women and children without pity are moral acts. But, he asked, who can remain restrained in an armed struggle, "who can hold in the human beast once it is unchained?"

Who indeed? By the time Sturzo returned to Europe the atomic bomb had been dropped twice, in his own words "an incubus, a spectre, a macabre portent: to kill, or rather to annihilate, over a hundred thousand non-combatants in a single blow, in a fleeting second, is something truly catastrophic."[3] Catastrophic, we notice, not evil, the consequence of a deliberate moral choice. Sturzo fails to drive home the conclusion from his own premise not from intellectual cowardice or fear of being unpopular, but for the same reasons which had made the Papacy act as it did.

The following year, he published *Nationalism and Internationalism.* Although still insisting that it is our duty to subordinate politics to morality, he puts forward an interesting and within its own terms, unanswerable apologia for the conduct of the Catholic hierarchy (and indeed himself) during the war. The Church tolerates "conditions of fact" which are beyond its powers to modify. Fundamentally, what really occupies the clergy, bishops and Pope is, above all, spiritual assistance to the population and its armies. Therefore they are concerned not to question the necessity of war but to support it "in order not to engender in the faithful distrust towards a clergy apathetic, critical or detached from the common cause."

Is this something which was later to develop into "emergency ethics"? In other words, the principles enunciated in his books remain valid but cannot be applied in the real world of death, destruction and sacrifice? Perhaps we have indeed reached "a level of collective sinfulness in which we *cannot* do right." Slavery was a "condition of fact" in the Roman Empire but there was no conflict because the early Church did not look upon it as morally wrong. Had it done so, Christianity would have remained a Jewish sect. Sturzo describes a permanent feature of Catholicism in much the same way as D'Arcy Osborne. As Watkin himself had repeated: gold without alloy is unusable.

There are no rules. There was another, more important person, who did not act precisely as one would have expected. Pope Pius XII is generally thought of as someone so cautious that he could not bring himself even to appear to violate the Lateran Treaty by involving himself in politics. However, barely a few months after the declaration of war, he consented to play a major part in a plot to depose the Führer. His decision, taken alone, without any consultation whatsoever with his Secretary of State, was both courageous and foolhardy. It has been described as being one of the "most astounding events in the modern history of the papacy."[4] By means of a military coup, dissident German generals were to overthrow Hitler by force, Pius XII was to approach Chamberlain through the British Minister at the Vatican, and to act as mediator for a just peace between the Allies and the new government of Germany. This hazardous venture failed in its early stages and disintegrated into something like farce when King George VI, on being told what was going on, cheerfully remarked that his cousin, the Queen of Yugoslavia, had already told him that there was a scheme to "bump off" Hitler.

It was not a farce for Pius XII. Reports of the coming German advance into Western Europe had reached the Vatican. It was a last, almost desperate bid for peace on the part of a man whose true character we hardly know.

Watkin would have been delighted if Hitler had been bumped off together with Mussolini and Stalin. The prospect of their triumph was as repulsive to him as it was to Russell. It was hard for someone with his impetuous and sometimes violent temperament to remain quiescent in the face of the violation of much he so passionately believed in. He was perhaps what Evelyn Underhill would have called a "quasi-pacifist." He had no (theoretical) qualms about taking human life in self-defence, or professional forces fighting professional forces in defence of their own or another's country. He hoped that one day human beings would see sense and organize an international armed police force which could be called upon to keep the peace. What he objected to was conscription and modern total war which inevitably involved the massacre of thousands of innocent men, women and children. One could kill a soldier, he used to say, but not his wife, his parents, aunts, uncles and remote cousins.

Tom Burns was not concerned with these distinctions. Indeed his brother Charles, a distinguished child psychiatrist, unfairly accused him of having turned into a Fascist militarist! He himself gave his allegiance to Watkin as President of *Pax*. If modern war is wrong, then it is the duty to refuse to take part in it even if the country were invaded. Tom, who thought otherwise, spent the war in Madrid as press attaché at the British Embassy where Sir Samuel Hoare was ambassador. Bernard Wall, who had once proclaimed in the pages of the *Colosseum* that we had less excuse to fight than we had in 1914, spent most of the war years in the Foreign Office writing reports on Italian affairs under the auspices of Arnold Toynbee and Watkin's former tutor, Sir Alfred Zimmern.

"Publishing is in chaos," Frank Sheed wrote to Watkin at the end of September 1939, adding that Dawson had had a nervous breakdown and was in a nursing home and too ill to write. His own wife, Maisie, very sensibly took herself and their two young children off to America where they stayed throughout the war. The firm had a branch in New York and poor Frank spent much of his time crossing and re-crossing the Atlantic.

Many boarding schools left London and Roehampton was among them. The convent took over an hotel on the seafront at Newquay in Cornwall. The Sacred Heart was more or less an enclosed order. It must have been a daunting task for the nuns to find a place to go to, organize the move, and arrange the accommodation as best they could to suit the pupils and the community. The number of pupils was considerably diminished. The foreigners had departed, some to fight against us, others to join the Resistance. A few Irish remained, travelling back and forth from what most people thought to be their shamefully neutral country. Joseph Kennedy was recalled but he must have spoken well of the school since his successor sent his daughter to Newquay. The nuns now looked out not upon terraces and statues but on a promenade where forlorn stragglers from a hot summer lingered in bathing suits and sucked ice creams.

The convent rose to the occasion with calm efficiency and without surrendering anything of its central purpose. A retired priest arrived as chaplain, one of the best rooms was set aside as the chapel and furnished as a fitting place for Catholic worship. The retreat from centuries-old Catholic practice had not yet begun. The nuns recited the Little Office, Mass was celebrated every morning, solemn Benediction sung every evening, the Angelus repeated twice daily. However, the extreme strictness of the ancien regime was forced to give way to a more relaxed order of the day. Constant surveillance was no longer possible, nor the moving from place to place in long silent files.

Teresa and Magdalen shared a bedroom, and Watkin, who lived not so far off, came to stay at a local bed and breakfast and took them both out to tea and long walks. They went together to the headlands and under his direction and in secret fear of the arrival of an angry farmer, collected rabbit snares and threw them over the cliff. Teresa was then preparing for Oxford entrance, enabled to go to the university because Aunt Sissie, had left her a much diminished legacy.

In the spring of 1940 the convent moved to a far more suitable place, Stanford Hall, on the borders of Warwickshire, not far from Rugby. This was a William and Mary house owned by Lord Braye whose family had converted to Catholicism in the nineteenth century. The chaplain moved with the school and a room over the stables was converted into a chapel with ordinary chairs serving as choir stalls for the nuns. The lay sisters, novices and a few other nuns lived in a separate part known as the Community, the teaching nuns slept on camp beds set up in various places in the main building. The children nursed vain hopes that one day a nun would oversleep and be discovered in her night gown.

Just before the Germans entered Paris, Edda's old friend Ponty, now a monk of Downside, returned to Oxford on a melancholy visit. He had recently heard of the death of Philip Fowke, he wrote to Watkin. As he looked at the stairs in the corner of the front quad and then at the window of Cork's room in the Garden quad, he felt like a revenant. It was hard to realize that only Edda and himself were left of the NCC. "When we all used to discuss life and death so short a time ago, it certainly never entered my head that all but two of us would have solved the mystery in less than thirty years. It makes one feel old and rather lonely. And one cannot help speculating as to the nature of the next meeting – in circumstances which are already no matter of speculation for them. It's all very queer and passing very quickly. Anyhow, I'm sure all is well with Philip."

There is an undertow to this letter. When last they had looked out at the Garden quad from Cork's rooms they had been children of Empire, secure in the knowledge that the British Navy would police the seas. Since then there had been two wars and now they faced possible defeat and perhaps the end of all speculation about life and death for them too. Edda was Ponty's convert but no longer the eager, obedient Catholic he had accompanied to Abbots Hall to woo Helena on that summer's day in 1912. By chance the past had become alive again and in this hour of doubt and danger Ponty wished to finish what he had begun, to give some reminder to Edda, make sure that all would be as well with him as it most certainly was with Philip Fowke.

That same June, in 1940, when our troops were pouring back from Dunkirk, Perpetua got a job as a secretary at what was then called the Passport Office. This was in reality the London headquarters of MI6, the Secret Intelligence Service, Britain's principal overseas intelligence gathering organization. She had been sponsored, at Watkin's request, by Alfred Zimmern. When she started work, after passing a man with a revolver, for we were then expecting invasion, she was taken to sign the Official Secrets Act and warned of the dire penalties that would befall her if ever, waking, sleeping or in her cups, she gave away an inkling of the nature and location of her work. When she asked if eventually she would be able to tell her grandchildren, she was assured that "for ever" was meant to be taken literally. This she took very seriously indeed and for five years neither to her family nor in the pages of her diary gave the faintest hint of what she was doing. She was in fact in the military section where she was at the receiving end of Enigma and much else.

Perpetua remained in London throughout the entire war, coming back to Dorking only on her days off. From the first week in September London was bombed with high explosives and incendaries every night. Although two hundred windows of her office had been blown out by a bomb which had exploded in Birdcage Walk, Perpetua assured her father that she worked in a place that had a large shelter with twelve stories of reinforced concrete above it. The Science Museum, the Tate Gallery, Battersea Power Station, all the large shops in Oxford Street and Piccadilly and five major hospitals had been badly damaged or completely demolished. She was not frightened of death, she told him, but of being injured.

But she was really frightened of both. The worst sound in the world, she wrote to Watkin, was the sound of a falling bomb. It seems like an eternity before it explodes and everything shakes. Why should people be born to die before they have had time to live, before they have had time to find out the answer to life, if there is one? She met her father and Teresa at Oxford and judging from an undated letter written from his home must have spoken to him about what was on her mind. Watkin was incapable of intellectual dishonesty and words of false comfort. He always found it difficult, he replied, to *talk* about the depths of things, he was afraid of saying something that might do harm. He understood her difficulties *only too well*.

"I have never had any realisation of an afterlife. It has <u>seemed</u> impossible," he continued. "This in fact is my chief reason for hating an anaesthetic, that it seems to be an annihilation. On the other hand, an afterlife follows from man's present contact here and now with God. The entire spiritual life and growth in the depths as recorded by the mystics is a testimony to a progressive union with an Eternal Good beyond time and therefore beyond the bodily death which time brings. It can't be an illusion. It is experienced as a reality more certain than our experience of the sensible world we can see and touch which, after all, has been doubted."

"If the animal of a day has at the deepest core of his being this need for the Eternal which cannot be explained by his nature as a reasoning animal organically evolved, it must be because the Eternal Value exists and can be attained by him. Why does the death of a hero leave us with a sense of triumph? Because we obscurely feel that he has reached his goal beyond the earthly defeat."

"We cannot look for survival to the surface life, but need to go down the fathomless depths of the spirit. Indeed strictly there is no *next* life as opposed to the present. There are two lives or two levels, both *present* here and now. There is a natural life in time and space and the life of the spiritual depth in contact with Eternity beyond the scope of the surface self and life to grasp. I felt this very obscurely once. But to the mystics it is an intense and a solid reality. I believe them as a man without musical ear believes in the beauties of music. It is because our age lives in the breadth of life not the depth that it cannot find 'present Eternity', the treasure hidden in the field of the spirit. Eternal life is here and now but for most of us is normally subconscious. It must be held to by the root of the will in the dark, that fine point of the spirit of which by various names the mystics tell us. At its greatest, art comes close to this life, religion lays hold of it. The attitude I adopt in the face of doubt is this: I adhere to God in Himself, in *all* His revelations to man and in the darkness of His infinite greatness *above* them all and infinitely exceeding them all. *The hand does not let go* though it often seems to have slipped out of ours."

Perpetua had need of his counsel. On the night of November 7, 1940 the United Services Club where she was living received a direct hit. Four floors were destroyed including the dining room where she had been eating shortly before. Fortunately she was sleeping in the basement and had gone early to bed.

That same year Watkin wrote a book entitled *Catholic Art and Culture*. It was to become one of his most successful but it very nearly died at birth. On December 31, 1940, he received a most distressed letter from Frank Sheed. Their offices in Maiden Lane had been hit by an incendiary bomb. He hates to tell Watkin but the manuscript of his book was burnt. There was no other copy and Watkin was in despair.

In the January of the new year he went to stay at Downside where the monks were unfailingly good to him. His "box" had long gone. Its place had been taken by something his children called his "Daddy bag". This was a large bag made out of some soft material, not unlike the receptacle with wooden handles in which women carry knitting or embroidery. He slept naked and did not bother with pyjamas. The bag contained his razor, soap, a sponge, a hairbrush, a change of underclothes, his missal together with his breviary for, like the priest he had wished to be, he recited the Day Hours from the Divine Office. He took with him also the book he was reviewing, a pen and an exercise book, writing paper and stamps and that was all. He wore a black plastic mackintosh as a dressing gown and his shoes for slippers. He never wore suits, only a short shabby jacket and odd pairs of trousers. To save money he travelled where he could by coach.

He would arrive at the front door of the Abbey as Father Daniel described it, "often in a Mendip mist which made him seem altogether like a visitor from another planet." This was to echo something Tom Burns had long ago remarked. Watkin came to me, Burns wrote, "as a carrier of other-worldly, other time values: a sort of goblin or gnome from the woods where the soul wanders when it is granted a little leave of absence."

Christopher did not care to have relations who could be compared with goblins or gnomes. In two years time he was to be ordained priest and to go up to Cambridge, to read history. He was already teaching in the school and about to finish his edition of the *Wells Cathedral Miscellany* to be published by the Somerset Records Society. In a controlled way, his relationship with his father was rather sad. Their interests were so similar, their characters so different. Watkin was very proud of Christopher and all his achievements, and totally unaware that his presence at Downside for long periods was a strain for his son. As unselfconscious as Christopher was socially alert, Watkin had no idea that he cut a peculiar figure or that Christopher had classes to prepare as well as his monastic duties.

Very quick, very amusing and highly knowledgeable, in the years to come Christopher was to appreciate his father's thought, if not his personality, far more than he did at this time. He was grateful to him for opening his eyes to natural beauty, art, literature and history. But in 1941 the past was still too close. Emmeline had been stupidly dealt with, his mother slighted and the whole family so deeply troubled. There are some scars, he wrote to one of his sisters, that time can never heal. His considered verdict, written many years later, was that his father, like Newman, possessed more intelligence and insight than his character could sustain. Now he calmed him down and strongly recommended that if possible he should write *Catholic Art and Culture* all over again.

The next letter Watkin had from Sheed was written on board ship going back to America. No, he answered in reply to a request from Watkin, he could not reconstruct the chapter order out of his head. He admires Watkin for attempting to rewrite his book but owing to the firm's losses he could no longer afford to pay him the usual quarterly retainer fee of £50 or pay for his typist. Watkin must have worked from notes or rough copies because *Catholic Art and Culture* was rewritten and published by Burns and Oates in 1942 with the *Imprimatur*. It was greatly enhanced when another edition with over forty illustrations came out after the war in 1947. This "brilliant and eloquent essay", as one reviewer called it, is not yet another book on aesthetics. It is a discussion about how, over the centuries, Catholic Christianity expressed itself in the world that confronted it and is one of the most interesting and thought-provoking books he ever wrote although it could have done with some pruning and cries out for an index. Some chapters were to be the inspiration for Section VI of Robert Lowell's poem *Quaker Graveyard in Nantucket*.

An excellent memory is a useful tool to pass examinations and indispensable for success in many directions. But it does not necessarily give its possessor understanding. This comes, as Watkin would say, from contemplation of what the object of our contemplation actually is, not what one would wish it to be. He grasps what Catholic Christianity was attempting to express and examines its different phases, starting with the Church of the catacombs and ending in modern times.

Since we are limited human beings, Watkin points out, there will always be tension and even conflict between the vertical movement towards God and the horizontal movement of human interests and natural knowledge. The Church of the catacombs lived in retreat from a hostile world. After the conversion of Constantine, it was the mission of Catholic Christianity to go out and conquer it, to mould and assimilate the pagan civilization by which it was surrounded.

Watkin shapes his material by dividing his survey into five essays or discussions about the period he is looking at. The first he calls the Christian spring, which made its appearance during the autumn of classical culture. This is followed by chapters on the summer of medieval Christendom and then on the Renaissance, and the disintegration of the medieval order, which he calls the late summer. Then comes a fascinating essay on Baroque culture, which he calls autumn. This is succeeded by the winter of the modern world. It is a very rich book but controlled by the discipline of his treatment.

The chapter on autumn, the age of Baroque, was his longest and came in for the most comment. Baroque art was not then popular and what was wrong with the modern Catholic Church was too often laid at the door of the Counter-Reformation. Watkin loves Baroque culture, particularly in what he calls its early autumn in the seventeenth century. Never, not even in the later Middle Ages, had mysticism played such a powerful part in Catholic life. Devotion passed easily from the Divinely human to pure Divinity beyond image and concept.

He insists that Baroque was the heir and continuation of Gothic and that since it represented a more adequate balance between the vertical and horizontal movements, in fact post-Reformation Christendom expressed the Catholic ideal more fully than the medieval. "It will teach us how to be free without being lawless, to be humanist without being secular, to rise high yet range far, to live a life hid with Christ in God yet regard no human interest as alien." When this Baroque religion–culture crashed after the French Revolution, Christendom fell with it. Watkin analyses the reasons for its ruin, the inadequate responses to the forces ranged against it and, in his final chapter entitled "Winter", the reasons why it cannot be raised from the dead.

The longest review was carried by *The Times Literary Supplement*. It might seem, its writer concluded, that Watkin's book ends in pure pessimism. But in fact this is not so. The author maintains that the union of form and matter which creates an organic religion–culture is as mortal as that of plants, animals and human beings. But its form, that is the revelation of God, cannot die or become obsolete and sooner or later will be embodied in a new, far-wider culture which will incorporate Western scientific knowledge and the thought of the East, both Christian and theist. The cycle of the seasons leads to another spring, but not to the delusory Second Spring of the nineteenth century which turned out to be merely a St Martin's Summer. This spring will be the age of the Spirit, not unlike that predicted by the twelfth-century monk Joachim of Flora, but without his illusions.

Watkin had glimpsed this years ago as an undergraduate at Oxford and had later poured out his convictions into the autobiographical notebook he kept in 1916. Then he had foretold an inrush of the Spirit into our civilization culminating eventually in a new synthesis of religion and natural knowledge. He was not alone in thinking along these lines. Beneath the more superficial certainties of Catholicism as it was then popularly presented, there ran a current of thought which was trying to express a consciousness that we were moving into a different stage of Christian history. That "explorer of the spiritual world", as Watkin called Evelyn Underhill, in one of her last letters referred to an awareness of "some great movement in the supernatural, some vast and transforming action of the Spirit which will end the present chaos." As the century drew to its close, this conviction became more widely articulated.[5]

For some reason the exiled and soon to be betrayed Poles fastened on Watkin's book. Their Ministry of Information in London wrote a sad letter to his publishers asking permission to produce a Polish edition. "In the present abnormal circumstances they freely confess that they are unable to make payment but promise to reimburse you later if and when they ever get back to Poland."

The disasters, the hopes and the fears of war turned many minds to religion. Before he had even finished rewriting *Catholic Art and Culture*, Watkin completed a commentary on Lauds and Vespers which he called *Praise of Glory*. It was published by Sheed in 1943.

He had long argued that the Divine Office, once part of regular Catholic worship, should be restored to daily use. Its neglect by the laity and its replacement by shapeless and sentimental devotions had been due to lack of education and failure to provide good translations. Priests were bound to recite the Divine Office daily but this was plainly impractical for the majority of people. Watkin suggests that those parts of the Office most suitable for daily prayer, either public or private, are not the generally commended Prime and Compline, lovely as they are, but Lauds and Vespers. Lauds, whose very name means praise, is the office of dawn, of cockcrow, and bids us rise from sleep. To this morning praise, the evening praise of Vespers or Evensong corresponds, a second burst of praise before the birds go to sleep and light fails. The rest of his book is a commentary or meditation on the psalms, prayers and hymns which make up Lauds and Vespers for each day of the week.

In August 1940, a few months after the fall of France, Cardinal Hinsley launched a movement called "The Sword of the Spirit" and asked Dawson to be Vice-President. Although inaugurated by Hinsley it was intended to be a lay movement, an inter-denominational, international crusade to awaken Christian spiritual and social values in a time of crisis. It hoped to promote justice in war and after victory urge that peace should be in accord with the five points already set out by Pius XII. It would resist racialism, class hatred, extreme opinions of either left or right. "Not tanks," Hinsley wrote to Dawson, "airborne forces, mines, torpedoes but strong manly help will unite our nation and win victory." Politicians, he added, plus moral degeneracy, plus treachery had brought about the fall of France.

Hinsley may have shared the opinion of many Catholics that France collapsed because of the widespread use of contraceptives. But whatever the underlying reason the immediate cause was military failure. Bismarck was right. Wars are won by blood and iron, not by speeches and resolutions, however manly. Those who worked so hard to make the Sword of the Spirit a success were the very people who relied in the first place upon the sword of the flesh. The last thing its promoters wanted was to be identified with pacifists or even quasi-pacifists like Watkin.

To start with everything went off remarkably well. In the December of 1940 *The Times* published a joint letter in favour of the movement signed by the Archbishops of Canterbury and York, Cardinal Hinsley and the Moderator of the Free Churches. It was the start of a joint Christian campaign which included as part of its programme the five Peace Points already put forward by Pius XII. Next May two large public meetings were held at the Stoll Theatre in London, the first chaired by Hinsley, the second by Archbishop Lang.

Fortnightly bulletins were published for one of which Dawson wrote a poem called "Prayer to St Michael": "Our armies are broken/ The saints are dead/ The Prince of evil/ Lifts up his head." Dawson was a reclusive scholar and no committee man but he was ably assisted by the Chairman, Richard O'Sullivan, K.C., Barbara Ward and Professsor Beales from London University.

If the tide had been taken at the flood, the history of the relationship between the Christian churches in this country might have been different. Unfortunately the whole enterprise was wrecked on the rocks of Roman Catholic intransigence and folly. Co-operation between Catholic and Protestants even about social questions was thought to be dangerous, to repeat the Our Father was *communio in sacris* and utterly forbidden. Archbishop Amigo of Southwark, the man who had denied Tyrrell Catholic burial, informed Bishop Bell of Chichester, one of the leading lights on the Anglican side, that the Catholic Church could not be regarded as just one church among many. She alone had divine authority to decide what Christian social principles were. Before long Rome itself directed that full membership of the Sword of the Spirit must be confined to Roman Catholics only and non-Catholics would have to form a separate organization. From then on the movement lost its impetus. Hinsley resigned from the Presidency in 1942 and died the following year.

Watkin was not surprised. He approved of the movement from the first and wrote for it. Of course it was not by force alone that victory could be achieved. But he knew very well that it would be politics and not the Pope who would decide the peace terms and feared that the very breadth of the Sword's agenda would deprive it of thrust.

There had been no attempt on the part of either Helena or Edda to equip their daughters for marriage. They had been trained for nothing except to prepare for the worst. It was taken for granted that they would somehow go to the university if they wished or take some other qualification to enable them to earn a living. Like their mother, they neither cooked nor cleaned and not until they were married and it was too late did they grasp the terrible implications of the fact that human beings have to be fed every few hours.

In her adolescent years Perpetua used to grumble about having a father who knew all about Aristotle but no idea how to mix a cocktail. Helena was thought to be the worldly one but she too knew nothing about cocktails and her sole piece of advice, recounted with much amusement, was a cautionary tale told to her by the nuns over fifty years ago. One of their pupils was about to get engaged, Helena thought probably to a peer of the realm, but anyway to a most eligible *parti*. Alas, on handing his future bride into her carriage, he noticed a large hole in the heel of her stocking and the engagement was never announced.

Teresa was not particularly fond of darning but nevertheless she married Ronald Chapman at the age of twenty in 1942 when she was still an undergraduate. Although not a peer of the realm he turned out to be a most eligible *parti* because he had been led into the Church through reading his future father-in-law's *The Catholic Centre*. His mother was the adopted child of the artist G. F. Watts and his second wife. The first had been Ellen Terry. Ronnie had been brought up in the painter's home, Limnerslease, at Compton, near Guildford. Watts was to be the subject of his first biography and he described his childhood there in a subsequent novel. Since his poor sight prevented him from serving in the Forces, the wedding was a quiet one and to his great relief, Edda was not required to wear morning dress.

CHAPTER TWENTY-TWO

Taking Advice

The Catholic Church teaches, as one of her fundamental claims, that she is God's authentic mouthpiece to teach about Faith and Morals. If she is wrong in this, she is a liar and Christ is not God and the Resurrection never happened and the Blessed Sacrament is a myth.

Soon after the end of the war all Helena's and Edda's daughters were grown up and before long followed Teresa's example and got married. Christopher went up to Christ's College, Cambridge to read history. He was elected a scholar of his college, made a Fellow of the Royal Historical Society while he was still an undergraduate and took a First in both parts of the Tripos. Christ's offered him a College Fellowship but he was needed to teach at Downside where in a short time he was appointed a housemaster, known of course, by his monastic name, Dom Aelred.

Perpetua remained in London and in the last year of the war had to put up with flying bombs followed by the rockets. She did not marry the man she was in love with in 1939. She had made up her mind that on her release from MI6 she would take advantage of those family connections which her father had so foolishly cast aside. As early as 1942 she took her courage in both hands and wrote to Edda's first cousin, Bruce Ingram, the editor of *The Illustrated London News*. She received a favourable reply and that letter changed her life.

Bruce was the second son of Emmeline's old antagonist, her brother William, "a man of great capacity and restless, indomitable energy" as *The Times* obituary put it. William had been a most successful manager of *The Illustrated London News* devoting himself to the problem of printing engravings and the introduction of a machine that could turn out 6,500 copies an hour. He was also proprietor of *The Sketch*, a slightly down market version of the *News* whose founding in 1893 had been opposed by his mother and sisters. William saw to it that they reaped none of its profits. In 1900 he appointed his son Bruce, then only twenty-two, as editor of the more prestigious paper in succession to Clement Shorter.

It was an act of inspired nepotism. Bruce was to control *The Illustrated London News* with great distinction for sixty-three years, from the reign of Victoria to that of Queen Elizabeth II. He had inherited all the drive, energy and force of the Ingram personality. In the Great War he was awarded the MC, the military OBE and was mentioned three times in dispatches, yet somehow he kept sufficiently in touch to hold on as active editor and to supervise the publication of an additional weekly supplement. He liked to be first in everything. As early as 1906 he published the first photographs to be transmitted over telegraph wires; his was the first paper to use the photogravure process and to publish a picture of the summit of Everest taken from an aircraft. In 1922 he tried to secure the sole rights to publish the reports and photographs of Tutankhamun's tomb but to his chagrin was forced to share these with *The Times*. During the General Strike of 1926 he arranged to have the paper printed in Paris and not a single issue was missed.

From the start he determined to meet the challenge of an increasingly illustrated popular press by the sheer quality of his own publication. He had a sharp eye for the kind of talent that appealed to the educated middle class both at home and scattered across the globe. He spotted Chesterton very early on and appointed him to write the "Our Notebook" feature which he did for thirty years, to be succeeded by Arthur Bryant.

Bruce's grandfather, Herbert Ingram, had had a stroke of luck when a dreadful fire broke out in Hamburg in 1842 just before the first number of *The Illustrated London News* went to press. Bruce had hardly been appointed editor when in January 1901 the old Queen fell mortally ill and presented him with a difficult problem. He had not only to produce special numbers to be prepared in advance but an enlarged edition of the ordinary number whose publication could not be delayed. But what if the Queen remained at death's door while it was being put together but died before it reached the bookstalls? Bruce solved this with ingenuity and tenacity. He prepared two numbers, both twice the size of the usual issue, one referred only to the Queen's illness, the other to her death. In those days photography was still little used and most news was covered by drawings. Bruce directed the operation personally by remaining in his office for three nights and four days. He later covered the Queen's funeral with an enormously successful "Panorama Number", double the size of the ordinary page. From that time his reputation as a resourceful indeed brilliant editor was unchallenged.

One of the people on the stand outside the door of St George's Chapel on the day of that funeral was, as we know, Edda. A little over ten years separated the cousins but until Perpetua entered Bruce's life they had never met, although it was possible that Bruce had seen Edda as a baby when he visited Grandma at Mount Felix. Bruce was a rich man. He was an art collector and owned probably the finest collection of Flemish and Dutch pictures and drawings in private hands. During the war he gave one of his Van de Veldes to sell in aid of the Nelson Fund, and both commissioned and presented the Battle of Britain Roll of Honour to be permanently placed in the Royal Air Force Chapel in Westminster Abbey. In many respects he was the sort of person Perpetua would have liked for a father but since his temperament was so different and his understanding of religion so slight, he would have been quite unable to help her in the way she needed. In the crisis to come it was not to Bruce but to Edda that Perpetua turned.

In 1946 she started a job in the editorial department of the paper. It was here she met another, younger cousin, Hugh Ingram. Hugh was the grandson of Sir William Ingram's younger brother Charles, the man Emmeline used to refer to as a fool. His son, Hugh's father, was named Lewis, an odd man with a passion for flying kites. According to newspaper reports, he had once flown one to the height of 32,000 feet. As a former Secretary of the Kite and Model Aeroplane Association, in 1941 he advised the Ministry of Aircraft Production to fly very large kites instead of barrage balloons. This proposal was gratefully received but not adopted. Lewis was at Eton but did not make any mark either there or in his later life. He appears to have done nothing very much except sit alone in a room upstairs drinking champagne and reading. He found time, however, to father five daughters and this one son, Hugh, who had worked at *The Illustrated London News* before the war and taken up his old job after it. He and Perpetua liked each other, loved each other and wished to spend the rest of their lives together.

Unfortunately Hugh was just divorced. He had married unhappily and while he was in the army in Italy decided that he could not endure the thought of coming home and living again with his wife. In leaving her he had also to leave his two very young daughters. These he loved but just because he loved them, made up his mind that it was best for them all if he made an absolute break and never saw them again.

Helena was horrified at the thought of Perpetua marrying a divorced man. There was little hope of obtaining a decree of nullity but Perpetua trod the path so many troubled and even desperate Catholics had taken before her. She consulted the Jesuits at Farm Street, the Oratorians in Brompton Road, the Dominicans at Oxford. They were all kind, spoke a great deal about Almighty God and the law of the Church, and were as accommodating as their consciences would allow. Since, however, they assumed that Hugh had been validly baptised, his marriage was indissoluble. Of course, it could be that the Protestant clergyman either failed to say the right words in the right order, to use only natural water, or to make sure that this natural water actually touched the baby's skin, in which case the sacrament would be invalid. There was another, less remote possibility. If a sufficient number of people, perhaps four or five, could be found to attest that before Hugh married he was heard to say that he was doing so unwillingly and would divorce if it did not work out, then the ceremony would have been null.

The scribes and Pharisees were sincerely repeating what their books and their lectures on moral and pastoral theology had told them to repeat and Perpetua ceased to consult them. She blamed herself for her folly in making the attempt since she had already heard what she thought to be a lot of well meaning nonsense on the subject of contraception.

As early as 1941, thinking about getting married, she had written in her usual straightforward manner to ask advice from her father's old Oxford friend, Ponty, who was now Dom Dunstan Pontifex and at Downside. He was later to be made Prior.[1] Her mother, Perpetua said, had told her that if she practised birth control she would be acting against the law of God, therefore condemned by the Church and unable to go to Confession and Communion. She would *hate* to give up her religion but she is certain that under modern conditions, birth control was in some cases a necessity. These she very clearly instanced and pointed out that the problem was exacerbated by war-time conditions. The safe period was unreliable and anyway impractical. She would have asked her father about the matter but sometimes his views were strange.

Ponty's reply was immediate and very kind. He would like to meet her and discuss the whole matter. When he read her letter "he could not help thinking of St Perpetua's father and relations urging her in the name of commonsense and common charity to think of her baby – and not to be a fool and be martyred. The Catholic Church teaches, as one of her *fundamental* claims, that she is God's authentic mouthpiece to teach about Faith and Morals. If she is wrong in this, she is a liar and Christ is not God and the Resurrection never happened and the Blessed Sacrament is a myth. Therefore – *if birth-control is right* you need have no regrets about giving up a false religion." Birth-control is wrong not because of any ecclesiastical legislation but because it is against natural law. To use a thing which is made for one purpose when it is made for another is to flout the maker. Just as our digestive machinery is clearly made for nourishment, so our sexual machinery is clearly made for babies. He believes the Romans used to make themselves sick in order to enjoy again the pleasure of eating. This was to frustrate the primary purpose of food and put the secondary, the pleasure of eating, in its place. No amount of difficulty can make a wrong thing right. Babies would be desperately needed after the war. Couldn't she wait until then to get married? A big sacrifice, a big act of faith, but not impossible!

It is fortunate for most of us that the written advice we may have given from time to time is unlikely to have survived. To our eyes, over sixty years later, Pontifex's arguments do not stand critical examination. Nor had they convinced Perpetua. She regretted even asking the clergy and now turned to her father.

"Whenever you are depressed or in difficulties," Watkin had told one of his children when she was still at school, "you can always write and I will answer." Perpetua's situation drew from him some of the finest and most revealing letters he ever wrote.

Watkin almost never referred to his own conduct but he was painfully aware of "things done and done to others' harm," as T. S. Eliot put it. But if he was on difficult ground so was Perpetua. Of all his children she had been the one to feel most bitter about his conduct, had blamed him most severely and urged her mother to leave him. One very odd thing emerges from the letters they exchanged. As we know, Watkin loved his children, not enough indeed to separate from Zoë but even at the height of his passion with sufficient strength to make sure that they understood that he would never desert them. Yet although these letters throw a great deal of light on Watkin's thoughts about the relationship of religion and ethics and some indeed on his own conduct, not once is the existence of Hugh's little children mentioned and it is difficult to know what to make of this.

On the central point at issue Watkin repeats over and over again that he is no use to Perpetua because he simply cannot make up his mind on the question of divorce. The fact is that traditional Christian ethics have always been uncertain about those middle values which "lie between religion at the top of the scale and pure animal pleasure at the bottom of it." Absolute indissolubility is difficult to defend but the present situation of wholesale divorces and broken homes is bad. He sees powerful arguments on both sides. Are marriages without religious faith or genuine love permanent and sacramental unions? His marriage to Helena was a loving and sacramental union of such a nature not to admit of divorce. "I know I did in the first instance sacrifice your mother and you all to what I wanted for myself – a very grievous sin against the law of love."

It is this which determines our relationship with God. Are we acting for or against the love of God and our neighbour? "For years now I have not swerved from the conviction that this is the absolute natural law, valid equally in all ages and for all men and in all situations." Above all, he fears that because Perpetua cannot accept the moral teaching of the Church she may reject the inexhaustible treasure of *religious* truth found in her faith and practice. "As year follows year the adoration of God – not by feelings which shift and may even for a very long time be quite atheistic – but by the deep *will* which is the true self and our immortal soul- means more and more. I do *beg* you [underlined three times] don't give up the worship of God – don't let priests put it over to you that the essence of religion – the adoration of our heavenly Father – must depend on one's belief about the right sexual code."

He reminds Perpetua of those Gentiles in the past who were convinced of monotheism but could not accept the Jewish law. "What is more ridiculous than to suppose that to eat beef is morally right but to eat pork a grave sin? Yet how mistaken a Gentile would have been had he relapsed into paganism and rejected the God revealed to the Jews on that account. Better never touch pork and worship God."

He could not tell her the rights and wrongs of divorce, he wrote in September 1947, "but I can say with the utmost conviction of mind and spirit, hold fast to God in trust. This is my last birthday before sixty! Looking back on a life in many ways misspent – caring for nature more not less than when I was young – *I know that God is* [underlined six times] and to adore Him is the highest fulfillment and satisfaction – deeper than feeling – so deep in fact that we cannot express it, that is why it is so hard to persuade another of it. I am so afraid that you might just drift away and away." He wishes he could see her. "I know that there is a presence of God in the [Catholic] Church – not found in such fullness elsewhere."

Reverend Mother Archer-Shee had written to Perpetua telling her that if she married Hugh, she would be helping to drive nails into the hands and feet of Our Lord. Distressed, Perpetua sent the letter to her father to read. His response is interesting because it approaches the question in a different way from most people. For Reverend Mother Archer-Shee, he wrote, all such difficulties are settled by the Gospel and the Church and it is hard to answer such a sincere and heartfelt plea. But he cannot share her devotion to the human Christ. "God – the ineffable incomprehensible Godhead as experienced by many mystics – this for me takes the place Jesus occupies in her religion." This remark, whose significance probably would not have been appreciated by Perpetua, is an important reminder of Watkin's approach to the mystery of the Incarnation.

In his most recent book, *Catholic Art and Culture,* he spends some time discussing the meaning of the devotion to the Sacred Heart of Jesus, the Order to which Reverend Mother Archer-Shee belonged. He points out that the earlier emphasis of this Counter-Reformation devotion was theocentric. The human Jesus and the Jesus now in the Blessed Sacrament is still both victim and priest, offering himself to God's glory. Jesus is not present in the tabernacle primarily to help and console us or even to be adored by us, but to offer with us and on our behalf the sacrificial worship of God which is the essence of prayer.

This understanding gave way to a more man-centred view. The Sacred Heart came to represent Christ's human love for his fellow men. His presence in the tabernacle was thought of more as an aid and comfort to us than the Christ who as our representative is offering himself to God's glory. This relapse into a more exterior and superficial understanding is the cause of much of the sentimentality and execrable art which surrounds the devotion and repels so many people.

Reverend Mother Archer-Shee, soaked in nineteenth-century French Catholicism, would not have understood this. Nor would she have understood Watkin's next suggestion. If he had been answering her letter, he told Perpetua, he would have asked her a simple question. Would she have told any relation of hers who was serving in the last war in Bomber Command that he was driving nails into the wounded hands of Jesus by massacring innocent Germans and their children?

This was typical of Watkin but not the kind of response Perpetua could ever have made nor would it have served her purpose. But she was very grateful to her father for his insistence that she must follow her conscience and not allow herself to become a victim of religious terrorism or to feel threatened by what he called "the blasphemous fear of a bogey god."

Christopher's attitude was quite different. He had written her a very loving but severe letter. "I know only too well," he said, "that there are worse sins than adultery but nevertheless adultery will kill the love of God in the soul (i.e. the real you, the centre of your personality) and will for all eternity keep you from attaining the happiness for which you are made and in which all human happiness is but a shadow."

Watkin reassured her. "For myself," he wrote, "I never think of the next life to fear or hope anything. It has never been real to me, just something to believe. God here and now, that is my religion and I can but trust that when I have to face death which I dread so much, not from fear of hell but fear of the unknown and the feeling that one might turn to nothing, God will give me a sense of certainty He has so far withheld. But I could not fear love."

He was he said, compiling the index for Dawson's "magnificent Gifford Lectures" later to be published by Sheed under the titles of *Religion and Culture and Religion and the Rise of Western Culture*. When they met, Dawson had lent him a book of extracts from the seventeenth-century Anglican divine Peter Sterry, who was steeped in the sense of God's love and beauty present everywhere even in the least thing. Sterry's hell, Watkin told Perpetua, is not hell at all, it is simply a purification, purgatory. Everything for Sterry is God's love and His love in us and God's beauty – love inside things. Sterry was one of Cromwell's chaplains and attended him on his death bed, "which throws a very different light on Cromwell's religion than the usual notion of it. It is sad that so much Catholic religion should fall far short of this trust in God's love."

Helena was being told by some priests that if Perpetua married Hugh she must not visit her or see her grandchildren should there be any. If only her mother, Watkin wrote, "would trust her wholly admirable mind and heart rather than seek advice from the clergy." Refusal to see her daughter or her children "is a clear breach of the absolutely certain law of charity and any priest who tells her not to do so is preaching immorality."

Time has its revenges. The Second Vatican Council would shatter these hard and fast moral certainties. Before twenty years were out priests themselves would be openly questioning the validity of the traditional marriage discipline "because it had little to do with marriage as it is now understood." How we are to understand it, has not yet emerged.

In the event, with Bruce and his wife as witnesses, Perpetua and Hugh married at Chelsea Registry Office in June 1948. They had been to Mass together first. Christopher wrote to her a most affectionate letter. She knew his views but she also knew that "I will always think of you, love you and help you in any way I can if ever you need it." He will be singing High Mass and will offer it for her, "I don't mean as a last minute appeal to heaven to stop you (would to God it could!) but also that God will give you all the happiness he can and in the end make it all right." He will not write to her about the matter *ever* again unless she brings it up first. He would hate to pester her or let this come between them. She is, and always will be his dearest sister, whatever happens.

None of Perpetua's family was present either at the Registry Office or at the reception and in after years were to regret this deeply as a sin against charity, which indeed it was.

The honeymoon was spent in Anglesey and Watkin hoped they would visit Pantafon. "At this time of year the rhododendrons will be out by the lake and the water lilies and the yellow iris." He had climbed Snowdon last year and gave them advice on the ascent. Because of his childhood memories he had wanted to take the Watkin Path but had climbed up the Llanberris way because it was easier and come down by the most beautiful route actually within the crater of the volcano.

Very soon the fact that in Catholic eyes Perpetua and Hugh were not married at all was forgotten and everybody, including Helena and Christopher, visited them as if they had been joined together at Brompton Oratory and received a congratulatory message from the Holy Father himself.

Children rarely read their parents' books. One of Watkin's daughters was horrified when a fellow guest at a party informed her that he had read her father's *The Balance of Truth* in the war while serving in the army in the Far East. He found it most interesting and hoped that she would be able to clarify those parts he found obscure. This was a short book, published by Hollis and Carter in 1943, that prolific year when *Catholic Art and Culture* and *Praise of Glory* came out also.

Its dedication had caused some awkwardness not only to Helena but her children as well. It was Watkin's habit to dedicate his books to each of them in turn according to their age. Having gone through the others, he dedicated this one to his child by Zoë and completely ignored the difficulties which arose from those who either had no idea he had two families or any notion that Helena had given birth to one of that name. Watkin was unyielding. He could not give the child legitimacy, only love and recognition.

In this book Watkin returns to a discussion about the grounds of our knowledge, the truth and value of human experience. It may not be an easy book to read but the rigorous philosophical arguments of the first chapters are illuminated by his commonsense and enlivened by his references to politics, poetry, painting and the curiosities of human behaviour across the centuries. He reflects upon the stages by which "faith meritorious without works was gradually superseded by works meritorious without faith." Never before had humanity been so empty within as it was today.

The book was written in the middle of a war whose outcome was yet uncertain. In his opinion, eventually the future would bring a new world-order analogous to the Roman Empire which would, from necessity and self-interest, impose peace on the world. Provided they are regularly fed and watered, more people are content to live in cages than Western liberals imagine. The Roman Empire sheltered the advent of Christ, this new empire or super-state would shelter the gradual construction of a truly Christian society.

For some reason *The Balance of Truth* was published by Hollis and Carter without the *Imprimatur*. After the war, in 1947, Watkin wrote another book for Sheed, who was very much back in business and insisted that it should be applied for. Watkin entitled his new book *Catholic Contemplative Christianity*. It is not a book about contemplative prayer. He is asking us to contemplate Christianity, to reflect upon it, to look upon its doctrine and life with an inner eye as an organic whole. Sheed sent the book in page proof to the Westminster Diocesan censor and a copy of his report still exists.[2] The tone is as sharp, the attitude as narrow and as arrogant as it had been all those years ago when Watkin submitted his *The Philosophy of Mysticism*.

There were ten objections, many trivial and exhibiting the paranoia of a priestly caste for whom any criticism is an attack upon the faith. The author's theology was disturbing. Above all, the censor cannot accept Watkin's interpretation of the Redemption and his emphasis on the invisible union of every human being in charity with God. The Catholic Church is essentially a visible Church, united in the profession of the true faith as many papal encyclicals have taught.

As we know, this invisible union is central to Watkin's understanding of the Redemption. All those whose will is turned towards God and away from themselves, whatever their religious label or lack of it, form part of a vast hidden sea of the spirit, united one to the other already, sharing the life of God here and redeemed from the nothingness of self-love. Watkin calls this participation the Total Christ, its opposite, adherence to the nothingness of self-will, the Total Adam. That is the human battle ground, the struggle between light and darkness which is the leitmotif of St John's Gospel.

Sheed had an office in New York and hoped that the American censor might be more enlightened. Although more courteous, he was even less so. Like his English counterpart, he was quite sincere but had seemed to have lost touch with the depths of his own religion. At least seventy-three pages were doctrinally objectionable. "It is not a book that can be made harmless by the excision of a few passages, the mentality and spirit of the whole is definitely not in accord with Catholic mentality."[3]

With a single, and in the event, disastrous exception, Watkin was never again to write a book dealing directly with doctrinal questions. But he had already found an outlet for some of his most considered and succinct work on Christian doctrine elsewhere. In May 1940, when our troops were being evacuated from Dunkirk, he received an unexpected letter from an old school friend, Paul Shuffrey. Shuffrey was the newly appointed editor of *The Guardian* (not to be confused with the *Manchester Guardian*), an Anglican paper founded in 1846 by a group of distinguished disciples of the Oxford Movement which included Newman's brother-in-law, James Mozley and R. W. Church, later Dean of St Paul's. Shuffrey told Watkin that he had never forgotten his kindness to him when they were together at St Paul's School, he had read Watkin's books with admiration and he wondered if he would write for him. They agreed that because of the bigotry that still existed on both sides of the Reformation divide, it would be best if Watkin's work was in general unsigned. For ten years Watkin wrote many of the *Guardian*'s leading articles and reviews, and was enabled to discuss the meaning of Christian doctrine with more freedom and truth than his own communion would permit. Shuffrey reported widespread speculation about the authorship among readers.

None of this brought in much money. During the war, in desperation, he did something that remained on his conscience until the end of his life. He sold for timber the long avenue of fine trees that led up past the lodge to Pantafon. This was done in violation of his often expressed horror at the ever increasing destruction of natural beauty. When challenged by his remorseless children he would mutter yes, yes, yes, but what could I do, and seeing his distress, even they would leave the matter alone.

Pantafon itself remained, a white elephant. If he could help Perpetua in the things of the spirit, she could and did, to the end of his life, help him in worldly matters. She got him to write out exact details for estate agents, and found out the prices of Welsh property both for rent and for sale. Sir Michael Duff of Vaynol made inquiries on behalf of his sister. She was interested in taking a long lease but asked Watkin to put in a third bathroom since she did not like having a bath on the same side of the house as the servants. She would be lucky to find any, Watkin remarked dryly. He would hate to sell it to a speculator and if he had only himself to consider would rather live in two rooms than have such a beautiful place damaged. On Perpetua's advice the property was taken out of the hands of local agents and transferred to London. An advertisement appeared in *The Times*: "Between Caernarvon and Llanberis. Beautifully situated 300 feet up with magnificent views of countryside and sea. Attractive COUNTRY HOUSE WITH REGENCY CHARACTER. Lounge hall, 3 reception, 12 bedrooms, 2 bath rooms, central heating, electric light, parquet floors; Adam fireplaces; stabling, garages for 6, lodge and cottage; well-timbered gardens, kitchen garden, small trout lake and stream, parkland, farmland and woods about 58 acres. Excellent sporting facilities."

It was sold three years later and converted into three houses. Watkin received five thousand eight hundred and five pounds, fifteen shillings and fourpence.

CHAPTER TWENTY-THREE

The Little Boy

"My God, what have we done?" the co-pilot of the aircraft which dropped the atomic bomb wrote in his logbook as he watched the mushroom cloud rise over Hiroshima on the Feast of the Transfiguration, August 6, 1945.

Germany and Japan had been defeated but the Western world was not to reach those broad sunlit uplands suggested by Churchill's vivid imagination. The dark shadow of Soviet Russia dominated Europe and the weapon that had ended the war threatened the people who had first used it.

The Continent had been closed to the English for five years but increased material prosperity meant that those who had never before thought of going on holiday abroad now crossed the Channel in droves. For Watkin it was the other way about. Poverty cut him off from what he had once taken for granted and in the years to come he was dependent upon the kindness of others for his visits abroad. He was therefore very pleased in 1950 to be asked to lecture at a *Pax Romana* Congress in Amsterdam. It was here that a Dutch newspaper reporter caught sight of him and wrote an account which sent his children into fits of laughter. Watkin was then sixty-two. He was, the reporter said, one of the most striking and picturesque figures of the Congress. "An elderly man with a slight stoop and a head of beautiful but primitively combed white hair. His clothes are too big and his collar always in conflict with his awkwardly knotted tie. He speaks fast and with great vitality. One sees him often by himself standing in a quiet corner with his eyes closed or sitting on the steps of the majestic staircase. And this is the same man who is famous for his sublime books on art, philosophy and Catholicism." At the end of the interview he tripped over the carpet.

Of all Watkin's expeditions abroad after the war his visit to the United States gave him the most pleasure. It was Frank Sheed who thought of a lecture tour and organized the whole thing as a boost both for his firm's books and for Watkin. His trip lasted a month from November 13 to December 13, 1956, and he enjoyed every moment of it.

It started, however, with a typical Watkin misadventure due entirely to his neurotic fear of not arriving in time. It appears that he was booked to sail on the *Queen Mary* but in order to be absolutely certain that he would not be late for the first two lectures changed to another ship which he was told would get there a day earlier. Needless to say, it turned out to be making its last trip before being scrapped, ran into appalling weather, and arrived in New York a day and a half late.

It did not seem to matter. "The whole of the New York Office fell in love with him," Sheed wrote to Perpetua with kindly exaggeration, "and my son Wilfred was quite delighted with his lecture at Columbia." The liking was mutual. Watkin was natural, easy to please, happy to go to parties, to enjoy the Panorama of the Wonders of the World, to watch student plays and to drink sherry with the cast. He cannot have been an accomplished lecturer but it may be that his vitality and amusing asides made up for the uneven pace of his delivery. He had about eight subjects in his repertoire, each selected according to his audience.

American lecture tours are notoriously exhausting but Watkin never complained of tiredness in the notes he kept at the time. He gave nineteen lectures in all to college students besides impromptu talks and seminars, travelled by train from New York to Chicago, to South Bend, Indiana where he was given "such a kind welcome" in a professor's house and shared the Thanksgiving lunch with his host's family. He then returned to Chicago, took the afternoon train to Minneapolis, Minnesota, where he stayed for a week lecturing at various colleges sometimes being driven eighty miles each way and returning to his base at Minneapolis at midnight. He left for Chicago on a "mild fine day, three hundred miles along the Mississippi", lectured again and two days later returned to New York. Off then to Boston and Philadelphia and as his tour drew to an end, back to New Jersey and lastly to Manhattan to see the Empire State Building from the top of which he had "a magnificent view of New York together with a conjunction of the setting sun and rising moon."

He returned home a happy man. *Commonweal* had given a party in his honour, he had visited his friend Dorothy Day at the office of the *Catholic Worker* and just before he left he had seen her again with Thomas Merton's friend, Robert Lax, at her farm on Staten Island where she had presented him with an Indian coat from California. He had met too a great admirer of his work, the Carmelite friar Father William McNamara, before long to get permission from Pope John Paul II to start what he called his "perilous adventure". This was the foundation of the Spiritual Life Institute, a contemporary interpretation of contemplative hermitic community for both men and women under vows.[1]

"I fear it must be your fate," Sheed once wrote to Watkin, "to influence people who influence great numbers, rather than to reach great numbers yourself. Nor do I think there is much chance that the men whose thought is enriched by yours will make very spectacular acknowledgement of the fact. But moving about all the time I am constantly meeting people, professors and such like, who speak with real excitement of what your work has meant to them."

Soon after the end of the war the author and critic Neville Braybrooke met Watkin at a Newman Conference in Manchester. On Sunday morning they wandered about the city together trying to find a church where they could hear Mass. At length Watkin said they must forget about Mass and return to the Conference because their first duty in charity was to support their fellow speaker. Another remark remained with Braybrooke. "When we die," Watkin said, "the questions at the Last Judgement will not be did you commit adultery or covet another man's wife. The question will be – how much did you love the woman?"

At this time Braybrooke was editor of a literary review called *The Wind and the Rain*. It was for this review that Watkin wrote his controversial essay on Shakespeare, "He Wanted Art", which he included in his next book, *Poets and Mystics*. This consisted of thirteen essays eight of which were revised and enlarged pieces he had already published, five entirely new. Nearly all his subjects are poets or mystics or both: Shakespeare; Thomas Goodwin, a leading Puritan divine, preacher before the Long Parliament and one of Cromwell's chaplains who, contrary to what one might expect, wrote the first book specifically treating of devotion to the Sacred Heart; Julian of Norwich; Margery Kempe; the poet Richard Crashaw whom Watkin compares to a Christian Keats; the influence of his father, William Crashaw, on Richard; the seventeenth-century writer on contemplative prayer and mystical theology, Augustine Baker; John Smith, the Cambridge Platonist and contemporary of Goodwin; the early twentieth-century French Carmelite, Elizabeth of the Trinity; Henry Vaughan; the poet, Ruth Pitter. There is an introductory essay on the relationship between mysticism and poetry and another essay on drama and religion. It is among the most interesting of Watkin's books but again cries out for an index.

Watkin had called his essay on Shakespeare "He Wanted Art" from the well-known verdict of Ben Jonson. It came in for the most criticism. One writer called it "an egregious failure", another the only "inept piece of work Watkin has ever written". Some went to the opposite extreme and praised "an extraordinarily acute analysis of the plays" and "the cleverest and most satisfactory of the analysis of the great poet, his genius and his foibles that has yet been written." Watkin had used the terminology of Claudel to make the distinction between 'animus' and 'anima', that is between the clear logical and abstract reasoning of the kind employed for example in the exact sciences and the obscure intuitive faculty which informs both poetry and mysticism. Shakespeare, he maintains, is both a Forsyte and an Ariel. "He has his place among the world's great artists second to none but not among the world's great *men* or most perfect artists." For all his unsurpassing poetry he was a Forsyte, a careerist, a social climber, a genius and a hack. When his inspiration failed he allowed sad stuff to creep into his writing because he lacked artistic conscience.

Christopher thought that had his father only concentrated his gifts he would have become a most successful historian. Certainly Watkin possessed an immense knowledge of the past, its cultural achievements and political structures. He was a shrewd judge of character and had painfully acquired the art of controlled narrative. His mind moved with precision between centuries, snapping up relevant facts with the ease of a fish snapping up bait. In 1957 the Oxford University Press published his *Roman Catholicism in England from the Reformation to 1950* for the Home University Library series. It was an unexpected success.

"I think it much the best account of the whole period that I have seen," Dawson wrote in a letter from Budleigh Salterton, "and that on some controversial subjects like the Elizabethans and persecution you have been much fairer and more judicious than other Catholic writers . . . even Philip Hughes seems bigoted by comparison." Reviewers agreed with him. One, evidently surprised that such a book could be written by a Roman Catholic, praised its brilliance and objectivity; the Anglican *Church Times* called it a "candid and disarming narrative." Bédoyère was particularly impressed by the postscript with its analysis of the nature of religion and the pitfalls that await all ecclesiastical historians, of whom he was one.

In a speech to the House of Commons at the beginning of the war Chamberlain had declared that "whatever be the lengths to which others may go, His Majesty's government will never resort to the deliberate attack on women and children and other civilians for the purposes of mere terrorism."[2] We know what was done to cities like Hamburg, Berlin, Dresden and Tokyo by "conventional" high explosives and incendiaries. "Our plans are to bomb, burn and ruthlessly destroy in every way available to us," Brenden Bracken, Minister of Information and Churchill's protégé, told the press at the Quebec Conference in 1943. "As to atrocities," Bernard Shaw remarked a year later, "we have rained 200,000 tons of bombs on German cities and some of the biggest have no doubt fallen into infant schools and lying-in-hospitals. Can we contend that the worst acts of the Nazis . . . were more horrible?"[3] But perhaps they were.

As the war continued and news filtered through about gas chambers designed for the wholesale elimination of Jews, gypsies and others, together with reports of the deliberate killing of old people and mental defectives, many people thought that all methods to put an end to such

The Little Boy

evils were legitimate. There were some, however, who doubted the wisdom of using Satan to cast out Satan.

Among these was George Bell, Bishop of Chichester, the sole member of the Anglican episcopate publicly to condemn the indiscriminate bombing of Germany. Watkin, who had met Bell at an ecumenical conference before the war, wrote to congratulate him on his stand. In reply the Bishop told him that he had received a great many letters of support, far more than those denouncing him. The outburst of disapproval in the press "may in itself be the sign of a guilty conscience."

In the climate of the time, it was extremely difficult to get most people to consider the matter objectively. In 1942 the Anglican, Ashley Sampson, drew up a manifesto protesting against the horrors of total warfare from the air, and the humbug of practising it while professing to fight for the cause of Christianity. He suggested a negotiated pact with Germany to abstain from the bombing of all but strictly military objectives. He got few signatures. Neither Canterbury nor York would sign, nor disappointingly for Sampson, would George Bell.

Watkin knew from experience that he would not get the backing of Dawson for any public protest of this kind. But he persisted and the following year wrote to enlist the Bishop's support for another appeal against the bombing. He was touched by Watkin's letter, Bell replied, and shared his sorrow at the remorseless bombing but having "said my say and my opinion being so well known," did not really feel able to act again. "I only wish I could see some way to prevent this woeful killing of children."

Bell's protest against indiscriminate bombing was part of his whole attitude towards the war which he had held from the start. The Church was not the "spiritual auxiliary" of the state. It had its own ends as a religious community and as such must preach basic Christian principles. This was to turn out to be a difficult, perhaps impossible, position to maintain and very probably cost him Canterbury.

The Church of England is a state creation. When in 1943 Bell asked the Archbishop of Canterbury to raise the question of the bombing offensive in the House of Lords, Temple refused. "I am not at all disposed," he said, "to be the mouthpiece of the concern which I know exists, because I do not share it."[4] Both men were deceiving themselves. Bell persuaded himself that war could be waged successfully without violating Christian morality. Temple was a realist. He rejected what he called the "kid-glove school" and without admitting it, had therefore to temper Christian morality to the needs of the hour. He told a newspaper correspondent that he thought it would be wrong to fight the war ineffectively. "When it is all over," he added, "we shall have to find some way of showing justice and mercy."[5]

"My God, what have we done?" the co-pilot of the aircraft which dropped the atomic bomb wrote in his logbook as he watched the mushroom cloud rise over Hiroshima on the Feast of the Transfiguration, August 6, 1945.[6] The bomb was code-named "Little Boy". Estimates vary but it caused the eventual death of about 140,000 people. Thousands more were left irradiated, blinded, mutilated, scorched and naked. A second bomb, nearly twice the size of the first and called "Fat Man", was dropped on Nagasaki three days later killing about 70,000 with the attendant consequences. "The physicists have known sin," Robert Oppenheimer was to remark, "and this is a knowledge they cannot lose."

Ronnie Knox had spent the war working on his greatly undervalued translation of the Bible. While we were still fighting he had, in public at least, kept silent about the British bombing of Germany. He was appalled, however, by the destruction of Hiroshima and Nagasaki and expected immediate and widespread condemnation from all civilized people followed by unequivocal moral guidance from the Catholic Church. After waiting in vain he felt so strongly about the matter that he wrote, in haste, a short book entitled *God and the Atom*.

His was a self-contained and rather private character. He did not usually comment on public events but on this occasion he felt very deeply indeed. The carnage of the First War and the loss of his closest friends had changed his attitude towards life. He never defended the just war theory. All war was evil. But Hiroshima was a shock. The dropping of this new kind of bomb, he said, was an outrage, an act against faith, hope and charity. We had conquered in the name, not of the Sign of the Cross in the heavens, but an evil mushroom shaped cloud "which hung like a mocking question mark over the future of our race." And the religious authorities were "ready to pronounce their benediction on an orgy of mass-murder." His fear of Modernism, his search for an unassailable doctrinal authority, had led him as a younger man to adopt the conventional Catholic apologetic of the time. The re-union of the churches was not merely impossible, it was unthinkable. "The mysteries of the Christian religion," he once said, "come to us in majestic isolation as known facts guaranteed to us by an authority which does not abide our question." That satisfied him no longer. There was no majestic isolation. Previous answers "seem glib, too 'slick'; there is something machine made about them," he was to write in an unfinished book on apologetics he did not live to complete.[7]

In 1956 he celebrated his last Mass at Mells, served by Christopher, ready to take over should Knox's strength fail. Christopher visited him on his death bed and said that he looked just like Newman. Perhaps it was fortunate that Knox left the scene when he did. He had had some success with his interesting book, *Enthusiasm*, and did not live to witness the almost complete disregard of his translation of the Bible nor, unlike his friend and biographer Evelyn Waugh, the doctrinal and liturgical disintegration of the post-Conciliar Church and the flight from the priesthood.

Evelyn Waugh called *God and the Atom* a masterly essay. It fell flat. We had won the war and most people simply did not want to be bothered to consider either the means by which victory was achieved or any of the other questions Knox raised. As Waugh pointed out, it was five years before "the public to whom it was addressed awoke to the fact that they themselves were threatened by the invention they had applauded." Then complacency gave way to fear and fear to a debate that dominated the sixties and seventies of the last century.

One wonders why, if Knox's essay was so convincing, neither its author nor Waugh used his influence to came out publicly and condemn the use of nuclear weapons. Michael de la Bédoyère was not a man to shirk difficulties. His troubled editorship of the *Catholic Herald* was coming to an end. The subject of nuclear warfare came up again and again in the correspondence columns of his paper. "How," he asked, "was the ordinary citizen's conscience to be formed in a subject matter of such extreme complexity?" To clarify minds, including his own, in 1959 he and Charles Thompson, the editor of *Pax*, got together to produce a short book called *Morals and Missiles*. Bédoyère wrote the Introduction. There were seven contributors: Watkin, Canon Drinkwater, Bede Griffiths, Christopher Hollis, Compton Mackenzie, Archbishop Roberts, and the German Dominican, Father Stratmann.

Drinkwater imagines a lively conversation between three priests each holding a different view; Bede Griffiths stresses the power of non-violence and seeks a technique of passive resistance which would endure all the Communists could inflict and also convert them; Compton Mackenzie declares his conviction "that Britain could save the world by completely disarming herself and thus, by a blazing act of faith, abolish war". As befits a politician, Christopher Hollis is tentative. He draws a distinction between absolute pacifism to which he thinks the Church is not committed and discusses other various responses to the nuclear threat.

Archbishop Roberts was a man of humour, sanctity and courage who had renounced the see of Bombay in favour of an Indian. Raymond Goffin, Richard's father, then Deputy Publisher of the Oxford University Press, once visited the Archbishop in Bombay. It was a hot day and Roberts offered tea. Prohibition was then in force. The tea pot poured out a stiff whisky and soda.

His independent views on contraception and nuclear warfare rendered Roberts a thorn in the side of ecclesiastical authority who as a consequence treated him disgracefully. The Apostolic Delegate in London, Archbishop O'Hara, delated him to Rome for serving on the Council of *Pax*, forbidden to priests. He was denied the right to take part in the official ceremonies when he returned to his former see of Bombay for Pope Paul's visit there in 1964. As a Jesuit and a former archbishop, however, he was answerable to the Pope only and went on quietly and doggedly repeating what he believed to be true.

He suggests in his chapter in *Morals and Missiles* that the confusion among Catholics comes from our inability to perceive moral principles. We turn to the Church and do not receive clear-cut teaching, but are not our hands and limbs also part of the body of Christ and did not His renunciation of violence carry a lesson for nations as well as individuals?

In his contribution, Stratmann describes the hardening of the Christian conscience to the point where it will accept universal conscription and adapt itself to total war and all that that implies. He urges Gandhi-like passive resistance and a general acceptance that Christians follow Christ without taking up arms.

Watkin's essay, on a subject long pondered over and most deeply felt, was a powerful piece of writing and the one which was the most difficult for the Catholic war party to refute. It was later printed as a pamphlet and distributed by *Pax*. He starts by stating clearly what traditional Catholic teaching on a just war actually is and applying it to the present situation.

There are seven conditions, *all* of which must be satisfied if a war is to be justified. The cause must be just, the war waged by lawful authority, the intention of the government declaring war must be just, war must be the only possible means of securing justice. Three conditions remained. The employment of immoral means renders war unjustifiable, there must be reasonable hope of victory, the good to be achieved by victory must outweigh the probable, not to speak of the certain, evil effects of war.

Watkin argues that a major war against the Communist bloc could not fulfil these three last conditions. No cause, however just, however great the value to be achieved by victory, can justify the wholesale massacre and mutilation of millions of innocent non-combatants and the likely effect upon generations yet unborn. If slaughter on this scale is not immoral, then morality has no meaning.

Watkin continued: many Catholics, perhaps most, persuaded themselves that such is the evil of Communism, that any means could be employed to prevent its spread. Those who urged this unconsciously adopted the Marxist view that material force is more powerful, therefore in the last analysis more real, than spiritual. If this were true, if matter were actually more powerful than spirit, it "would not be easy to maintain that the ultimate and fullest reality is God. The historic victory of the Cross, though the centre of their religion, seems to them irrelevant to the realities of the contemporary situation, something which cannot be continued, in a sense repeated, today."

Watkin goes on to point out that religion is still alive in Russia, that

Marxism has failed to suppress the deeply rooted freedom of the human spirit, or to prevent its congenital aspiration after God. The act of faith demanded by the present situation is therefore supported by an empirical observation – the failure of Communism in its strongest and longest held citadel to defeat the forces of the spirit. In fact, while Watkin was actually writing his essay, Richard Goffin was inside the Lenin Library organizing for the British Council the first large exhibition of British books to be held in Soviet Russia. Early one morning an old man came up to him, handed him a card and asked him to write out the Lord's Prayer in English.

There are those, Watkin continued, who maintain that while it is immoral to drop the bomb it is necessary to possess it as a deterrent against aggression. Watkin thinks this a bad argument. An insincere bluff will not serve its purpose, a genuine intention to act immorally is self-evidently wrong.

He now grasps the nettle. If what he asserts is true, why have not Catholic bishops throughout the world plainly and unambiguously forbidden any participation in such a war? No false notions about edification or loyalty should prevent us from saying the truth. It is an historical fact that bishops have consistently supported all wars waged by the government of their country. He himself knows no instance of a national hierarchy condemning any war undertaken by its government however patently unjust.

What however of the Bishop who is not a national citizen, the supreme shepherd of Catholics throughout the world? Why has the Pope not implemented his opposition to atomic war by pronouncing it immoral for Catholics to participate in it? We must be realistic. Such a pronouncement is most unlikely and the reasons for refraining from making it are weighty. Watkin makes his point by giving an historical example. In 1130 Pope Innocent II presided over the Tenth Ecumenical Council. It forbade as immoral the employment in warfare of bows and arrows – the very weapons which were later to win the battles of Crécy and Agincourt. All the rulers of Western Europe were Catholics. None of them took the least notice. Today the majority of Catholics would disregard any papal condemnation of the use and preparation of nuclear weapons and oppose the small minority who obeyed. So the Catholic body would be rent asunder and Catholicism equated with disloyalty to the civil power.

It could be argued that even if the Pope were to accept the defection of a multitude of Catholics as Our Lord accepted the flight of the Apostles rather than compromise His divine mission, the crucifixion of the Church would achieve a victory analogous to the victory of the Cross. That was his own personal belief, but to expect the Pope to share it is a different matter. Our Lord's choice of His own death was His alone. On the Pope's choice would depend the lives and even the faith of Catholic multitudes.

Moreover, the papal curia is a bureaucracy on which the Pope depends for the Church's administration. Not for them the venture of naked faith and the prospect of disobedience on a colossal scale. Catholic moral theology has provided clear and sufficient guidance based on principles determined by the use of human reason. It is up to each of us to decide the matter for ourselves.

The calm, analytical tone of Watkin's essay was not reflected in his conversation. The whole subject agitated him in the extreme. It infuriated him to hear bishops and priests going on and on about the wickedness of contraception and divorce while remaining silent about mass murder. The canon lawyer who so carefully distanced himself from *Morals and Missiles* in the *Clergy Review* took the trouble to point out in another section of his magazine that it was legitimate for a person troubled by a persistent cough to take a lozenge before Holy Communion. Watkin, however, admitted, as few nuclear protesters did, that because of his "human weakness, natural fear and weak faith" he could not "help *feeling* a security behind the atom piles of our anti-Soviet alliance. But reason and faith condemn it."

He was exasperated when Thomas Merton told him that his superiors had forbidden him to publish the book he had just written about nuclear war. "I just can't believe," Watkin wrote back, "that any superiors whatsoever have [the] right to forbid protests against the most appalling wickedness in human history." He had been driven to the conclusion that when the state was concerned, the Catholic hierarchy teach *sheer immorality*. This remark was also underscored by Merton who was facing personal problems at this time. He wanted to escape to his hermitage. Soon he would find out what it meant to fall in love. He did not "feel snug in the Church". Perhaps with his temperament he would not have felt snug anywhere. Watkin too wished to distance himself from a Church which accepted the wholesale massacre of non-combatants as the price of victory. He told Merton that he would not pay the least attention to the ethical pronouncements of any organization which did not unequivocally condemn such weapons of war. He was utterly disillusioned with "the moral guidance of the Church and its legal authoritarianism." But his unease, like Merton's, lay far deeper than that. Their exchange of letters is revealing.

" Christian thought is largely hampered by fear," Merton wrote. "It does not dare . . . to realize our *immediate* union with God in the order of grace." He suggested that Watkin should select and edit passages from the work of the seventeenth-century Benedictine monk, Augustine Baker, whose writing on contemplation they both admired. "There is no question," Merton said, "that the mystics are the ones who have kept Christianity going, if anyone has." He himself would write the Preface. For various reasons this project came to nothing but Merton sent him a signed copy of his *New Seeds of Contemplation*. Watkin found the book to be "a disconcerting blend of profound teaching on mystical contemplation and defence of the letter of Catholic orthodoxy." This last was far from convincing and included, he was sorry to say, belief in everlasting suffering.[8] If it is true that the superficial self disappears at death like smoke up a chimney, he scribbled in pencil at the end paper of the book, it cannot then survive to be alienated in hell.

Watkin does not seem to raise this particular question with Merton, but tells him that he differs from him "profoundly and absolutely" about his view of the cosmic role of man and a *human* incarnation of God. Merton states that man contains within himself the meaning of the cosmos and tells us that "the love of the *Incarnate* Son of God is a force that gives spiritual life . . . to the evanescent material universe." In the light of our knowledge of the immensity of the universe, Watkin finds such a view of man utterly unthinkable. Alice Meynell saw what even Teihard de Chardin, otherwise so scientific, did not see. She speaks in one of her poems of other incarnations of the Word. A difficulty becomes an impossibility if we think of Jesus and Mary as the central figures, not simply of the earth, but the universe.

"But for the fact, so abundantly witnessed, of mystical contemplation, indeed one might say of all genuine prayer," he wrote to Merton in the course of their discussion about *New Seeds of Contemplation*, "I should, I know, have lost all religious faith and become an agnostic. For I cannot *see* how to reconcile the scientific view of the world and man's history as I find it stated by Catholic writers competent in science, with the religious view. I must just hold to both, knowing that truths of reason and truths of spirit must be in agreement even if that harmony is not visible to me here and now."

His own family were divided on the issue of nuclear war. Catherine and Magdalen agreed with him and joined the Campaign for Nuclear Disarmament. The rest, except for Catherine's husband, Keith Davenport, were against him as were his other sons-in-law. Three had been on active service. Hugh Ingram served abroad in the Royal Artillery. Richard had joined the RNVR from Oxford and served in Combined Operations. Keith was in the Sherwood Foresters. He had been on the retreat to Dunkirk and later fought his way up Italy. They had seen more dead bodies than Watkin was likely to encounter, and undertaken more responsibility for the lives of others than he had ever done in his life.

Christopher was in a very different position. His father was a free-lance, he a member of a monastic community. He had managed to combine a heavy teaching schedule with his own work, had been elected as a Fellow of various learned societies and completed his edition of the *Great Chartulary of Glastonbury Abbey* to be published in three volumes. In 1962 he was appointed Head Master of Downside School.

Not long before his death, he discussed his father's character in letters to Magdalen. He himself shared, he wrote, neither Watkin's innocence nor, in some ways, his integrity. The most shameful act of his own life had been the taking of the anti-Modernist oath before he could be ordained as sub-deacon. He had betrayed both God and himself, and he compared what he did to Cranmer's perjury on his appointment to the See of Canterbury.

This was too severe. Catholics had found themselves trapped between Roman obscurantism and the dilution of liberal Protestantism. Christopher was, like Newman, his father and many educated Catholics, a Modernist in von Hügel's sense. He did not by any means agree with a number of their conclusions but neither then nor later could he give assent to the ludicrous fundamentalism of the Biblical Commission or stomach *Pascendi* or *Lamentabili*. When Cranmer took his oath of obedience to the Pope he was already secretly, and as his brave death would finally show, sincerely committed to an interpretation of Christianity which would in this country largely supplant the religion brought to us by St Augustine. Christopher was faced by acceptance or departure from the Abbey. He took the oath in much the same way and with the same mental reservations as a Church of England clergyman assents to the Thirty-nine Articles. "It is difficult to be guileless," Thomas Merton was to write to Watkin.

As head master of a well-known public school it would have been impossible for Christopher to encourage any kind of resistance to conscription, then still in force, or to express doubts about the morality of nuclear weapons to pupils who were in the Combined Cadet Force and some of whom preparing for careers in the Services. While he appreciated the strength of his father's position, he did not share it.

In October 1958 Angelo Guiseppe Roncalli, the Patriarch of Venice, was elected Pope at the age of seventy-seven and took the name of John XXIII. There were some who groaned. He was the bishop who had complained about scantily dressed women on the Lido. Nothing would change. Soon he announced his intention to summon a General Council. "The holy old boy doesn't realize what a hornet's nest he's stirring up," Archbishop Montini of Milan remarked to a friend. As Pope Paul VI he was to be severely stung.

CHAPTER TWENTY-FOUR

Opening the Windows

"Peter's bark has slipped from its mooring," Watkin wrote in one of his Christmas letters as further reports of the reforming party's triumphs came through, "and is off on a voyage – but where?"

" T hat great and ancient power, the Church Catholic which dates her origin from the first preaching of the Gospel, which was founded by the Apostles, . . . has been taken captive by her enemies, blinded and set to servile employments – to make men good citizens and to promote the enlightenment and comfort of the world . . . " So wrote Newman in his essay on the fall of Lamennais. A modern nun has stated the matter more succinctly. "My religion knows only a horizontal dimension now."

Strictly speaking, there can be no compromise between these two positions but a balance between them was at the root of many of the sometimes bitter controversies which surfaced during and after the Second Vatican Council. The one accepts the religious premise. The other in effect denies it. The one knows that God exists and that we are capable of union with Him. The other has fallen for that most beguiling of all apostasies, enlightened and compassionate atheism. In the name of humanity the supernatural is insidiously surrendered and we end up with the modern version of the Tower of Babel, the Millennium Dome.

General Councils are not general in the sense that they include those Protestant, or semi-Protestant churches founded in the sixteenth century and later. The two thousand five hundred bishops summoned to gather in Rome from all over the world were in communion with the Pope. However, numbers of "observers" from the Reformed churches were invited to attend which they did in some numbers and caused nervous Catholics to complain that they exercised too strong an influence not only on the debates but on the final documents. A profounder but less urgent Conciliar loss was the absence, as participants, of the Great Church of the

East, the other lung of Catholicism, severed by the eleventh-century Schism. This absence was to some degree compensated for by the presence of those churches of Eastern Christendom in communion with Rome but for the most part these were regarded by their fellow Catholics as rather unusual birds that had flown into their enclosure.

Before the Council met and while the bishops and universities throughout the world were sending in subjects for discussion, Darton, Longman and Todd asked Watkin to write *The Church in Council*, an historical study of the previous twenty Ecumenical Councils. Watkin explained the background of each, the actual issues in contention and was frank about clerical manipulations. This time the publishers had provided an index, that vital tool for reading an author whose mind moved so easily between centuries and personalities.

Preparations took three years and the Council did not convene until the autumn of 1962. That summer Michael de la Bédoyère was sacked as editor of the *Catholic Herald* in what he described as "rather curious circumstances." He returned from a three-month lecture tour of America only to be informed that his services were no longer required. It is probable that the tension between a blinkered hierarchy and an increasingly articulate laity was intensified by the prospect of the Council and the debates already taking place. At that time free speech was no more acceptable in the *Herald* than it was in *Pravda*.

From the first moment of his appointment, Bédoyère's intention as editor had been, in his own words, "to clear, little by little, an area of greater religious freedom in this country." To do anything else was to cut off the Church from the people, not solely non-Catholic Christians, but many good and intelligent Catholics who were kept in a state of blind docility and intellectual ignorance. In fact, as Bédoyère himself came to recognize, his departure from the *Catholic Herald* was providential. Most Catholics had little idea what the Council was all about but he understood that the present time was one of the most important in the history of the Church, perhaps *the* most important moment since the Council of Jerusalem opened up the Jewish world to what was to become Christianity. Within five months of his dismissal he founded a small monthly magazine, available by annual subscription only, which he called *Search*.

A keen ecumenist, discriminating, tolerant of opinions widely different from his own, Bédoyère was just the man for the moment. As the biographer of von Hügel, he foresaw the difficulties that the Council would face and as the author of *The Archbishop and the Lady*, a book written round the correspondence between Fénelon and Mme Guyon, he grasped their significance. It seems that he had inherited his journalistic flair from Labouchère, and a light touch combined with depth of religious thought from Algar Thorold. Making use of connections made during his twenty-eight years as editor of the *Herald,* he published short articles, reviews, summaries of Conciliar speeches and letters from many parts of the world.

It was *Search* which in 1964 published Archbishop Roberts's once notorious article admitting that he considered the condemnation of contraception on the grounds of natural reason no longer valid. "This one honest and brave man," as Watkin described him, had however broken the clerical taboo and his article prompted Cardinal Heenan, on behalf of the English bishops, to repeat that the Church's teaching was God's law and as such unalterable. Despite strong episcopal disapproval, Bédoyère's venture thrived and was one of the most sensible and informative publications to emerge from that troubled and confused time.

When they assembled in Rome, most of the British and American bishops were in for a shock. Now that the pendulum has swung in the opposite direction, it is difficult for many people to believe just how intransigent the Catholic Church in Britain remained right up to the eve of the Council. The Sheringham nuns had forced Catherine to go to Confession after she had joined in the Lord's Prayer at her grandmother's funeral, Helena felt herself bound to confess that she had attended Evensong at St George's Chapel with one of her sons-in-law. Catholics could not act as bridesmaids or pages at Protestant weddings, books on moral theology warned nurses against calling in non-Catholic ministers to pray with the dying. In time, a Conciliar decree was to state that other religions beside Christianity are supernaturally revealed and involved in the salvation of the world but those who had been taught otherwise had a long way to travel.

The British contingent was therefore ill-equipped to evaluate the thought of its more progressive brethren from northern Europe. According to the American journal *Commonweal,* some of them were having their minds broadened by attending study circles in scriptural and reformist theology. For many, the conflict remained one between Catholic and Protestant and had little or nothing to do with reform or contemporary restatements of basic Christian doctrine. To the Bishop of Salford, Catholic dogma was as certain as the multiplication table and far from being "fellow pilgrims" as they were now being called, Anglican bishops were laymen, even their blessings at public meetings of doubtful efficacy.[1] Many therefore did not grasp the implications of John XXIII's opening remarks about the substance of doctrine being one thing and the way in which it was presented another. The Pope may not have done so either. He was doctrinally and devotionally at heart a 'Garden of the Soul' Catholic of the kind later, in some quarters, to be looked down upon. Père Congar once asked if people could "refresh at one and the same time from St Paul and the Month of St Joseph?" But it is the genius of Catholicism that they can.

David Worlock, later Archbishop of Liverpool, who kept a secret diary throughout the Council, rightly described what happened at the opening sessions as a bloodless revolution. It did not take long for most of the English bishops to see which way the wind was blowing and according to Warlock, change tack accordingly, although he reported that poor Cardinal Godfrey, the Archbishop of Westminster, was heard to complain about the unfairness of criticizing people for loyally upholding what they had previously been taught as true.

Watkin was astonished at what was happening. It was "something one could never have foreseen or believed possible," he wrote to Magdalen after he heard that the Papal Curia and the old guard had been routed by the progressives, "and the outcome is with God. Certainly the election of Pope John seems a divine intervention." But the time would come when Watkin would think that the Pope had been fortunate in the hour of his death, though not the manner of it.

Once Roman Catholics took a certain quiet satisfaction in the doctrinal difficulties of other churches, now it was plain that they were all in the same boat, as Father Gregory Baum, theological adviser to the Archbishop of Toronto pointed out. The solution to doctrinal and disciplinary questions, he wrote, "is elaborated in a truly human process which, although guided by the spirit, goes through all the stages of discussion, disagreement, uncertainty, tentative suggestions and inadequate proposals analogous to the advance in any branch of human wisdom." That was not the kind of approach Catholics were used to.

"Peter's bark has slipped from its mooring," Watkin wrote in one of his Christmas letters as further reports of the reforming party's triumphs came through, "and is off on a voyage – but where?"

The Pope's health, however, was failing. In the spring of 1963 he fell dangerously ill and by May the world knew that he had not long to live. "A terrible blow," Watkin wrote, "never has a pope been more indispensable." In June, Iris Origo stood with thousands of others while a Mass was celebrated in St Peter's Square for the old man who lay dying so close to them. No one present, she wrote, believer or not, "could fail to have a sense of what was meant by the 'communion of the faithful' or to receive a dim apprehension of his own vision of one flock and one shepherd, of the love of mankind as a whole."

"What a wonderful life and death," Helena wrote to Watkin. "Probably he has done more good in these four years than others have done in a life time." Watkin watched the coronation of the former Archbishop of Milan on a neighbour's television. "A fascinating piece of ancient pageantry," he wrote in a letter, "surviving in our dreary mechanical world. Yet strangely remote. The Pope seemed like an idol of some ancient religion coached by priests to go through an elaborate series of ritual gestures – not a living human being. No wonder Pope John disliked the *Sedia Gestatoria*. As always a dilemma – a ceremony rich in historical and aesthetic appeal but a remoteness from life, the appeal of a living religion to living men and women. Could not the archaic solemnity be succeeded by some kind of informal meeting with Catholic bishops and non-Catholic religious leaders?" He hoped that Pope Paul VI would let Pope John's work continue.

The new pope not only wished to do so but himself had contributed to the reforming agenda before the Council started. However, he had neither the temperament nor the power to control the forces released by the summoning of the Estates General.

Eighteen years later the recently elected John Paul II had the courage to speak out. "Realistically it must be admitted," he said on February 7, 1981, "with deep pain and distress, that many Christians today are troubled, confused, perplexed and even deceived; ideas which contradict the revealed truth of all time are spread abroad; veritable heresies abound, creating doubt, confusion and revolt; the liturgy has been damaged, [people] plunged into intellectual ethical relativism and thus into permissiveness; Christians are tempted by atheism, agnosticism and vaguely moralistic illuminism by a sociological Christianity without defined dogma and without objective morality."[2]

For years, owing to the kindness of a friend, the Goffin family was able to spend its holidays "wandering in gladness" as Coleridge put it, far up on the Quantock hills. Watkin would join them on his way to and from Downside and to his delight pass close by Alfoxden House where William and Dorothy Wordsworth lived in 1798. The nearest village was Nether Stowey. Here Coleridge, Sara, and their baby Hartley had lived in a cottage in the street opposite the home of the poet's patron, Tom Poole. Watkin would recite with relish passages from *Frost at midnight* or *This lime-tree bower my prison* and with wide gestures intone *The Ancient Mariner* by the sea at Watchet.

It was here, too, in the autumn of 1964, when they were about to go into the church at Bridgwater for Mass, that Magdalen, to her dismay, caught sight of her own words on a placard advertising that Sunday's edition of *The Observer*. Intending to provoke discussion, Constable had recently published three books about religion. Each one contained chapters written from the inside by believers acting, as it were, as counsel for the prosecution. *Objections to Christian Belief* had already come out, likewise *Objections to Humanism*. *Objections to Roman Catholicism*, with an introduction by Bédoyère, contained seven essays. John Todd wrote on the worldly church, Frank Roberts on authoritarianism, conformity and guilt, Professor Finberg on censorship, Rosemary Haughton on freedom and the individual, G. F. Pollard on scholasticism and Archbishop Roberts on contraception and war. This last was an act of integrity and courage typical of the man. All other priests asked to contribute had declined. Each of the writers was asked to sell the copy-right to Constable lest the Church should apply pressure to make an author withdraw any essay.

Bédoyère had asked Magdalen to contribute a chapter on superstition. Watkin sensibly pointed out to her that superstition should be distin-guished from credulity. She started the innings therefore with an essay entitled *Some Reflections on Superstition and Credulity*. She understood the meaning of superstition to be a belief or practice inspired by an unworthy view of God, credulity as an uncritical, ill-founded belief in supposed occurrences which are in fact contrary to any known truth at a given time. To believe in eternal torment is to be superstitious, to believe that the Holy House at Nazareth flew to Italy with all its furnishings is to be credulous.

In order to discharge her brief she had, unlike most of the other contrib-utors, to discuss fundamental theological issues including what are called the Four Last Things, that is death and judgement, hell and heaven. It was this part of her essay, even more than the part dealing with visions or hallucinations, especially Fatima, that caused the uproar which followed publication. J. S. Mill had quite rightly pointed out that compared with the doctrine of endless torment for the lost, any other objection to Christianity sinks into insignificance.

"Unless a man is born of water and the Holy Ghost he cannot enter the Kingdom of Heaven." No one now takes these words of Christ literally. Although the Church has ceased to believe that actual membership of the visible church is necessary for salvation, it still teaches the existence of an everlasting state of positive suffering for all those who die in mortal sin and a state of natural happiness called limbo for embryos, babies and young children up to the age of reason who are deprived of the beatific vision because they are not baptized and therefore still in the power of Satan.

Looking back over the years since *Objections* was published, two things are plain. First, almost no Catholic priest attempted seriously to discuss the issues Magdalen's essay raised. The old certainties were already disappearing into that mist of doctrinal confusion from which we have not yet emerged. In Sheed's words, the Church was turning from being a teacher into a question mark. We do not hear many sermons today about hell, limbo, original sin, indulgences and little about contraception. The verse referring to purgatory has been cut out of a popular hymn.

Secondly, it was the manner of Magdalen's presentation, her laughter and obvious enjoyment of the follies which Catholicism shares with all living religions, that provoked the wrath of the clergy and the shock of the laity. She came from a highly unusual background where such matters had been talked about since her childhood, she had little idea of the offence and perplexity they would cause. Pope John had urged Catholics not to linger behind "the ramparts of our faith" and she had been only too happy to oblige. Watkin had long ago supplied the ammunition, she fired it. But as Helena pointed out at the time, it would have been better to have done so with less obvious relish. A respectful and tentative approach would have received a more intelligent response from the guardians of the flame.

One of these was Father Charles Davis, editor of the *Clergy Review*, a Professor of Dogmatic Theology at Heythrop College and author of the much praised *The Study of Theology*. An admired theologian, the most respected of all Sheed and Ward's advisers, he was chosen to review *Objections* in the *Catholic Herald*. His comments were a masterpiece of controlled ambiguity. He did not think the book disloyal. He respected the sincerity of all the contributors and thought each chapter should be assessed on its merits. Magdalen's essay was the only one that really got under his guard. He disliked intensely her "irreverent arrogance" and her theology made him wince. But he could not say that it was not on the whole sound or her targets were not well chosen.

At this time the BBC ran a televised discussion programme called *Meeting Point* and invited Magdalen to speak. She reiterated some of the points she had made in her chapter which were intended to be rebutted by a priest. The TV appearance together with the wide publicity given to the book meant that Magdalen received a deluge of letters, the majority of which were from puzzled and faithful Catholics who in contrast to the hostility of the Catholic press, were largely in favour of what she said and rejected the priest's evasive attempts to defend the doctrine of eternal torment.

When in the December of 1964 a telegram arrived from Christina Foyle inviting Magdalen to be one of the guests of honour at a lunch at the Dorchester to mark the successful publication of *Objections*, she thought at first that it was one of Christopher's practical jokes. It was not and if the Catholic party managers had kept quiet the occasion would never have become the plaything of the media who were delighted when at the last minute Archbishop Roberts was prevented from speaking. Everyone thought that it must have been Heenan's doing but it turned out that the person directly responsible was the Provincial of the English Jesuits who had asked the Archbishop "to reconsider his acceptance". This he quite rightly did, remarking sadly to the press that he had only wanted to make some nice jokes. His speech was read out together with Evelyn Waugh's amusing response to the luncheon invitation. "I would gladly attend an *auto da fé* at which your guests were incinerated. I will certainly not sit down to a social meal in their company."

Watkin was unable to be present and he had to be satisfied with a request from Bédoyère for him to contribute a chapter in the next symposium he was planning to edit. Perpetua represented the family at the table of honour. It was good of her to support Magdalen just then because recently things had gone most unexpectedly and disastrously wrong for Hugh and herself.

In May 1950, Bruce Ingram had celebrated his half century as editor of *The Illustrated London News*. It was the peak of his career. He was knighted, received an Honorary D.Lit. from Oxford, and a dinner in his honour at Claridges. Mr Attlee, the Prime Minister, was present together with the French Ambassador and the Duke and Duchess of Gloucester. Bruce regaled His Royal Highness with the story of how when King Edward VII died he published a picture of the death bed scene before anyone else by acting as a model for the artist. The King's head was drawn from photographs but Bruce himself spent the evening before Press Day lying covered with a blanket on a bed in his office. Queen Alexandra, he told the amused Duke, signed and accepted the original drawing.

When he was eighteen Hugh Ingram had gone straight from Stowe to work for Bruce as one of his sub-editors and steadily made his way up the ladder. The two men, although they shared many interests, were unlike in character. Bruce, accustomed to command since he was twenty-two, was a benevolent dictator. To the end of his life he personally selected most photographs for a particular number of the paper. He would get down on his hands and knees, arrange the photographs on the floor as he wished them to be presented and woe betide anyone who altered them. Perpetua wrote some of the captions and, more importantly, was a tremendous personal help to Bruce and his second wife who died before he did, as had his only son. Hugh was editor-in-waiting, unable to make any important decisions, but in reality running the paper from day to day while taking care not to make this obvious.

Bruce lived in some splendour at Great Pednor Manor, Buckinghamshire, surrounded by his animals and his collection of beautiful objects. He celebrated his eightieth birthday by giving two Van der Veldes to the National Maritime Museum but still clung to office. He died at his home of a heart attack in Perpetua's presence during the bitterly cold January of 1963. He was eighty-five. He left his portrait of Mary Tudor as a princess by Hans Eworth to the Fitzwilliam Museum, Cambridge together with all his Flemish and Dutch drawings and Nelson's favourite picture of Emma Hamilton, a pastel by Schmidt which hung in the day cabin on *Victory* at Trafalgar, to the National Maritime Museum.

The Illustrated London News had been sold to the Ellerman family just after the First War and as recently as 1960 had been bought, together with *The Times*, by Lord Thomson of Fleet. It was housed in a large building in the Strand called Ingram House. Unfortunately, it was soon to change its name. Even before Bruce's death the Managing Director had tried in vain to get Hugh to force Bruce to retire and take his place. Now it was

Hugh's turn. Just before he left for his summer holiday in 1963 the Chairman told him that he had absolute confidence in his editorship. On his return he was summoned to the board room and bluntly informed that he was to be superseded by a younger man; no reason was given, there was no expression of regret. This sort of thing may be common enough today but times were different then and *The Illustrated London News* was supposed to be a gentlemanly paper. Hugh was so shocked that he was physically sick all night and Perpetua feared he might have a stroke. He had been with the paper for thirty-six years but since he had had no contract, all Thomson offered him was the obligatory one year's salary.

Watkin was disgusted by the fact and manner of Hugh's dismissal. He understood that there had been pressure from Thomson to give the paper "a shake-up". He expressed his admiration for Hugh's refusal to lower the flag and drop the traditional standard. "For some a hundred and twenty years, " he wrote, "Ingrams have continued the Ingram creation and made *The Illustrated London News* what it is, deservedly honoured throughout the English-speaking world."

Perpetua immediately got in touch with Mr (later Lord) Goodman who thought that Hugh had been "very shabbily" treated. They had no legal position, but Goodman, in his own words, somehow shamed the Thomson organization into granting reasonable compensation. Hugh had suffered "a grave injustice". Goodman stated the real cause of the sacking with subtle innuendo. "Hugh is so obviously a person of integrity and high standards and I am not altogether surprised that they decided that he might be awkward to deal with if they want to make changes of which he does not approve."

That was the truth. Thomson was right, not Watkin. The English-speaking world as Watkin understood it, was finished. The language would become international but in a different form. The middle class whose patterns of speech and common literary background provided the readership of *The Illustrated London News* would soon barely exist.

Perpetua wrote to her father that Hugh's sacking had perhaps saved his life. The misery of working for Thomson would sooner or later have killed him. But the blow was a bitter one all the same. She had enjoyed her life as the wife of the future Editor of *The Illustrated London News*. She had attended the Coronation with Hugh who was in the Abbey as a journalist and acted as hostess at parties Bruce was too old to attend. It was an unhappy woman who chatted so politely to Robert Speaight about his biography of Eric Gill that afternoon at the Dorchester.

20 The East Beach, Sheringham about 1900. The tall house on the cliff was Augustine Birrell's, named The Pightle. Loudwater was next door.

21 Watkin, *left*, talking to Christopher Dawson on the Yorkshire Moors, 1930s.

22 Jack Hornby, the son of A. N. Hornby and Watkin's Aunt Ada.

23 The graves dug by the Canadian Mounted Police by the Thelon River in the Northern Territory, Canada, June 1929.

24 Watkin's mother, Emmeline Heakes, looking into her crystal ball, 1920s.

25 Perpetua, Teresa, Mrs McDowell with two dogs on the lake at Pantafon, 1932.

26 Watkin's bookplate. The text is from a Latin Hymn by Thomas Aquinas: "The shadow has given way to truth, light overcome darkness."

27 Frank Sheed with the enlarged edition of his *Theology and Sanity*, 1980.

28 Michael de la Bédoyère in his sixties. From a sketch by his son, Count Quentin de la Bédoyère,

29 Sir Bruce Ingram photograph by Baron, 1950. Sir Bruce was to edit *The Illustrated London News* for sixty-three years, from the reign of Victoria to that of Queen Elizabeth II.

30 Perpetua and Hugh
Ingram, 1950.

31 "Watkin at the
Waterfront", Hoboken, USA.
Published in *Jubilee,* January
1957. Watkin was on a lecture
tour.

32 Watkin and Teresa
Chapman with her son, Peter,
1953.

33 Catherine Davenport, Fairmead, 1957.

34 Watkin at Torquay, January, 1960, aged seventy-two.

35 Helena at Fairmead, 1960, aged seventy-eight.

36 Richard Goffin, *left*, at the Frankfurt Book Fair, 1965. Centre: Siegfried Taubert, Director of the Book Fair; *right*, Dr Schröder, West German Foreign Minister. Richard was Director of Book Promotion at the British Council and in charge of the British National Stand at Frankfurt for many years.

37 Samuel Shepheard in old age in the grounds of Abbots Hall.

38 Christopher Dawson talking to Alec Guinness at Boston College, USA. They were celebrating Dawson's seventieth birthday.

39 Christopher Watkin (Dom Aelred) when he was appointed Head Master of Downside School in 1962.

40 Magdalen at Silcocks, 1996.

CHAPTER TWENTY-FIVE

Making a Clean Break

*"Harvard has always considered Catholicism intellectually
contemptible," Stillman, a convert himself, wrote to
Dawson, "socially negligible, and dangerous politically."*

édoyère kept his word. James Mitchell, Constable's excellent editor,
made arrangements for the publication of another book, to be called
The Future of Catholic Christianity. So was Watkin unwittingly
drawn into a bitter and at times silly controversy which was none of his
making and did him a great deal of damage.

There were ten contributors. The first was Yvonne Lubbock, the author
of *Return to Belief*, a widely-read account of her spiritual and intellectual
journey from agnosticism to Catholicism. Her essay was entitled *Belief is
Being* and Bédoyère thought it the most interesting in the book. This was
followed by chapters from Bernadine Bishop, the daughter of Bernard and
Barbara Wall, Magdalen, John Todd, T. L. Westow, Andrew Boyle,
Daniel Callahan, Ronald Brech and Archbishop Roberts.

Watkin's essay was the last. His contribution was really a distillation
of his religious approach crammed into a short space. He knew that in the
confused and often acrimonious atmosphere of the time, it would please
neither the conservatives nor the progressives. He called it *The Wisdom
of the Spirit: A Platonist's Faith*. He started with a quotation from Father
Cornelius Ernst, a well-known Dominican theologian who had pointed
out, in the pages of the *Catholic Herald* that, as a matter of common
knowledge, the Roman Catholic Church was going through a period of
volcanic doctrinal upheaval. Watkin compares this period of confusion,
doubts and dismay to the condition of a contemplative who is being withdrawn "from a prayer of affections, images and concepts into a bare
adherence to God beyond all images and concepts." It is a descent from
the surface and letter of prayer into the depth of its spirit, or if another
metaphor is preferred, an ascent to its summit.

As time passed, this idea of a "corporate dark night" was to be echoed by others. Ruth Burrows, the well-known Carmelite writer on contemplative prayer, also perceived it. "Today," she wrote in an article on St John of the Cross, "we have our own peculiar 'night' in that what we had assumed were religious certainties, basic principles perhaps, have collapsed; in the West the Church we loved, in which we have invested, is rapidly losing credibility and we may well be wondering what is certain, what is reliable."[1] Her own teaching answers the question. "I have only one short life in which to love," she wrote as the concluding prayer in her book, *Living Love,* "in difficulty and pain, trusting in the dark and nonseeming." This is what Watkin was saying.

As a result of this upheaval, he continued, many dogmatic and moral pronouncements hitherto considered to be immutable because they were divinely guaranteed, are being exploded. The letter is being discredited and the elaborate structure of theological and moral doctrine is crumbling before our eyes. The urgent question today is whether this letter contained a void or an inexhaustible substance of spiritual reality. That it contains inexhaustible spiritual reality is his faith and he wished to convey it to all who are disturbed, disheartened or reduced to despairing doubt by the collapse of the traditional presentation of doctrine and morals.

The arguments which followed were familiar to anyone who knew his books. He discusses the philosophical basis for any metaphysic, the reasons why he does not adhere to the then fashionable philosophies of linguistic analysis and existentialism but instead to the fundamental principles of Platonic Aristotelian philosophy as developed from Plato onwards, but with emphasis rather on the Platonic than the Aristotelian constituent.

Unlike rational knowledge, spiritual knowledge cannot be precisely formulated but with it alone are scripture and the Church concerned. However, the letter is inevitable, indispensable, and therefore good. To neglect or despise it is folly because "it is the necessary translation and expression of the spirit in the imaginative and conceptual orders in a particular environment or climate of opinion in relation to scientific knowledge, and political or social organization." But if it is made an end in itself or looked upon as immutable, infallible and divinely revealed, it may in time become a servitude or incredible and then it kills, as St Paul tells us.

Scriptural statements are human and fallible translations of spiritual insights into conceptual terms or presented in and through poetical and often mythical imagery. When we study the letter of scripture, the superficial meaning intended by the human writer, we are confronted by errors not only of factual statements but even of moral and theological teaching. However, when we turn to the spirit of scripture we become aware of a profound and consistent orientation to God, a story of humanity finding God in experiences too deep for adequate enunciation but to be assimilated by prayer. The fundamental fact about the Church is that she exists for prayer, to unite us to God here and now. It is prayer that discerns the spiritual truth which is the veritable deposit of faith. Watkin ended by stating his long-held conviction that the present breakdown of the Church was opening the way to the eventual advent of the Third Kingdom of the Spirit which would succeed the dispensation of the Son.

Magdalen's chapter, *The Broken Pitcher*, argued that the Conciliar decrees made plain that the hitherto exclusive claims of the Roman Catholic Church to doctrinal authority could no longer be upheld in the form they were previously understood. Abbot, later Bishop B. C. Butler, had pointed out in his two pre-Conciliar books on the nature of the Church and its infallible authority that, objectively speaking, the Church was essentially the one single visible ark of salvation existing to the exclusion of all other societies. To abandon these claims would mean that the Church has been wrong since Pentecost and must lead to doctrinal liberalism of an extreme kind. They had been abandoned, doctrinal liberalism was rampant, some other basis for doctrinal authority was in the process of being worked out.

How the book will be received, Helena wrote to her, depends upon the type of Catholic who reads it. It was reviewed that March 1966, in the *Catholic Herald* by a man who did his best to make sure that nobody did.

Father Charles Davis was still Professor of Dogmatic Theology at Heythorp College, still a highly respected popular theologian and editor of *The Clergy Review*. People had no idea that he was leading a double life, on the verge of apostasy, his mind, as he himself described it, becoming more and more twisted and dishonest. His was a cautionary tale.

He had started his early training for the priesthood at a junior seminary when he was a boy of fifteen. From there he had gone to St Edmund's, Ware, studied theology in Rome and then returned to England to teach in two other seminaries. He was, from boyhood to early middle age, a product of a devout but very narrow system which tended to be suspicious of secular knowledge. Davis had never attended an ordinary university nor experienced daily contact with intelligent contemporaries who held views completely different from his own. He was soaked in what was beginning to be called "curial theology" or "unhistorical orthodoxy", much of which was in fact, as Abbot Butler had shown, the previous teaching of the Catholic Church.

The Council changed all that. Davis was summoned to Rome as a theological expert, witnessed the struggles between the old guard and the new, read books and heard opinions he had never encountered before. In his own words, he realized that "there was a fundamental conflict within the Roman Church on the whole question of Christian truth." From then onwards he was to "suffer agonies as a theologian in the Catholic Church."[2]

Until it happens, none of us know how we would actually behave in a tight corner. And Davis was in a very tight corner. He was a priest, presumably hearing confessions and certainly celebrating Mass, a well-known theologian who had to answer questions and form minds. His review of *The Future of Catholic Christianity* seems to have been written by a fundamentally honest man who simply did not know how to escape from the situation in which he found himself.

He had not been trained to think along Watkin's lines: the mystical approach was regarded by many as a subtle escape route from the institutional church. He adopted a tone of patronizing mockery towards Watkin's chapter, suggesting that the idea of a doctrinal crisis was a peculiar one, Watkin's love of the old Mass eccentric and any idea of a Third Kingdom of the Spirit an agreeable absurdity. Once again, he reserved his main fire for Magdalen and her "remarkably able, lucid and effective writing" in the course of which she explicitly rejected the essentials of the Christian faith. "Ludicrous", Canon Drinkwater remarked in the pages of *The Universe,* but few believed him. Neither her essay nor her father's, Davis said, had anything to do with the serious theological thinking that was going on in the Church. The book contained some good things written by the others, but as a whole it was deplorable, disastrous and unredeemable.

Sheed could not understand how his revered old friend could have got caught up in such an enterprise. When he came to write *The Church and I,* he told Watkin than since he was uncertain of Watkin's views about the Church with regret he could no longer include him in the list of the five contemporaries who had "shaped him most."[3] Father Michael Hanbury, a learned monk from Farnborough Abbey, editor of the Benedictine Quarterly *Pax* and a friend of over thirty years, wrote to Watkin in some distress to say that he had read the review and, as he delicately put it, sincerely hoped that it would not damage his reputation for Catholic orthodoxy. They all thought very highly of Davis at Farnborough and he supposed that Magdalen had left the Church.

Watkin replied at once. The substance of his chapter was not destructive but an attempt to penetrate below the more superficial zone of conceptualization to the underlying insights of the spirit. "Father Davis' writings," he remarked with truth and psychological insight, "contain plenty of doctrinal restatements and reinterpretations, though he contrives to disguise from himself as well as his readers the extent and nature of the revolution in which he is playing a part." Magdalen had not left the Church. In fact, she and her two children had accompanied him to Mass and Holy Communion a few days ago. She is going to have a portion of her chapter read on the BBC. He would be grateful if Hanbury would show this letter to any other member of the community who had been influenced by Father Davis' review.

But the net was closing in. The sharp-eyed Heenan had already remarked some dangerous tendencies in Davis' thought and insisted that the *Clergy Review* should be controlled by an editorial board. In November, Davis wrote a very able defence of clerical celibacy and in December announced his intention of getting married. He was going to leave the Church, which was in the process of disintegration, torn by tension and incoherence, its institutional faith in truth incompatible with biblical criticism and modern theology. It must die in order to live again. From the depth of his being he wanted to be free from the oppressive and tormenting Roman Catholic system and to rejoin the human race. He remained a Christian but a "disaffiliated" one, free from any authoritarian structure whatsoever.

Watkin's first reaction was admirable. He was amazed, he wrote to Magdalen, to read about the manner of Davis' departure and to understand that he was engaged to be married. He feared that his admirers might lose their faith. It was very sad. Whether Davis' admirers lost their faith or their heads is open to question, but his defection was felt by them to be a "ghastly blow and an indescribable sorrow." The impulsive Father Herbert McCabe, the editor of the Dominican periodical *Blackfriars*, announced in its pages that the Church was quite plainly corrupt. His fellow Dominican, Father Lawrence Bright, assured his fellow Christians that the only body of thought they could support today was Marxist, and Paul Johnson, editor of the *New Statesman*, asked if the Church could survive Davis' departure which might prove far more momentous than Newman's going out in the opposite direction. The Church, Johnson observed, was in a state of intellectual paralysis. Pope Paul should abdicate, his successor chosen by a truly representative body, the Vatican abandoned and its headquarters moved to a tolerant country like Holland.

Watkin's second reaction to Davis' behaviour was one of anger and disgust. What humbug! Here was a man who had condemned them out of hand, who had prevented people even considering their work and was now saying something along the same lines himself. Indeed Davis was. "The Church in its existing form," he told an *Observer* reporter, "seems to me to be a pseudo-political structure from the past. It is now breaking up and some other form of Christian presence in the world is under formation." Expressed in different terms, that had been the thrust of Watkin's essay. Davis had said that the Church's institutional faith was incompatible with biblical criticism and modern theology. So Magdalen had remarked. His review had verged on hysteria just because he secretly shared many of the opinions that he had condemned.

The editors of the *Catholic Herald* and the *Universe* were caught on the wrong foot. It all proved too much for the *Herald*'s editor, Desmond Fisher, who had given Davis and his future wife hospitality in their hour of need. He resigned. "It is, I think," he wrote to Magdalen, "better to make a clean break than to muddle along with a split personality at work." Bédoyère would have understood.

Davis did not leave the Church in order to get married. It is more likely he got married in order to leave the Church. He needed the support of a loving wife. His fiancée had also been a Catholic. Before they married she gave a newspaper interview in the course of which she remarked that she and Charles had come to the conclusion that if you reject even a part of Catholic teaching, you must reject it all. In other words, if you drop one stitch the entire fabric will unravel. She was expressing a widely-held opinion, using the same arguments Ponty had put forward to Perpetua all those years ago. The philosopher Anthony Kenny, later Master of Balliol, had left the Church two years before, not for Davis' reasons, although they played a part, but because he was uncertain about the existence of God and could no longer believe in the Christian creeds. He remarked in an autobiography written many years later that he was old-fashioned enough "to believe that if the Church had been as wrong in the past on so many topics as forward-looking clergy believe, then her claims to impose belief and obedience upon others, are, in the form in which they have traditionally been made, mere impudence."

Is one then to go out into the wilderness because claims to teach truth in the forms they were traditionally made turn out to be ill-founded? Watkin did not think so. "In this time of theological transition," he had written to Magdalen long ago, "patience is the most urgent necessity. However crushing the burden of ecclesiastical officialdom the Roman Catholic Church is the Church founded by Christ and preached by the Apostles." His view was remote from the outpourings of Davis and his disciples. The difficulties occasioned "by the new world view opened up by science and prehistory and the traditional presentation of theology" he advised her now, "is a call not to reject but to go *inwards* by a faith which is not blind swallowing of formulas and externals . . . but an *adherence* of the deepest self, the root and centre of will and intuition to God as He is, and beyond any revelation of Himself He has made and can make to man on earth. A doctrine prayed is somehow very different from a doctrine thought about, stated in a catechism or textbook. It becomes no longer a barrier, baffling and restricting, but a door leading into a vast distance where the things of God are felt, not clearly seen."

While Watkin was struggling to make his voice heard, Christopher Dawson was far away in America. In 1958 he had been invited to become the first Professor of Roman Catholic Studies at Harvard. The Chair had been endowed by the Catholic layman, Mr Chauncy Stillman, in order "to cultivate the understanding of the theology and closely related studies of the Roman Catholic Church." This was to break new ground. Never before in the history of the United States had there been anything like it, a Chair of Roman Catholic Studies in a Divinity School which was Protestant in tradition and outlook. "Harvard has always considered Catholicism intellectually contemptible," Stillman, a convert himself, wrote to Dawson, "socially negligible, and dangerous politically."[4]

Dawson felt that he had at last received the recognition denied him by his fellow countrymen. In turn, his wife Valery was given an opportunity to escape from her restricted and demanding life. The sadness, as Dawson's daughter, Christina Scott, subsequently pointed out, was that it all came too late for her father. He was now sixty-nine and had been a semi-invalid for years. But he was determined to seize the chance and the appointment gave him the vitality he normally lacked. There were other difficulties.

What Dawson said was very interesting but he was a poor lecturer. His voice was low and monotonous and he spoke in an old-fashioned, upper-class English manner. Nor were his expectations realistic. His students were post-graduates but such a mind as his was too challenging and some of them simply could not keep pace with his massive learning. An assistant had to be appointed to act as interpreter.

Taken all in all, however, the whole enterprise was a success, the crowning success of Dawson's life and of Valery's also. He had opened the eyes of his largely Protestant and provincial students to the immense spiritual, historical and artistic scope of Catholicism. She had been awarded an honorary degree as Doctor of Laws by Cardinal Cushing at Regis University. Both she and her husband had travelled together far across the American continent, given interviews to the press, been honoured at public receptions, replied to speeches and shaken hundreds of hands. This was achieved at a cost. At the end of 1959 Dawson suffered a small stroke. He was not incapacitated but it was a warning. In the winter of 1962 he suffered another, speech became difficult and his hand-writing altered. It was a cruel blow. That June he resigned his Professorship, in July sailed to Southampton in the *Queen Elizabeth* and disembarked in a wheelchair.

So, at the thin end of life, the old friends met again. Two volumes of Dawson's Harvard lectures were being published in the United States under different titles although, as Watkin sardonically pointed out, most modern Catholics wanted neither his religion nor his culture. Watkin would go by bus and train to Budleigh Salterton, stay the night and take up his task of correcting typescripts, galleys, compiling indexes and encouraging publishers to re-issue Dawson's earlier books.

He was perplexed about his own work. Weidenfeld and Nicolson had invited him to write a book on Roman Catholicism. Once he would have leapt at the chance, now he hesitated. He was seventy-six. Had he the sustained energy to write a long book requiring research? Besides, and this weighed heavily with him, his own position was an uneasy one, poised between the fundamentalists and those progressives whose tendency to substitute earthly welfare for union with God were pulling up Christianity by its very roots. Eventually, he turned down the proposal.

When Dawson remarked that Watkin was a Greek and he a Roman, he meant presumably that Watkin's mind was more speculative than his. Dawson was not strictly speaking a theologian nor a philosopher but a brilliant exponent of past religion-cultures. The cast of his mind was conservative and cautious in a way that Watkin's never was, even in his Aloysian days. Their friendship, a reviewer wrote after Watkin's death, accounted for the direction and much of the accomplishment of Dawson's work. Watkin provided Dawson not only with comradeship but with mental, intellectual and spiritual stimulation. "One may say that if there had been no E. I. Watkin there would have been no Dawson as he is known to the scholarly world."[5]

"What a contrast," Watkin wrote in a letter to Magdalen, "between Dawson's understanding of *past* history and his complete incapacity, even when in the best of health, to look in the face the problems of the present and the possibilities of the future." Unlike Dawson, Watkin thought that there would be no restoration of Catholic culture as history has known it. In any event, the large migration of non-Europeans and the consequent building of mosques and temples would radically affect our way of life and diversify our religious consciousness. The present position was both a breakdown and a breakthrough. "The breakdown of traditional [Christian] orthodoxy," he continued, "has accompanied and released a breakthrough of spiritual insights whose operation and apprehension has [hitherto] been restricted and impaired by conceptual formulations now become more or less untenable." The religion of the future would be much what Catholicism has been to Judaism, a dispensation of spirit, released from the letter. "There is a substance of mystical religious truth, truth experienced by prayer to which we must hold for *dear life*. Otherwise there is but barren scepticism."

As time went on Dawson became unable or reluctant to communicate continuously. He lived shut up in himself, Watkin wrote, a pathological exaggeration of his natural temperament. They saw each other for the last time a few days before his death on May 25, 1970. Watkin had tears in his eyes when he told the nurse that he was taking leave of his oldest and best friend. Dawson had very much disliked the changes in the Mass and thought the translation utterly inadequate. His funeral therefore was celebrated at Budleigh Salterton in the old Latin rite. "Always and always," Watkin wrote to Perpetua, "a sense of darkness and the impenetrable beyond." Later his body was taken to Yorkshire to be buried beside his parents in the churchyard at Burnsall, the place below them in the valley which Dawson had pointed out to Watkin as they had travelled to Hartlington together in that long ago summer of their Oxford finals.

CHAPTER TWENTY-SIX

The Twilight Catholics

The time had arrived for self-expression, experiments, opportunities to try out new approaches and long suppressed ideas. The laity were to be empowered, the focus of the parish was to be not the altar but the promulgation of justice and peace, outreach and interfaith dialogue.

I n July 1968, Pope Paul issued his long awaited encyclical, *Humanae Vitae*, in which he condemned as intrinsically wrong all forms of birth-control except the rhythm method.

Watkin thought abortion wrong, except in rare cases, since it entailed the destruction of a human being in the very early stages of development. Contraception was a different matter. He described the condemnation as a bombshell, although the Pope was but repeating what the Church had always taught.[1] It was a bombshell only because extensive leaks from the papal commission set up by John XXIII to examine the matter suggested that the majority had been in favour of setting aside the former teaching. Archbishop Heenan himself apparently thought so and was dropping hints in that direction in order to prepare people for a *volte face*, but he would have found it hard to explain how what was God's law one day could be contradicted the next. He was spared the task but considered that the adverse reaction to the Pope's ruling was the greatest shock the Church had suffered since the Reformation. "Many lay theologians left the Church," he wrote in the last volume of his autobiography, "while new-style priests and nuns began to practise the evangelical virtues unhampered by vows. Outraged by the lack of love in their own communities," he added acidly, "they sought Christ in each other's arms."[2]

On the whole Helena's generation accepted the Church's teaching and followed it as she herself most certainly did. By the nineteen thirties and beyond, however, richer and more worldly Catholics increasingly had put the prohibition to one side. Some left the Church, some gave up going to Confession altogether or simply failed to mention the matter. Others slept in different rooms, on sofas downstairs or struggled with the rhythm method but by the time the Pope made up his mind many had ceased to care what was decided one way or the other. This attitude was rarer among poorer Catholics and those of all degrees who still clung to the idea that the Church was literally infallible in faith and morals.

Anthony Kenny had worked as a priest for some years in a Liverpool parish and knew what he was talking about. Reviewing *Objections* in *The New Statesman* a few years after his defection he asked how, if artificial contraception were to be declared not to be intrinsically immoral, the Roman Catholic Church could ever be taken seriously again. "If a doctrine taught so solemnly and at the cost of so much suffering can turn out to be mistaken, what reliance can be placed on any moral doctrine?"[3]

Watkin, it may be remembered, had been very anxious that Perpetua should not feel that she had to leave the Church solely because she had married a divorced man. He now feared that the publication of *Humanae Vitae* might force those with tender consciences to abandon their religion because they could not accept a decision about a matter of secular ethics, the arguments for which were in any case ill-founded. He therefore wrote an article which he called *Catholic Morality* in order to "give some guidance to perplexed and troubled people." This he sent to *The Tablet*.

The former editor of the paper had been Douglas Woodruff. A cultivated and widely informed man of conservative views, his instinct was to shield the Church from what he considered to be destructive criticism. He even objected to some passages about Newman in Ronald Chapman's life of Father Faber and tried to persuade the author to remove them. He had supported the Council as far as he could in the pages of *The Tablet* but as the paper's historian Michael Walsh pointed out, "for him Vatican II destroyed the institution which he loved from his earliest years."[4]

The publication of *Humanae Vitae* faced his successor, Tom Burns, with a difficult challenge. Bishop Butler had altered his former views about contraception. He later told Burns that since the encyclical had not been "received" by the Church, he thought it was therefore invalidated.[5] In any case it was known that the Pope had overridden the majority opinion of his own special advisors and Tom wrote an editorial opposing it. For this, the paper was accused by some of disloyalty. Watkin's article was too long and no doubt too radical to publish, but now stung by the criticism and anxious about his standing as editor, Burns wrote to ask him if he could make use of his "historical illustrations and well-phrased points" in order to rebut the charge.

Shortly, what Watkin had said was this: The encyclical had divided the faithful, delighting some but dismaying, even tormenting others. We must therefore carefully examine the nature and scope of papal authority and its relevance to natural ethics. The Church has always claimed to teach a detailed moral code revealed to her by God and to apply it to the solution of moral problems, deciding with divine authority whether conduct is moral or immoral. She has further claimed that this competence extends to the natural law, that is, the law determined by our natural reason. "No believer," the Pope says, "will wish to deny that the teaching authority of the Church is competent to interpret even the natural law." This, however, is precisely the issue to be determined in the light of indisputable historical facts.

On more than one occasion the official Church has radically altered her previous moral teaching. Watkin goes on to instance examples which are well known today but at that time usually glossed over or even denied. The taking of interest was once as persistently and emphatically condemned both by popes and Ecumenical Councils as contraception. This condemnation was based upon a fundamental economic error and after a number of modifications, finally abandoned. Watkin follows with an interesting account of the *volte face* over the morality of religious perse-cution and capital punishment for heretics and the employment of torture. It took the Church nineteen centuries to convince itself that slavery was a violation of the natural law.

When the Pope speaks about natural law, that is law within the scope of reason, his decision, Watkin pointed out, is worth only the facts and arguments produced in its support. There is no external code engraved on stone tablets or promulgated by papal rescript. Moral codes, however, are not the same thing as moral principles. Ethical pronouncements, even when proved to be mistaken in the letter, often point to genuine moral insights underlying the discredited formulas.

Far from turning away from the Church, we never needed her more. However deplorable the aberrations of the ecclesiastical magisterium in the lower order of natural reason, she has consistently protected prayer in all its depth and breadth. Prayer and worship involve moral attitudes. It is through prayer, the human spirit's union with Divine Love, that we are enabled to distinguish between letter and spirit, to perceive "the law of God written into men's hearts."

In fact, the encyclical did indeed contain some of Watkin's "underlying moral insights", warnings which tended to be ignored because the reasons given for the absolute prohibition of artificial contraception were uncon-vincing. As the century progressed many societies came to accept gross sexual immorality, not as human weakness, but legitimate self-expression.

The sacred centre of the Catholic religion was the Mass. It was this which gave it its identity, its radical separation from the Reformed churches. In his autobiography, Tyrrell, not yet a Roman Catholic, describes the effect a high Anglican Mass had on him. "I felt instinctively what I long afterwards understood clearly, namely: the difference between an altar and a communion table was infinite; that it meant a totally different religion, another order of things altogether, of which I had no experience."[6]

It is not easy for those brought up in a modern scientific culture to believe in miraculous births, angelic visitations, prophetic dreams, resurrections from the dead and ascensions into heaven, that is, to accept the literal truth of the world picture into which the seed of Christianity was sown. Scientific knowledge cannot and does not alter spiritual truth, but it makes its presentation difficult.

We have to be lured into belief, led into that dimension of spirit akin to poetry which enables us to begin to understand the meaning of what cannot be expressed in ordinary language. As Tyrrell perceived, Catholic worship presents us with a different order of things, something beyond human companionship or the togetherness of the common meal, rather a numinous experience that draws us into the mystery that is God. The former low Mass, the spoken Mass in the old rite, uniquely combined solemn ritual worship with a large measure of Quaker silence. It had little to do with bells, incense, or vestments as those who have heard it on battlefields, in prison or in other desperate circumstances could testify.

The practice of Watkin's faith was centered on the Mass and the Office. During the war, for Helena's sake, the Abbot of Downside allowed Christopher to celebrate Mass in the house at Dorking, in those days a rare privilege. In July 1944, as the family were assembling, someone whispered to Watkin that the radio had just announced the overthrow of his old enemy, Mussolini. He shook his head and waved his arms violently across his face as if to push the news away. These things were of no importance, it was the Mass that mattered.

It cannot be said that Watkin faced the question of liturgical reform altogether realistically. He saw the need for greater lay participation, which was why he was so pleased with Canon Carter's insistence that his congregation should sing the Mass every Sunday. He thought that most of the sacraments should be in the vernacular but was convinced that the Mass itself must be celebrated in a sacred language and was dismayed by the failure of Catholic schools to make sure their pupils understood sufficient Latin. A sacred language helped to preserve the unity of the Church; it was no idle boast that wherever a Catholic went in the world, he or she could hear the familiar words of the Mass substantially as it had been celebrated in Western Christendom for over a thousand years.

On the other hand, he sometimes muttered about the absurdity of nuns daily reciting their office in a language of which they were largely ignorant and he was conscious of the need for non-European countries to fit the Mass into the framework of their own cultural forms and traditions. It should never be allowed to become merely an archaic rite but have "the appeal of a living religion to living men and women." He did not always face the implications of his own thought. He never realized what a release Mass in English would be for thousands of people and how much an increased active, physical participation in the liturgy might mean to those whose cast of mind was very different from his own. The time for reform had arrived but because of the heavy hand of Rome and the sheer complexity of the issues involved, these matters were not generally discussed. When everything came out into the open it was too late, the momentum for change was too powerful and a great work of religious art was dismantled just at the time when it was most needed.

Pope John had died before any conciliar decrees could be agreed upon. It was Pope Paul VI who promulgated the Constitution on the Sacred Liturgy. The Council Fathers had listened very attentively indeed to their fellow pilgrims, and many had come to feel that they had somehow missed out on the original Reformation. As a result the document, as far as it concerned the Mass, has been called a half-hearted attempt to combine a community eucharistic meal with the solemn sacrifice offered to God for the living and the dead. There was no suggestion that the old Mass should be replaced by a new rite. On the contrary, it was to be preserved and fostered. It was, however, to be revised and simplified, and scriptural reading extended to provide "a richer fare at the table of God's word." Some vernacular was to be permitted but Latin was to be preserved together with the treasure of sacred music and Gregorian chant was to be given pride of place.

It was left to a comparatively small number of highly motivated progressives to drive liturgical reforms in a direction not originally envisaged either by the authorities or the faithful. At the first Reformation, to use Watkin's expression, the Roman Catholic Church in this country collapsed like a pack of cards. The population was compelled into Protestantism by the power of the Crown and the complicity of the clergy. The second Reformation was, for diverse and complex reasons, a collapse from within and once again the shepherds fled. Watkin had brought himself to accept the idea of an occasional low Mass celebrated in English provided the translation was not in too vulgar a tongue. High Mass, however, should always be sung in Latin. Hardly had he forced himself into docility before the Pope declared both rites to be obsolete.

In 1969 the Pope promulgated the official New Order of the Mass and declared that the old Mass, misleadingly described as the Tridentine, in fact substantially the one brought to us by St Augustine, should be no longer publicly celebrated. There was to be a new rite, celebrated in a spoken language, "a simple, communal, intelligible service prescribed for all churches" as the *Catholic Truth Society* pamphlet put it. Pope Paul elaborated his decision in a speech of great interest and remarkable frankness.

The entire liturgy was to be desacralized for the sake of verbal meaning "suited to the greater number of the faithful, even children and persons of small education." We are," he said, " parting with the speech of the Christian centuries; we are becoming like profane intruders in the preserve of sacred utterance. We will lose a great part of that stupendous and incomparable artistic and spiritual thing, the Gregorian chant. We have reason indeed for regret, almost for bewilderment. What can we put in place of the language of angels? We are giving up something of priceless worth. Why? What is more priceless than these loftiest of the Church's values?" The answer, he continued, will seem banal, prosaic. "Yet it is a good answer because it is human, because it is apostolic." The liturgy was to be converted into everyday speech because children, young people, the world of work are fond of plain language, easily understood.[7]

So it came about that the entire liturgy was dismantled and like the base Indian, the Roman Catholic Church "threw a pearl away greater than all his tribe." Before long the "People's Missal" would define the Mass as "the assembly of the People of God under the presidency of the priest to celebrate the memorial of the Lord." The Roman Catholic Church survived the Reformation. The decisive break with the past came after the Second Vatican Council.

This was the sixties and seventies and the clergy were as much liberated as anyone else. The time had arrived for self-expression, experiments, opportunities to try out new approaches and long suppressed ideas. The laity were to be empowered, the focus of the parish was to be not the altar but the promulgation of justice and peace, outreach and interfaith dialogue. Many of the clergy were only too pleased to think of themselves as Presidents of the Assembly rather than priests forever according to the order of Melchizedek. Like the Protestant Bishop Hooper, some derided "the golden vestments of Popery" as ecclesiastical millinery and at house Masses experimented with bread brought from the kitchen. The difficulty was to know what to do with the crumbs.[8]

Practical problems arose. A fundamentally different kind of liturgical celebration, as the Protestant reformers well understood, requires a fundamentally different kind of church. Previous buildings were obviously unsuitable for the direction Catholic worship was taking. Of what use were high altars and rood-screens when what was needed was a central altar with people gathered round? Watkin heard that Archbishop Dwyer of Birmingham was planning to get rid of Pugin's great screen in St Chad's Cathedral, lost his temper and accused him of wanton destruction. The Archbishop wrote to assure him that the screen was safe, but two years later it was ordered to be removed and saved from burning only by the joint efforts of a local architect and the City Engineer. It found a home in an Anglican church in Reading.[9]

The Anglicans were indeed astonished at what was happening. Some were gratified by this tardy conversion but others were disquieted. If Rome collapsed, where were the Anglo-Catholics to go? It was as if the days of Cranmer and Archbishop Grindal had returned. All over the world Catholic bishops allowed rood-screens, paintings, pews, statues, altar rails, tabernacles, altars themselves to be dismantled, destroyed or obscured by a "holy table" thrust towards the chancel.[10] There was no longer to be any sacred space, no "place where Thy glory dwelleth" as the old Mass once proclaimed. The idea of "a house of God" was not incarnational, merely the survival of a mediaeval perversion. It was accepted that the congregation might talk loudly, gossip and laugh before and after Mass just as if the Blessed Sacrament were not present. Indeed, since some churches thrust it into an insignificant corner, devotionally speaking, it hardly was.

Churches came to resemble church halls, complete with office furniture, an abundance of microphones, notices pinned on the walls together with children's pictures and at the appropriate season, the introduction of carefully placed Christmas trees. In a number of parishes, the Mass became very like any rather low church Protestant service, indistinguishable when heard on the radio.

Much of the "re-ordering", as Eamon Duffy has pointed out, sprang from crass philistinism, the cultural impoverishment of a Catholic community "which had little inherited sense of the value or meaning of art and which distrusted formality as a mark of elitism." Beyond that, "there lay the collapse within the culture of any broader sense of the decorum of symbol, a profound lack of ease with the heightened speech and the loss of the charged sense of the sacredness of holy things, which is the soul of liturgy."[11]

Far from being given pride of place, "that stupendous and incomparable artistic and spiritual thing", as the Pope described Gregorian chant, all but disappeared together with the language of angels. The surviving Benedictine monasteries came to sing nearly all the Office in English and reserved the beauty of the Latin Office for the production of compact disks sold to support the foundation which for the most part had ceased to make use of it. Catholics in the majority of parishes might be Baptists or Methodists for all the knowledge they acquired of the Church's accumulated treasure of hymnody and music down the ages. Copes and chasubles were sold, wooden chalices became fashionable and Holy Communion was no longer received kneeling but given out standing, frequently by young men and women in casual clothes.

"All the most intelligent and best priests are leaving," someone once said in Watkin's presence. They thought he was asleep but he opened his eyes. "The most intelligent perhaps," he said, "but not the best." For the most part, the laity greeted the departure of so many priests at first with shock, then with disapproval, gradually with resigned amusement but only in exceptional cases with respect. There was a certain amount of *schadenfreude*. These were the people who only yesterday were telling them that the world had no greater privilege to offer than ordination as a Catholic priest, who once gave out edifying figures about the number of elevations of the Host there were over the globe every minute and whose manuals explained that all sexual sin was considered to be mortal.

According to a recent commentator, himself a Benedictine monk, "the mask was bound to slip". If one asked the hundreds who have abandoned their vocation over these forty years the majority will tell you that they left the priesthood to stop the pretence, to be free to be themselves, "to break out of the stifling world of clericalism which was condemning them to be to be hypocrites and Pharisees."[12]

This testimony does not fit the thought and behaviour of the many priests who played such an important part in Watkin's life and who did not, as far as one can tell, feel themselves to be hypocrites and Pharisees. Yet there is no doubt, and Watkin's letters confirm it, that the post-Conciliar Church was far more human than the stuffy, self-centred clericalism which preceded it. The scattered remnants of the Sacred Heart nuns were much easier to get on with than they ever were in their glory days at Roehampton. In general, those who remained were much more relaxed, and convents and presbyteries far more homely than they had been in the past. This extended to the celebration of marriages and funerals. Gone was the mean spirited service once so grudgingly extended to those who married a non-Catholic, likewise the cheerless austerity of the requiem Mass. But at a price.

Always the same dilemma, Watkin remarked after watching Pope Paul carried up the nave of St Peter's. Life offers us one thing at the cost of another, very rarely both. Marriage services were more human because they were less holy, requiem Masses less austere because to a large extent they ceased to be insistent, repeated, humble pleading that the dead person might be united to God despite his sins. Death was no longer felt to be transcended. A redeemed human being was not welcomed into paradise by choirs of angels so much as congratulated by his friends and relations on the good life he had led.

This was the reason why Watkin was so profoundly troubled by the path the post-Conciliar Church was taking. The suppression of the ancient liturgy was not solely an act of cultural vandalism but a symptom of a far deeper malaise. The fact, he wrote, "that the changes in the Mass do not favour contemplation and reverential adoration damns them as radically irreligious."

The fundamental issue between religion and secularism was whether or not there existed a second and deeper dimension than that of which science could take cognizance. It is to this spiritual dimension that with varying degrees of understanding, the religions of the world have addressed themselves. If this dimension does not exist then religion is illusory, as Watkin was for ever pointing out.

But if it does exist, attempts by so-called Christians, and now Roman Catholics to give religious colouring to what are basically efforts to improve our lot in this world are to misconceive religion's very nature and purpose, which is to unite us to God now and for all eternity. The clergy were cutting off the bough they were sitting on.

Before long the majority of nuns who still remained in their convents abandoned the habit. Greatly diminished numbers and scattered objectives soon made it necessary for the Sacred Heart order to leave the school at Tunbridge Wells. Like those unfortunate pre-Reformation Catholics who had at great expense erected new rood-screens only to have them smashed and vandalized on the orders of Henry VIII's commissioners, they left behind a newly-built and useless chapel of which they had recently been so proud.

The Jesuit seminary at Heythrop was sold. It moved to Farm Street in London and the seminarians wrote words and guitar music with "a modern sound" and a "modern message" to accompany the new service. According to the biographer of Father Martin D'Arcy, once Master of Campion Hall, Oxford, and Jesuit Provincial, the traditional training melted away. The students wore hippy clothes, invited their girl friends to supper, disregarded their old dress, rules and customs together with solemn Masses, prayers, meditation, spiritual exercises, poverty and obedience.[13] "We are both growing old," D'Arcy wrote to Watkin, "and seeing an insidious humanism replacing the glory of past belief and the Imitation of Christ." Living now in spiritual exile at Farm Street, because of his age, he was given special permission to say the old Mass. "We share the heart-ache over what is happening to Christendom," he wrote in his last letter to Watkin before his death in 1976. "I hope to fight the good fight to the end." Between 1964 and 1976 over a hundred members of the English Province alone had abandoned their vows.

Cardinal Heenan had the reputation of being an excellent pastoral bishop and he undoubtedly was. But like the majority of those in high office, both in church and state, he preferred prevarication to scandal, and untruthfulness to anything that might injure simple people's faith in the institution he represented. He had a devotion to the old Mass and was hard put to defend what was happening. In 1964 Evelyn Waugh wrote to him to complain about the distressing changes in the language and rite of the Mass and invited him to dinner at his Club so that they could discuss the matter. Flattered perhaps, for once Heenan's guard slipped. They must meet, he replied, Waugh was right. The Mass, he said, " is no longer the Holy Sacrifice but the Meal at which the priest is the waiter. The bishop, I suppose, is the head waiter and the Pope the patron."[14] It was not a position he could maintain and remain Archbishop. Next year he was to write a Pastoral Letter assuring the faithful of the immense gain the new service had brought and that "millions who hitherto were mere bystanders are now taking an active part in the Mass." Double-faced, was Waugh's comment. In a personal interview a year later, Heenan assured Magdalen that the old Mass would continue to be said and that seminarians would be taught it. This was not the case and both of them knew it.

One should not be too hard on the Archbishop. He genuinely loved the old Mass but he feared schism within the Church even more than he feared scandal. There was a steady, well-organized and deeply felt opposition to the new service led by the Latin Mass Society and the followers of Archbishop Lefebvre, and it was never to die. The danger of schism was a real one and whatever his personal opinion, the Archbishop, like Pius XII in a different context, would go almost to any length to preserve the unity of the Church.

Like the rest of the episcopate, Heenan had been a conservative at the beginning of the Council and later became a progressive. He was soon disillusioned. He came to believe that without some form of divine intervention, it seemed unlikely that there would be a Church left by the end of the century.[15] At that time, he was among the few priests in high office openly to state that the root of the trouble lay in the loss of faith in the supernatural, above all, in a rejection of prayer. Here at least he was close to Watkin. So was Helena's brother, Samuel Shepheard. Educated at Beaumont and Stonyhurst, he was a staunch Catholic and sat glowering at Abbots Hall – old, impotent and amazed.

Samuel had lived there alone with his dogs ever since his mother's death in 1939 and that was nearly thirty-five years ago. He was determined to stay in his old home until the end and took steps to ensure that he did. Let it all go to rack and ruin, it would see him out. Most of the house was shut up and the grounds left to themselves. He kept the drawing room door locked and its windows shuttered. He saw no reason to move anything so the furniture remained exactly as it was on the afternoon his mother died. Most of the bedrooms were locked. He himself slept in the old night nursery, a shotgun by the iron bedstead. The dining room was turned into an estate office and he ate by the Aga in one of the inner kitchens, using the *Eastern Daily Press* as a tablecloth, afterwards rinsing his plate under the scullery tap. He saw to it that the stove in his mother's conservatory was kept alight and tended her plants. Someone came in once or twice a week to do some cooking, sweep the floors and do a bit of dusting, but that was all.

After the war he had tried to keep the hunt going but it soon petered out. When he got too old to manage the property himself, he employed a bailiff who lived in the farmhouse by the water meadows. He had once given shooting parties but it was a long time since he had preserved game and the most he could do was to ask a few neighbours to walk round and enjoy a bit of rough shooting in his overgrown woods. Until she became too infirm to travel, every year Perpetua or Catherine drove Helena to stay at Cromer so she could visit the brother to whom she remained obstinately fond. She and Samuel would sit side by side in the afternoon sunshine on the bench outside the front door and talk stiffly to one another, strangers in all but blood. The grassed-over flowerbeds were indistinguishable now from the distant meadow. Behind them both, the unpruned shrubs mingled with the stems of the clematis which had already reached the upper storey of the house, covering the windows like a huge beard. Helena remembered everything as it had once been but said nothing of this to her brother as he sat bent over his thumbstick in his tattered coat.

Year after year Christopher used to stay at Abbots Hall for a fortnight to fish the river. He had loved the place since he was a boy and his sisters wondered if he had hopes that Samuel would leave it to the Abbey. He liked being alone, he told them, as much as his uncle and took melancholy pleasure in observing the fallen rhubarb crocks among the cabbage stumps in the desolation that was once the kitchen garden, and fighting his way through brambles, elder and lilac to reach the edge of the pond where Philip had once planted water lilies for Maria Pasqua. It was bed at nine and Mass next morning served punctiliously by Samuel in the chapel.

Rumours reached him that a table had been placed in front of the altar at Cromer church and that the altar rails, benches and the statue of the Sacred Heart had been thrown out, as well as two pictures which had served as a reredos together with other beautiful objects collected by Squirrel.[16] This was where Helena had been married. His parents had given the church a crucifix and a monstrance in memory of his little brother Martin. He understood that there was no such thing as Benediction there now and that all the Latin hymns were completely disregarded. Norfolk was then still in the diocese of Northhampton and he and those who thought like him with justice referred to their Bishop and his successor, Alan Clark, as Cranmer. You can't teach an old dog new tricks, Samuel told Christopher, getting up at the most sacred part of the Mass, shaking hands and grinning like a lot of monkeys.

The time came when the priest's words "I will go unto the altar of my God" dissolved into "good morning everyone". Samuel told Christopher that he was now too old to have people to stay. So the chapel was closed, not to be opened until his own body rested there on the night before his funeral.

For over fifty years he had dismissed Edda as a hopeless husband for Helena. Now for the first time they signalled to each other in the darkness, sharp points of light between men who before had little more in common than their names on a marriage certificate.

CHAPTER TWENTY-SEVEN

Exactly What Happened

Muffled by scarves, in thick jumpers, duffel coats, trousers, stout shoes and wearing rubber gloves they looked for all the world like people searching for dead bodies in the aftermath of some dreadful disaster.

As time passed it began to look as if the Catholic Church, like the Communist system, could not be reformed without being destroyed. "We must have faith," Watkin wrote from Downside towards the end of 1969, "that we are witnessing not a death agony but the birth pangs of a new and more interior dispensation." Only a religion based on personal prayer could exist in our secular and irreligious environment and hold fast against man's self-worship.

Christopher's position was a difficult one. He very much disliked the vernacular Mass and the changed rite. "I find it a torment," he wrote, "but it is my duty to go through with it. The English translation is as barbarous as it is incomplete." But he was a monk under a vow of obedience to his abbot and moreover the head master, a very successful head master, of a thriving public school. He had made his choice long ago and was prepared to accept the consequences. At the time of the Charles Davis débâcle he wrote to Magdalen, remarking that such folly was very sad. "Why are some people so immature that they will not realize you have to take good things *on the terms offered*?"

"I understand only too well your feelings about the liturgy," he wrote to his father, "they are really mine but unless I accept what I cannot alter, I get no peace of mind." It was all so painful that he did not like to discuss the matter. "I think of Shakespeare's Duke of York in *Henry VI*," he ended his letter. "'Through these wounds my soul doth fly to Thee.'"

He now appreciated his father's work far more than he had done when he was younger. Few people could have been more unlike in temperament yet so close to each other in their approach to religious truth. The fundamental difference between them was that Christopher, because of his profession, clung to the authority of the institutional Church while Watkin gave it less weight.

Yet even in this they were fundamentally at one. "What is life on earth at best but a life of clouds and shifting lights; that is a trust and faith in the mysteries of which we see only the outer surface?" Christopher now quoted to him from an unexpected source, Cardinal Manning. "A veil is spread over the face even of the Church through which the realities of the hereafter are faintly discovered."

When Catherine married Keith Davenport in 1954, both she and her husband made their home with Helena at Fairmead. She was now seventy-two and the arrangement was a good one. Helena was looked after until the end of her life and able to enjoy the company of her grandchildren. Perhaps her happiest years, certainly the most tranquil, were spent after the war at Dorking. In 1939 a maid called Nellie came, as it were a replacement for Hetty, and was the mainstay of the household for over forty years.

Like Watkin, Helena made the rounds of her family, went on holiday with Catherine and the children and abroad with Christopher or Perpetua. Edda's long visits tired her as his presence always had done but she minded not at all the numerous letters which arrived in Zoë's enormous handwriting. Nellie would pack Watkin some lunch and together with his flora and his breviary he would spend the day on Box Hill looking for wild flowers, just as he had done at Baden and by the Starnberger See before the old world died. Gräffin Hertha had told him that the sorrow in this life outweighed the joy. He had not believed her. When he was younger he had cried out in passionate denial when the Church referred to this world as a vale of tears. It's *not, not, not*, he would say to his children, who already feared it might be. Now he himself was not so sure. The sad, pleading, *Salve Regina* was one of the loveliest of all the anthems to Our Lady.

Helena's slim figure and the upright bearing that she owed to the retired drill sergeant employed by the Roehampton nuns made her appear much younger than she actually was. She was always delicate and spent long periods in bed. The priest would come from the other end of the town to bring her Holy Communion. Things are very casual now but in those days a special table covered by a white cloth was prepared in Helena's bedroom. On this would be placed a crucifix and two blessed candles. Still fasting, she would await the priest's arrival with a black mantilla over her head. It was accepted then that people never held any unnecessary conversation with a priest known to be carrying the Blessed Sacrament. One or two of the children then at home would look out for him anxiously, standing side by side at the front door and trying not to giggle because he had requested that they should wear hats when they accompanied him up the stairs.

The subsequent turmoil in the Church did not bother Helena in the least. She was no longer the stiff, exceedingly reserved woman she had been when she married Edda. Her children, she said, had worn her down. Right to the end she greeted all that was happening with equanimity, and her particular kind of rather dry humour. She had a great friend named Mabel Tottie, a nun at Greyshott, a convent well known as a centre for retreats. "The Reverend Mother has just decamped," she wrote to Edda not long before her death. "Mabel hasn't mentioned it but her letters have been much more cheerful than usual, the excitement must have bucked her up."

She visited her children regularly until her late eighties, after that she was not strong enough to come any more and remained at home devotedly looked after by Catherine, helped by Nellie.

"Your mother's dispostion is so perfectly right," Watkin wrote to Perpetua in 1969, "holding on to life but prepared if need be to leave it – assured of a better life beyond. Would to God," he added, "I had that confident faith. I NEVER HAVE. Faith in God, yes, yes, yes, in survival no more than to hold the belief and pray accordingly."

Towards the end of that year Helena had a slight stroke. She recovered the use of her arm and hand but gradually grew weaker from that time onwards. In November Edda came to see her at Dorking. It was the last time they were to meet and perhaps Helena knew it.

"Just a word to tell you," she wrote to him, "that I miss you very much and hated parting from you." She wrote again for his eighty-fourth birthday in 1972 and enclosed a new £1 note. Her writing was very wobbly. "My dear one, I can only write to you a word but you have all my love and best wishes for your birthday. If only I could write more, I have so much to say and to thank you for. Very best love, dearest one, Helena. Get something you would like with the enclosed." He never did but left the note in its envelope where it remains to this day. She died, aged ninety, on Christmas Eve 1972.

Helena had asked to be buried beside her family at Erpingham and this was done in early January 1973. One of her children had a particular horror of seeing her mother placed in a hole in the ground. Owing to a mistake in writing down the time of the funeral she and her family sat out the entire service waiting in the car in Aylsham market place and arrived at Abbot's Hall just as Samuel was saying a thankful goodbye to the mourners.

Perpetua feared that there had been an accident and anxiety took away the edge of her grief. Watkin was not present. Since the disintegration of the liturgy he no longer attended his local parish church but at Mass times went to pray in the chapel of the Catholic orphanage close to his home. He spent the time of Helena's funeral there, he told Perpetua, and in the evening was driven to Brixham to hear a Latin requiem in the old rite celebrated by a priest from the Society of St Pius X.

In her turn, Perpetua told him how Uncle Samuel had stood at the foot of the grave supporting himself with two sticks. Both she and her father shared a love of animals. Aquinas, he once told her, asserted that there could be no love or friendship possible between mankind and animals. "*We know very well that it is.*" The grave digger had once worked at Abbots Hall and when he started to shovel earth over the coffin his yellow retriever rushed over and lay at Perpetua's feet. As she fondled his head through her tears, she told her father, the dog gave her two licks and ran back to his master. "It was a very real comfort and something I shall remember for the rest of my life – only a sign, but a very real and significant one – that love has absolute dominion over death." She followed this with advice to marry Zoë as soon as he could for the sake of his children. It could not affect the five of them. Their involvement with it all was past and long ago completely forgiven.

At this time Zoë decided she would like to be called by her second name, "Ella". She and Watkin were married in early February. Watkin was eighty-four, Ella sixty-nine. "The ceremony," Watkin told Perpetua, "was at one o'clock at Marychurch, when in any case the church is usually shut for the luncheon hour." It remained so sad, he added, that the marriage had been made possible only by her dear mother's death. If only the old state of things could have remained. "We were fortunate in Canon Meiklem, so kind and thoughtful throughout. I can't however say the same of the marriage service – in English and completely unlike the old. I'm glad I was not asked to address God with the familiar 'you'. I could not have done it. The cats should have attended with bows round their necks."

The loss of their mother was an irreparable blow to all her children, particularly to Perpetua who was so close to her and had none of her own. Their anchor was gone, the one person who had remained calm throughout the strains and stresses of their troubled childhood, the war years and the ups and downs of their adolescence. There was never any suggestion that she was one of them, as it were an older and wiser elder sister. She lived in her world, they in theirs. It was she who taught them their first prayers and to learn by heart the mediaeval hymn "Come Holy Ghost Creator Come" which was to remain with them for the rest of their lives.

At the end of the same year that they had gathered together for her funeral at Erpingham, Samuel had a heart attack and was forced to go into Aylsham hospital. The house was empty and on the afternoon of December 19 his bailiff was feeding the cattle across the road when he saw smoke rising from the roof of the Hall. He raised the alarm immediately and four fire engines extinguished the blaze before it reached the lower floors. A fault was found in the electric wiring.

The news that Abbots Hall had been on fire came as a shock to Helena's children. Their father's conduct, his peculiar interests, his eccentricities and his poverty had alienated him from his rich and successful family. Only Cousin Phil had stayed faithful. But their mother's old home had remained there in the background even after it became forbidden territory. When they were young it had given them a kind of security. It had been a normal solid house with servants, regular meals, beautiful gardens and people who did not raise their voices.

Samuel died on the very day of his sister's funeral the year before. Christopher visited him the previous afternoon and saw immediately that the end was near. Samuel recognized him but was very weak, very quiet and held his rosary between his fingers.

Erpingham churchyard is a lonely even desolate place in the winter. The wind comes sweeping over the flat fields and dashes itself against the flint tower, so tall that it can be seen for miles. Helena's burial had taken place on a cold but calm day, Samuel's in weather so wild and wet that Christopher's voice could hardly be heard above the roaring of the wind in the trees.

The blackened rafters of Abbots Hall were protected by tarpaulin. The dining room table was almost exactly as their uncle had left it, covered with letters, bills and account books, cheque stubs and old Christmas cards. An unknown hand had made room for a tea tray. Whoever it was must have still been in the kitchens because the tea was hot and poured out by Samuel's solicitor, not Purdy any longer, but a man they had never seen.

Conversation was not animated and after a short while the executor nodded at the solicitor who moved a pile of papers to the centre of the table and signalled to the family to sit down on the chairs already provided. The wind rattled the window frames and the long brown arms of the clematis slid backwards and forwards over the panes as if searching for entrance. High above them the tarpaulin rose and fell making a faint booming sound like guns far off at sea.

The main provisions of Samuel's will were briefly described before the distribution of copies to each of the family. It was fairly short considering the size of the property. Christopher was not mentioned. Each of the nieces was left a small legacy, the rest went to charity. Christopher was silent. Seeing this, Perpetua spoke out. Abbots Hall, she said, was their mother's home known to them since they were children. They would like permission to take away all family papers and photographs. On their honour they would remove nothing of commercial value.

This was accorded and still Christopher said nothing. He was determining in his mind to walk down the unused and overgrown drive to the front gate for the last time. Alone with Teresa he left the house as dusk was falling. "The rain was pouring down," he wrote to his father, "and the wind howling through the trees and darkness was setting in. It seemed like the end of an epoch and I felt like Gurnemanz in *Parsifal*, 'time here becomes space.'"

Watkin was shocked at this turn of events. A large fortune obtained partly because their mother had been forced to sell land to her brother at a time when the agricultural depression had rendered it almost valueless, now left away from her children and grandchildren. To crown it all, their grandmother's jewellery to be sold for charity. "My blood boils at the cruel wrong done to your mother and her children – who are also mine." No wonder nothing had been left to Downside. Their uncle had disliked intensely the new services with which the monks had replaced both the Mass and the Office. At least Perpetua's prompt action had secured the family papers. They must let him know *exactly what happens*.

Christopher gave them instructions. He knew the house well. Philip Shepheard's diaries were in the long corridor leading to the bathroom, Samuel's in the hall. The cupboards and chests there were stuffed with wills, albums, indentures, photographs, letters, account books and pictures drawn for Maria Pasqua when her children were young. The glass was filthy but they must take down all the framed reproductions of her portraits painted in Paris in the eighteen sixties. They must search the attics, and the book room, the stables, the outhouses, the chapel and above all, the hay loft. Here were all the papers to do with their grandfather's first wife about whom he never spoke.

Towards the end of January 1973, the 'weird sisters,' as Ronnie called them, met again at Abbots Hall. They had given themselves two days to accomplish their task and took with them three bin bags each. The Aga was out, the house bitterly cold. Maria Pasqua's plants in the conservatory were already dead. Muffled by scarves, in thick jumpers, duffel coats, trousers, stout shoes and wearing rubber gloves they looked for all the world like people searching for dead bodies in the aftermath of some dreadful disaster. The dust lay thick in the unused rooms and the house smelt of wet dogs, mice and something like recently extinguished wicks of tallow candles. The carpets were covered with dried mud brought in by firemen, police, ambulance men and the funeral party itself. For company's sake the searchers stayed together.

Christopher had been right about the entrance hall. It was here, on a table not far from where the spiders made their home in the lantern of the *Peggy* wrecked off the Hazebro's in 1772, that they found the packet of letters Zoë had written to their mother those years ago when she was alone at St Mary's. That evening, exhausted, they read them silently and without comment over coffee in the lounge of the *Red Lion* at Cromer. Who had taken them over to Abbots Hall and for what purpose, they could not tell.

Except for the removal of the shotgun, no one had attempted to clear up their uncle's bedroom. A pillow was on the floor, the sheets thrown back and an unemptied bottle of stale urine lay under the bed together with a copy of his great grandfather's translation of Juvenal. Samuel had liked to keep his windows open all the year round. His wardrobe was marked with droppings from birds which he allowed to nest in the space on top where women keep their hats. The floor was still scattered with downy feathers from last year's hatchings. On his chest of drawers a coloured picture of the Sacred Heart faced a photograph of his long lost love, Eileen. These they took, the Juvenal also, emptied the bottle and covered the bed with a sheet.

CHAPTER TWENTY-EIGHT

Full Circle

Twice he wrote to remind both Perpetua and Magdalen of the words of the French Dominican scholar, Sertillanges: "We exist, this is a fact. Before us stretches the vast universe and beyond our vision, called by the name of our great God, the mystery."

Perpetua once said that to describe Watkin on paper would be like picking up leaves beneath an oak tree. He lived for nine years after Helena's death and continued to make the rounds of his childrens' homes until he was almost ninety, arriving as always with his plastic mackintosh and his Daddy bag packed with his breviary, missal, writing paper, and razor.

After Helena's death Catherine and Keith Davenport continued to live at Fairmead with their children. Keith was a businessman but his real interests lay in philosophy and linguistics. Not for him the shallow dismissal of metaphysics as unimportant. He agreed with Watkin that the fundamental question was not particular creeds but the existence of another order of being or dimension of spirit which humanity could objectively experience. At weekends they both would go out to a country pub and talk and talk over their drinks but no arguments could convince Keith that such an order existed, not even after an expedition to Chartres together, Watkin's share paid by an old friend. Keith lived and died a reluctant agnostic.

Watkin was hard up. Perpetua had spent months if not years tracing some of Grandma's famous trusts which were activated when he was still a boy living alone with Nana at Mount Felix after her death. Eventually sufficient was gleaned from the past to enable him to buy a small annuity. For the rest he depended upon stocks and shares about which he was surprisingly knowledgeable. But he still had a wife and two children to support and it was a struggle to make ends meet.

His address book is covered with little sums, how much he paid for fish for the cats, a fountain pen, his coach fare, Christmas presents for his children, grandchildren and Hetty, whom he never forgot. These sums are scattered with anguished cries of distress. "If only, if *only*, I could sell more copies of *Neglected Saints*." This was a book he had written for Sheed who had also got him a hack job correcting articles on philosophy for an American junior encyclopaedia. Sometimes the comments are sadder. "The modern church has *separated* me from Almighty God."

In one way Watkin was the easiest of visitors. He thoroughly enjoyed good food and wine but was perfectly content with bread and cheese and a glass of cider. Nor was there the least difficulty in entertaining him. His conversation was still punctuated by gusts of laughter. Although their length diminished as his strength gradually failed, he would still walk for long distances and sit for hours reading a book, in his usual fashion shouting out every now and then, "Rubbish. Absolute rubbish," or "I didn't know that, did you?" to retreating backs.

In many respects Watkin was far freer from the tyranny of self than most people. But this had its disadvantages. The world of ideas was so real and present to him and his consciousness of what was going on around him so slight that he made a nuisance of himself without being aware of it. Once, anxious to continue a discussion, he followed one of his daughters into the lavatory and when he realized what he had done was so overcome with embarrassment that he could not stop appologizing to his son-in-law. He shared with Bertrand Russell a Victorian prudishness about referring to natural functions, including sex, and spoke of them only in a low, conspiratorial voice.

When trousers with a zip instead of buttons came on the market, Teresa bought him a pair. He retired to try them on and before long she heard first groans and then loud cries coming from behind the locked door. "Ronnie? Where's Ronnie? Get Ronnie," he called out. "These trousers are very *dangerous*." The zip had stuck. No farmer himself, he hated the spraying of weeds. The Chapmans lived in the country then. One spring a tractor was driven into the field behind the house and started to poison the buttercups. Watkin ran to the fence waving his arms and shaking his fists and shouting "Murderer! murderer!" at the astonished driver.

This was an exception. On the whole Watkin's violent outbursts had ceased. He happened to be staying with Magdalen at the time of the Cuban crisis. He had long thought that human beings could no more be trusted with atomic weapons than monkeys with a box of matches. On the evening of Friday, October 26, 1962, at the White House, President Kennedy asked his Secretary of State if he thought "people in this room realize that if we make a mistake there may be two hundred million dead?"[1] Acutely aware of what was at stake, Watkin remained absolutely calm, reading Enid Blyton aloud to the children or sitting, as was his habit, with his eyes closed.

Ronnie Chapman's life of Faber had been a success and now he began work on a very different man, George Tyrrell, a subject which interested Watkin very much. In his opinion Tyrrell's work was not acceptable as it stood but it conveyed many powerful and brilliant insights which anticipated much that was being said by Catholics then. "He was a pioneer," he wrote in 1963, "with the pioneer's inevitable mistakes and tendency to headlong action." If completed, Ronnie would have written an excellent and much needed biography but tragically his eyes deteriorated so much that that he had to leave the Bodleian Library and abandon the task. He also, for the time being, abandoned his faith. Watkin lamented that he had lost his only convert and Christopher blamed Tyrrell.

That was not directly the case although Ronnie's study of Tyrrell's thought coincided with the collapse of old-style Catholicism. His difficulties may have been accentuated by his near blindness and delicate health but they were fundamental. He could not believe that a good God could have created a world soaked through and through with so much innocent suffering. Watkin, as we know, was very concerned with this difficulty which in his early essay on the problem of evil he had called the most powerful challenge to Christian theism. His views were not unlike those of Teilhard de Chardin who thought evil the inevitable accompaniment of creation.[2] Watkin reminded Ronnie that Socrates had said that evil of necessity haunts this lower world. If it had been possible for God to have made our world without suffering, Watkin maintained, then He would have done so. That He has not therefore proves He cannot. Philosophically, evil is an unreality. Once we admit that evil as a positive entity, then we have to admit that either there is a radical dualism in the constitution of reality, as did the Manicheans, or that evil is a reflection of the Divine Nature, which would be a denial that God is God. Ronnie was unconvinced. Crows pick out the eyes of newly-born lambs. Religion was an illusion. He was to return to the Church but for a time drifted into scepticism and despair, and published a book of poetry that he called *This is My Winter*.

In one sense, it was Watkin's also. He valued only two of his books: *A Philosophy of Form* and *Poets and Mystics*. He felt *in tenebris,* lost and powerless, in a false position, caught between the moral and doctrinal fundamentalism of the defenders of the old Mass and those who believed the purpose of the Church was to develop social consciousness. Most people seemed quite unable to grasp that freedom of theological interpretation could exist side by side with passionate defence of the former liturgy. It was precisely because the letter of scripture and creeds had proved to be so fallible that he treasured the profound and beautiful liturgy which enables us to understand their interior meaning. Religion was like poetry: as Christopher had pointed out, it was an art, not a science.

The authority of theologians was dubious because they attempted to set up as norms of absolute truth particular formulations of an experience too deep and obscure for such a formulation. He faced both ways, Watkin wrote to a correspondent, because he looked in both directions. "In one direction I see the spiritual, aesthetic and philosophical treasure in Catholicism, on the other I am aware of the scientific world pattern. But knowledge in the breadth of human experience cannot really contradict knowledge in its depth." Because at present it was not possible to have a conceptual integration of the scientific and rationalist view of Ultimate Reality and our relationship to It, does not mean that one has to reject one or the other.

Watkin's letters over the post-Conciliar period are a most interesting running commentary on the times. If anyone had a mind "that feeds upon infinity," it was his. Profound, amusing, angry, occasionally unfair, they illuminate the reflexions of a man searching for truth until the very end. He thought that the physicists might give us a clue to much that is perplexing or seemingly impossible in the Christian tradition. In a letter written as early as 1962 he refers to the opinion of a well-known physicist that other psycho-physical universes may exist which interpenetrate with our own. Today such speculations are widely discussed.[3]

Yet the letters are more than a running commentary. They were also a twitch on the string. "However my life has turned out," he wrote in old age to Magdalen, "whatever success or failure has been in my work, I know it has been amply worthwhile if I have helped you to hold fast to God."

Behind the rigorous questioning, however, there is a sense of betrayal, of being deceived by a false prospectus, that a new firm was trading from the old premises. Halévy had asked him why he became a Catholic and Watkin had more or less avoided answering. Catholicism, Newman once remarked, is a deep matter, "You cannot take it in a teacup." Watkin could not, even if he would, explain to an unbeliever the multitude of complex reasons that had led him to the Roman Church. It was love of the past and the ancient liturgy; when he heard Compline sung by the monks of Downside after his conversion, he thought himself back at Fountains. Above all, it was the attraction of the Church's long tradition of mystical theology, the recognition which had never left him, that God was particularly present in Roman Catholicism. Moreover, the Roman Church seemed to him then to be a fixed and certain religion, a citadel against the encroaching secularism of the age. In his letters he refers constantly to that conversation he had with the Archbishop of Canterbury in the garden at Lambeth. If you want that kind of certainty, Davidson had told him, you must go to Rome. He had gone to Rome and look what happened.

Yet what had happened was only what he himself had foretold would happen. There was in him an unresolved ambiguity towards the Church from the very beginning. He wanted authority but he had spent much of his life undermining it. As an emotionally insecure young man he sought a Church whose pedigree went back to the Apostles and which was able to defend the creeds with certainty and consistency. But what he wanted psychologically and spiritually was not being propounded in a manner his reason could accept.

Even as a new convert he had recognized the inadequacy of the Catholic response to the challenge of secular knowledge. His first book, published when he was still in his twenties, was *Some Thoughts on Catholic Apologetics: A Plea for Interpretation.* This was an attempt to present the Christian creeds in a way that neither denied nor suppressed the certain conclusions of modern knowledge in all its branches. In other words, as Martindale had smelt out, he was a Modernist in the sense of von Hügel's definition of the movement, a never quite finished "attempt to express the Old Faith and its permanent truths and helps – to interpret it according to what appears the best and most abiding of elements in the philosophy and science of the later and latest times."

Prophets are notoriously wrong abut dates and details of what their deepest intuitions perceive. In August 1916 Watkin had solemnly recounted his conviction that sooner or later, perhaps after a long period of moral, social and intellectual anarchy, there would be an inrush of the Spirit and a new, more interior realization of the Catholic faith would replace the old. This thesis, expressed in one way or another, runs through all his books.

At the first Reformation, Catholic apologists often failed to defend the faith convincingly because no satisfactory theory of doctrinal development had been worked out. At the second Reformation, modern scholarship and commonsense made a literal interpretation of the Bible frequently untenable and dealt a mortal blow to any fundamentalist understanding of Christianity. From the very beginning of his Catholic life, and in the face of opposition and obscurantism, Watkin understood the crucial importance of clarifying the nature of revelation. His position has since been vindicated by Conciliar constitutions and papal encyclicals.

He was quite obviously one of the foremost precursors of the Council. The dismantling of the liturgy, however, the folly of the bishops in conniving at the destruction of churches and their furnishings, together with their encouragement of a movement which tended to substitute the love of man for the love of God, blinded him to its considerable achievements many of which, ironically, he himself had pioneered.

With conscious exaggeration, B. C. Butler, the Abbot of Downside, once described pre-Conciliar Catholicism as "the best of all possible religions and everything in it an intellectual scandal."[4] The time had come, he was now pointing out, for the English Catholic public to be given an adult introduction to the problems that faced biblical scholars. The picture of Jesus which emerges from the Gospels is self-authenticating. There was almost nothing historical science could know about Jesus, he explained, except what was mediated to us by the Primitive Church. We see him through its eyes or we see him not at all. This statement goes to the heart of the matter and raises questions which have as yet to be satisfactorily answered. The primitive church was Jewish and expressed itself within the sometimes bizarre imaginative world of contemporary Judaism which has to be interpreted before it can be stated as Christian doctrine.[5]

For many, Butler's approach opened the way to what Archbishop Heenan considered to be pastoral sadism. "We shall not," he wrote, "increase the faith of our people nor bring them closer to Christ by banishing the Angel Gabriel and poking fun at the Magi."[6] But whose fault was this? Children grow slowly into adults and the long years of censorship and repression, on insisting only too often on the literal truth of the plainly impossible, left Catholics unable to cope with an entirely different way of looking at things.

Some thought that since it had turned out that little or nothing was really known about St Joseph, devotion to him should cease. Others wondered if it was right for cribs to be given such a prominent place in churches at Christmas since the infancy narratives were evidently something called midrash, which they took to mean pious fiction. Some were pleased at the diminished rôle the archangels and seraphim played in the new Mass because good and evil spirits were surely no part of the Christian faith.

They may or may not be part of the Christian faith, Watkin commented, but they were certainly part of its founder's. Again and again he points out that since Christ was truly man his insights of spiritual truth were necessarily imagined and conceptualized within the limitations and imperfections of first-century Judaism. This approach, later to be endorsed by Pope John Paul II in his encyclical *Faith and Reason*,[7] applied to Jesus' eschatology, or what are called the Four Last Things, that is death, judgement, hell and heaven. This released Watkin from what he described as the element of religious terrorism which disfigured the surface of the Gospels.

It was a matter that touched him nearly. Nana was a Presbyterian and may have frightened him with descriptions of hell although Watkin never accuses her of this. The Gospels make plain that the Sadducees held the older view that the dead existed, or semi-existed, in a shadowy world called Sheol, which resembled the classical Hades where no communion with God was possible. "The world of shadows all my company", as the psalmist so sadly describes it. The Pharisees, on the contrary, taught an eternity of either bliss or torment according to personal merit. This was the theology taught by the earthly Jesus, but as Watkin wrote, we worship the Risen Lord "who knows that God is love and never vengeance."

A theologian whom Cardinal Hume greatly admired, his fellow Benedictine Bede Griffiths, states the matter explicitly. The self, the separated individual self, has to die if the true self is to be found. This was the final sacrifice Jesus had to make. As he lay dying on the cross, he cried out "My God, my God, why have you forsaken me?" This, Griffiths writes, is the last trial of every spiritual person, to surrender his image and concept of God and to face the Reality which lies beyond all images and concepts. Only then could Jesus say, "It is finished."[8]

Many of Watkin's old friends were dead. But Bernard Wall, the former spirited editor of *Colosseum* who had argued about Mussolini all those years ago, was still alive and shared Watkin's love of the old Mass. Wall was one of the organizers of the international appeal to Rome for its preservation signed by so many writers and artists from all over Europe and America. Watkin's old friend Hugo Yardley, one of the founding members of *Pax*, loved it too. Yardley's son fed him fearful reports of the removal of splendid Renaissance ornaments from Baroque churches in Rome. St Peter's, Santa Maria Maggiore, St John Lateran, St Paul's without-the- Walls, had all taken on the office furniture aspect which so fittingly expressed the spirit of the new liturgy.

Bédoyère died in 1973. However Tom Burns, a younger man, continued to steer *The Tablet* through choppy waters, giving much space to an appreciation of Watkin and his work on the occasions of both his eightieth and ninetieth birthdays. On his eightieth birthday Watkin sent in a translation of a poem entitled "A Country Walk" by the fourth-century Latin poet Tiberianus. It was his final contribution to a journal for which he had written, often anonymously, over so many years.

From the nineteen sixties onwards the Sheeds' Catholic Evidence Guild of its very nature faltered and gradually faded away. It had been founded to present and explain Catholic doctrines and practices. That was no longer possible. Frank and Maisie spent their time between London and New York where Sheed and Ward had their American office. They had both welcomed the Council with open arms and now struggled valiantly but not convincingly to make sense of what Frank called "the chaos which now is."

The management of the London branch of their publishing house was handed over to Sheed's son-in-law who eventually became a Marxist and the firm developed into what Wilfred Sheed, Frank and Maisie's novelist son, referred to as a left-wing bookshop. Wilfred thought that this period in his father's life the most heroic. Everything he had lived and worked for seemed to be in ruins yet he stuck to his guns.

Sheed's was naturally a black and white legal mind but a shrewd and penetrating one, excellent while working within the terms of a Catholic apologetic that existed now only in patches. He was exceedingly touchy about the application of historical methods to the New Testament and hated the very word midrash. Nor did he follow Watkin's keen interest in the speculations of the physicists about the nature of matter.

Sheed was not excited by the prospect of interpenetrating universes. Moreover, he was shocked and surprised by Watkin's vehement repudiation of the authority of Pope Paul to desacralize the liturgy. The Pope, he wrote in a letter, may have used those words but for both Maisie and himself the Mass in English was a great experience, more vivid and more mysterious than it ever was in Latin. Not only did he feel closer to his fellow human beings but closer to God. Watkin may scoff and despise him. He can only bow his head.

In his turn, Watkin could only bow his head before Sheed's acceptance of the Church's unique authority to legislate in the moral field. When Wilfred's marriage failed in the late sixties, both Frank and Maisie set their faces resolutely against any idea of his marrying again in his former wife's lifetime. That was before annulments, or what amounts to Catholic divorces, were granted on psychological grounds. Then it was all right for Wilfred to marry in church. This fudge was as distasteful to Watkin as any suggestion of a fallible Christ was to Sheed. So they clashed, but gently, not as ignorant armies but as men who had thought deeply and endured much in the battle for truth.

Watkin continued to go through the work of both Sheeds, answering questions, and making suggestions first for Maisie's autobiography and then for Frank's. He had been thinking, Frank wrote, of all Watkin had done for him over the years to build his understanding of God. "I find it hard to think of anyone to whom I owe more." But time was running out. Maisie died in 1975. "The letter you wrote to me after her death," Frank told Watkin, "pierced to the very essence of her mind, her work and our marriage. And one sentence stays in my head – your desire to clasp my hand." This was never to be. All plans to meet failed so the old friends continued to write to each other instead, Sheed from what he called his shallows to Watkin's depth. The last letter came from New York in 1978. Was St Teresa of Avila aware of her Jewish blood? How did she feel about Jews? Watkin was ninety. This time there was no answer.

If I get to heaven, Frank once told Perpetua, it will be only by holding on to your father's coat tails. But Watkin still had no conviction that survival after death was possible. If only he could have a certain conviction of this, he would be at peace. He found it difficult to understand how the Hebrew prophets for whom conversation with God was all in all could be reconciled with an eternity of separation. Death still remained for him the supreme evil as it had done since he was a child. Christopher might be longing to leave this world of images and shadows but he was like the

Irish monk who had told St Bridget that he feared the long journey into the dark. That had been an admission made in the ages of faith, a reaching out across the centuries to the plangent cry of a modern atheist poet against total emptiness for ever, "the sure extinction that we travel to . . . no sight, no sound, No touch or taste or smell, nothing to think with, Nothing to love or link with. The anaesthetic from which none come round."[9] Watkin may never have read Philip Larkin but how deeply he shared his feelings.

He thought that no man had a better son than Christopher. If he knew at the last that he was facing death he would wish to have him by his side. But Christopher had his work cut out. His father could no more accept the dumbing down of the Catholic liturgy than a Walt Disney version of the *Divina Commedia*. He had been on the verge of tears after hearing what he thought must be Canon Meiklem's last Latin sung Mass at Marychurch. "In fact," he wrote to Christopher, "I felt as the Northern Rebels must have felt when for a brief moment Mass was restored to Durham Cathedral."[10] He obstinately refused to go to any Mass not cele-brated in the old rite and spent instead the time before the Blessed Sacrament. Father Leander Donovan, Christopher's former novice master, now an old and sick man himself, travelled regularly to Torquay with Christopher to celebrate Mass in the house, hear Watkin's confes-sion and try to calm his troubled mind.

Yet the depth of him was untouched. He who scattered Israel would gather Israel in. But not in the way we expect. Twice he wrote to remind both Perpetua and Magdalen of the words of the French Dominican scholar, Sertillanges: "We exist, this is a fact. Before us stretches the vast universe and beyond our vision, called by the name of our great God, the mystery."

In 1975 Christopher resigned as Head Master of Downside School. Why is not altogether certain. Perhaps he was just tired. His ship had coin-cided with a period of unprecedented religious and social instability. Few head masters could have faced such a difficult term of office and come out of it so well. He went to Beccles in Suffolk where the Benedictines served a fine parish church. The following year he was appointed, most appro-priately, titular Abbot of Glastonbury. The decision to go to Suffolk was painful to his father since the distance between them would be so much greater. However, Downside itself had lost its savour although the monks were as kind and welcoming as ever. He told his children to their amuse-ment that on one of his visits a young monk had come up to him before Mass and politely asked him if he would like to take part in the "commu-nity meal". The language, Watkin remarked, of Tyndale, not of St Thomas More whose stained-glass window was so prominent in the abbey church.

When Watkin was eighty-nine a visiting professor from the University of Iowa and a colleague from Exeter University unexpectedly asked him to revise both his essay on Julian of Norwich, which he had written for Sheed's anthology *The English Way* in 1933, together with his later chapter on her Norfolk contemporary Margery Kempe, published in *Poets and Mystics*. This he did. He had come full circle. It was his last published work, a slim booklet with a well-designed cover entitled *On Julian of Norwich and in Defence of Margery Kempe*.

The regular rounds to visit his children continued until Watkin was almost ninety. He used to come to Richard and Magdalen twice a year. He thoroughly enjoyed his visits especially his trips to Hall's second-hand bookshop in Tunbridge Wells where he sometimes found books he had long been seeking. Every evening he would play a card game called "The Black Widow" as eagerly as a child and like a child, really minded when he lost. Each morning before lunch he would walk with a carrier bag for nearly a mile along the lane to the village pub, have a glass of cider, talk to anyone who was there and return carrying a filled bottle of "Uncle Bob", a still, strong cider of which he was very fond. When he reached the front gate he would shout out, "Here I come. Here I come with Uncle Bob."

In October 1977 he planned to stay as usual. It might be, he said, the last time he would be strong enough to undertake the journey. He wanted to visit his friends at the *Chafford Arms* and the village shop and bring back Uncle Bob to lunch. But Uncle Bob never came again. Watkin's ninetieth birthday was celebrated at Torquay. Christopher went to visit him with bottles of wine and took him out to see some churches round Exeter. Ella explained that although he was mentally alert he had aged considerably and he himself told Magdalen that he found it increasingly difficult to wash and put on his clothes.

For many years Watkin had shared a sofa bed downstairs with his cats, sleeping beneath a portrait of his father who had been painted wearing a plum coloured evening coat and gazing out of a darkened window, Pantafon perhaps, or Loudwater. Now Watkin's hand was not sufficiently steady for him even to attempt to shave himself, so Ella thought it best for him to grow a beard. That was how his children found him when they came.

The meeting with Ella, which had taken place soon after Helena's death, had not been easy. The gap was too great, the memories too dense, her presence too overwhelming, to give them space to express the good wishes they sincerely felt. She spoke a great deal, their father was for the most part silent, saying almost nothing when they took them both out to lunch or for drives over Dartmoor. It was as if Helena's children belonged to another life, a world so remote from the one he lived in Devonshire, that the two could not mingle.

As a homesick young man in Germany, Watkin could never see the

Plough in the winter sky without remembering it as it hung high over the sea at Sheringham.

Then he had prayed that if he *had* to die, let it be there. He had to die and it was not at Sheringham but in Torbay Hospital on March 2, 1981. His death certificate recorded his occupation as Roman Catholic Philosopher. (Retired).

No one had ventured to ask Watkin about his funeral arrangements but of his own accord he had brought himself to write twice to Christopher on the subject. He wanted a Latin requiem in the old rite, but the *Dies Irae* was to be omitted. "Neither antiquity nor beauty," he had written, "can justify what is to me sheer blasphemy against the goodness and love of God." So this was done at Marychurch. Few people were present beside the family. Christopher had driven down with Dom Philip Jebb, now Head Master of Downside School. He was Belloc's grandson and some of Helena's children had last seen him at the celebration for the old man's eightieth birthday at King's Land. Canon Meiklem's successor, Monsignor Anthony Gilby, who had given Watkin the Last Sacraments, was there also. Perpetua had had a recent hip operation and experienced great difficulty in walking down a slope to his grave in Torquay Cemetery.

Ella found herself unexpectedly well off. Watkin had left her the house together with his library, which included his valuable collection of illuminated missals, books of hours and incunabula accumulated in the days of his prosperity. She lived to ninety-six and when she became ill was looked after in a nursing home for many years. She did not consider herself worthy to be buried beside Watkin and chose to be cremated.

When he was parish priest at Beccles, Christopher's life took an unlikely turn. Difficulties had arisen within the local Council and he was persuaded to stand as an Independent candidate. As headmaster he had served on numerous committees and acquired the skill of conducting business with speed and efficiency. Before long he was elected Mayor of Beccles and enjoyed his term of office. He took pleasure in the ceremonial and traditional robes but unlike his great-grandfather who had been Mayor of Manchester, he wore the Benedictine habit and abbatial cross under his lace cravat and chain of office. Teresa and Ronnie had moved to Norfolk and Teresa was sometimes able to act as his Lady Mayoress. He chose a woman as chaplain, a local Salvation Army officer.

In 1989, now over seventy, he returned home to Downside. He died in early May 1997, three months after Perpetua. Before he left Beccles he had organized a subscription for the erection of a beautiful rood beam in the church. The figures were taken from the disused church of St John, Maddermarket in Norwich, the city and county which had played such a large part in the lives of both his parents. Our Lady and St John stand on either side of the crucified Christ. Beneath is written *Sic Deus Delexit Mundum:* God so loved the world.

Appendix to
Chapter Fifteen

Those who care about the details of the negotiations between Great
Britain and Ireland over Home Rule may be interested in an exchange of
letters between Watkin and Augustine Birrell in 1931. Watkin was then
translating the first volume of Halévy's *The Rule of Democracy,
1905–1914*, which started with the victory of the Liberal Party after ten
years of Tory dominance with the Irish question still unresolved. The
Prime Minister, Campbell Bannerman, appointed James Bryce as Chief
Secretary for Ireland, a man not particularly sympathetic to the Irish
claims. Bryce was then sent to Washington as our ambassador and Birrell,
then President of the Board of Education, took his place. Birrell, who
Halévy described as "a witty man of letters and a professional sceptic",
had not been a success at the Board and his new appointment was
"certainly regarded as a victory by the Nationalist leaders. Had he
renewed negotiations with them? If he had, had at least a conditional
agreement been reached?"

Watkin would not, one presumes, repeat the first part of this remark
but he was curious about the second and wrote to Birrell for clarification.
Birrell replied from London on January 26, 1931.

"When Bryce in 1906 went to the US, the Irish parliamentary leaders
(Redmond and Dillon) took occasion to interview Campbell Bannerman
to find out who he was thinking about to succeed, *no sort* of agreement
or bargain was or could be made, for the Party was pledged already to
bring in a Home Rule Bill on lines acceptable to the Irish leaders. It was
only a question of the *personality* of the new man. I had been for a year
at the Education Office and in charge of the Education Bill and somehow
or other had created a favourable impression on the RCs. But as I say,
what passed between Redmond, Dillon and C.B. I never heard. You may
take it from me that there was *no* bargain or agreement – for there was
need of none."

Birrell died before this volume came out in 1934.

Notes

CHAPTER ONE   Making Money

1   *Dictionary of National Biography* (hereafter *DNB*), vol. X. Reprinted 1937–39.
2   *DNB*, vol. XV. Reprinted 1937–38.
3   Henry Vizetelly, *Glances Back Through 70 Years*, Kegan Paul, Trench, Trubner and Co Ltd, 1893.
4   Isabel Bailey, *Herbert Ingram, Esq. Founder of the Illustrated London News*, Richard Kay, 1996.
5   *DNB*, vol. XVII.
6   MS Diary letter home. Letters to Edward Watkin and Nathaniel Wedd, August–September, 1860.
7   Stanley Weintraub, *Victoria, Biography of a Queen*, Unwin Hyman, 1987.
8   *Chicago Journal*, September 8, 1860.
9   *Illustrated London News*, September 29, 1860.

Sources

Goffin, Magdalen. *A Manchester Man: The Diaries of Absalom Watkin, 1789–1861.* Alan Sutton, 1993.
Shorter, Clement. *CKS An autobigraphy.* Privately printed, 1927.
Yates, E. H. *Fifty years of London Life: Memoirs of a Man of the World, 1831–1884.*

CHAPTER TWO   Spending It

1   David Hodgkins, *The Second Railway King. The Life and Times of Sir Edward Watkin, 1819–1901*, Merton Priory Press, 2002.
2   J. Ridley, *Lord Palmerston*, Constable, 1970.
3   David Hodgkins, *The Second Railway King. The Life and Times of Sir Edward Watkin, 1819–1901.*
4   MS diary Edgar Watkin. Voyage to Australia and back, 1875.
5   MS diary Edgar Watkin. Voyage to India, 1902.

Sources

Bailey, Isabel. *Herbert Ingram, Esq. Founder of the Illustrated London News.* Richard Kay, 1996.

Goffin, Magdalen. *A Manchester Man: The Diaries of Absalom Watkin, 1787–1861.* Alan Sutton, 1993.
Shorter, Clement. *CKS: An autobiography.* Privately printed, 1927.
Watkin, Edgar. Mss Diaries. France, 1873. Voyage to Australia and back, 1875. Voyage to India and Burma, 1895. Voyage to India, 1902.
MS letters, Edgar Watkin, Ann Ingram, Sir Edward Watkin.
Family albums.
Newspaper reports.

CHAPTER THREE **A Public Scandal**

1 *DNB*, vol. X. Reprinted 1937–39.
2 Letter from the Oriental Institute, Chicago, to Perpetua Ingram, 1993.
3 Article *Daily Telegraph*, January 14, 1911.
4 Letter from the Oriental Institute, Chicago, to Perpetua Ingram, 1993.
5 Legal correspondence and statements formerly in the possession of Perpetua Ingram.
6 *Stockport Echo*, April 3, 1888.
7 *Pall Mall Budget*, April 7, 1892.
8 George Dow, *Great Central, vol. 2. The Dominion of Watkin, 1884–1899.* Ian Allan, London, 1962.
9 Margaret de Bunsen, *Nana Walker and the Babington Smith family.* Privately printed, 1980.

Sources

Manchester Evening News, March 24, 1892; April 6, 1892; April 11, 1892.
Blackpool Herald, April 8, 1892.
Unpublished Article, "*Folly or Foresight*", Perpetua Ingram, 1968.
MS letters between Sir Edward Watkin and William Ingram, 1891–92.

CHAPTER FOUR **The Watkin Path**

1 Adrian Vaughan, *Railwaymen, Politics and Money: The Great Age of the Railways in Britain*, John Murray, 1997.
2 Sir E. W. Watkin, *Canada and the States: Recollections*, Ward Lock, 1878.
3 E. A. Mitchell. Edward Watkin and the Buying-out of the Hudson's Bay Company, *Canadian Historical Review* XXXIV (3), 1953.
4 T. Whiteside, *The Tunnel Under the Channel*, Simon and Schuster, 1992.
5 F. Barker and R. Hyde, *London As It Might Have Been*, John Murray, 1982.
6 C. A. Williams, Gladstone, Lloyd George and the Gladstone Rock, *Caernarvonshire Historical Society Transactions*, 1999 (60).
7 John L. Jones, *Welsh Hymns and the Liberal Path.* Country Life, January 17, 1980.
8 David Lloyd George, *War Memoirs, Vol. 2, second edition*, Odhams Press, 1938.

Sources

Dow, George. *Great Central, vol. 2. The Dominion of Watkin, 1864–1899.* Ian Allan, 1962.

DNB, vol. X.

Gernsheim, H. and A. Gernsheim. *Queen Victoria – a biography in word and picture*. Longmans, 1959.

Greaves, John Neville. *Sir Edward Watkin, 1819–1901. The Last of the Railway Kings*. The Book Guild Ltd, 2005.

Hodgkins, David. *The Second Railway King. The Life and Times of Sir Edward Watkin, 1819–1901*, Morton Priory Press.

Longford, Elizabeth. *Victoria RI*. Weidenfeld and Nicolson, 1964.

Reid, Michaela. *Ask Sir James*. Hodder and Stoughton, 1987.

St Aubyn, Giles. *Queen Victoria: A Portrait*. Sinclair Stevenson, 1991.

Tuchman, B. *The Proud Tower*. Hamish Hamilton, 1966.

Wilson, A. N. *The Victorians*. Hutchinson, 2002.

MS Gladstone letters to Sir Edward Watkin.

MS family letters, papers and legal documents.

CHAPTER FIVE **A Coffin the Size of a Child**

1   E. I. Watkin, MS poems, Pantafon, 1903.
2   Michaela Reid, *Ask Sir James*. Hodder and Stoughton, 1987.
3   E. I.Watkin. Another Dialogue of the Dead: a conversation between Herod and Churchill, 1966. This was sent to Paul Johnson, then editor of the New Statesman. Eventually he turned it down.
4   E. I. Watkin, *Christopher Dawson, 1889–1970*. Proceedings of the British Academy, LVIII.

Sources

de Bunsen Margaret. *Nana Walker and the Babington Smith family*. Privately printed, 1980.

Brownrigg, Lt. General Sir Douglas. *Unexpected. A book of memories*. Hutchinson, n.d. (A contemporary of Watkin at Lord Normanby's.)

H. and A. Gernsheim. *Queen Victoria: A biography in word and picture*. Longmans, 1959.

Longford, Elizabeth. *Victoria RI*. Weidenfeld and Nicolson, 1964.

Reid, Michaela. *Ask Sir James*. Hodder and Stoughton, 1987.

St Aubyn, Giles. *Queen Victoria: A Portrait*. Sinclair Stevenson, 1991.

MS letters Mr and Mrs Gladstone to Sir Edward Watkin.

MS family letters, papers and legal documents.

MS Watkin Diary of a visit to Switzerland with his mother, August–September, 1900.

MS Watkin notes on his visit to Spain. 1904.

CHAPTER SIX **The City of Bells**

1   Christopher Dawson, *Memories of a Victorian Childhood*. First published in *The Wind and the Rain*, Spring, 1949.
2   MS letter Watkin to author, August 3rd, 1978.
3   Jeremy Lewis. *Cyril Connolly: A Life*, Pimlico, 1998.
4   Magdalen Goffin, ed. *The Diaries of Absalem Watkin: A Manchester Man. 1789–1861*. Alan Sutton, 1993.

5   F. von Hügel, *Selected Letters, 1896–1924*, J. M. Dent, 1927.
6   MS letters Martindale to Watkin, 1920–32.
7   MS Watkin diaries, January–June, 1911.

Sources

Bédoyère, Michael de la. *The Life of Baron von Hügel*. J. M. Dent, 1951.
Knox, R. Francis Urquhart. *Dublin Review*, January, 1935.
Martindale, C. C. Review of *The Modernist Movement in the Roman Catholic Church* by A. R. Vidler. *Dublin Review*, January, 1935.
Mortimer, Mrs. *Peep of Day*. Together with a biographical sketch, n.d. Simpkin, Marshall, Hamilton, Kent and Co., n.d.
Scott, Christina. *An Historian and His World. A Life of Christopher Dawson. 1889–1970*. Sheed and Ward, 1984.
Sire, H. J. A. *Father Martin D'Arcy. Philosopher of Christian Love*. Gracewing, 1997.
Urquhart, obituary. *The Times*, September 18, 1934.
Watkin, E. I. *Christopher Dawson, 1889–1970*. Proceedings of the British Academy, LV11.
Watkin, E. I. Impressions, MS diary, 1916.

CHAPTER SEVEN   **Prophesying Doom**

1   Christina Scott, *An Historian and His World. A Life of Christopher Dawson, 1889–1970*. Sheed and Ward, 1984.
2   He had already translated a treatise on mystical theology by Hugh of Balma and another on *Spiritual Conceits and Mystical Enigmas* by Johannes Angelus Silesius. The typescripts are extant.
3   MS diaries, E. I. Watkin 911–12.
4   Ibid. Philip and Gladys were to be the grandparents of the pianist Philip Fowke.

Sources

Dawson, Christopher. *Memories of a Victorian Childhood*. First published in *The Wind and the Rain*, 1949.
Watkin, E. I. MS, *Fairyland: A Comic Operetta in Two Acts*.
Contemporary letters and telegrams.

CHAPTER EIGHT   **Joy**

1   *Introduction to Mr Wu and Mrs Stitch: The Letters of Evelyn Waugh and Diana Cooper*, ed. Artemis Cooper, Hodder, 1991.
2   MS diaries, E. I. Watkin, 1911–12.
3   Walter Lord, *A Night to Remember*, Longmans, 1956.

CHAPTER NINE   **I am the Master of My Own Life**

1   Magdalen Goffin, *Maria Pasqua*. Oxford University Press, 1979.
2   MS letters between Emmeline Watkin, E. I. Watkin and Philip Shepheard.
3   Christina Scott, *An Historian and His World: A Life of Christopher Dawson. 1889–1970*, Sheed and Ward, 1984.

Sources

Watkin, Edward Ingram. *Some Thoughts on Catholic Apologetics. A Plea for Interpretation.* Manresa Press, 1915.

CHAPTER TEN   *Dulce Et Decorum Est*

1   Ray Monk, *Bertrand Russell: The Spirit of Solitude,* Vintage, 1997.
2   Mentioned in eight volumes of war cuttings 1914–18 assembled by Emmeline with Helena's help.
3   E. I. Watkin, *A Little Book of Comfort in Time of War,* Catholic Truth Society, 1914.
4   Magdalen Goffin, *Maria Pasqua,* Oxford University Press, 1979.
5   MS letters to Helena and Edda from Phil Shepheard, April/May 1915.
6   Ronald Blythe, *First Friends,* Viking, 1999.
7   Alan Wilkinson, *The Church of England and the First World War,* London, 1978.
8   Ray Monk, *Bertrand Russell: The Spirit of Solitude,* Vintage, 1997.
9   Ibid.
10   MS letters Claughton Pellew to Helena and Edda, 1916–18.
11   Jane Badini, *The Slender Tree: A Life of Alice Meynell,* Tebb House, 1981.
12   Luigi Sturzo, *Nationalism and Internationalism,* Roy Publishers, New York, 1946.

Sources

Collins, Ian. *A Broad Canvas: Art in East Anglia Since 1880,* Parke Sutton Publishing, 1990.
Coppard, George. *With a Machine Gun to Cambrai. The Tale of a Young Tommy in Kitchener's Army.* Imperial War Museum. HM Stationery Office, 1969.
Gaspari, Cardinal. MS letter, November 22, 1916.
Goodall, Felicity. *A Question of Conscience.* Sutton, 1997.
Joliffe, J. *Raymond Asquith: Life and Letters.* Collins, 1980.
Keegan, John. *The First World War.* Hutchinson, 1998.
Lambert, Angela. *Unquiet Souls: The Indian Summer of the British Aristocracy, 1880–1918.* Harper and Rowe, 1984.
Meynell, Sir Francis. *My Lives.* Bodley Head, 1971.
——. *DNB,* Supplement 1971–80.
Morrison, Stanley. *DNB,* Supplement 1961–70.
Nicolson, A. *The Hated Wife. Carrie Kipling, 1862–1930.* Short Books, 2001.
Roberts, John Stuart. *Siegfried Sassoon.* Richard Cohen Books, 1999.
Scott, Christina, *An Historian and His World: A Life of Christopher Dawson, 1889–1970.* Sheed and Ward, 1984.
Von Hügel, Baron F. *The German Soul.* J. M. Dent, 1916.
Ward, Maisie. *Gilbert Keith Chesterton.* Sheed and Ward, 1944.
Watkin, E. I. *Little Book of Prayers taken from Liturgical Sources,* Catholic Truth Society, 1916.
——. MS Impressions, June 16–September 1, 1916.

CHAPTER ELEVEN   **A Season of Good Will**

1   *Times* obituary, November 26, 1933.
2   Letter to Watkin, July 15, 1920.
3   Dom John Chapman, *Spiritual Letters*, Sheed and Ward, 1935.
4   *Times Literary Supplement*, June 17, 1920.
5   Anonymous Report Westminster Diocesan Council of Censorship, 1919.
6   Letter, June 14, 1927.
7   MS letters, Christopher Watkin (Dom Aelred) to author, 1967–97.
8   MS memoir by Christopher Watkin (Dom Aelred).

Sources

DNB, Supplement 1931–30. Augustine Birrell.
Goffin, Magdalen. *Fighting Under the Lash*. Downside Review, July 1978.
Watkin, E. I. *A Philosophy of Mysticism*. Grant Richards, Harper, Brace, 1919.
Watkin, E. I. *Poplar Leaves*. Cornish, 1918.
Waugh, Evelyn. *Ronald Knox*. Chapman and Hall, 1959.
MS letters Mrs Tatham to Watkin, 1910–56.

CHAPTER TWELVE   **Thirteen Vicarage Gate**

1   MS letters Father Cuthbert to Watkin, 1919.
2   Evelyn Waugh, *Ronald Knox*, Chapman and Hall, 1959.
3   The problem of evil and suffering concerned Watkin until the end of his life.
    In 1932 he published his *Bow in the Clouds,* and his friend the Italian priest,
    Don Luigi Sturzo, then in exile in London, wrote to congratulate him on his
    "beautiful book". However, he did not agree with the philosophical basis of
    Watkin's argument about the existence of evil. Their interesting exchange on
    this subject is kept in the Archivo Luigi Sturzo in Rome together with the rest
    of their correspondence. Watkin still maintains, as against Sturzo, that evil is
    a privation, an absence of due good, a universal frustration of harmonious
    development whose extent and deep rootedness theists tend to minimize. It
    is something quite apart from the misuse of human free will. His last letter to
    Sturzo on the matter is written in July, 1935. It is about suffering "whose
    grim visage," he was later to write, "lost Darwin his faith and made Jefferies
    deny his own vision." That God enables us to overcome and utilize disease,
    he concedes. That God actually sends disease as something good and accept-
    able, he denies.
4   Watkin MSS letters to Thomas Loome, August to September, 1969.
5   Alec Vidler, *A Variety of Catholic Modernists*, Cambridge University Press,
    1970.
6   MS letter von Hügel to Watkin, 5/6 August, 1921.
7   Wilfred Ward, *The Life of John Henry Cardinal Newman*, vol 1. p. 198, vol.
    2 p. 647, Longmans Green and Co. 1921.
8   Michael de la Bédoyère, *The Life of Baron von Hügel*, J. M. Dent, 1951.
9   Letters to the author, 1980–90.
10 The originals of all the von Hügel material referred to in this chapter are kept
    at the University of San Francisco.
11 Watkin letter to Thomas Loome, September 10, 1969.

12   *The Guardian,* September 21, 1945.

Sources

Cuthbert, Father, ed. *God and Supernatural.* Longmans Green and Co. 1920. Abridged edition, Longmans, 1936.
Dawson, Christopher. *The Spirit of the Oxford Movement.* Sheed and Ward, 1933.
Goffin, Magdalen. *Fighting Under the Lash.* Downside Review, July 1978.
Jodock, Darrell, ed. *Catholicism Contending with Modernity. Roman Catholic Modernism and Anti-Modernism in Historical Context.* Cambridge University Press, 2000.
Newsome, David. *The Victorian World Picture.* John Murray, 1997.
Prestige, G. L. *The Life of Charles Gore.* Heinemann, 1935.
Scott, Christina. The Vision and Legacy of Christopher Dawson. *Downside Review,* October, 1996.
Ward, Maisie. *Insurrection versus Resurrection.* Sheed and Ward, 1937.
Vidler, Alec. *The Church in the Age of Revolution.* Pelican History of the Church, vol. 5. Penguin, 1961.
Von Hügel, F. *Selected Letters, 1896–1924.* J. M. Dent, 1927.

CHAPTER THIRTEEN   **The Blue House**

1   John Murray published Edgar Christian's diary under the title of *Unflinching* in 1937. The whole story has been told in detail by George Whalley, *The Legend of John Hornby,* John Murray, 1962. Also by Clive Powell-Williams in *Cold Burial,* Penguin Books, 2000. Most of Edgar's letters to his parents at this time are now in the possession of the author.
2   Bernard Ward, *The Sequel to Catholic Emancipation,* vol. 2, Longmans, Green, 1915.
3   Penelope Fitzgerald, *The Knox Brothers,* Macmillan, 1977.
4   Christina Scott, *An Historian and His World: A Life of Christopher Dawson, 1889–1970,* Sheed and Ward, 1984.

Sources

Bunsen, Margaret de. *Nana Walker and the Babington Smith family.* Privately printed, 1980.
Hanbury, Dom Michael. Algar Thorold. *Dublin Review,* First Quarter, 1955.
Sheed, F. J. *The Church and I.* Sheed and Ward, 1974.
Watkin, E. I. *Mr Thorold's Editorship.* Dublin Review, June 1934.
MS letters Edgar Christian to his parents, 1927–28.
MS letters Dawson to Watkin, 1919–65.
MS letters C. C. Martindale to Watkin, 1920–32.
MS letters Algar Thorold to Watkin, 1925–36.
Watkin, E. I. MS diary, January 1–March 25, 1926.

CHAPTER FOURTEEN   **Making Waves**

1   F. J. Sheed, *The Church and I,* Sheed and Ward, 1974.
2   Wilfred Sheed, *Frank and Maisie: A Memoir with Parents,* Chatto and Windus, 1986.

3 Maisie Ward, *Insurrection Versus Resurrection*, Sheed and Ward, 1937.
4 F. J. Sheed, *The Church and I*, Sheed and Ward, 1974.
5 Tom Burns, *The Use of Memory: Publishing and Further Pursuits*, Sheed and Ward, 1993.

Sources

Edwards, David L. *Poets and God*. Darton, Longman and Todd, 2005.
Griffiths, Bede. *The Golden String*. Harvill Press, 1954; Fontana, 1964; Fount Paperbacks, 1979.
Moorman, Mary. *William Wordsworth: A Biography*. Vols 1 and 2. Oxford, Clarendon Press, 1957 and 1965.
Order: An Occasional Catholic Review. Vol. 1, May, 1928; Vol. 2, August, 1928; Vol. 4 November, 1929.
Pearce, Joseph. *Literary Converts*. HarperCollins, 2000
Watkin, E. I. *The Bow in the Clouds: An Essay towards the Integration of Experience*. Sheed and Ward, 1931, second edition, 1954.
MS letters T. F. Burns to E. I. Watkin, 1928–74.
MS letter T. F. Burns to author, August 30, 1984.
MS letters, Dawson to E. I. Watkin, 1919–65.
MS letter Bede Griffiths to author, November 14, 1984.
MS letters Emmeline Heakes, 1930.
MS letters Christopher Watkin (Dom Aelred) to author, 1967–97.
MS letters Leo Ward to E. I. Watkin, 1919–32.
MS diary, E. I. Watkin, February–March 1931.

CHAPTER FIFTEEN **Kicking Into Touch**

1 Elie Halévy, *A History of the English People in the Nineteenth Century*. Vol. 5. *Imperialism and the Rise of Labour*. Ernest Benn, 1929. Translated from the French by E. I. Watkin.
2 Part of letter Watkin to Halévy, October 31st, 1927. In the author's possession.

Sources

Goffin, Magdalen. *"My volume, your volume, our volume."* Downside Review, October 1985.
Halévy, Elie. *Correspondence 1891–1937*. Editions de Fallois, Paris, 1996. Edited Henriette Guy-Loë.
MS letters between E. I. Watkin and Elie Halévy, 1927–34, in the author's possession.
MS letters Christopher Watkin (Dom Aelred) to author, 1967–97.

CHAPTER SIXTEEN **The Mark of the Beast**

1 Article 43 Lateran Treaty, February 1929.
2 The cause for the beatification of Luigi Sturzo was begun in 1995.
3 Archivio Luigi Sturzo. Istituto Luigi Sturzo, Rome. Correspondence between E. I. Watkin and Sturzo, 1926–37. Most of the originals in the possession of the author.

4 Undated letter Barbara Barclay Carter to Watkin. Archivio Luigi Sturzo.
5 Kevin L. Morris, *Fascism and British Catholic Writers, 1924–1939*, New Blackfriars, part 2, February 1999.
6 In his professional capacity, Count Michael de la Bédoyère dropped the two French accents on his name. The younger generation have restored them.
7 Article by a former editor of the *Catholic Herald*, Desmond Albrow. *Sunday Telegraph*, February 21, 1988.
8 Kevin L. Morris, *Fascism and British Catholic Writers, 1924–1939*, New Blackfriars, part 2, February 1999.

Sources

Barclay Carter, Barbara. *The World of Ideas of Don Luigi Sturzo*. Blackfriars, 1943.
Binchy, D. A. *Church and State in Fascist Italy*. Oxford University Press, 1941. Reissued 1970.
Brandon, Piers. *The Dark Valley: Panorama of the 1930s*. Jonathan Cape, 2000.
Conquest, Robert. *The Great Terror*. Macmillan, 1968.
——. *Reflections on a Ravaged Century*. John Murray, 2000.
Cornwell, John. *Hitler's Pope. The Secret History of Pius XII*. Viking, 1999. Penguin, 2000.
Rhodes, Anthony. *The Vatican in the Age of the Dictators, 1922–1945*. Hodder and Stoughton, 1973.
Sturzo, L. *Church and State*. Geoffrey Bles. The Centenary Press, 1939.
——. *Morality and Politics*. Pax pamphlets, No. 3. 1938.
Ward, Maisie. *The Wilfred Wards and the Transition*. Sheed and Ward, 1934.
MS letters Augustine Birrell to Watkin.
MS letters Count Michael de la Bédoyère to Watkin, 1934–65.
MS letters Charles Diamond to Watkin, 1931–33.
MS letters Mary Bottrill to Watkin, December 1933–March 1934.

CHAPTER SEVENTEEN **Bordering on Genius**

1 Article by Antonia White in the Roehampton–Woldingham Association News, 1964.
2 H. J. A. Sire, *Martin D'Arcy. Philosopher of Christian Love*, Gracewing, 1997.
3 Miranda Seymour, *Ottoline Morrell: Life on the Grand Scale*. Hodder and Stoughton, 1992.
4 Article by a contemporary of Vivien Leigh reprinted in the Roehampton Woldingham Association News, 1989.
5 Teresa Chapman (Watkin) A Memoir. MS 2001.
6 Quoted by reviewer *Irish Press*, June 19, 1935.
7 Letter, Bede Griffiths to author.
8 Sir Colin Lucas, article in the *Daily Telegraph*, February 2, 2001.

Sources

Spurling, Hilary. *The Girl from the Fiction Department: A Portrait of Sonia Orwell*. Hamish Hamilton, 2002.

Watkin, E. I. *A Philosophy of Form.* Sheed and Ward. First edition 1935, second edition 1937, third edition 1950.

MS letters Tom Burns to Watkin.

MS letters Algar Thorold to Watkin.

MS letters E. I. Watkin to Perpetua Ingram (Watkin), 1934–67.

CHAPTER EIGHTEEN **There Are No Rules**

1 Maisie Ward, *Insurrection Versus Resurrection,* Sheed and Ward, 1937.
2 MS Memoir, Christopher Watkin (Dom Aelred).

Sources

Watkin, E. I. *Theism, Agnosticism and Atheism.* Unicorn Press, October, 1936.

Watkin, E. I. *Men and Tendencies.* Sheed and Ward, May 1937.

MS letters Zoë Bowen to Helena Watkin, October–November, 1936.

MS diaries Perpetua Ingram (Watkin.)

MS letters Christopher Watkin (Dom Aelred) to author.

MS diary E. I. Watkin, various dates in the 1930s.

MS letters E. I.Watkin to Perpetua Ingram.

CHAPTER NINETEEN **Only Connect**

1 Contemporary Catholic attitudes are brilliantly described in Bernard Bergonzi's novel, *The Roman Persuasion,* published by Weidenfeld and Nicolson, 1981.
2 Letter E. I. Watkin to Barbara Barclay Carter, February 15, 1937. Archivio Luigi Sturzo, Istituto Luigi Sturzo, Rome.

Sources

Colosseum. Edited by Bernard Wall, March 1937.

Conquest, Robert. *Reflections on a Ravaged Century.* John Murray, 2000.

Morris, Kevin L. Fascism and British Catholic Writers, 1924–1939. *New Blackfriars,* January/February, 1999.

Sturzo, L. *Morality and Politics.* Pax Pamphlets, no. 3. James Clarke and Co. Ltd. 1938.

MS letters Watkin/Sturzo, Sturzo/Watkin. Archivio Luigi Sturzo, Rome.

MS diaries, Perpetua Ingram.

MS letters E. I. Watkin to Perpetua Ingram.

CHAPTER TWENTY **To Reckon in Centuries and Plan for Eternity**

1 Letter Donald Attwater to Watkin March, 1936. This is part of a considerable archive about the early history of *Pax* in the author's possession.
2 Unpublished thesis by Dr Valerie Flessati entitled *Pax: The History of a Catholic Peace Society in Britain 1936–1971.*
3 *Gaudium et Spes.* "Any act of war aimed at the destruction of entire cities or extensive areas along with their population is a crime against God and man himself. It merits unequivocal and unhesitating condemnation." Despite these strong words, the Council did not forbid the production of atomic weapons. In June 1982 Pope John Paul II told the United Nations Special Session on

Disarmament that deterrence could be morally acceptable if seen as a stage on the way to nuclear disarmament.

4   Quoted by Owen Chadwick, *Britain and the Vatican during the Second World War*, Cambridge University Press, 1994.
5   Letter to author from Dom Daniel Rees, 1994.

Sources

Binchy, D. A. *Church and State in Fascist Italy*. Oxford University Press, 1941. Reissued 1970.
Goffin, Magdalen. *Maria Pasqua*. Oxford University Press, 1979.
Watkin, E. I. *The Catholic Centre*. Sheed and Ward, 1939. Reprinted 1943.
Search, September, 1963, Vol. 11, No. 5.
Zahn, G. C. *German Catholics and Hitler's Wars*. Sheed and Ward, New York, 1962.
Diaries, Perpetua Ingram.
MS letters Michael de la Bédoyère to Watkin.
MS letters E. I. Watkin to Perpetua Ingram.
MS letters Maisie Ward to Watkin.

CHAPTER TWENTY-ONE   **Our Armies are Broken, the Saints are Dead**

1   Bertrand Russell, *Principles of Social Reconstruction*, George Allen and Unwin, 1916.
2   Letter Bertrand Russell to Robert Trevelyan, quoted by Roy Monk in *Bertrand Russell: The Ghost of Madness 1921–1970*, Vintage, 2000.
3   L. Sturzo, The Atomic Bomb and International Politics, *People and Freedom*, September–October, 1945.
4   The historian Harold Deutsch, quoted by John Cornwell in *Hitler's Pope, The Secret History of Pius XII*, Viking 1999; Penguin 2000.
5   Watkin makes a distinction between apocalyptic and mystical religion. Mysticism seeks a Kingdom of God already in the soul, apocalyptic seeks a Kingdom of God which will come in the future and take possession of the world. For a long time he believed, as indeed the liturgy suggests, that before the close of human history there would be a transformation or glorification of the present order. This he stated in many of his books. He came to believe that this was an impossibility because of the intrinsic limitations of gross matter. "Beauty alone in the natural order brings the supernatural and the Divine into this lower world and manifests it there," as he replied to a correspondent in 1974. He still looked for the Third Kingdom of the Spirit but it would be manifest in the widespread knowledge of mystical theology and the prayer of quiet given to the faithful generally. Since the Second Vatican Council and the realization that we are moving into another stage of Christian history, there has been a growing interest in Joachim of Flora. In 1999 there was a Congress organized by the International Centre of Joachimate Studies in Italy. The theme has been taken up recently by contributors to the *Catholic Herald*, *Times*, and *Tablet*.

Sources

Berry, P. and Bostridge, M. *Vera Brittain. A Life*. Chatto, 1995.

Scott, Christina. *An Historian and His World. A Life of Christopher Dawson 1889–1970.* Sheed and Ward, 1984.

Sturzo, L. *Nationalism and Internationalism.* Roy Publishers, New York, 1946.

Watkin, E. I. *Catholic Art and Culture.* Burns and Oates, 1942. Revised edition with forty-one illustrations, Hollis and Carter, 1947.

Watkin, E. I. *Praise of Glory.* Sheed and Ward, 1943.

Letters and papers of Perpetua Ingram, with reference to her work at MI6.

MS letters Perpetua Ingram to Watkin.

MS letters Watkin to Perpetua Ingram.

MS letters Frank Sheed to Watkin, 1932–76.

MS letters Evelyn Underhill (Mrs Stuart Moore) to Watkin, 1932–41.

MS letter Father Dunstan Pontifex to Watkin, June 11, 1940.

MS letter Watkin to Ruth Carter, December 22, 1974.

CHAPTER TWENTY-TWO **Taking Advice**

1 MS letters between Father Dunstan Pontifex and Perpetua Ingram, August 30, September 3, 1941.
2 Censor's Report, Archdiocese of Westminster, 1947.
3 Report from the Office of the Censor of Books, Archdiocese of New York, 1948.

Sources

Ingram, Sir Bruce Stirling, *Dictionary of National Biography*; *Illustrated London News;* Newspaper reports.

Watkin, E. I. *The Balance of Truth.* Hollis and Carter, 1943.

Watkin, E. I. *Catholic Contemplative Christianity.* Page proof, Sheed and Ward, 1947.

MS letters Paul Shuffrey to Watkin, 1940–55.

MS letters Watkin to Perpetua Ingram, 1934–79.

MS letters Watkin to author.

MS Letters Christopher Watkin (Dom Aelred) to Perpetua, 1947/1948.

CHAPTER TWENTY-THREE **The Little Boy**

1 *Passionate Pilgrims. The Story of William McNamara,* ODC *and the Spiritual Life Institute.* Spiritual Life Institute, 2001.There are foundations at Crestone, USA and at Skreen, Co. Sligo, in Ireland.
2 A. J. P. Taylor. *English History, 1914–1945.* Clarendon Press, 1965.
3 *Daily Mail.* January 6, 1944.
4 Ronald C. D. Jasper, *George Bell, Bishop of Chichester*, Oxford University Press, 1967.
5 Martin Boyd, *Much Else in Italy.* See *The New Stateman*, July 30, 1965.
6 Log book of Captain Robert Lewis, co-pilot of the B 29 bomber "Enola Gay". Report, *Daily Telegraph*, March 26, 2002.
7 Ronald Knox, *A New Apologetic.* The Month, 1959. See also the Knox Centenary number of *Priests and People*, vol. 2, no. 10, December 1988.
8 MS letters from Watkin to author, August 28, December 10, 1962.

Sources

Hastings, A., ed. *Modern Catholicism. Vatican II and After*. SPCK, 1991.

Hurn, David Abner (pseudonym). *Archbishop Roberts, s.j. His Life and Writings*. Darton, Longman and Todd, 1966.

Iremonger, F. A. *William Temple: Archbishop of Canterbury*, Oxford University Press, 1948.

Thompson, Charles S., ed. *Morals and Missiles. Catholic Essays on the Problem of War Today, with an Introduction by Michael de la Bédoyère*. James Clarke and Co. 1959. Second and third impressions, 1960, 1961.

Watkin, E. I. *Poets and Mystics*. Sheed and Ward, 1953. Watkin has left a heavily corrected text.

Watkin, E. I. *Roman Catholicism in England from the Reformation to 1950*. Home University Library. Oxford University Press, 1958.

Waugh, Evelyn. *Ronald Knox*. Chapman and Hall, 1959.

Watkin, E. I. MS account of his American lecture tour, 1956.

Watkin, E. I. MS letters to Thomas Merton, 1962–64. Thomas Merton Studies Centre.

MS letters from George Bell, Bishop of Chichester to Watkin, February 23, 1944 and March 8, 1945.

MS letter from Neville Braybrooke to author, 1984.

MS letters Thomas Merton to Watkin, 1962–64. Thomas Merton Studies Centre, Bellarmine University, Louisville, Kentucky.USA.

MS letters Frank Sheed to Perpetua Ingram.

MS letters Frank Sheed to Watkin.

CHAPTER TWENTY-FOUR   **Opening the Windows**

1 See the interesting and unusual correspondence in *The Times*, October–November, 1949. A selection of these letters from both sides of the Reformation divide together with the anonymous leader which prompted the discussion was later reprinted as a separate pamphlet entitled *Catholicism Today*, Times Publishing House, 1949. It was reviewed, when his opinions were more conservative, by Bishop B. C. Butler, then Abbot of Downside, in the *Downside Review*, First Quarter, 1950. Butler attended the Council as President of the English Benedictines, and made some valuable contributions to the debates which were unfortunately still conducted in Latin despite American offers to finance a simultaneous translation system.

2 Pope John Paul II, February 2, 1981 to the first meeting of "Mission of the People for the Eighties". Published by Association Noel Pinot.

Sources

Bouyer, L. *The Decomposition of Catholicism*. Sands, 1970.

Longley, Clifford. *The Warlock Archieve*. Geoffrey Chapman, 2000.

Objections to Roman Catholicism. Edited with an Introduction by Michael de la Bédoyère. Constable, 1962. Later published (Pelican) Penguin, 1966. American, German, Italian, Spanish, Dutch, Polish and Norwegian editions.

Origo, Iris. *Images and Shadows*. John Murray, 1970.

Search, passim, June 1962–July/August 1968.

Watkin, E. I. *The Church in Council.* Darton, Longman and Todd, 1960.
MS papers about Sir Bruce Stirling Ingram.
MS letters between Perpetua Ingram and (Lord) Goodman.
MS diaries Perpetua Ingram.
MS letters Perpetua Ingram to Watkin.
MS letters Watkin to Perpetua Ingram.
MS letters Watkin to author.
MS letters/articles about *Objections to Roman Catholicism.*

CHAPTER TWENTY-FIVE   **Making a Clean Break**
1   *The Tablet*, December 12, 1991.
2   *The Observer*, January 1, 1967.
3   Letters from Sheed. The five were Belloc, Chesterton, Martindale, Knox, Dawson.
4   Christina Scott, *A Historian and His World: A Life of Christopher Dawson, 1889–1970*, Sheed and Ward, 1984.
5   R. E. Lamb, University of St Thomas, Houston, USA. *Canadian Catholic Review*, February 1985.

Sources

Butler, B. C. *The Church and Infallibility.* Sheed and Ward, 1954.
Butler, B. C. *The Idea of the Church.* Darton, Longman and Todd, 1962.
Davis, Charles. *A Question of Conscience.* Hodder and Stoughton, 1967.
The Future of Catholic Christianity. Edited with an Introduction by Michael de la Bédoyère. Constable, 1966. Pelican (Penguin), 1968.
Kenny, Sir Anthony. *A Path from Rome.* Oxford University Press, 1986.
Search, passim, June 1962–July/August, 1968.
MS letters Dom Michael Hanbury to Watkin.
MS diaries Perpetua Ingram.
MS letters Perpetua Ingram to Watkin.
MS letters Christina Scott to author, 1981–2001.
MS letters Watkin to Perpetua Ingram.
MS letters Watkin to author.
M/S letters/articles about *The Future of Catholic Christianity.*

CHAPTER TWENTY-SIX   **The Twilight Catholics**
1   See J. T. Noonan's *Contraception,* Harvard, 1966. Also Quentin de la Bédoyère's, *Autonomy and Obedience in the Catholic Church*, T&T Clark, 2002.
2   Cardinal J. C. Heenan, *A Crown of Thorns: An Autobiography 1951–1963.* Hodder and Stoughton, 1974.
3   *New Statesman,* January 1, 1965.
4   Michael Walsh, *The Tablet: A Commemorative History, 1840–1900,* Tablet Publishing Company, 1990.
5   Tom Burns, *The Use of Memory: Publishing and Further Pursuits*, Sheed and Ward, 1993.

6 George Tyrrell, *Autobiography and Life of George Tyrrell,* arranged with supplements by M. D. Petre. 2 vols. Edward Arnold, 1912.
7 Papal Allocutions, November 19 and 26, 1969. Published in English editions of *L'Osservatore Romano,* November 27 and December 4, 1969. Reported in *The Tablet,* December 12, 1969.
8 For what a sincere and conscientious priest felt at the time see Owen Hardwicke's *Living Beyond Conformity,* Columbia Press, 2001. Also, from a different viewpoint, Anthony Faulkner's *To Travel Hopefully: Wrestling with Vocation,* Darton, Longman and Todd, 1994.
9 MS letter Archbishop Dwyer to Watkin, May 25, 1967. For the fate of the screen see article *Catholic Herald* by Brian Brindley, August 14, 1998.
10 The "re-ordering" and selling-off of churches in this country has been recorded in many papers including the *The Listener, The Spectator, The Daily Telegraph, Priests and People, The Catholic Herald* and *The Tablet.*
11 Eamon Duffy, *Holy Pictures. Priests and People,* December 1995. There are many vigorous Catholic parishes still in existence but they are very different from those common in pre-Conciliar times. *One Cog: A History of St Augustine's church in Tunbridge Wells, 1838–1995* by Edward Marchant, 1992, is a fascinating and delightfully frank account of a Catholic parish as it was formerly.
12 Brian Green, *Vessels of Clay. Priests and People,* August/September, 2002.
13 J. A. Sire, *Father Martin D'Arcy: Philosopher of Christian Love,* Gracewing, 1997.
14 *A Bitter Trial: Evelyn Waugh and John Carmel Cardinal Heenan on Liturgical Changes,* edited by Scott M. P. Reid, St Austin Press, 1996.
15 *Times Literary Supplement,* December 22, 1973.
16 The rumour was true. When Christopher (Dom Aelred) visited the church in 1976 he found it as bare as a Methodist chapel. Only the statue of Our Lady of Walsingham remained.

Sources

Chapman, Ronald. *Father Faber.* Burns and Oates, 1961.
Thomas Ellis, Alice. *The Serpent on the Rock.* Hodder and Stoughton, 1994.
Wilson, Prue. *My Father Took Me to the Circus. Religious Life from Within.* Darton, Longman and Todd, 1984.
MS letters Father Martin D'Arcy to Watkin, 1920–75.
MS letters Perpetua Ingram to Watkin.
MS diaries Perpetua Ingram.
MS letters Christina Scott to author, 1981–2002.
Watkin, E. I. T/S *Catholic Morality,* August 1968.
MS letters Watkin to Perpetua Ingram.
MS letters Watkin to author.
MS letters Watkin to Christina Scott, 1969–78 .
MS letters Christopher Watkin (Dom Aelred) to author.

CHAPTER TWENTY-SEVEN   **Exactly What Happened**

Sources

MS letters Perpetua Ingram to E. I. Watkin.
MS letters Christopher Watkin (Dom Aelred) to E. I. Watkin.
MS letters E. I. Watkin to Christopher (Dom Aelred).
MS letters E. I. Watkin to author.

CHAPTER TWENTY-EIGHT   **Full Circle**

1 Martin Walker, *The Cold War*, Fourth Estate, 1993.
2 See Teilhard de Chardin's comments in his unpublished *Comment Je Crois*. "God seems to have been unable to create without entering into a struggle against evil." Evil is not the will of God, Teilhard says, but He could not simply do away with it at this stage of evolution "not because of any defect in power or goodness or love but because of the nature of creation itself." *Teilhard Reassessed*, ed. A. Henson, Darton, Longman and Todd, 1970.
3 Stratford Caldecott, *Second Spring*. No. 4. 2003. Keith Ward, The Quantum Leap, *The Tablet,* April 2, 2005. See also *Kierkegaard's God and Hawking's Universe* by Julia Watkin, published by the Religious Experience Research Centre, Westminster College, Oxford, 1997. Dr Watkin was a daughter of E. I. Watkin and Zoë and lecturer in philosophy at the University of Tasmania. She died in 2005, having completed her book *Kierkegaard*, published by Continuum in 1997, reissued in 2005.
4 *The Tablet*, May 2, 1966. Quoted in an article by David Goodall, The Impact of the Council, *Ampleforth Journal*, October 1966.
5 Father J. Daniélou, *The Theology of Jewish Christianity*, Darton, Longman and Todd, 1964.
6 Cardinal J. Heenan, *Council and Clergy*, Geoffrey Chapman, 1966.
7 Pope John Paul II, *Faith and Reason,* Catholic Truth Society, 1968. *The Tablet* November 2, 2002.
8 Bede Griffiths, *Universal Wisdom. A Journey through the Sacred Wisdom of the World*, selected and Introduced by Bede Griffiths, Fount, 1994.
9 Philip Larkin, *Aubade*.
10 November 1569. A rebellion in the early years of Queen Elizabeth I. England beyond the Trent was still very Catholic in sympathy.

Sources

Butler, B. C. *A Time to Speak*. Mayhew-Mcrimmon, 1972.
Griffiths, Bede. *A Human Search. Bede Griffiths Reflects on His Life*. An Oral History, ed. John Swindells. Burns and Oates, 1997.
Leonard, Francis. *Fools for Christ's Sake. Being a Short Account of the Catholic Evidence Guilds in England and Wales*. Mel Publications, 2000.
——. *Search*. May/June 1966.
Sheed, Frank. *The Church and I*. Sheed and Ward, 1974.
Sheed, Wilfred. *Memoir with Parents*. Chatto and Windus, 1986.
Watkin, Christopher (Dom Aelred) *Registrum Archidiaconatus Norwyci*. Norfolk Records Society, 1946–1948.
——. *The Heart of the World*. Burns and Oates, 1955.

——. *The Enemies of Love*. Burns and Oates, 1958. Gracewing, 1994.

Watkin, E. I. *Neglected Saints*. Sheed and Ward. New York, 1955. Ignatius Press, 1994.

——. *On Julian of Norwich and in Defence of Margery Kempe*. Preface by Marion Glasscoe. University of Exeter, 1979.

——. *Tablet* Tributes, September 29, 1986 and September 16, 1978.

——. Obituary March 14, 1981. Obituary, *Times,* March 12, 1981. E. W. F. Tomlin.

MS letters Frank Sheed to E. I. Watkin.

MS letters Frank Sheed to author. None of Watkin's letters to Frank or Maisie seem to have survived.

MS letters Christopher Watkin (Dom Aelred) to his father.

MS letters Christopher Watkin (Dom Aelred) to author.

MS letters E. I. Watkin to Christopher Watkin (Dom Aelred).

MS letters E. I. Watkin to Perpetua Ingram.

MS letters E. I. Watkin to author.

MS letters Christopher Watkin (Dom Aelred) to Perpetua Ingram.

Index

Index

Index

Index

Index

Index